THE BOOK OF EMPERORS

MEDIEVAL EUROPEAN STUDIES XIV
Patrick W. Conner, Series Editor

OTHER TITLES IN THE SERIES:

Sir Gawain and the Green Knight
Translated by Larry D. Benson
with a foreword and Middle English text edited by Daniel Donoghue

Perspectives on the Old Saxon Hêliand:
Introductory and Critical Essays, with an Edition of the Leipzig Fragment
Edited by Valentine A. Pakis

Cross and Cruciform in the Anglo-Saxon World:
Studies to Honor the Memory of Timothy Reuter
Edited by Sarah Larratt Keefer, Karen Louise Jolly, and Catherine E. Karkov

The Cross and Culture in Anglo-Saxon England
Edited by Karen Jolly, Catherine E. Karkov, and Sarah Larratt Keefer

Cædmon's Hymn and Material Culture in the World of Bede
Edited by Allen J. Frantzen and John Hines

The Power of Words: Anglo-Saxon Studies Presented
to Donald G. Scragg on his Seventieth Birthday
Edited by Jonathan Wilcox and Hugh Magennis

Innovation and Tradition in the Writings of the Venerable Bede
Edited by Scott DeGregorio

Ancient Privileges: Beowulf, Law, and the Making of Germanic Antiquity
Stefan Jurasinski

Old English Literature in its Manuscript Context
Edited by Joyce Tally Lionarons

Theorizing Anglo-Saxon Stone Sculpture
Edited by Catherine E. Karkov and Fred Orton

Naked Before God: Uncovering the Body in Anglo-Saxon England
Edited by Benjamin C. Withers and Jonathan Wilcox

Hêliand: Text and Commentary
Edited by James E. Cathey

Via Crucis: Essays on Early Medieval Sources and Ideas
Thomas N. Hall, Editor, with assistance from Thomas D. Hill and Charles D. Wright

THE BOOK

of

EMPERORS

A TRANSLATION OF THE MIDDLE HIGH GERMAN

Kaiserchronik

EDITED AND TRANSLATED BY

HENRY A. MYERS

2013 · WEST VIRGINIA UNIVERSITY PRESS

20 19 18 17 16 15 14 13   1 2 3 4 5 6 7 8

A condensed version of chapter 38, "Charlemagne," appeared in vol.
  1 of the 5th edition of *The Global Experience: Readings in World
  Civilization* (Upper Saddle River, NJ: Prentice Hall, 2006).

PB 978-1-935978-70-1
EPUB 978-1-935978-87-9
PDF 978-1-935978-86-2

Library of Congress Cataloging-in-Publication Data
Kaiserchronik.
The book of emperors (Kaiserchronik) / translated and edited by Henry
  A. Myers. -- 1st ed.

p.   cm.

Includes bibliographical references and index.
ISBN 978-1-935978-70-1 (pbk. : alk. paper) — ISBN 1-935978-70-5
  (pbk. : alk. paper) — ISBN 978-1-935978-87-9 (e-pub : alk. paper) —
  ISBN 1-935978-87-X (e-pub : alk. paper) — ISBN 978-1-935978-86-2
  (pdf : alk. paper) — ISBN 1-935978-86-1 (pdf : alk. paper)
I. Myers, Henry Allen, 1934- II. Title.
PT1551.K2M94 2013
831'.2--dc23
2012027188

Cover design by Than Saffel
Book Design by Than Saffel with Nathan Holmes

Cover image: The Emperor Otto I (912-73) Presenting a Model of His
Church at Magdeburg to the Enthroned Christ in the Presence of Saints
Peter and Mauritius (?) and Other Saints. 962-968. Ivory, 5 1/8 x 4 7/16 x
5/16 in. (13 x 11.3 x .8 cm). Gift of George Blumenthal, 1941 (41.100.157).
The Metropolitan Museum of Art, New York, NY, U.S.A. Image copyright
ⓒ The Metropolitan Museum of Art. Image source: Art Resource, NY

To my wife, Nancy,
and children, Terry, Daniel, Lisa, and Allen,
neglected, but not forgotten,
during the half century 1961–2010 that this work
has been in progress

Table of Contents

The Book of Emperors *continued*

Acknowledgments

This translation intends to provide a useful source of intellectual history. The *Book of Emperors* is a primary source without equal for an account of the ideology of the Holy Roman Empire in medieval Germany. Intended to be chanted or read in verse form to an audience without much education, it tells the story of Roman, Byzantine, and German emperors with a great admixture of fiction to make them interesting to twelfth-century hearers. It is a uniquely early work of popular history.

I am indebted to many people in the United States, Austria, and Germany for encouragement and support in this project, beginning with Edgar Nathaniel Johnson, my advisor at Brandeis University, whose own dissertation published as a book, the *Secular Activities of the German Episcopate, 919-1024*[1] has stood the test of time. He encouraged me to "do something worth doing" for my dissertation. The "something" turned out to be the modification of basic concepts of government and politics by medieval historians from Saint Augustine and Orosius in the fifth century to the *Book of Emperors* in the mid-twelfth century. The final work for that project—I will attempt to show in my "Introduction" that the *Book of Emperors* is the best English name for it—seemed worth translating then in 1961, and—since scholarly debate has picked up concerning it in the intervening decades—even more so now.

In 1966–1967, I had a sabbatical year from Lowell Technological Institute, where I was teaching German, to pursue medieval-language, paleographical, and editing studies at the Institute for Austrian Historical Research in Vienna. Both the director, Professor Heinrich Fichtenau, and his assistant, Herwig Wolfram, who joined me in a number of scholarly undertakings in the 1970s, gave me every encouragement in my project of preparing an annotated English translation of *Die Kaiserchronik*.

---

1.   Lincoln: University of Nebraska Press, 1932

Beginning in 1969, I taught a variety of history and political-theory courses full time at Madison College, which became James Madison University in 1977, and work on the project proceeded a bit slowly. After two drafts, the third and what was intended to be the final version of the translation underwent constant revision for two decades until, with a summer grant from James Madison University's College of Arts and Sciences, it neared completion in 1995, with the general introduction, chapter introductions, and notes following in 2003. I am obliged to my wife, Nancy, for proofreading the first version, typing it in 1967, and for proofreading subsequent versions and revisions as they emerged. Mrs. Belinda Babb of the Madison College Political Science Department typed the second version and introduction in 1971–1972, and a succession of conscientious and dedicated student assistants, working under the direction of JMU History Department secretary Paula D. See, typed revisions until what had been the typescript entered the computer age. I would like to acknowledge the sometimes quite considerable logistical support from past Political Science Department heads Paul Cline and the late William R. Nelson, and History Department heads, the late Raymond C. Dingledine, Jr., and above all its present head, Michael J. Galgano, who has offered me assistance with this project in every way imaginable.

Particularly for materials to support the introductions and notes, I am indebted to the Interlibrary Loan Program both at Lowell Technological Institute in the 1960s and at James Madison University since then. In particular, I would like to acknowledge the patient, decades-long and efficient efforts to procure books and copies of articles by Janis Pivarnik, the late Tom McLaughlin, Anna Lee Newman, Debra Ryman and Susan Huffman. I am indebted to Carrier Library's Gordon Miller for instruction and guidance in tracking down elusive sources since the earliest days of computer searches. Somewhat unusual incidents of encouragement and support have been legion. In June 1967, I was made to feel very welcome at the library of the monastery in Vorau, Austria, which houses the oldest (ca. 1185–1190) surviving manuscript of the work, and kindly left alone with that parchment treasure for as long as I cared to stay. Later that same year, the University of Munich Library sent me a microfilm of the typescript of an important 1958 dissertation on the actual German history in the *Book of Emperors*. Unfortunately, it could not be read with the lenses normally used in American microfilm machines; however, many decades later Mikki Butcher, in charge of microfilms at JMU's Carrier Library, diagnosed what kind of lens it would take and got one for me.

I would like to express thanks to Stephen Chappell, who teaches Greek and Roman history at JMU and offered significant improvements in the translation when it touched on matters of Roman history, also to William van Norman of the JMU History Department for clarification of some items of comparative mythology. I received financial support from Madison College in the form of summer "mini-grants" awarded in 1974 and 1975. I would like to express especially heartfelt thanks to Dean David Jeffrey and the JMU College of Letters and Sciences for a summer grant in 1995 and to both Dr. Jeffrey and Dr. Galgano for approving semester leaves in the fall of 2006 and the spring of 2010, which enabled me to complete the project. It was actually almost finished, when, in February 2004, a fast-spreading fire destroyed my house, containing the manuscript in hard copies, a hard drive, and "back-up discs." I owe a sincere expression of thanks to the JMU History Department staff, again Dr. Galgano, Department secretaries Jane Crockett and Judith Hollowood, and student assistants Sarah Carver, Joshua Durbin, Lindsay Matt, Lindsay Breitenberg, Ashley Raybourn, Janelle Hores, Katelyn Belcher, and Matthew Cain for assistance of many sorts in reconstructing the typescript, sometimes from charred fragments. I am also indebted to Mrs. Crockett and Mrs. Hollowood for ongoing assistance in completing several paperback, JMU trial house editions of this annotated translation of the *Book of Emperors* (*Kaiserchronik*) and computerizing them for advanced classes in medieval and German history. Mrs. Hollowood and Sarah Walker, student assistant, proceeded with integrating the final corrections into the text and standardizing the format of this work, which was skillfully completed by Ms. Laura Wisman, Dean Jeffrey's administrative assistant. Pam Brock, executive editor of *Madison*, the James Madison University Magazine, executed the duties of copyeditor, while Dr. Hilary Attfield went beyond her role of acquisitions editor to shepherd the *Book of Emperors* through the West Virginia University Press to final completion.

Henry A. Myers
James Madison University
Harrisonburg, Virginia

Editor's Note

This translation is based on the Middle High German text edited by Edward Schröder as *Die Kaiserchronik eines Regensburger Geistlichen*, MGH, series *Deutsche Chroniken* (Frankfurt: Weidmann, 1892; repr. WBG, 1964 and 1969). Schröder himself gave precedence to the Vorau Manuscript. Detailed information concerning the thirty-three surviving manuscripts and fragments can be found in his introduction to his MGH edition, pp. 1–78.

Introduction

1. The Book of Emperors and its Treatment of History

The *Book of Emperors* is the first history of the Roman Empire of any sort written in the West since antiquity and the first attempt at a world or universal history in any Western vernacular language. It assumes that world history funnels naturally enough into Roman history, and it makes no distinction between the ancient Roman Empire that fell in the West in *AD* 476, the Carolingian Empire inaugurated well over three centuries later, and its Germanic revival, still known in the English-speaking world as the Holy Roman Empire, which dates from the tenth century. On the contrary, it seems consciously to obliterate these distinctions, in order to show the contemporary empire of the mid-twelfth century as having a millennium-long history all of one piece. Its author was an anonymous monk in Regensburg, Bavaria, who took up the monumental task of setting down in German the whole story of the Roman Empire, including a bit of Biblical and ancient Greek background, as he thought it worthwhile for laymen to know. He seems to have written his work between 1152 and 1155, at least no later than 1165. Since his narrative stops short in describing events of 1147, he came quite close to making good on his stated intention of bringing his account "down to this very day for anyone who wants to listen."[1]

More than eight centuries later, we are quite familiar with the genre called popular history. The academic eye, upon catching the writer in the act of using questionable methods to hold the interest of non-scholarly readers, easily distinguishes the work from its entirely serious counterpart.

---

1.   Line 20. This and subsequent line citations are to the Middle High German text edited by Edward Schröder as *Die Kaiserchronik eines Regensburger Geistlichen* for the MGH series *Deutsche Chroniken I* (Frankfurt: Weidmann 1892; repr. WBG, 1964 and 1969).

The popular historian might be guilty of presenting doubtful hypotheses as assumed facts, inserting bits of dialogue between historical personages that could not possibly have been recorded, or even of introducing a composite or made-up character or two. The genre often features gratuitous scenes of sex and violence designed to catch the attention of the reader. Popular history is so much a part of our world today that we may realize only with some difficulty that it is part of our medieval heritage, emerging as a general European phenomenon in the twelfth century, when a variety of writers took history out of the monastery and introduced it to a much broader public than before.

Geoffrey of Monmouth, although he kept one foot within the older tradition by writing in Latin, felt no hesitation in using myth, legend, or any type of handy and reasonably credible fiction in order to gain wider popularity for his *History of the Deeds of the Kings of England*, completed about 1147. Just a bit later, Henry II patronized the Anglo-Norman poet, Master Wace, and made him canon of Bayeux for writing his highly fanciful *Roman de Rou*, a poetic history in French of Rollo and the Dukes of Normandy. Still, no other author undertook a vernacular world or imperial history before our Regensburg cleric, who used foundation stones of imperial reigns found in Latin annals on which to erect a superstructure derived from popular legends, epics, and the anecdotal sermon material aimed at lay audiences. The *Book of Emperors* has a huge variety of sources. With regard to its imperial scope in presenting vernacular stories of emperors over a thousand-year period, however, it has no surviving predecessors.[2]

---

2. A work that shows some of the same characteristics is the half-century earlier *Song of Bishop Anno (Annolied)* a vernacular, verse saint's life but with a long introduction of world *and* Roman history, which is obviously intended to interest a lay audience. Our author in fact adapted some of that introduction into his own. The *Annolied*, however, jumps directly from the founding of Metz, Trier and Cologne in the days of Augustus Caesar to the story of Saint Anno bishop of Cologne (died 1075). It is probably the initial work of popular history in a tradition continuous from the Middle Ages but apart from its introduction it is not a world or imperial history. Henry A. Myers "The Origin of Popular History in Twelfth-Century Germany," *Journal of Popular Culture*, Vol. X (1977), pp. 840-847. Stephan Müller seeks to demonstrate the possibility that parts of the *Annolied* and the *Book of*

1.1. The tradition of world historiography in the Middle Ages: Augustine, Orosius, and Otto of Freising

Until the mid-twelfth century, the learned tradition of writing world history or imperial history, as opposed to the history of a tribe or the biography of any outstanding ruler, remained very much rooted in the pattern set down for historiography of this scope by Paulus Orosius, the noted student of Saint Augustine of Hippo. It flourished very much under the influence of the medieval "ascetic" value system, in the sense of a strong other-worldly orientation that focused on salvation and the hereafter, rather than the deeds of men, dismissing things of "this world" as disappointing, unimportant, or evil. In 417-418, Orosius completed *Seven Books of History Against the Pagans* at his teacher's request to respond to pagan accusations that Christianity had weakened Rome and to show that the Roman Empire was no worse off for the advent of Christian times. In *The City of God*, Augustine stated his intention of contrasting the history of "the heavenly city," meaning good angels, the Christian elect, and pious figures from the Old Testament, with the history of "the earthly city" or "the city of man, meaning all the rest of mankind guided by considerations of this world. Augustine, however, did not actually record very much secular history himself. Orosius, on the other hand, set down a detailed catalogue of world events from the beginning of historical time, as he thought of it, and determined to his own satisfaction that Christian times were less beset by calamity than pagan times, the recent (410) sack of Rome by the Visigoths notwithstanding.

Throughout his work, Orosius made an exception of the story of the Roman Empire when he presented most of world history as a grim array of catastrophes, relieved only by divine intervention on behalf of the elect. He could scarcely have done otherwise and kept his thesis intact. If Christian times were more free of military defeats and natural calamities than pagan

---

Emperors derive from a common lost vernacular source. *Vom Annolied zur Kaiserchronik: Zu Text- und Forschungsgeschichte einer verlorenen deutschen Reimchronik* (Heidelberg: Universitätsverlag C. Winter 1999), pp. 284-322.

times, then the Roman Empire—as the only state that had its beginning under the same ruler (Augustus Caesar) as did the Christian faith and that had existed during about the same period as the Church—must have had a fairly happy lot when contrasted with other states.

And what *had* to be true *was* true for Orosius. The last of his *Seven Books* deals entirely with the Roman Empire to 417. In it, Orosius describes a generally wiser, more just series of rulers than those found in previous and necessarily pre-Christian portions of the earthly city, such as the Assyrian Empire, the Greek city-states, and, above all, the Roman Republic, which the Roman Empire replaced under Augustus.

Orosius states expressly that the Roman Empire's world domination was divinely chosen for world power. For him, the God-ordained *pax Romana* brought worthwhile, earthly peace and justice to much of mankind, quite apart from its furthering of Christianity.[3] This exceptional place of the Roman Empire in world history was, of course, of less interest in the West after Rome had fallen. However, once the medieval Germanic Empire had gained a footing in the struggle for political power, imperial protagonists were to avail themselves of the view of history that tended to exalt the old Roman Empire and to maintain that their own empire was its continuation. In addition to the work of Orosius, Latin translations of writings of Eusebius of Caesaria, stemming from the 320s and 330s—when the first Christian emperor gave the faithful every reason to be thankful for his benign leadership—were readily available. They modified the negative outlook toward institutions of the empire as outgrowths of the city of man, which the ascetic tradition had fostered.[4]

Most widely-read medieval writers of world history—Cassiodorus, Gregory of Tours (in the early part of his *History of the Franks*), Isidore of Seville, the Venerable Bede, and Frutolf of Michelsberg—followed Augustine and Orosius, but generally imitated the latter more than the

---

3.   Paulus Orosius, *Historiarum adversum paganos libri* vii CSEL V; Book VI ch. xxii p. 428.

4.   Henry A. Myers in cooperation with Herwig Wolfram *Medieval Kingship: the Origins and Development of Western Monarchy in All Stages from the Fall of Rome to the Fifteenth Century* (Chicago: Nelson-Hall 1982) pp. 22-25; 164.

former in style and content.[5] All of these except Frutolf, however, wrote in the period when the empire in the West was defunct; and Frutolf was too much of a partisan of the interests of the Church against Emperor Henry IV to appreciate the special status accorded by Orosius to the Roman Empire among the dominions of this world. The historiographical tradition begun by Saint Augustine and Orosius reached its climax and approached its end in the work of Otto of Freising, probably the most painstaking and genuinely learned of all medieval historians. In a letter—which subsequently became the preface to his own *Chronicle* or *History of the Two Cities,* completed in 1146—Otto notes that he has modeled his history on predecessors written more than seven hundred years earlier.

> Of these, one [Augustine] dealt in a most perspicacious and well-ordered fashion with the origin, extension, and deserved ends of the glorious City of God; how it continually spread forth among the people of this world who were the City of God's citizens and princes. The other [Orosius] wrote, against those who showed an inane preference for pre-Christian times, a most useful history of times from the creation of the world to his own day, dealing with the varied and lamentable events in human affairs, with wars and threats of wars, and with the rise and fall of empires.[6]

Actually, even the genius of Otto of Freising encountered great difficulty in bringing into harmony the divergent views of history contained in the works of Augustine and Orosius, which were anything but as harmonious as the master-student relationship led many to suppose. Orosius was an incurable optimist, and, apart from assigning the Roman Empire a very special place in world history, had ironed out the kinks in the

---

5. Anna-Dorothee von den Brincken gives a full account of historical themes in all surviving Latin world chronicles of any significance and the relation of these works to each other in *Studien zur lateinischen Weltchronik bis in das Zeitalter Ottos von Freising* (Düsseldorf: Michael Triltsch Verlag 1957).
6. *Chronica sive historia de duabus civitatibus*, ed. Walter Lammers (Darmstadt: WBG 1961) *Prologus* p. 10.

history of the preceding century. He argued forcefully that Christian emperors, as long as they were Trinitarian rather than Arian, won their wars and achieved prosperity during their reigns as a matter of divine principle. Hence, Gothic invasions or no Gothic invasions, things were looking up for the Roman Empire of the early fifth century, and, under the pious Emperor Honorius, an era of peace between barbarians and Romans must be (and consequently *was*) dawning.

Augustine, on the other hand, by the time he was writing the concluding books of the *City of God,* showed little of the interest in the fate of the Roman Empire that he had shown in the first five books. His view of the role of the Christian emperor and the other institutions of imperial Rome had been much less sanguine than that of his student to begin with. He gradually let his discussion of what was to happen to Rome be absorbed in his description of what was to happen to the two cities at large. Consistent with his assignment to Orosius, Augustine forcefully rejected charges that Christianity was to blame for Rome's decline, but that is as far as he would go. Angenendt is accurate in his conclusion that Augustine "really was willing to concede to the empire only credit for preparing the way for the Christian faith."[7]

In spite of these divergences, Otto of Freising did achieve a remarkable degree of synthesis in drawing on the works of Augustine and Orosius as sources for his own world history. No one else had come even close to this accomplishment. Otto presented all portions of history—other than those in which one may readily discern the benevolent intervention of the divine hand—as a series of calamities brought on by man's material greed and lust for power, coupled with natural catastrophes aplenty. In this he followed Orosius closely and he set down this register of human events systematically and in as much detail as Orosius did. In doing so, however, he also maintained Saint Augustine's dominant interest in eschatological concerns, as Orosius was never able to do. Otto's conviction that the days of Germanic imperial glory were drawing to a close—as surely as those of

---

7. Arnold Angenendt, *Geschichte der Religiosität im Mittelalter* (Darmstadt: WBG 1997), p. 718.

Introduction

ancient Roman imperial glory had done—made it relatively easy for him to hold to Saint Augustine's otherworldly focus in viewing history. Unlike Orosius, Otto had no vision of a Christian empire as victorious and otherwise successful in this world if only the right people said enough prayers and exhibited enough piety.

The framework for presenting secular history for Otto of Freising, as for Orosius and medieval historians who followed him, often took the form of short biographies of rulers from which moral lessons could be drawn. Otto's ascetic viewpoint is consistent enough that the bright spots in earthly history—the triumphs of Christian emperors, notably Constantine I, Theodosius I, and Charlemagne—remain candles serving chiefly to heighten the reaches of darkness in this world. For Orosius himself, as well as Gregory of Tours and Isidore of Seville, the connection between the piety of a conquering Christian ruler and his political and military triumphs was the significant point of his biography. But for Otto, as for Augustine himself, the piety of a Christian emperor could be used to demonstrate a more profound point, namely the miserably insecure lot of even the mightiest of princes and the tribulations to which they could be subjected. In recounting the fate of Emperor Charles III, for example, Otto notes,

> It is said of this Charles that he was a most true Christian. Yet that ruler was plagued, particularly toward the end of his life, with misery against which neither faith nor piety protected him. After suffering physical and mental illness and forced to see the princes of the Empire transfer the imperial power to Carloman's son, Arnulf, whom they had elected as their king, Charles was forced to beg for mere subsistence from the new emperor.[8]

For Otto, the *mutatio rerum*, the fickleness of earthly fortune, is the one great existential fact that world history confirms over and over.

---

8. *Chronica*, op. cit., VI, ix, p. 446.

1.2. Mid-twelfth-century Germany: "deeds" replace the "two cities"

Extreme factionalism and the threat of civil war within the empire subsided around 1150, and, two years later, the accession of Frederick I, "Barbarossa," gave supporters of the empire cause for enthusiasm. Although the architectural and literary results of his patronage were to gain him recognition only later, his largely successful efforts to further the security of the empire and the prosperity of its inhabitants were acknowledged by contemporaries in Germany from the first. The dominant realities of imperial history during Otto of Freising's life through 1146—the date of his completion of the *History of the Two Cities*—had indeed been catastrophes. Civil war among the princes led to the interminable Guelph-Ghibelline strife, and, from 1138 on, the weak rule of amiable, impulsive Conrad III.

But then, after his election in 1152, the determined and capable Emperor Frederick I gave promise of introducing an era of peace and concord among previously warring forces, and—in looking toward Italy—of subduing elements in the city-states hostile to firm imperial rule. Otto was moved to adopt a new tone of enthusiasm for the accomplishments of young Frederick, who also happened to be his nephew. The former began writing a chronicle extolling the harmony between the church and the empire as evidenced by Frederick's subduing of heretical forces in Italy in cooperation with the Pope, which he called the *Deeds of Frederick*. The choice of title is most significant, for it points out the change in Otto's historiographical framework. History is no longer to be recorded only as the interplay of forces, divine and earth-bound, in which the will of man has normally a pathetic and uncertain role. Instead, history can now be recorded as the acts of great men.

Otto of Freising showed his consciousness of the new epoch when, in 1157, he wrote to Frederick in introducing his new work, "Since things have taken a turn for the better and the season of laughter has followed that of tears, as peaceful times have followed those of war,[9] I considered it

---

9.   paraphrasing Eccles. 3:4 and 3:6.

unworthy service—after having recorded the deeds of the other kings and emperors—to remain silent about yours."[10]

This, of course, gives a new twist to the *History of the Two Cities*, which, if it was indeed partly a record of the *deeds* of kings and emperors, contained very tepid acknowledgments of their worth and often wrote them off as exercises in futility. Otto now pays tribute to the success of the new emperor in achieving the political consolidation of his domains, and he lets no *mutatio rerum* detract from his hope-filled portrayal of the empire in the 1150s. Otto died in 1158, before completing his new chronicle of Frederick's reign to that point in time. He never made any attempt to extend his *History of the Two Cities* beyond 1146, possibly because he gave his new chronicle first priority for his available research and writing time, but possibly also because incorporating something of his new, optimistic outlook—which the budding career of Frederick seemed to presage for the empire—would have made a very incongruous final chapter in this otherwise harmonious work.[11] At Frederick's request, Otto sent him his *History of the Two Cities* with an introductory letter quite different from his original preface-letter to Isingrim, which had emphasized the work's Augustinian-Orosian view of history. His new preface glosses over the sad lines with which he repeatedly describes the fate of human strivings in that work. Instead he now states his approval of Frederick's "desire to know the ancient deeds of kings and emperors, in order to benefit the state, not only

---

10. Ottonis and Rahewini *Gesta Friderici imperatoris,* MGH ed. G. Waitz (Hanover and Leipzig: Hahn 1912; repr. 1978), Proemium, p. 11.

11. Otto's terrestrial history closes with his seventh book, to which he appends a list of popes and emperors. Following Augustine, he extends his history after this to include the fall of the earthly city, the advent of the new Jerusalem, and other eschatological depictions in an eighth book. As far as the form of his work is concerned, he would have had no problem in making insertions after the seventh book to bring his secular history up to date, but he had so conclusively demonstrated the finality of contemporary catastrophes and the impending end of the world at the end of his seventh book, that incorporating later material of the type used in his *Gesta Friderici* would have been more than a technical problem. He did add the names of the two popes since 1146 and that of Emperor Frederick in his list of popes and emperors.

for studying its defense with arms but also for gaining new ideas about courts and laws."[12] At very much the same time, the anonymous author of the *Book of Emperors* makes it clear with some fervor that for him deeds in the earthly city do indeed matter.

> Peace grew in the Empire. . . . The farms remained intact, unrobbed, and unburned, so that the son found his inheritance just as pleasing to behold as when it had been his father's. . . . Between the lords and their men there was fidelity and honor, there was joy and moderation, and there was unbounded happiness and satisfaction. No one belittled whatever had been passed on to them; rather did each man content himself with what his father had left him.

> In King Louis' time—the Book tells us this with certainty—the lords of the realm were faithful and true. They administered their domains well and kept their word: Owî! How quick they were to carry out their pledges! And that wonderful king gave them examples in his own rule. (15148, 15151-54, 15170-86)

With this comment on the reign of Louis the Pious, the author of the *Book of Emperors* sets down something of his idea of what the exemplary reign of a just monarch can accomplish. To be sure, his knowledge of the life of Louis is extremely sketchy. It is also quite true that much of Louis' reign was in reality marked by rebellions, one of which saw the emperor deposed in favor of his three eldest sons. For our author, however, these facts are of relatively little importance. He writes with a different vision of truth before him: the truth of the unity of the Holy Roman Empire, its past glory, and its potential for bringing about a satisfying life in this world, while supporting the Church in its task of saving souls for the next.

1.3. "I tell you this for sure"

"True," "truly," and "for sure" are favorite elements of the author's vocabulary. He writes with a sense of urgency, for he feels that truth is neglected

---

12. "Schreiben an Kaiser Friedrich," prefixed to *Chronica*, op. cit., p. 2.

in his own day: far too many people give credence to the shoddy improvisations of poets and singers of (what we would think of as normal) epics, for they lend credence to their fictions with beguiling phrases. The true story of the Roman Empire should be known so that the fabrications of those unscrupulous caterers to the public fancy can be exposed for what they are. He knows that far too often "ignorant people think that it is hard labor" (Line 6) to listen to veracious accounts such as his, preferring the verses of wandering entertainers even at the peril of losing their souls.

It is surely the case that by including a vast body of legend and un-factual tradition in his own work, while freely adding his own inspirations, the author of the *Book of Emperors* plays very fast and loose with the truth by modern standards, even for popular history. He rolls King Tarquin the Proud and his son, Sextus, into one monarch, who appears not in his right-ful place as the last king before the Roman Republic, but more than five and a half centuries out of sequence as an emperor between Nero and Gal-ba (4301-4834). He presents several emperors who are composite figures, one who was the father of a saint and pope according to legend but had no imperial associations, and a few others who are linked only faintly with any historical names at all. He mentions a few Byzantine emperors and skips the rest, while conveying the impression that he has omitted none before Charlemagne's time.

Worse, he deliberately distorts facts when he obviously knows better. For example, from the sources with which he gives evidence of familiar-ity, he must have been aware of the Investiture Controversy, the excom-munication of Henry IV by Gregory VII, the humiliation of the emperor at Canossa, and Henry's subsequent deposition of Gregory. Besides, the scene in the Canossa drama of penitent Henry, barefoot and shivering in the snow as he anxiously awaits word that the pope will receive him, was as familiar a mental image to any even half-educated cleric of mid-twelfth-century Germany as that of, say, Washington and his soldiers at Valley Forge is to modern Americans. And yet he gives no hint of knowing any of this in his rather detailed account of Henry IV's reign. As for the desertion of Henry IV's eldest son, Conrad—who had been crowned joint king with him in 1087 only to join rebellious vassals against his father eleven years later—or the similar act of Henry IV's second son (the future Henry V), who had been crowned joint king with his father upon Conrad's defection only to join rebel forces himself—our author has a much smoother account. In the *Book of Emperors* the only factual relationship of that civil war to its causes remains the fact that Henry IV left Germany to lead an expedition to Italy, setting off this time of troubles for the empire. According to the book, old Henry rode out hunting one morning and fell into the hands of unidentified enemies, who held him incommunicado for four days. The princes of the realm back in Germany, thinking him dead, mourned his loss and elected young Henry in his stead. Thus it was all a misunderstanding that led to hostilities (16790-16831). The whole account of the conflict is clear, interesting, consistent—and, for us, one of total misinformation.

In the early twenty-first century, we historians still have, to be sure, all sorts of substitutes for the literally true in defending ourselves or another historian we like from charges of inaccuracy. There is "true on a higher level," "figuratively true," "true in a broader sense," along with all the other kinds of almost-true or better-than-true. But the author of the *Book of Emperors* knows no such shilly-shally. Indeed the chief justification for assigning the position of *first popular imperial or world history* to his work, rather than attempting to fit it into the history of fiction out and out, is that he obviously intends for his audience to take what he says as literally true, however oversimplified or downright inaccurate he may know it to be. There can be no other reason for his meticulous attention to recording the number of years of an emperor's reign, often down to the months and days; for sometimes giving what purport to be exact statistics of battle participants and casualties; and for his continual interruptions of his narrative with phrases like "I am telling you the truth about this." In the best tradition of literally-true historiography, he waxes indignant over another author's intellectual slovenliness in recording that Theodoric the Ostrogoth and Attila the Hun once met.

If there is anyone who insists that Theodoric ever saw Attila, let him have the *Book* brought out: it was forty-three years after King Attila was buried at Oven [Buda] that Theodoric was born. He was raised in Greece, when he first buckled on his sword belt he was sent to Rome, and he was buried in Mount Vulcan [Mount Aetna]. And so you see that lie put to rest! (14176-14187)

Factual truth then, is supposed to be of the essence. It is also fairly clear that when a medieval cleric quotes the words of angels verbatim in their messages to emperors, or when he refers to written evidence in Rome to prove the truth of what he has to say, he at least hopes to be taken at his word. How then can we account for so much fiction in his narrative?

Part of the answer lies in the habit of medieval sermon writers of portraying historical personages simply as personifications of particular vices or virtues.[13] When they focused their attention on the benevolence of Christian governance or on the afflictions attendant upon excess pride, it did not matter much to medieval preachers what the real-life Emperor Philip the Arabian, in the first instance, or Emperor Justinian, in the second, had done besides exemplify the traits in question. In fact, following what *mattered* in giving life to an abstraction could lead a preacher equally well in a different direction: if *these* were the names that tradition had associated with particular virtues and vices, then *good stories illuminating these traits necessarily illuminated the historical figures themselves.* Parson Weems was operating on the same mental plane when he let his famous cherry-tree story illuminate both the virtue of truth-telling and the personality of Washington.

Another part of the answer lies in the author's estimate of what his audience will listen to and in his understanding of his medium, for this is a work for oral presentation in epic form before a lay audience not distinguished by learning. The up-and-coming proto-burghers of an expanding commercial city are, along with nobles and their favored personnel, likely hearers of this extended "song." If they are going to sit still and listen to history at all, they will do so only for something not only in their own language

---

13. Medieval sermons as well as saints' lives furnished a very large portion of the author's sources. See the discussion of sources below.

but interesting as well.[14] Imperial biographies, interspersed occasionally with deeds of the saints, must be gripping enough to compete with the heroic epics of secular origin. Not only must the stories be full of action, but they must serve the purpose of demonstrating the glory and peace-achieving nature of the Holy Roman Empire, while the ongoing *oneness* of crown and cross cannot stay out of sight for long. Therefore, all material that tends to confuse the point of harmony between church and empire—accounts of popes and emperors quarreling, for example—must be treated gingerly or omitted. A sparse narrative will need enrichment with insertions from reasonably similar stories, and these, in turn, may be enlivened by stirring, if generic, battle-scene descriptions, while the tedious connecting material can be reduced to a minimum and sometimes deleted altogether.

2. *The Value of the* Book of Emperors *as a Source of Intellectual History*

The value of the *Book of Emperors* to a student of history is much less as a source of historical fact, which it obviously is not, than as a record of intellectual history or the history of ideas. It is a forceful presentation of

---

14. Scholars paid relatively little attention to the author's likely audience beyond identifying it as one mostly of laymen, assumedly nobles, until Karl Bosl showed that in the author's lifetime an upwardly mobile proto-bourgeoisie or pre-patriciate lived in Regensburg, the author's home and then the most populous German city, a center profiting greatly from trade passing through and one where ideas as well as goods were traded about. At the same time, the ducal court patronized chivalric-courtly literature and many clerical writers flourished as well. *Frühformen der Gesellschaft im mittelalterlichen Europa* (Munich/Vienna: Oldenbourg, 1964), pp. 443-446, and Die Sozialstruktur der mittelalterlichen Residenz- und Fernhandelsstadt Regensburg; die Entwicklung ihres Bürgertums vom 9.-14. Jahrhundert. Bayrische Akademie der Wissenschaften, Phil.-Histor. Klasse, Neue Folge, Heft 63 (Munich: Beck, 1966), pp. 32-36. Christian Gellinek concludes reasonably enough that the ambitious, developing upper middle class in Regensburg and environs would have welcomed the painless, entertaining, historical learning offered by our author. "The *German Emperors' Chronicle*: An Epic Fiction?" *Colloquia Germania Internationale*, Heft 3 (1971), p. 232, and *Die deutsche Kaiserchonik: Erzähltechnik und Kritik* (Frankfurt: Athenäum Verlag, 1971), pp. 148-9.

the ideology of the Holy Roman Empire to the citizens of that empire at its height, and as such it has no parallel. It is only fitting that the Holy Roman Empire should have as its first history and presentation of its ideology a work that was also so full of fiction and could yet, like the empire itself, make such a striking demand to be taken seriously.

For the Holy Roman Empire (Voltaire's famous quip that it was neither holy, nor Roman, nor an empire, to the contrary) had its serious side in the world of ideas—however grotesque its claim to continuity from ancient Rome and its claim to represent the unity of Christian Europe may appear to moderns. As an idea, the empire lasted a little more than one thousand years—from the crowning of Charlemagne in Saint Peter's Cathedral on Christmas Day, 800, until the Hapsburg Emperor Francis II, at Napoleon's prodding after the Battle of Austerlitz in 1805—transformed its very sizable political remnants into the Austrian Empire on August 6, 1806. It had even nominal institutional continuity beginning only with Emperor Otto I in 962; but, from the Carolingian Renaissance, through the Crusades, through the Wars of Religion and beyond, its rulers—availing themselves of the magic of ancient Roman authority with widely varying degrees of success, perfected by its Christian mission—had a great deal to do with deciding the affairs of Europe.

2.1. The ancient law uniting church and empire

The popular ideology of any political unit is, in its simplest form, that body of assertions and theories that its people learn to believe concerning the origin, nature, and mission of their nation or state. The *Book of Emperors* gives us an insight into what this was at the apex of the empire by lending tangibility to the abstractions the empire was supposed to embody: security, unity, the rule of law, and the perpetual triumph of the Christian faith. Our author never isolated such concepts, but held all of them to be ideals striven for together. In its pages the empire and church are one, the imperial law is of ancient and divine origin, and the society under the imperial law has immutable goals. In contrast with the practice of Augustine, Orosius, and Otto of Freising, who regularly stepped back from their positions as historians in order to draw lessons for the reader from the material they were presenting, our author's ideological presentation is almost entirely contained in his narrative. The following examples demonstrate his technique of recasting history in order to deal with difficult problems raised by medieval political thinkers, or, more exactly, raised by the contradictions inherent in the myth of church and empire as one.

It was a cardinal point of the most outspoken advocates of imperial authority in the Middle Ages that the laws of ancient Rome antedated those of the visible Church and that the power of the empire was thus older than that of the papacy. Yet for Dante as for Marsiglio of Padua—the two most famous spokesmen for this position and the two who were to carry to an extreme the justifications for an independent secular sphere once demanded by the supporters of Henry IV against Gregory VII in the eleventh century—such a forceful insistence upon the primacy of the empire at the expense of the church turned out to be self-defeating. The empire of Dante and Marsiglio was deprived of much of its inspirational force when these imperial partisans sought to remove the empire from the authority of the church in everyday matters of who should obey whom. In attacking church claims to secular authority through emphasizing better imperial claims, they ultimately contributed to undermining the unity and hence the authority of the empire whose cause they sought to promote.

The approach of the author of the *Book of Emperors* a century and a half before Dante's *De Monarchia* is much more subtle. He, too, uses the evidence of history to extol the empire, but, drawing much more from feeling than from logic, he seems convinced that the church should never be the in the least belittled or condemned in comparison with the empire; lest the empire, which shares its mission with the church, be damaged in the hearts and minds of men. Instead of hammering home the point as Dante was to do, that God sanctified the laws of Rome with legitimacy through bestowing power on Augustus Caesar,[15] our monk describes what Augustus Caesar did as a lawgiver and lets it go at that. He tells of how the old Roman Empire was ruled by several pagan emperors with a profound respect for law,

---

15. *Monarchia*, ed. Prue Shaw (Cambridge University Press, 1995), I, xvi, p. 42.

and, instead of maintaining its significance as a predecessor of the church in introducing universal law, the primacy of Augustus' authority fades in the light of more vivid depictions of later lawgivers. In fact, throughout the *Book of Emperors,* pagan and Christian emperors alike can be judged equally well by the answer their lives give to the question: Did they keep the Imperial Law?

Among pagan emperors, for example, the author presents Titus in his traditional role of military conqueror, but he chiefly praises him for his devotion to the Imperial Law from the very moment of his election. As his first act of office, Titus "called for the Law of the empire to be brought before him; he would never render judgment except as the Law of the empire directed him." The emperor's personal subjection to this law is displayed when his strict and impartial enforcement of it procures him embittered enemies among the more unruly nobles—the ultimate crisis of conscience for the medieval sovereign. Titus, epitome of the just secular ruler, voices his pride in what he has done in spite of the ingratitude it has earned him. "Then mighty Titus responded, full of wisdom: 'If I judge the people justly according to the Imperial Law, so that you are moved to slay me because of it, there can be no great wrong in what I did.'"

In Trajan, too, the author shows an emperor's greatest virtue to be steadfastness in handing down judgments according to the Imperial Law, undeterred by crises. He characterizes evil emperors, on the other hand, not only by their persecution of Christians but by their tyrannical acts in violation of the law. To be sure, conscious or unconscious historical distortion is necessary here, for Roman law made the persecution of Christians quite legal for the most part between Domitian and Constantine. Regardless, the author has no desire to confuse his audience with observations that modify the sweeping points he desires to make concerning the antiquity and fairness of the Imperial Law, and so he depicts the persecuting emperors from Nero through Diocletian as victims of their private rage who have yielded to lust for arbitrary power.

Our author's Christianization of the Roman emperors begins unhistorically early and proceeds very gradually. He shows Constantine, the first overt and successful Christian emperor, carrying on the tradition of the best of his pagan forerunners by proclaiming the Imperial Law as his fixed standard. According to him, Constantine incorporated Pope Sylvester's advice into the law adhered to by his non-tyrannical predecessors. The day after Sylvester had baptized Constantine into the true faith he sang a mass in his presence, gave him the sacraments, and began the awesome association of the law with holy ritual.

> When the benediction had been said, the holy man took him by the hand and pointed out the way of justice for him. They revised the Law of the Empire and the King [Constantine] sent forth his edicts, just as they were written at Rome, that the people should no longer worship idols but should pray to the one true God, Who called forth Heaven and earth out of nothingness. (7986-7996)

Sylvester and Constantine go on to outline the entire political and ecclesiastical structure of the empire in accordance with the older law, in which they repeal nothing except the provisions for worship of the pagan gods, but to which they add a great deal. Sylvester, consulting together with the emperor, is shown establishing the Curia and outlining the duties of patriarchs, bishops, and priests in a pattern valid for all time; Sylvester even includes instructions for the office of cardinal, an office that, of course, was only a century old when our author was writing. On another day, after another church service, Constantine and Sylvester "made the Imperial Law more full" in its secular aspects. This time Constantine consulted with the pope concerning "dukes and counts, and all who were under them, providing for all the orders of knights, and how they should conduct their lives." Sylvester and Constantine continue at this for a full week.

This is one of the few difficult portions of the *Book of Emperors* to translate with accuracy, because the emperor and pope are so melted into one person that, for instance, it is not always possible to tell who is taking whom by the hand to sit down and work on the law, or, in formulating decrees, who is consulting with whom in the following passages: "He took him by the hand." "He consulted with him about the Imperial Law." The literal distinctness of personages is dissolved in a vision of empire and church as one in the setting down of precepts for Christian society.

2.2. True kingship

The *Book of Emperors* is much concerned with kingship as the art and science of discharging royal functions well. In the Middle Ages generally, the total being of the king was so nearly identical with the royal office that the question: "What are the functions of the king?" is really more the simple question: "Who is the king?" If the man under consideration is a true king, his functions—his practice of kingship—will follow as a matter of course.

All right, who is the king? On a conscious level for medieval people, the king is the man ordained to keep peace and render justice, to further the earthly happiness of his subjects. He is also the man ordained to defend and strengthen the faith, to help his subjects gain eternal bliss. On a less-conscious level, the king is the man whose life subsumes the experiences of his nation, making its- victories and sufferings those of his own person and enabling his people to sense these all the more keenly in his person, so that, for better or worse, the king personifies his people.[16]

In conveying a sense of what medieval kingship was all about, the *Book of Emperors* is of unique value as one of the earliest works for laymen that treats kingship in any depth. Its recurring prototypes of the good king inevitably show him to be the just and severe enforcer of the law: he is impartial, he is restrained, but his determination cannot be deflected. Trajan, for example, is such a prototype.

He handed down just judgments to the lord and to the serving man. His justice cost poor people no money at all. No man could gain such wealth or power as to be of avail against him. As for those miswrought and criminal rogues who richly deserved maiming or hanging, neither silver nor red gold was of any help to them: death was always awaiting them. No one dared

---

16.   For more examples in greater detail: Henry A. Myers, "The Concept of Kingship in the *Book of Emperors* (*Kaiserchronik*)" *Viator,* Vol. XXVII (1971), pp. 205-230.

offer him any sort of payment, and no one dared support guilty men. His was a kingly life. (5845-5858)

Then, once the author types such a ruler as a true king, he fills out his biography with stories to illustrate the defender of the peace in action. One day, a widow seeking justice against the murderer of her son approaches Trajan, one foot in the stirrup as he mounts to lead a mighty army against the Normans. The murderer had committed his crime in private vengeance, for his brother had been killed by the widow's son. Trajan weighs the possibility of putting off judgment of the case until he has returned from the Norman campaign, but the widow opens his eyes to the need for executing justice immediately. He dismounts, interrogates the accused, refutes the wretch's justification for having taken justice into his own hands when he should have sought the king's justice, condemns him, has him beheaded, gives his head to the widow, and goes off with the widow's blessing—she seems to be a Christian—to hand the Normans a stinging defeat. The fact that something like half a millennium separated the historical Roman Emperor Trajan from the earliest historical Norman invaders is, of course, irrelevant.

Elsewhere our author makes the same case in reverse by driving home what a good ruler is *not* by offering the prototype of a faulty ruler or tyrant. His typical bad ruler ignores the law and either rules by capricious whim or is so wrapped up in the temptations of palace life that he scarcely rules at all. For this purpose he recasts in a medieval mold all the old stories of Nero. In the most familiar of these, his alleged burning of Rome, Nero compels bands of knights to fight one another in a ghastly tournament amidst flames, to satisfy the wicked monarch's curiosity about how the Trojans must have looked and acted as the Greeks overcame them with fire. He presents a disproportionate number of Byzantine rulers in terms of unkingly attributes: greed, worldliness, and a cunning that alienates them from their subjects. Even Justinian displays insufferable arrogance here and—another common failing in the prototype of a mediocre-to-bad ruler—seduces the wife of one of his noble subjects, so that he is murdered with some justification in the author's eyes. Justinian, The Great Lawgiver, is incompatible with the author's Justinian, the near-tyrant, and so Justinian is not the great lawgiver at all. What worldly success he does have is the result of the perceptiveness and resourcefulness of his queen. Domitian presents a negative model of true kingship with one set of typically tyrannical traits—hatred of Christianity, a savage disposition, and rejection of Roman custom—as does that of young Henry IV with another recurring set of tyrants' traits—contempt for the nobility, indifference to crime, abuse of noble women, and neglect of the art of ruling. "He gave himself over to excess and often sat at the gaming table when he was supposed to be governing the Empire" (16558-16560).

The function of kingship in uniting the people and then heightening their sense of identity in the king's person is not noted explicitly in the *Book of Emperors*, but it plays a large unspoken part in many chapters nonetheless. For example, in recording an interminable series of wars against the Hungarians, the author ascribes victory to the divinely-aided, particular king or emperor: Arnulf, Louis the Child, Conrad I, Henry I, Otto II, and Conrad II—but the people of the empire, however vaguely described, subsequently share in his triumphs. While the victories appear *at the time of their original description* as the king's own, later kings often cite the same victories as those of their peoples or armies, invoking "our forefathers" in a collective sense to inspire their warriors not to be outdone by their ancestors.

The conquest of Jerusalem in "the Jewish War" was thought of in the Middle Ages rather much as the personal doing of Vespasian and Titus. Our author's Vespasian makes it clear that he won "the Jerusalemite lands" with his warshield (5104-5111), but by the time of Theodosius, Vespasian's personal victories with his warshield have become simply part of the "worldly honor that our forefathers won for us, fighting with their warshields" (13396-13398).

2.3. The Donation of Constantine and the translation of Empire

One of the thorniest problems in medieval political theory concerned the "Donation of Constantine." It was an eighth-century forgery according to which the Emperor Constantine, in return for being cured of leprosy by Pope Sylvester, turned over the secular rule of the empire in the West, along with all its sources of income, to the papacy. The document disturbed Otto of Freising and Dante alike, for, by the twelfth century, it seemed most unlikely that things had happened just that way. Otto of Freising wondered why—if Constantine had indeed left his empire to the papacy—others could point out that he had divided his empire among his sons.[17] Dante, writing about 1300, seems to have accepted the Donation's reality, although he roundly condemned Constantine for making the offer and Sylvester for having taken it.[18] Thus the controversy went on, evoking much ill feeling on both sides, until the philological acumen of Lorenzo di Valla in 1440 showed the document's eighth-century wording to betray its claim to authenticity, a finding which later evoked still more ill feeling all around.

The Donation presents no problem at all for the *Book of Emperors*. In telling of Constantine's conversion, the author suppresses the old story that this event followed the emperor's vision of the Cross in the sky before his victory at the Ponte Molle near Rome, an account that had rested on the excellent authority of Eusebius, Orosius, Frutolf, and others. Instead he lets Constantine's conversion to Christianity follow Sylvester's curing him of leprosy. This is evidently reward enough for Sylvester, and there remains no good reason for Constantine to turn the western empire over to the Pope at that point. Only much later in the story, after famine in Rome has given Constantine the thought of leading a mass emigration to found a colony, does he depart to found Constantinople at an angel's instruction. He leaves Sylvester behind to rule in his stead at Rome and to enjoy his imperial sources of income ("for you will encounter great expense in buying food"), *but only* until such time as the emperor shall come again. Then, once having made his departure, he resolves never to return. And so we see the Donation accounted for, but not made so firmly or irrevocably as in the old forgery. Then it quickly disappears from sight in the *Book of Emperors*. It seems that the pope following Sylvester—no name

17. *Chronica*, IV, iii, p. 306.
18. *Monarchia*, III, x, p. 130.

is given—is susceptible to bribery and so implicitly violates the Imperial Law and Constantine's trust. He makes good his mistake, however, and the point is not pressed. Such a combination of events, gives neither papal nor imperial partisans cause to raise the divisive issue of the Donation of Constantine.

As the author had allowed the identities of pope and emperor to fuse into one in the telling of how Constantine and Sylvester had perfected the Imperial Law, he employs an analogous device in bringing together Charlemagne and Pope Leo III. Here again, as a matter of political history, the relationship of pope and emperor had later given cause for much feuding between protagonists of clerical and of temporal supremacy within the Holy Roman Empire. Did the fact that Charlemagne came to Rome to save Pope Leo from the threats of his enemies make the church dependent on the empire? In other words, did Leo crown Charlemagne because he had no other choice? Or did the fact that the pope "moved the empire" from Constantinople to the West by crowning this roving, barbarian king as emperor mean that the empire in the West derived from papal authority?

Once more, the altered history in the *Book of Emperors* suppresses the divisive issue. According to its account, the Greeks had so wretchedly abused the imperial splendor by the atrocity of gouging out the eyes and cutting off the noses of a Byzantine emperor and an empress-dowager (Constantine VI and Irene) that the Roman princes vowed never to elect any more men from the Greek nation as emperors, "for they had been unable to maintain fidelity or even respect toward them" (14282-14292). Leo III and Charlemagne then enter the story as sons of the same father, the Frankish Ripuarian King Pippin. They are shown to be congenial brothers throughout, so that the question of whose will or necessity it was that Leo crowned Charlemagne becomes irrelevant. The author emphasizes the continuity of the empire from the first Roman emperors to the Carolingians rather than any transference of authority from the East. He presents his reduced number of Greek emperors more conspicuously for interrupting the flow of authority from Romans to Germans than for exercising any particular right to rule from Constantinople. In telling of Charlemagne's accession to imperial leadership, his narrative stresses "how sorely the imperial law of Constantine had been neglected," (14782-14783) assumedly under the Byzantine rulers; in order that Charlemagne could give new life to the narrative, an angel recites it for him: "Then the mighty Emperor left us many a good article of law of which God's compassion had given him knowledge, as he ruled the Empire in great esteem." Besides fitting Charlemagne into the tradition of imperial lawgiving from Augustus to Constantine, the episode illustrates the author's conception of Roman law as not really different from older Germanic law. When situations demanded new laws, the Germanic peoples held rediscovered old laws to be more valid than those decreed for the first time by a ruler.

2.4. Christian clemency and draconic law enforcement

Closely related to the topic of law, the perennial problem of balancing just retribution with Christian clemency is the subject of much dialogue in the *Book of Emperors*. In the famous legend of Pope Leo's blinding by his enemies, Leo speaks for forgiveness, Charlemagne for the strict administration of justice. When Leo tells Charlemagne that he looks to Heaven alone to exact vengeance and admonishes him "never to let ill befall any of them on account of this," his stern brother contradicts him.

> It would never serve God's honor if one were to spare murderers. Hai! How gravely that would damage Christendom! My titles are those of judge and ruler, and accordingly I am pledged to hand down judgments to my people. . . . With my sword I shall protect Christendom. They will have a cause for sore regret: either I will avenge your eyes, or I will renounce my sword. (14529-14540)

The temporal authority, then, may well forgive a crime against it, but only if such forgiveness *belongs* to it. No ruler should deal forgivingly with crimes against others or "against God."

The same question, but with much more subtle shading, is treated in an earlier story, that of the entirely fictional Empress Crescentia. She intervenes with a duke on behalf of a guilty seneschal whose false witness had caused the duke to order her drowned for the murder of the duke's son. The duke had never known her imperial identity when he had entrusted his son to her care, and when she appears again the duke does not even recognize her as the woman he had ordered executed. He has now promised Crescentia to forgive the seneschal, but when the latter finally confesses the stern duke nonetheless insists on the death penalty because, as he sees it, only his promise to forgive a crime against himself (his son's murder) can be held valid. He will not forgive "what he did to that poor woman [the unrecognized Crescentia] as a crime against God," i.e., what is not his to forgive. Forbidding any more discussion, he has the guilty man executed. Later, however, the earlier crime of her brother-in-law is exposed: he had succeeded in having the emperor condemn Crescentia, his innocent wife, for adultery. Crescentia had miraculously escaped both execution attempts. Both the seneschal and Crescentia's brother-in-law were enraged at her rejection of them. This time, however, Crescentia persuades the emperor to pardon the guilty man, and he does so, for in this instance the crime is hers and the emperor's to forgive (11435-12798).

All in all, the *Book of Emperors* seems rather heavily weighted on the side of strict punishment in balancing claims for the Christian ethic of mercy against those for law and order.[19] The author is usually content to see clerics make a pro forma plea for clemency before stern judges who will exact an eye for eye from the guilty man, as an example to those who might slip. In presenting his greatly idealized reign of Louis the Pious (see above) he loses his grammatical composure in an outburst over the severity of that sovereign's measures.

---

19. Gellinek goes a bit too far when he says: "Jesus does not figure even marginally [in the work]." The German Emperors' Chronicle . . . ," op. cit., p. 233. Jesus plays a part in the Tiberius story as "the great physician" of whom the emperor hears from afar. The author's Tiberius tries to invite Jesus to Rome to cure his illness, but Jesus is killed before the imperial messenger arrives in Jerusalem. At the end of the story, the words of Jesus about the destruction of Jerusalem are cited at length just before the (unhistorically early) Roman destruction of Jerusalem (690-764; 875-896). Still, his general statement that "the spirit of severity tinged by the genius of the Old Testament prevails almost everywhere" is on target. Ibid.

Thus with wise council did the King rule the Empire. He proclaimed a peace of God: for highway robbery the noose was the sentence, for murder the wheel—hai! What a peace that was!—the gallows for the robber; from the thief his eyes; from the disturber of the peace, his hands; for setting fires, the neck. (15138-15147)

Such a draconic notion of law enforcement on a small scale finds its parallel, naturally enough, in justified wholesale slaughter of "heathen" forces who defy the Church and empire (the destruction of Jerusalem and the massacre of its inhabitants is also neatly worked into this pattern). The author's account of the First Crusade is all too typical of the heroic strain in crusading chronicles in its thirst for pagan blood. After recounting in detail how Godfrey of Bouillon and his men went on to massacre women and children after defeating the Muslim forces, he notes, "God was helping His own that day!" (16710-16711).

2.5. Prayer-answering as within a feudal contract

But if we find frequent and gross omission of Christian forgiveness, love, and all that we may feel is the Christian ethic in this work with its large religiously based ideological component, our objection would probably seem beside the point to our author. A considerable part of the value of his work to us is his display of what he and his audience were looking for in their religion. In popular medieval Christianity, Christian ethics were, of course, extolled. In a contrast that could not be more marked with the liberal theology of the early twenty-first century, however, these Christian ethics were not the main thing the Christian religion had to offer. Far closer to the average man's consciousness of what his religion was all about was the divine promise of eternal salvation in the hereafter and of immediate help here on earth. It is in man's reaction to this promise—Does he believe in it? Does he let it work wonders?—that much of the dramatic impact of the *Book of Emperors* lies. The saints believe in this promise with a fervor fifty times as great as that of ordinary men, and they work miracles because the promise is real. Over and over the author depicts good Christians welcoming death at the hands of the impious, for this is clearly the road to sainthood.

In some of the episodes the author is content to depict bravery in the face of death in terms familiar enough in heroic portrayals from ancient times to our own. "I would be a happy man indeed, " the future Saint Sixtus tells Emperor Decius, "if I were worthy enough to earn the name of martyr. Then I should enjoy a splendid life forever and receive my promised crown." (6088-6191) But the author goes far beyond this routine tone in depicting the urgency of the pious in seeking torture and death for their faith. "I wish you well, Holy Father," shouts the future Saint Lawrence as the soldiers of Decius hasten the satisfied Sixtus away to his death, "but don't leave me behind you forever. What have I done to offend you? . . . Why are you deserting me like this? Let me enjoy a share of your holy martyrdom. . . . Master, don't abandon me in my misery, but let me come along with you!" (6209-6211, 6216-6217, 6222-6223).

Man was, of course, to avail himself of the Christian promise through prayer, and prayers are often spoken by historical personages in the *Book of Emperors*. Two aspects of the frequent prayers attributed to historical personages throw considerable light on just how men of the feudal age were apt to view themselves in relation to God and the saints. One is the frequent challenge to the deity to prove that it is indeed a deity; the other is the act of reasoning with the deity, pointing out what one has a right to expect as a prayerful Christian in search of assistance. This sort of thing can be found in the Old Testament, as when Moses reminds God of the promise of his Covenant, pointing out that if he does not give the Children of Israel the aid that they are counting on, in spite of their sins, the Egyptians will think that he is lacking in power.[20] This challenge would seem rather foreign to the spirit of the New Testament, however, which avoids putting this kind of pressure on God. Prayer has, of course, always been intended to produce a divine response, particularly when the victory or deliverance sought by the supplicant seems not to be forthcoming in the normal order of events. The supplicants in the *Book of Emperors*, however,

---

20. 20 Exod. 32:1-14.

are not so much supplicants as—like the children of Israel—holders of a contract. They have accepted the Christian faith, been baptized, and are placing trust in God directly or through a particular saint. Consequently they expect God or that saint to fulfill the divine part of the contract held by people who have met these conditions.

For example, when Saint Peter and Saint Paul are shown praying for Peter's success in an impending contest of wonders with Simon the Magician, the author records,

> With hearts and minds alike they reminded God the Good of what he had told his disciples when he left them in great sorrow: that whatever they asked for in his name he would surely give them, to the end that he should bar the devil from success in anything that would bring shame upon Christianity. (4221-4228)

Saints on earth can thus "remind" God of the divine promise, and once in heaven they themselves can be "reminded" of what is expected of them by those who believe in them. For our author, as with his general approval of Old Testament eye-for-an-eye law enforcement over Christian clemency, we see the Old Testament idea of holding God accountable for preventing calamities in the here and now prevailing over the New Testament idea that in *this* world evil may very well befall the blessed, who are promised rewards in heaven for their sufferings on behalf of the faith.

In the author's account of Pope Leo's blindness noted above, both of these characteristic aspects of prayer in the feudal age are in evidence. Charlemagne points out to Christ that he has done everything that an earthly ruler of the Romans can do, and he *reminds* Christ of the Resurrection, both as an indication that he is a true believer and that it is clearly within Christ's power to do all things. He concludes that it would be well for the evil people of Rome to be taught a lesson and given something by which to remember Christ's power: "Then they will know with certainty that Thou art a true God!" With Saint Peter, Charlemagne proceeds less subtly. There is no question but that his tone is appropriate only for addressing someone who has not kept his part of a contract. After reminding the saint of his heavenly office, he bids him,

> Think now, my lord, what I am going through! . . . Just look at your pope!
> I left him sound of body in your care, and now I found him blinded. If you do
> not heal that blind man today, I shall destroy your house [Saint Peter's Cathe-
> dral], ruin the buildings and grounds donated to you, and then leave him for
> you, blind as he is, and go back again to Ripuaria. (14714-14724)

Yet even here, in a passage that comes very close to exalting the empire against the church, the point is still that church and empire are one.
Immediately after Charlemagne's threatening "prayer" the pope's sight is
restored, but the latter explains to the congregation in Saint Peter's that this
miracle is the result of *all* of their prayers (14725-14748).

There are many similar instances that document the immediacy of
medieval man's religious experience. In spite of a great deal of magic and
the stress laid withal on a point that in our day tends to lose its appeal—the
notion that Christian magic is more powerful than pagan magic—there is
nothing mysterious, nothing in the least difficult to grasp about the Christian religion as practiced by the men the *Book of Emperors* portrays as de-
vout. The saints and angels encountered in its pages behave in quite com-
prehensible human fashion and speak the clearest of mortal idioms, never
with any double meaning, never with any need for interpretation.

When Pope Gregory, for example, prays for the salvation of Emperor
Trajan's soul some two hundred years after that exemplary pagan emperor's
death, an angel appears to Gregory and at first attempts to convince him
that there is no hope. Pagans, after all, are justly condemned permanently
to hell. But Gregory reasons with the angel and persuades him to modify
his total opposition to his plea, for the angel can understand why Gregory
feels as he does and makes a suggestion.

> Gregory, I'll tell you what you do. You are a proven servant of God, so let God
> give you the right to decide whether you will let this heathen suffer what he earned
> with his life or whether you will take care of his soul from now on—but with that

choice you must accept seven severe illnesses that you can never be healed of until you die. (6050-6058)

Here, as frequently enough elsewhere, the modern reader will find some loose ends to the story. As the gates of hell open and Trajan's soul comes flying back to his tomb, where he is turned over to Pope Gregory until Judgment Day, we are left to puzzle out just what the good Pope is going to do with the disembodied (or perhaps, re-embodied) soul of a Roman emperor from then on. But to stress this would again be very much beside the point, for the narrative in the whole work is woven of visionary elements that are distorted when isolated and pursued with cold reason. The vision of the Holy Roman Empire remained a vision only as long as no one attempted to sort out its assertions from its assumptions and to weigh the factual content in both.

To accept the ideology of the Holy Roman Empire at its height, a man was to believe that the imperial tradition stretched back to the Roman Caesars and that it was destined to hold Christian Europe together in a community under one law and one faith that were as inseparable as they were ancient. The *Book of Emperors* shows how substance could be given in an infinite variety of ways to the conceptions for which the empire stood. To be sure, the work also demonstrates why it was relatively easy for historians in the Renaissance, Reformation, and Enlightenment to unravel the visionary fabric of the Holy Roman Empire. To these later investigators, determining "true" and "truth" in history mattered less and less what vision one had and more and more whether this man really said *that* and whether *those* men really lived *then*.

3. Composition and Utilization of the Work

3.1. Authorship

A phenomenally large number of passages in the *Book of Emperors* use quite similar, occasionally identical, lines and phrases to those found in the German adaptation of the *Song of Roland* from its French original by one Priest Conrad, who identifies himself at the end of his work. This led the young historian, Heinrich Welzhofer in the early 1870s to conclude that Conrad was the author of at least most of the *Book of Emperors*.[21] The established philologist, Wilhelm Scherer, soon expressed some doubts about this,[22] but the theory of Conrad as author found its way to general acceptance in large part through Edward Schröder's advocacy of it in the notes and introduction to his *Monumenta Germaniae Historica* edition of the Middle High German text as *Die Kaiserchronik eines Regensburger Geistlichen* (Hannover, 1895).[23] Fixing Priest Conrad in Regensbug during the 1130s led to putting him in the service of the Bavarian Duke, Henry the Proud (1108?-1139), particularly since the *Book of Emperors* treats Henry's father-in-law, the Guelph Emperor Lothar II, with great enthusiasm.

Almost thirty years after Schröder's edition of the text appeared, however, the German *Song of Roland* was shown to be of much later vintage than originally supposed—stemming from about 1170 rather than 1130. In 1924, Carl Wesle pointed out that several of the virtually identical passages make perfect sense in the context of the *Book of Emperors* narrative, while fitting into Conrad's *Song of Roland* much less comfortably.[24] Thus Conrad borrowed from the *Book of Emperors*; since the *Book of Emperors* is not quite finished, it is unlikely that he was its author, too.

---

21. *Untersuchungen über die deutsche Kaiserchronik des zwölften Jahrhunderts* (Munich: C. Ackermann 1874), pp. 57-66.

22. "Rolandslied Kaiserchronik Rother" *Zeitschrift für deutsches Altertum und deutsche Literatur*" Vol. XVIII (1875), pp. 302-5.

23. Source as in note 1, pp. 50-60.

24. Carl Wesle "*Kaiserchronik* und *Rolandslied,*" *Beiträge zur Geschichte der deutschen Sprache und Literatur,* Vol. XLVIII (1924) pp. 223-258. The ghost of Conrad still occasionally haunts the pages of common English-language reference works; his must also be the shade of "a cleric who was employed at the Regensburg Court of Henry the Proud probably as a chancellery writer" in what may well be the only literary-historical work on the period billing itself as "a comprehensive systematic presentation from a Marxist-Leninist viewpoint" to touch on the authorship question. Ewald Erb, *Geschichte der deutschen Literatur von den Anfängen bis1160* (Berlin: Volk und Wissen Volkseigener Verlag 1965) Vol. II p. 717. *Wikipedia* as of January 21, 2010 was still citing Conrad as "not improbably" the author of the *Book of Emperors*.

Multiple authorship of the *Book of Emperors* has been asserted from time to time. Felix Debo thought that stylistic differences, as well as two different passages that sound like conclusions, pointed to two authors.[25] Schröder thought he could distinguish "Conrad," a second author and perhaps a third.[26] Subsequent stylistic research, however, has tended to support the idea that all sections of the work were either written or rewritten by a single author, whose unmistakable phrasing crops up even in clear adaptations of other writings from beginning to end.[27]

Nothing about the author is known except what can be derived from the internal evidence of his work, and this evidence suffices only to make him a probably aging cleric of Regensburg. That he was a cleric the evidence is massive, ranging from his clear conviction that theological disputation can be more exciting than scenes of battle to his use of the canonical hours. He is moved on occasion by such patriotic feeling for the Bavarians as assumedly only a Bavarian could show. His use of Regensburg local history and hagiographical tradition, for instance, is such that he must have received at least a substantial part of his education in that town; at one point he even notes the holding of a council "at Regensburg, the chief city." [28] He shows some geographical familiarity with Rome and with parts

---

25. "Über die Einheit der *Kaiserchronik*: eine kritische Vorstudie," dissertation, University of Graz (Graz: Leuschner & Lubensky 1877).

26. Op. cit., pp. 62-64.

27. Hans Ferdinand Massmann, *Der keiser und der kunige buoch oder die sogenannte Kaiserchronik* (Quedlinburg and Leipzig: Gottfr. Basse 1849-1854), Vol. III, pp. 393-4. A summation of arguments for single authorship is given by Ferdinand Urbanek, "Zur Datierung der *Kaiserchronik*," *Euphorion* Vol. LIII (1959), pp. 113-152, and this has prevailed as the majority opinion. Sections and passages which can nonetheless be cited to show multiple authorship are pointed out in the preliminary paragraphs and notes to individual chapters of this translation. Most of the scholarly discussion on the topic continues to revolve around questions of how much the author adapted his sources from the way he found them. There is a considerable range here from the "Crescentia" story, which he appears to have adopted in bulk from an earlier source with a few interpolations of his own to the chapter on Louis the Pious which is his own from beginning to end.

28. "Ze Regenesburch der houbestat," line 16822, in the story of the war between Henry IV and Henry V. The context does not quite make Regensburg into the "capital" of the empire, but it is not very far from doing so either.

of Hungary, which can be taken as evidence of some travels. The probability that he was at least in his fifties when he wrote is generally taken as fact because he recalls events of the 1120s and 1130s with a vividness that suggests that he experienced them as a mature observer. It is certainly true, as has been pointed out, that his work shows every sign of having been begun in leisure and finished in a hurry, for he deals with ancient Roman emperors much more fully than with German ones; however, even if this points to some knowledge of his own impending death, which is only one possible explanation, this need not signify an advanced age. Two different factors seem to bear a little—though not much more—weight in determining that he was in middle age or beyond at the time of writing. The first is his horror of gout, a disease seldom very acute in younger men, which he couples with leprosy as the epitome of sore affliction. The second is the great store he sets on the appeal of youth, while putting passages reflecting wisdom into the mouths of older men.

Some attempts have been made to glean a biographical detail or so about the author from the abrupt breaking-off of the *Book of Emperors*, although few since the fixing of the work's *terminus a quo* in 1152, discussed below. After the author tells of Saint Bernard of Clairvaux and how his preaching encouraged the nobles of Conrad III's court to undertake an expedition to the Holy Land, the words "The king hesitated no longer" (17283) are the last he recorded. The clause in question, *"der chuonich niht lenger netwelte"* could conceivably stand alone grammatically in Middle High German, as can its English rendering. Yet the author's style is to introduce some action by writing that so-and-so "hesitated no longer but hastened to" act in some way, indicating that this break-off was an unnatural stopping point for him. This observation has been variously used to suggest: (1) the author's death at the time of preparations in Germany for the Second Crusade, or soon afterwards; (2) his decision to go along on the Second Crusade; (3) his shock at the disaster the Crusade met, which rendered him unable or unwilling to continue; or, finally, (4) someone's decision not to record the outcome of the Crusade.

Since Conrad's departure for the Holy Land was in 1147, the first of these interpretations must obviously be ruled out if we hold that the bulk of the *Book of Emperors* was written after the accession of Frederick Barbarossa in 1152. As for the second interpretation, the author's participation in the Second Crusade remains a possibility, for indeed many clerics, including Otto of Freising, joined the Crusaders; however, if he did so, this is unrelated to his breaking off his work, for he must have returned from the Crusade to continue the task of writing even if he had begun his history before. The third interpretation has been forcefully argued,[29] but it rests on a most unlikely coincidence: that the news of the disaster of the Second Crusade reached Regensburg just at the time the author was writing about Saint Bernard and Conrad III. Even assuming that he had really been writing in the 1140s rather than later and that the coincidence of events was real, there is not much reason to suppose that this news would have sufficed to make him drop his stylus on the spot, never to take it up again.

Schröder advanced the fourth interpretation in 1895, and none of his false assumptions concerning dating or Conrad the Priest's authorship disproves it. He reasoned that whoever introduced the work to the public (he supposed an editor and cites two passages that look like last-minute additions) decided to leave the caesura so that "the broken-off ending could appear to the first readers in 1150 or 1151 as a highly suggestive dash, which the fresh memory [of the disaster] would explain sufficiently well."[30] Whether the *Book's* first readers, if indeed they were to be readers rather than the listeners the author seems to envision, were to receive the work in 1150 or five years later makes no difference in evaluating the interpretation. Instead, speaking chiefly against this premise is the fact that the *Book of Emperors* shows no inclination to leave this sort of potentially controversial subject to the audience's imagination: not only does the author elsewhere show himself bent on giving an all's-right-with-the-church-and-Empire interpretation of disasters, but even the two passages cited by Schröder as evidence of an editor show the same harmonizing tendency. Still, this much is certain: events of the Second Crusade were difficult for any Christian

---

29. Friedrich-Wilhelm Wentzlaff-Eggebert *Kreuzzugsdichtung des Mittelalters: Studien zu ihrer geschichtlichen und dichterischen Wirklichkeit* (Berlin: Walter de Gruyter 1960), p. 61.
30. Op. cit., p. 45.

apologist to cope with, and Saint Bernard's subsequent explanation that the expedition had failed because of the iniquity of its participants or the society they represented could not have been at all palatable to the author. The only inference to be drawn from the abrupt breaking-off of the work that does not do violence to considerations of time and the author's attitude toward recording events is, unhappily, of no help in telling us anything about him: that, at the point in question, our monk was puzzling over how to proceed with his account of the Second Crusade, and probably putting off its writing from day to day, when death or some sudden force of circumstances kept him from returning to his work.

3.2. Patronage

Although there is neither a dedication nor mention of a patron in the *Book of Emperors*, a figure of some wealth or authority must be assumed to have stood behind its writing—unless the author himself were a spiritual lord of high degree, which cannot be ruled out, but which his anonymity speaks against. It seems unlikely that a priest or monk would take it upon himself to spend years of his life writing such a novel work as this without special authorization. Procuring the necessarily immense quantity of parchment alone entailed considerable expense. One or several of the Bishops of Regensburg have been proposed as probable patrons. Schröder suggested Bishop Kuno of Regensburg, and some fifty-five years ago in her doctoral dissertation Irmgard Möller documented the extremely long history of involvement of the Bishops of Regensburg, not only as participants in the Investiture Struggle—the civil war between adherents of Henry IV and Henry V—and the Guelph-Ghibbeline strife, but also as often having actively contributed towards resolving the conflicts with compromise.[31] Certainly the reconciliation of this type of conflict is central to the ideology of the *Book of Emperors*. Most of the evidence linking the Bishops of Regensburg with patronage of the work comes, however, from an earlier period than its apparent time of writing. It remains quite possible that the idea of having

---

31. Irmgard Möller, *Die deutsche Geschichte in der Kaiserchronik* (Munich: typescript 1958), pp. 54 ff.

such a work as this written—to put the ideology of the Holy Roman Empire before an audience of laymen growing in influence—might have originated with one of them.

In 1959 Ferdinand Urbanek suggested Count Palatine Otto V of the House of Wittelsbach as one of the Bavarian notables in the 1150s with the likeliest inclination and the resources to support such a work as the *Book of Emperors*.[32] A passage in its portrayal of Charlemagne reflects the wording of a law promulgated by Frederick Barbarossa in Regensburg in 1152 in the presence of Count Otto V of Wittelsbach. This idiofact does much more to establish the Charlemagne chapter's *terminus a quo* than Count Otto V as the author's patron, although this dating does serve to eliminate suggested patrons from an earlier period. Urbanek bases much of his argument for Count Otto V as patron upon the chronicler's non-usage of Otto of Freising's *History of the Two Cities* as a source book of historical fact. Freising is also in Bavaria, something less than seventy miles from Regensburg, and the author might have normally been expected to have known of Bishop Otto of Freising's history and to have availed himself of it in order to protect himself against gross error in writing a vernacular history of the Roman Empire. He did not do so, although he used other Latin sources less adequate to his undertaking. Now Count Palatine Otto V was one of the few enemies singled out by Otto of Freising in his world history for personal attack in a passage, later expunged from some of the manuscripts, striking for its immoderate tone.

> Count Palatine Otto, the very similar son of a faithless, unrighteous father, surpasses all his ancestors in malice and troubles the Church of God without ceasing down to this very day. Thus, most remarkably, almost the entire descendants of this house are, according to I do not know what divine ordinance, *"in reprobum sensum tradita* [given over to a depraved mind]"[33]

---

32. "Zur Datierung der *Kaiserchronik*" op. cit., pp. 129-130.
33. Rom. 2:28, which introduces a comprehensive catalogue of vices: "Being filled with all unrighteousness fornication wickedness covetousness maliciousness; full of envy murder debate deceit malignity; whisperers backbiters haters of God despiteful proud boasters inventors of evil things disobedient to parents . . . etc."

so that among them one finds none or almost none who does not rage in public acts of violence or, completely blinded and unworthy of any spiritual or secular office, lapse into thievery and highway robbery, or eke out a wretched beggar's existence.[34]

This is strong language in anyone's book. Mid-twelfth-century Germany being a time and place where a nobleman did not let a personal insult go ignored if he could help it, what better retort could there have been than for Count Otto to sponsor a work of world history that, through its appeal to laymen, might easily eclipse the scholarly work of the attacker? The Wittelsbach family had every reason to supply the author with as many sheepskins as he needed to write on and to see to it that he was given plenty of free time and perhaps a handsome reward for his labor.

Actually the author's non-usage of Otto of Freising's work does not quite prove what it might be expected to, for although Otto of Freising wrote "1146" as the year in which he brought his *History of the Two Cities* to a close, there is no evidence of his book's having been read and used by others before he sent it with some additions and corrections to Emperor Frederick Barbarossa in 1157. The changed times made him introduce his work to Frederick with a letter that obviates the pessimistic tone of his work. And yet, while Urbanek rested too much of his case on the non-usage of Otto of Freising's work in the *Book of Emperors*, the basis of his proponency of the Wittelsbach family as furnishing a patron still stands. If Otto of Freising inveighed against Otto V of Wittelsbach so heftily in his world chronicle, it is most likely indeed that he expressed a marked dislike of the man in other occasions. And although Otto of Freising's work may not have been released to the public for eleven years after he wrote it, some knowledge that he had written *some* book of world history very likely made its way from Freising to Regensburg.

The only really sure *terminus ad quem* for the *Book of Emperors* is 1165. In that year Charlemagne was made a saint, a fact that the author,

---

34. Excursus on the alleged treason of Count Berthold of Scheyern one of Count Otto of Wittelsbach's ancestors in aiding the invading "Huns" (Magyars) in 955. *Chronica* VI xx pp. 462-4.

who refers to Emperor Henry II as "Saint Henry," would not have let pass unnoticed had he written after the canonization. There is thus nothing to keep the author from having begun his work around 1152 under Count Otto V, who would not need to have known of the blast against his family's honor specifically in the *History of the Two Cities*, or after 1157 under his son Otto VI (later Duke of Bavaria), who most certainly would have been confronted with the inflammatory passage.[35] At the moment of my writing (fall of 2011), one of the Wittelsbachs then remains the leading contender as patron of the *Book of Emperors*, perhaps following up on a suggestion from one of the bishops of Regensburg.

3.3. Sources

Concerning the sources of the *Book of Emperors*, a great deal is known approximately, relatively little—except near the beginning and end of the work—exactly. For almost thirty years, Hans Ferdinand Massmann, the poet, patriot, founder of gymnastics clubs, and scholar, conducted an intensive search for sources. In 1848 and 1849, he published the first complete, edited version of the Middle High German text in a synoptic collation of twelve complete and seventeen fragmentary manuscripts in two volumes—the *Book of Emperors and Kings* or the so-called *Chronicle of Emperors*—and followed these in 1854 with a third volume of 1192 pages containing commentary on all aspects of the work. His success in tracing the immense influence of the *Book of Emperors* (see below) was great; in identifying sources, less so. This was not his fault, for those who took material from the *Book of Emperors* in later times usually did so without adding or subtracting much. The author himself, however, was much more of an innovator *vis-à-vis* his source material, with a few notable exceptions, and the connections in the latter case are much more difficult to trace than in the former. Massmann's findings do show that the author's eclecticism knew few bounds in his search for usable material—that he ventured from

---

35. E. E. Stengel proposes Otto VI in "Die Entstehung der *Kaiserchronik* und der Aufgang der stauferschen Zeit," *Deutsches Archiv*, Vol. XIV (1958) pp. 395 ff.

the lives of saints, to Josephus, to pagan legend retold with a thin veneer of Christian moralizing, and retrieved material from many unknown sources as well. He considered the possibility that a whole, lost, German vernacular source, the *Chronicle* (*Cronica*) noted in the Prologue, preceded the *Book of Emperors*,[36] which now seems unlikely. On the other hand, his fierce partisanship led him to cite the few real, surviving German-language sources used by the author as having instead been derived from the *Book of Emperors*, for Massmann regarded the work as long as he lived rather much as his own fief, and he defended its every claim not only to fame but also to originality with passion and steadfastness.

Some forty years later Edward Schröder noted in his *Monumenta Germaniae Historica* edition of the Middle High German text that relatively little new material had been identified in terms of sources since Massmann's edition, although important work had been done to help straighten out the relationship between what was source and what was derivative.[37] It was Schröder who cautioned most clearly about speaking of the author's use of sources as if he were writing with open Latin chronicles in front of him. When we say that material from Suetonius is found in the work of Orosius, we mean that Orosius read the relevant portions of Suetonius' *Lives of the Caesars* and made extractions of facts and events as he desired soon afterwards. When we say that material from Orosius is found in the *Book of Emperors,* however, we mean that the author *could* have read Orosius' work. More likely a long chain of writing and telling through the media of sermons, epic song, and lives of saints conveyed the account to him with many omissions and embellishments. Furthermore he was quite possibly writing down years later what he had heard or read at a much younger age.

In the early twentieth century, a few more source fragments were unearthed, but then, in 1940, Ernst Friedrich Ohly published his dissertation

---

36. "Eine deutsche Vorlage?" in op. cit., Vol. III, pp. 324-7.
37. Schröder discusses demonstrable written sources, both German and Latin in pages 50-73 of his "Einleitung" and gives these succinctly in his footnotes to the text. His only significant error remains his assertion that Priest Conrad's *Rolandslied* served the author as a source of convenient phrasing.

as a book, *Sage und Legende in der Kaiserchronik*. His very comprehensive analysis reviews and evaluates every important supposition of Massman, Schröder, and others concerning sources in the *Book of Emperors* up to the Charlemagne narrative, while demonstrating new identifications of sources in some instances. Ohly is the first commentator to show the real familiarity with medieval preaching and minor theological didactic writings that his predecessors could only sense would be most useful in establishing the book's sources. Ohly found the author's use of saintly legend even greater than had been supposed and showed that often in adapting the story of a saint for the *Book of Emperors* the author would enlarge—and sometimes add outright—a ruler's role, reducing the role of the saint himself considerably. This type of legend, he found, was the source of some 10,000 verse lines of the first 14,281 lines dealt with in his investigation, with heroic epics of a secular nature accounting for some 2,500 lines and little "apart from the dry skeletal bones" traceable to Latin chronicles.[38] Ohly's work also deals with the author's probable motivation for composing original sections and sees the work as planned from beginning to end—in contrast with Schröder and other critics who approach it from a literary

---

38. *Sage und Legende in der Kaiserchronik: Untersuchungen über Quellen und Aufbau der Dichtung* (Münster 1940; repr. Darmstadt: WBG 1968), p. 234. Apart from space considerations, Ohly's confining of his work almost entirely to sources for stories of Roman and Byzantine emperors was due to the fact that from the account of Charlemagne on the author's use of sources changed somewhat; increasingly ". . . the small individual fact comes into its own right." p. 7. Sources for the German history in the *Book of Emperors* had been more accurately and completely given by Schröder in part on the basis of Heinrich Welzhofer's *Untersuchungen über die deutsche Kaiserchronik* (Munich: 1874). Welzhofer showed that the author made extensive use of the *Würzburg Chronicle* (Chronicon Wirziburgense) and the *World Chronicle of Frutolf* of Michelsberg (until 1896 given in the literature as the work of Ekkehard of Aura its continuator after 1103). Not much else has turned up here. Irmgard Möller's dissertation on German history in the *Book of Emperors* (see note 30) locates two new likely sources for the Charlemagne story but generally deals with questions of parallels rather than those of sources. This is also true of Robert Folz who includes the *Book of Emperors* Charlemagne story in his *Le Souvenir et la Légende de Charlemagne dans l'Empire germanique médiéval* (Paris, 1950). Publications de l'Université de Dijon VII.

standpoint and emphasize the work's unevenness—and lets accident account for changes that the author can be seen or assumed to be making in his treatment of sources.

Because the type of material used as source in the *Book of Emperors* varies so widely from story to story, as does the degree of freedom the author takes with it voluntarily or involuntarily, I thought it advisable to give in the introductory paragraphs before the individual chapters some idea of sources used, if they are known, along with some basic facts from the normally accepted history of the subject presented.

3.4. Influence

In contrast with the intricate problem of sources, the question of how much influence the *Book of Emperors* had on later German medieval historians is relatively easy to answer. The interest of modern students in it is, as noted above, more profitably linked to its worth as a document of medieval intellectual history than anything else. However, the value of any document of intellectual history cannot be separated from the impact it had on contemporary and succeeding ages, so that its popularity in medieval Germany is worth demonstrating at least in broad outline.

By 1895, thirty-three surviving manuscripts and fragments of the *Book of Emperors* had been catalogued, which, particularly if the enormous size of the work is considered—at 17,283 lines it is the longest work in German before 1200—attests in itself to its popularity.[39] The oldest-surviving

---

39. As a "best seller" it could not compete with a work such as the thirteenth-century *Schwabenspiegel*, discussed below, which was needed by a substantial body of public officials for ready reference and survives in two hundred copies. Against histories, however, it held its own. By way of contrast, the now famous *Annals* of Lampert of Hersfeld, one of the chief sources for the reign of Henry IV through 1107, reached the sixteenth century in only six manuscripts. Gregory of Tours, the only source of Merovingian history through the end of the sixth century worth mentioning and one of the most widely read medieval historians in modern Europe and the Americas, survived the Middle Ages in no more than forty manuscripts and fragments. The best description of the manuscripts and fragments of the *Book of Emperors* in relation to each other is still in Schröder's introduction to his text, op. cit., pp. 7-33.

manuscript of the *Book of Emperors*, in the Augustinian Monastery at Vorau, Styria, Austria, dates from before 1190. At least four intermediary manuscripts preceded this copy from the lost original copy, itself no more than thirty-five years old by then.[40] Although later many changes affecting the content of the work were made, the first alterations concerned style alone. The increasingly high standards regarding purity of rhyme and meter induced a partial re-writing (B) of the original text (A) in the early thirteenth century and another in the mid-thirteenth (C, taken directly from A, not from B), although A with its assonances and strained meter was recopied, whole and in part, sometimes fairly accurately, sometimes with massive scribal error, as late as the mid-fifteenth century.

The first proven borrowings from the *Book of Emperors* were those of historically minded poets, who were considerably weaker historians in any currently recognizable sense than its author. Conrad the Priest incorporated a vast number of lines and phrases from the *Book of Emperors* into his adaptation of the German version of the *Song of Roland* about 1170. Before 1174 in the Netherlands, Heinrich von Veldeke—regarded by subsequent writers as "the real founder of the court epic" for his *Eneit*—cited from it,[41] as did the anonymous Rhenish author of *Moriz von Craun* about 1210, who was concerned with tracing the course of chivalry from Greece to Rome to contemporary France and beyond. Around 1200 the Bavarian Master Otte cited the *Book of Emperors* a number of times as authority for his *Eraclius*. More than most of that generation of courtly poets, Otte was demonstrably a writer who "attached value to the historicity of his

---

40. Pius Fank, Librarian of the Vorau Monastery, proves rather conclusively that this manuscript was planned by the monastery's Prior Bernhard I, who was also its main copyist and illuminator. *Die Vorauer Handschrift: Ihre Entstehung und ihr Schreiber* (Graz: Akademische Druck- und Verlagsanstalt, 1967), pp. 11-55. In a postcard I received from him in June 1967, in response to an inquiry, the Rev. Fank indicated that the project was carried out "before 1190," which, given the dates of Bernhard's priorship (1185-1202), would narrow down its dating to 1185-1190.
41. M. C. O'Walshe, *Medieval German Literature* (Cambridge, Massachusetts: Harvard University Press, 1962), pp. 137-138. Heinrich's Eneit is an adaptation of Virgil's *Aeneid* over a circuitous route.

narration."[42] Although he used more of Conrad's *Rolandslied* than of the *Book of Emperors*, the great Wolfram von Eschenbach of *Parzival* fame showed some familiarity with the Charlemagne-Leo story and adapted some dialogue for characters of his own creation out of the Constantine-Helena-Sylvester chapter from the *Book of Emperors*.[43]

Apart from the *Book of Emperors* itself, the genre of vernacular imperial or world history did not come into its own in the German-speaking lands until the thirteenth century. Even then, prose history in form as well as content was slow and uncertain in its arrival. In the twelfth century the overwhelming preponderance of anything written down in vernacular books had been rhymed, at least half-heartedly, although the use of Latin prose was common both for literary and practical purposes.[44] Not long after 1200, an awareness began to dawn on the German public—then enjoying a high point of vernacular poetry unparalleled for centuries to come—that poetic form was best restricted to poetic matter. There are epic portions of the *Book of Emperors* that readily lend themselves to verse presentation. The material of a didactic, informational nature, on the other hand, could be recognized by some literati even then as being better off without the encumbrance of rhyme and meter, which were substandard in the original version A and still well below the technical poetic standards of the time in the revisions B and C. Consequently, while some hands continued to copy the *Book of Emperors* in verse form until the sixteenth century simply because they found it this way, others took parts of it and rewrote them in prose.

The first German history book in prose form, the Saxon *Weltchronik*, was completed about 1230 by Eike von Repgow, a knight, tax assessor, and

---

42. Eberhard Nellmann, *Die Reichsidee in deutschen Dichtungen der Salier- und frühen Stauferzeit: Annolied – Kaiserchronik – Rolandslied – Eraclius.* (Berlin: Erich Schmidt, 1963), *Philologische Studien und Quellen*, Heft 16, p. 13.
43. Samuel Singer, *Wolframs Willehalm* (Bern: A. Francke, 1918), pp. 38-9 and 43-4.
44. Perhaps this is surprising, perhaps not. It may be recalled that while the Greeks were quite interested in their own history, they satisfied themselves with historical narratives in poetic form for more than four centuries, until Herodotus introduced prose form in his *Histories* in the second half of the fifth century, *BC*.

also author of the *Sachsenspiegel*, a work on the legal tradition of his native Eastphalia. Eike, who wrote in Low German, incorporated some stories from the *Book of Emperors* into the final version of his *Weltchronik*. Evidently these inclusions were well received, for a copyist of Eike's work in the fourteenth century grafted almost the entire *Book of Emperors* onto it. When he did so, he took a rhymed version as he found it—as Schröder notes—without being the least deterred by repetitions and contradictions between Eike's prose inclusions from the *Book of Emperors* and the original text.[45]

But Eike's venture into German prose as a medium for recording world or imperial history was still not much followed during the thirteenth century. The first, still anonymous, continuations of the *Book of Emperors* were also in verse. In the 1260s, a Bavarian writer brought the *Book of Emperors* up to the death of Emperor Frederick II in 1250, and another, this time Swabian, anonymous continuator about 1280, brought the work up to 1276 and thus the first years of the reign of Emperor Rudolph I. Not even a man possessed of the greatest imagination could have treated the conflicts of Frederick II with the Church—which ultimately brought the downfall of the Hohenstaufens and ushered in the Imperial Interregnum—satisfactorily in terms of the church and empire as one. The despairing tone of the first continuator is at a sharp variance with that of the old author of the book. He is obviously a Hohenstaufen partisan and laments Frederick's passing with "Woe! When shall we have his like again?" Neither continuator appears to be a cleric. The second continuator, however, quite in the original author's vein, makes an effort to depict a generally approved transfer of imperial power from the Hohenstaufens to Rudolf, the first Hapsburg emperor. He asserts that a search was made far and wide for more of the Hohenstaufen kin to lead the empire, but in vain (II, lines 1-251).

---

45. Schröder, op. cit., pp. 13 and 77. The same copyist also made inclusions from the thirteenth-century papal history of Martinus Polonus (Martin of Troppau), and did so very justifiably. The *Book of Emperors* has much less to say of the history of popes than its Prologue indicates. This version was further brought up to date with sketches of popes and emperors through the mid-fourteenth century. The oldest manuscript of this type was destroyed by fire in Strasbourg during the Franco-Prussian War, but survives in two copies.

The latter part of the thirteenth century saw the influence of the *Book of Emperors* most clearly to the south, where the two most significant Austrian "world chroniclers" used it as a source. In the 1270s the Viennese historian Jansen Enenkel modeled his *Weltchronik* upon it, and somewhat later Ottokar of Styria used both the original work and the two continuations as sources for his *Weltchronik*.[46]

That users of the *Book of Emperors* thought of it as a source of history and in connection with law and theology, rather than as a work of epic literature, is clear from the way it was bound into larger codices almost entirely with works of the former category. In Vorau, it took its place as the first work in the codex now famous simply as the "Vorau Manuscript," to introduce a variety of vernacular selections on historical and theological topics. The concluding work in this configuration is Otto of Freising's Latin *Gesta Friderici*, which thus served to continue the historical narrative broken off in 1147 in the *Book of Emperors* by taking up the reign of the new emperor, Frederick Barbarossa—whatever the antipathy between Otto of Freising and the probable Wittelsbach patrons of the *Book of*

---

46. Continuations I and II are appended to Schröder's text, pp. 393-416. The second continuator shares his original predecessor's eclectic instincts. From a literary standpoint, it is difficult to think of two more diverse German writers under the Hohenstaufens than the very direct, often downright blunt, original author of the *Book of Emperors* and the most subtle and refined of all Middle High German poets, Wolfram von Eschenbach, who nonetheless adapted some material from the *Book of Emperors*. For his part, the second continuator inserts a short passage from Willehalm, mentioning Wolfram as needed to describe adequately Rudolf's reception by the German princes. He also introduces phrasing from Wolfram's *Parzival* as well (II, lines 314-328, pp. 414-5.)

Enenkel's usage is evident throughout his work, although in Massmann's less than impartial judgment, his efforts indiscriminately "exploited, re-rhymed, and watered down" the *Book of Emperors*. Ottokar's use of it is only by inference, for no manuscript of his *World Chronicle*, noted by contemporaries, survived the Middle Ages. The inference is sound, however, for he demonstrably drew on it through the first part of the second continuation of his *Austrian Chronicle*. Also in Austria, the anonymous author of *Der kleine Lucidarius*, a satirical work that already mourns the passing of the chivalric age in the 1280s, shows familiarity with the *Book of Emperors*.

Emperors might have been.[47] In other libraries, the *Book of Emperors* also served itself as a continuation. Rudolf of Ems's mid-thirteenth-century history of creation and Old Testament times, usually referred to as his *Weltchronik*, [48] was sometimes used as a reference work, balanced by the *Book of Emperors*. For medieval Germans the latter work took care of meaningful history after the birth of Christ about as well as Rudolf's did for history before it. Heinrich of Munich[49] in the mid-fourteenth century borrowed extensively from Rudolf of Ems and the *Book of Emperors* for his own *Weltchronik*, extracting both directly from it and from Enenkel's recasting of some of its stories; he also brought it up to date through the death of Emperor Louis IV in 1347.

Apart from Eike's prose reworkings from the text, the *Book of Emperors* was independently rewritten in prose, the first book in German to undergo this process. In the same sort of balance as with Rudolf's *Weltchronik*, it bore the title the *Book of the Kings under the New Covenant (Buoch der kunege niewer ê)* and was bound into codices before the *Schwabenspiegel*—the Swabian counterpart to Eike's *Sachsenspiegel*—usually with a corresponding *Book of the Kings Under the Old Covenant (Buoch der kunege alter ê)*, based on the Old Testament. The thought of the writer or compiler was to use the reflections of law in history as an introduction to the description of their present-day law and custom. The prose author shows little ability to keep the narrative enlivened by his choice of phrases, but, literary considerations aside, such a didactic utilization of the work as his was certainly close to the original author's intent. The prose writer

---

47. Karl Konrad Polheim discusses the logical arrangement of the twenty-three works in *Die Struktur des Vorauer Handschrift*, as an introduction to the second volume of the facsimile printing of all but the final, Latin part of the manuscript. The *Kaiserchronik* constitutes the first volume; the shorter vernacular works, the second (Graz: Akademische Druck- und Verlagsanstalt, 1953-1958).

48. It is not only a too-generic name —for many other works are called by it with more justification—but an out-and-out misnomer, for its thirty-thousand lines take it no farther in world history than the death of Solomon.

49. He is generally now cited by this name; he preferred to call himself "Heinrich of Bavaria" (von Beierlant).

makes the connection explicit with statements like "We derive sound law of the land from Trajan in this book and other books." [50]

A bit of criticism as to the historical accuracy of our original author could be implied by the fact that the prose author considerably condenses the narrative, particularly in the section dealing with Pope Sylvester I, which takes up a disproportionate amount of the narrative allotted to the reign of Constantine in the original, the legend of Crescentia, and the fictional Emperor Faustinian. Historical criticism on his part is not clear, however, for in these three instances he directs the reader to the original *"Coronica"* to read the full story he has condensed. With Henry of Munich, on the other hand, a certain critical sense in extracting from the *Book of Emperors* is quite evident: he not only reduces the Faustinian story to a few sentences but corrects the account from another source by referring to Faustinian not as emperor but simply as Saint Clement's father, which, according to church tradition, he was. To be sure, Henry allows fresh inaccuracies into his work.

From the fifteenth century on, much of the utilization of the *Book of Emperors* by vernacular historians involved drawing on its original sporadically and, in the same new work, making use of accounts derived from it via other sources. For example, the Strasbourg priest, Jakob Twinger von Königshofen, writing in the middle of the 1380s, noted in his introduction to his *Alsatian Chronicle* that while there was a sufficiency of Latin chronicles, "there are few such books in German, although intelligent laymen enjoy as much as do learned clerics reading about such things." His book was thus aimed at middle-class people with some education who

---

50. These prose versions have not been counted with the thirty-three manuscripts of the *Book of Emperors*. Five all-prose versions survived the Middle Ages, none independent of a *Schwabenspiegel* manuscript. The *Schwabenspiegel* itself is assigned an origin in the 1270s. One manuscript (no. 3 in Schröder's list, op. cit., pp. 9-12) is a half-verse, half-prose version of the *Book of Emperors* in a codex with the *Schwabenspiegel*. That manuscript is from the mid-fourteenth century, while the surviving all-prose versions are still later. Four are dated: 1445, 1450, 1419, and 1429 in a sequence, as Massmann describes them, op. cit., Vol. III, 55-56. The fifth is undated, but in its orthography it is not significantly different from the previous four.

wanted to read history themselves, rather than the audience to whom the original author had intended his book to be read aloud. In proposing to write a new chronicle for his literate public, Königshofen lists sources at the outset. He intends to extract from the Latin works of Eusebius (i.e. the translations and adaptations by Jerome, Rufinus, or both), Martin of Troppau (see note 45), and Vincent of Beauvais (i.e. his *Speculum historiale*), and also "from other books written in German." From the latter group he makes inclusions not only from the prose rewriting of the *Book of Emperors* and from the original, but also partly relies on Eike von Repgow's borrowings from the original.

The effect of individual chapters from the *Book of Emperors* on later historiography was enormous, particularly where a later historian took the perpetuation of local tradition of accounts found in it upon himself. To take only one example, Massmann was able to follow the author's detailed account of a Bavarian Duke named Adelger, who was supposed to have won a decisive victory over the Romans under Emperor Livius Severus, "through all Bavarian history books," and these he lists individually from the mid-fifteenth century through 1807. It is obvious from the later titles and headings that the legendary nature of the narrative was recognized, but not fully until the mid-seventeenth century. Because of the favorable position accorded Bavaria in the *Book of Emperors*, it was perhaps natural for its influence to have been felt there longest.[51]

If we discuss the work's influence after the Enlightenment, much, of course, will depend on our definition of "influence" on succeeding generations. More often than not in treating intellectual history, particularly that of the Middle Ages, we assume the influence of a book to have terminated when scholars deal with it as a source document to shed light on ideas in its century of origin—as, say, John of Salisbury's *Policraticus*—rather than as a work, which, through its information or persuasive message, could be expected to change people's minds about something—as only a few medieval books of the caliber of Thomas Aquinas' *Summa Theologica* are still expected to do. (Students in a college class in medieval or Renaissance

---

51. Op. cit., Vol. III, pp. 786-819.

Introduction

intellectual history may now read Torquato Tasso's *Jerusalem Delivered* to gain insight into the nature of the crusading spirit in sixteenth-century Europe as distilled by centuries of romantic legend and aroused by Don Juan of Austria's victory over the Turks at Lepanto. They read it not with the thought of absorbing its direct influence by imitating its style, vicariously savoring the irresistible charms of pagan women of the East, or resolving to go along some time with a Christian force to help clear Jews and Saracens out of the Holy Land.) Yet it would be false to let this clear distinction apply to the fate of the *Book of Emperors.* Massmann did not gather and publish the manuscripts and his notes to the Middle High German text out of purely scholarly motives, but with the conscious mission of making his people more aware of their Germanic cultural heritage in a manner not so very unlike the original author's own desire to inspire the inhabitants of the medieval empire with the glories of their German-Roman past.

Schröder notes that Massmann's research was "probably motivated by the patriotic commitments of the then-new Society for Research in Older German History." Generally reserved and sparing of praise, he calls his edition "a work done with a diligence commanding respect and with touching dedication."[52] Ohly's judgment of the three massive volumes is the same: "the result of a life's work full of dedication and supported by genuinely patriotic inspiration."[53]

It might be belaboring an already familiar point to demonstrate that the whole matter of bringing neglected German medieval texts before the public in the early nineteenth century was very much part of the German scholars' patriotic movement, at least until the disillusioning Revolution of 1848. It is worth noting, in connection with the question of the influence of the *Book of Emperors,* however, that a number of famous scholarly German patriots, including Karl Lachmann and F.H. von der Hagen, played some part during the 1830s in bringing the work to public attention. Heinrich Hoffman von Fallersleben, the poet who would later write *Deutschland,*

---

52. Op. cit., p. 2.
53. Ohly, op. cit., p. 1.

Deutschland über alles, copied a whole manuscript of the *Book of Emperors* in 1824 and published excerpts from it in 1830. In fact, it seems that his enthusiasm for the work exceeded proper bounds: he once borrowed from von der Hagen one of its few genuine twelfth-century manuscript fragments, which Massmann had acquired as his own but left in von der Hagen's possession, and then refused to return it.[54]

In the 1870s a Bavarian court official undertook the last recasting of the whole *Book of Emperors* to suit the assumed taste of a contemporary non-scholarly audience. He eliminated parts of the narrative that he felt were not suitable for his readers' education and inclinations; he added anecdotes to the stories of rulers from entirely extraneous sources; and he presented the result in a smooth nineteenth-century idiom. Thus, under the modern term "editor," he treated the *Book of Emperors* in exactly the same fashion as medieval adapters had treated it after the twelfth century.[55] The practice of excerpting the work in a fashion aimed at a popular audience also continued not only through the nineteenth but into the twentieth century. In 1926, Walter Bulst published a modern German version of its stories of German emperors from Charlemagne through Lothair of Supplinburg. In it he used rather much the same combination of pure rhymes and assonances as the original. He did so with the explicit aim of giving non-scholars access for the first time—treating in his own popularizing work Maier's earlier popularizing work as nonexistent—to a venerable source illustrating imperial glory in the German literary heritage.[56]

---

54. Schröder, op. cit., p. 17.

55. Oberappelationsgerichtes-Sekretär Joseph Maria Maier, *Der Kaiser und der Könige Buch oder die sogenannte Kaiserchronik in freier Prosa-Bearbeitung* (Munich: L. Unflad, 1878). It is a commentary on the inelasticity of the compartmentalized scholarly mind that Schröder, who is willing to discuss *Book of Emperors* text variations, revisions, and early adaptations of this or that version at greatest length, humorlessly dismisses this contemporary attempt at popularization as "a hapless contrivance of a later period," op. cit., p. 4, note 4.

56. *Die Kaiserchronik,* edited as no. 18 of the series, *Deutsche Volkheit* by Walter Bulst (Jena: Eugen Diederichs, 1926), esp. his "Nachwort," pp. 99-100.

While the mainstream of *Book of Emperors* adaptations ran toward popularization of the work until the end of the sixteenth century, we catch a glimpse of a small, muddy fork of the river running in the direction of superficially increasing its scholarly appearance. The author, we recall, purports to be authoritative—and no foolishness about it; yet in Germany, much later than in most other European countries, writing in the vernacular rather than in Latin had a stigma attached to it in the eyes of the learned. Near the end of the twelfth century some enterprising scholar took it upon himself to begin translating the *Book of Emperors* into Latin. We say "began translating" advisedly, because only the Latin for the very first part of the work is known, and we have no idea how far he went with his project or whether he intended no more than a translation of that beginning.[57]

Some medieval German writers maintained that it was much more difficult for them to communicate on heavy subjects in their inadequate vernacular than in Latin. Eike von Repgow, for example, proves that this was most certainly true for him: he wrote his *Sachsenspiegel* first in Latin and then, at his patron's urging, translated it into German. A complete translation of the *Book of Emperors* into Latin conceivably could have been justified on the grounds that it was thus more truly in the universal idiom even among Germans themselves; however, there is no evidence that one ever existed. Medieval Germany also knew considerable pretense in the use of Latin to impress the half-educated, and the book's author himself is not entirely free from this sin.

Four centuries after the Latin translation of the beginning appeared, a Latin *Book of Emperors* was alluded to—and probably invented out of thin air—in a daring, if mildly ludicrous piece of scholarly one-upmanship, all the critical scholarship of Renaissance and Reformation

---

57. The surviving fragment deals with the Roman gods and days of the week, breaking off with the account of the bells, which warned the Senate of revolt (lines 75-216). Massmann, who printed it (op. cit., Vol. III, pp. 296-302), sought to prove that it was part of a lost Latin source for the author. The reverse relationship, however, was demonstrated in 1873 and has not been challenged since.

notwithstanding. For it was in 1594 that one Christian Tegernseer passed off his bad reworking of the rhymed version C of the text as what he called the *"Cronica Romanorum Regum;* that is, the perfectly true description of the history and great deeds of all the Roman Emperors and Kings, what each one undertook and completed during his lifetime . . . all recorded with the greatest diligence and with unsparing application of effort and labor, and further put into rhyme . . . translated from the Latin work of the highly and widely esteemed historian Paulus Jovius into our German language."[58]

4. *Stylistic Considerations*

4.1. *The author's style: scholarly urgency*

The style of the *Book of Emperors* combines a number of elements that seem discordant at first, but that ultimately harmonize with one another quite well. The author's chief role is that of the didactic historian who knows the history that others only claim to know. Hence his style can be characterized in part as that of a man bent on speaking with authority.[59] To this end, he seems on occasion consciously to separate himself from his audience, presenting himself as a man whose educational level is several notches above that of his listeners, but one who will nonetheless make every effort to mediate between his intellectual realm and theirs. Sometimes

---

58. Massmann describes the manuscript at length, op. cit., Vol. III, pp. 26-28. The title, which in the manner of the sixteenth and early seventeenth century lets its subtitle run on as an advertisement, appears in slightly different words on the first two pages; also cited by Schröder, op. cit., p. 25. Whether the real-life Paulus Jovius or Paolo Giovio (1483-1552), whose purchaseable talents as a Latin stylist had been much in demand as long as he lived, really had anything to do with a Latin version of the *Book of Emperors* is to be doubted. More than likely his was simply a handy, Latin-sounding name, belonging to a famous and safely dead historian. On Jovius' own remarkable career as the first journalistic historian among Italian humanists, see Eduard Fueter, *Geschichte der neueren Historiographie* (Munich: Oldenbourg, 1936), pp. 51-55.
59. Gellinek shows this aspect of his style in his article and book, cited earlier.

he inserts factual minutiae that have doubtful relevance to the narrative but that underline his own learning. At his worst in his scholarly role, he is not above resorting to outright charlatanry: "so many men were killed"—he remarks in connection with a battle description so re-tailored from his sources as to make the result almost entirely his own invention—"that the *Book* has no number for them." Elsewhere his phrases tend to dispel any doubt that his reading of sources was rewarded with exact findings. He turns philology, particularly proper-name etymology, to good purpose here. Augsburg, he notes, derives from Augustus Caesar's name (661); the term "Saxons" from the type of long knife (*sahs*) that they carried (341-2). These were traditional name origins and are sometimes even taken seriously today. But while his learned posture leads him to disavow unsanctioned folk legend, he cannot bring himself to criticize bizarre etymologies where the tradition of clerical writing does not. Thus, for example, the Lateran Palace derives its name, according to him, from the broad toad or frog (*lata rana*) that sprang from Emperor Nero's mouth at the termination of his magically induced pregnancy (4151-4154).

The author's habit of viewing most of the major events of history in terms of a few outstanding personages reflects partly his uncritical following of ancient and earlier medieval historians who did the same thing. It might also be partly a conscious stylistic device, shared with the great sermonizers of the Middle Ages who were interested in biographies for the moral illustrations that they provided. Invasions, persecutions, periods of prosperity, conquests—all these tend to be, for the author, part of the personal history of a great man. There are exceptions when peoples, such as the Huns, Greeks, and Saxons, occasionally introduce action without being personified in a leader. By and large, however, his overall impression of a ruler as just or unjust leads him to fill in the sketch of his reign according to a stereotype of *what a just or unjust ruler does* with scant regard to whether Nerva, Justinian, or Louis I really did these things. His whole peoples or nationalities, too, act very much according to a preconceived model and show heroism, perfidy, or avarice as a group in the same way that his rulers do as individuals—a device or approach to history that necessarily plays havoc with the historicity of narrative to which he lays claim.

There is no hint of the modern connection between learnedness and detachment in the author's mental world. On the contrary—and this is another distinct element of his style—he seems to want to seize his hearer by the arm and make him listen to his accounts of battles, martyrdoms, crusades, and doctrinal disputations. Naturally enough, he displays a strain of evangelism in expounding the oneness of the Christian-Imperial fabric. Here his tone is one of admonishment: threats of hellfire, contrasted with the promise of heavenly bliss, flow quite readily from his pen. His style conveys the attempt to show himself sharing excitement with his audience in vicariously experiencing the horrid crimes and just punishments with which his history is filled. His frequent practice of dropping the role of narrator for an instant, to admonish his hearers to listen to him and to believe what he will say, has led to identifying "gleeman" (*spielmännische*) elements in his work.[60] In this respect, he does indeed seem to be imitating the very court singers whose fabrications he denounces; however, the attempt to involve one's hearers directly in a narrative by shouting at them, as it were, that the story coming up is a good one was no monopoly of secular performers in the Middle Ages. It is more correct to speak of an independent sermonizing element in his style, more familiar to be sure in the work of thirteenth-century revivalist preachers, such as Berthold of Regensburg, but stretching back to beginnings as old as the art of preaching in the West.[61]

Some literary histories compare the author's style with that of the minnesingers, who followed him by half a century. This is basically an unfair comparison, because the study and mastery of style was a necessary precondition to the practice of the minnesinger's art by those poets good enough to produce works that are still remembered. Our anonymous cleric of Regensburg, who wrote before German vernacular style became the studied discipline that it was for Walther von der Vogelweide or Neidhart von Reuenthal, had much worse models to imitate; further, his message

---

60. Marta Maria Helff, *Studien zur Kaiserchronik* (Leipzig/Berlin: Teubner, 1924), esp. pp 59-64.
61. This point is well documented throughout Ohly's work.

dictated his style in a fashion quite foreign to that of the minnesinger. If one insists upon the comparison, the author inevitably will be found crude and heavy-handed; however, his narrative does contain considerable visual imagery, and his love of recording action makes him impatient with the occasionally overlong descriptive passages that characterized subsequent Middle High German epics.

4.2. This translation

However rapidly the author's style may alternate between the scholarly-exalted and the entertaining-immediate, a modern reader applying a little empathy can, if this translation achieves its aim, feel what he is trying to do. He wants both to instruct and entertain, simultaneously maintaining a position of authority and exciting the emotional participation of his readers. I have attempted to keep this translation as close to the original as the limits of modern idiomatic English allow. In so doing, I have followed most of the syntactical conventions for rendering medieval Germanic sentences into English (eliminating pleonasticisms, giving relative pronouns antecedents, using conjunctions to show relationships between clauses, and other mechanisms such as these). The reader should know that any division of a medieval Germanic work into sentences in a modern language has an arbitrary element to it. Medieval German writers were much less guarded than moderns about where they picked up a thought and where they dropped it; further, they left many more questions of emphasis to the discretion of the reader. In their verse works, metrical division in their lines conveyed much of the division of thought for which we require punctuation. This is even more true of emphasis: words in certain metrical positions are to be emphasized more than others, which sometimes in translation can be done only by a different device, such as italics or the addition of a modifier; while sometimes one can get by with an appropriate transposition of words within a clause.

Although main and subordinate clauses are distinguishable enough in medieval German verse, clauses of the same type will frequently appear in rows, one after the other, with the task of emphasizing the comparative importance of one or the other left up to the reciter. This type of construction, parataxis, is typical of early Middle High German verse in general but particularly frequent in the *Book of Emperors.*[62] A translator should, of course, put himself in the reciter's role to arrange such clauses so that their comparative weight is clear; again, however, the subjective element cannot be entirely excluded. I have had the advantage of being able to refer to the work of Massman and Schröder, who punctuated their editions of the Middle High German text, but neither of these is free from a number of demonstrable errors in connecting one phrase with another, which I have sought to correct. In other respects, like Schröder and almost every other commentator on the work in the last century, I have given the Vorau Manuscript preference over the others, as both the oldest and closest to the original of the complete manuscripts, but have, of course, made corrections from others when some error, usually scribal in origin, was evident in it.

A happy trend in the translation of medieval works over the past few decades has been toward dropping the archaic vocabulary in which they were once presented to the English-speaking public. Particularly in printing works that were originally intended for immediate comprehension by an unlearned public, there is no excuse for forcing the modern reader to plod through texts with a dictionary at his or her fingertips. Still, of course, there are limits to how modern the form of presentation should be. Nouns that represent objects that were common in the medieval world but have since disappeared from the contemporary scene cannot be replaced by others: *"diu"* must remain "serving woman" or "bondmaid" as surely as *"halsperc"* must remain "hauberk." When no reasonably common English word has survived, as is the case with a number of medieval titles, articles of dress, and instruments of torture, I have found it necessary to give a single word in the original with a short phrase in translation: I have translated a "crowel," for example, as "a claw-shaped fork with hooked tines." Such instances are rare, however, for we have not lost sight of *that* many things from the medieval world.

---

62. Helge Eilers, *Untersuchungen zum frühmitteldeutschen Sprachstil am Beispiel der Kaiserchonik. Göppinger Arbeiten zur Germanistik*, no. 76 (Göppingen; Kümmerle, 1972), pp. 103-4.

A few words that in medieval German recur with peculiar frequency I have let stand in their modern English form, such as "*helt*" ("hero") and "*ere*" ("honor"). Although the context might justify substitutions, with the thought that the reader will soon enough become aware that—in some cases—a "headstrong hero" is a rather set phrase for an ambitious knight, and "hero" alone can connote both our kind of hero and an absolute brute; while "honor" sometimes has the same meaning as in modern times but often means nothing more than a wide reputation, particularly one that leaves others intimidated. For much the same reason, the words "king" (*chuonich*) and "emperor" (*cheiser*) are translated as they are found, regardless of which title is more appropriate from a modern perspective. The author *tends* to reserve the title "emperor" for good pagan emperors and for Christian emperors who have been crowned by the pope, while using "king" for rulers the rest of the time; however, the reader will see that this rule is not a hard and fast one and thus infer, I think correctly, that even for a writer as concerned with imperial ideology as he is, the importance of keeping the terms "emperor" and "king" separate was not consistently on his mind. Only with Constantine and again with Charlemagne does the author really differentiate between the same figure as "king" before his consecration to imperial office by the pope and as "emperor" afterwards.[63] The whole framework of his narrative is one of imperial reigns, and yet he uses "king" far more often than "emperor" in designating rulers during these reigns. What appears to be an inconsistency is probably more a reflection in the mid-twelfth century of an as-yet undefined idea of a king, as distinct from an emperor, in his relation to the German kingdom and the Roman Empire as revived by Germans.[64]

Since the author included his occasional Latin phrases more for their scholarly flavor than for the information they impart, I have left them as they are and given English translations in parentheses or brackets. Rather

---

63. E. Nellmann, op. cit., p. 104, n. 21; further discussion in Rüdiger Schnell and Skoukje Vedder, "'Kunic' und 'Keiser,'" in Schnell, ed., *Die Reichsidee in der deutsche Dichtung des Mittelalters* (Darmstadt: WBG, 1983), pp. 428-9.

64. Herwig Wolfram, review of Nellmann (see preceding note), MIÖG, Vol. LXXII (1964), pp. 179-181; in Schnell, op. cit., pp. 216-221 (219).

than grapple with the problem of what are difficult Latin phrases for the reader and what are not, I have given even the probably easy ones this way. Rhyme-induced words and phrases I have not ventured to change except where indispensable for clarity. For proper names, I have followed these rules: place names, including those that have changed since the Middle Ages, I have simply given in the form most likely to be familiar to an English-speaking reader; names of historical personages I have normally given the same way if these are familiar historical names, e.g. Vespasian, Gregory, Charles, Louis, or if it is clear that the Book's distortions are the result of gradual erosion through transliteration or scribal error, for instance, his "Athenor" as "Antenor" and even his "Signator" as "Vercingetorix." On the other hand, where he or an immediate source seems to have consciously Germanized a foreign name, "Mathilda" as "Mähthild" or "Otho" as "Otto," for example, I have given his German form, as I have with generally less familiar historical and pseudo-historical names. There are also a few borderline cases, which are individually noted. His frequent exclamation, "Owî!" I have retained as it is. It denotes astonishment, something like "Wow!" in our own day; it should not be confused with the lament, "Owê!" which I have given as "O woe!," not quite having the nerve to employ the etymologically closer "Oi-vay!"[65]

I have let the paragraphing follow the divisions of the original except where modern usage requires a new paragraph for the words of a new speaker. Such divisions are set off in the manuscripts with very little divergence from each other by the simple device of starting a new section with a large capital letter. Assumedly these points are where the man reading aloud to his audience would pause slightly. Ideas guiding how the *Book of Emperors* should be thus divided are different from those that would guide a modern writer in dividing it, but since he put the breaks there himself, I saw no pressing reason to change them.

To make the work read more smoothly, I have kept the interruptions of footnotes in most chapters to a minimum. As is done with

65. Owî! is by far his favorite interjection. W. F. Tulasiewicz cites thirty-two Owî!s and only ten Owê!s in the work. *Index Verborum zur deutschen Kaiserchronik* (Berlin: Akademie-Verlag, 1972), p. 233.

sources, essential historical facts concerning the people and events dealt with by the author are given in the introductory paragraphs to the individual chapters. For the material in these paragraphs, I have made much use of the invaluable works of Massmann and Ohly, some use of Schröder's notes to the MGH edition of the text, and some use of scholarly publications on individual aspects of the work, which will be noted in the bibliography.

4.3. This title

Some explanation is perhaps due as to why this work should be titled the *Book of Emperors* in translation rather than the *Chronicle of Emperors*. Both the *Book of Emperors and Kings* (*Der Kaiser und der Könige Buch*—usually given in archaic spelling) and *The Chronicle of Emperors* (*Die Kaiserchronik*) were in eighteenth and nineteenth century usage until the latter won out. It is not difficult to see why it did. For one thing, it is shorter and consequently handier to use. For another, within the medieval understanding of the term, it was not only a chronicle but a source of—in fact, the mother of all—German chronicles.

The work could be designated a chronicle with no qualification, as "chronicle" was understood in the twelfth and thirteenth centuries. First called *Cronica*, it became *Coronica* in the thirteenth century, the extra syllable added as a concession to meter. Königshofen, who both used this "*Coronica*" and wrote a "*Cronik*" of his own, defines the genre: chronicles are "books about times which in them tell of emperors, popes, kings, and other great men, of the sort of lives they lived, of various events, and of noteworthy things which happened to the men themselves or occurred during their times."[66] Thus the contemporary definition was broad enough to justify calling this work a chronicle, even with the fourteenth century—during which Königshofen wrote—placing more rigid demands on scholarship than did the twelfth.

---

66. Cited by Massmann, who preferred "The Book of Emperors and Kings" as the title; he prefixed "Imperial Chronicle" with the so-called op. cit., Vol. III, p. 254.

Further, since it does not make good on its promise in the Prologue to treat all of the popes from the beginning of the empire to the present day, but limits its framework rather much to emperors—among whom a few non-emperors are accorded the imperial title—*Chronicle of Emperors* would not have been a bad contemporary title. An English-speaking twenty-first-century public, however, expects something quite different from a work under the heading "chronicle"—namely, a work of history in which the ordering of events in chronological sequence is at least a large part of the writer's goal. Misinformation and honest (even sizeable) mistakes in dating must be tolerated in the definition; otherwise, we would have to deny that William of Malmesbury and Henry of Huntington wrote chronicles, and we would have precious few medieval chronicles.

What disqualifies this particular work from being a chronicle in the modern sense is the airy indifference its author displays to the whole chronological principle over huge portions of his work. He obviously thought his work sufficient as a chronicle of history for the unlettered audience for which he wrote, and, as noted above, there is every reason to accord him the title of first author of a world history or history of the Roman Empire in the vernacular since antiquity. And yet it is not the principle of narrating historical events in sequence that guides him. Instead, ideological considerations move his pen on every page and subordinate the whole matter of historical sequence. As a portrayal of good and bad types of rulers, model kings and tyrants, it is much closer to the mirror-for-princes genre than to that of chronicles. This is particularly true in the substantially larger part of the author's work, where he deals with ancient Roman and Byzantine emperors in 14,282 lines—although the chronological principle does play more of a part in his stories of German emperors, the final 3001 lines.

But did the author not decide the title question by calling his work "*Cronica?*" In his opening lines, after invoking the deity, he says straightforwardly enough:

A book has been written in German which tells us all about the Roman Empire. Its name is *Cronica*, and it tells us of the popes and the kings, both good and bad, who lived before us and guided the Roman Empire down to this very day. I shall recite for you what it says just as well as I can. (15-25)

We find him calling *his own* book *"Cronica"* only if we read these lines of his Prologue as a modern-style preface, in which the author tells his public a little bit about his own book, the text of which will follow. This, however, is not the way these lines relate to the rest of the work. At many points the author plays an intermediary between his source book (the *Cronica*) and his audience, opening chapters with "The Book tells us that . . . ." and, as we have seen, voicing astonishment at what numbers his source book gives for participants or casualties in battle. He constantly calls out "Owî!" to show his own excitement with what he is finding in his purported source book. It is as though he has his source book open on a table close by, glancing at it from time to time to jog his memory as he chants his own "song" to his audience. As indicated earlier, the search for a separate, earlier German-language chronicle was abandoned long ago, but the image of it was real enough to make scholars as serious as Massmann and Welzhofer look for it for a long time, and, at the end of the twentieth century, a young scholar reopened the search with some passion.[67] The way our author keeps referring to his source book may add weight and authority to his words, but the point is that his probably made-up source book, which he calls "chronicle," is not the same thing for him as the work that his audience will hear him chant, complete with shouts of amazement about the wonders found in his source. Sometimes he cites plural sources as "the books," occasionally as a "song," but never does he indicate that his own *"Cronica,"* is what he is reading or chanting.

Another reason for not simply calling this work "The Emperors' Chronicle" in English, in deference to "Die Kaiserchronik" as its most common German title, is the fact that "Die Kaiserchronik" no longer refers unambiguously to it. In 1955, Irene Schmale-Ott showed in her study of

---

67. If Stephan Müller's claim in his 1997 dissertation, published as a book in 1999 (see note 2), that the introductory parts of the *Song of Anno* and the *Book of Emperors* may well derive from the same, now lost, German-language source holds up, then that earlier source must have been the original source, *Chronicle*.

Ekkehard von Aura that a distinct chronicle of German emperors, which had long been included as part of "Recension C" of Ekkehard's Latin *World Chronicle*, was written by a different anonymous author, distinguished by his pro-Henry IV leanings, where Ekkehard was one of that emperor's most consistent detractors.[68]

That work soon took on the name, *"Kaiserchronik,"* as well it might have done, for it deals with emperors clearly as a chronicle both by medieval and present-day standards, as it reports, for example,

> *A.D.* 1097. Emperor Henry [IV] returned from Italy and came to Regensburg in Bavaria. There he stayed for a while and permitted some Jews who had been forced to be baptized to return to their Jewish rites. At the beginning of December Emperor Henry conducted negotiations aimed at peace with the nobles. A comet appeared. In this year the summer was very fruitful, while the winter was mild and brought much sickness. There were very severe floods from heavy rainfalls and rising rivers.

> *A.D.* 1098. When the Emperor initiated investigations in Mainz concerning the wealth of Jews who had been murdered, and the priest [Bishop of Mainz] and his relatives were accused in connection with this money, the bishop went full of resentment with his people to Thuringia.[69]

This excerpt is typical of the work's style and content as a chronicle, extending its coverage from the reign of Charlemagne to that of Henry V. By the late 1960s, calling this work *Kaiserchronik* reflected general usage. Eckhard Müller-Mertens refers to this work at great length in his book on the development of the concepts of German kingdom, kingship, and empire. He considers it to be a very early manifestation "of a definite

---

68. "Ekkehard von Aura," in *Die deutsche Literatur des Mittelalter: Verfasserlexicon,* ed. W. Stammler and K. Langosch, Vol. 5 (Berlin: De Gruyter, 1955), col. 188. She covers the topic at much greater length in "Die Recension C der Weltchronik Ekkehards," *Deutsches Archiv für Erforschung des Mittelalters,* Vol. 12 (1956), pp. 363-387, and "Untersuchungen zu Ekkehard von Aura und zur Kaiserchronik," *Zeitschrift für bayrische Landesgeschichte,* Vol. 34 (1971), pp. 403-61.

69. *Frutolfi et Ekkehardi Chronica, necnon Anonymi Chronica Imperatorum,* ed. and trans. (bilingual ed.) Franz-Josef Schmale and Irene Schmale-Ott (Darmstadt: WBG, 1972), p. 216.

German imperial consciousness and a consciousness of the historicity of the German empire." He calls it simply *"Die Kaiserchronik,"* seeing no need to differentiate it at all from our subject work.[70] The recent catalogs of Wissenschaftliche Buchgesellschaft, a major publisher of scholarly medieval texts, refer to the ex-Ekkehard work also as *Kaiserchronik*, again with no apparent need to distinguish it from our subject work. It would seem to be only a question of time until *that* chronicle becomes the "German Imperial Chronicle" or the "German Emperors' Chronicle" in the English-speaking world as well.

When preceded by a modifier, the ex-Ekkehard chronicle now goes by "Die anonyme Kaiserchronik" in German.[71] Our subject work is, of course, anonymous, so that in the long run this designation will not distinguish the two from each other. Surely both works cannot go comfortably through the twenty-first century with essentially the same name. Possibly a shortening of Schröder's *Die Kaiserchronik eines Regensburger* Geistlichen into something like "Die Regensburger Kaiserchronik" will prevail, while in deference to Bishop Otto of Bamberg, its likely patron, the ex-Ekkehard chronicle will go by "Die Bamberger Kaiserchronik" in German or "The Bamberg Chronicle" in English generally, as it already does in I. S. Robinson's recent biography of Henry IV.[72] Possibly there will be a reversion to Massmann's *Der Kaiser und der Könige Buch* for our subject work. This would mean that the likely alternatives for an English title would include "the Regensburg Chronicle of Emperors" or "the Book of Emperors and Kings." While our author uses the title "king" more often than "emperor," he actually takes up very few kings who were not emperors. His book is basically stories about emperors who illustrate models or types. The shorter English title, "the *Book of Emperors,*" consequently seems both adequate and preferable on the basis of aesthetic brevity, the truth-in-packaging principle, and the matter of keeping it more distinct from "the other" *Kaiserchronik.*

---

70. *Regnum Teutonicum; Aufkommen und Verbreitung der deutschen Reichs- und Königsauffassung im früheren Mittelalter* (Berlin: Akademie-Verlag, 1970), e. g., p. 349.

71. See note 70.

72. Henry IV of Germany, 1056-1106 (Cambridge University Press, 1999), pp. 327, 343, 345, 349, and 352-3.

Prologue

The Prologue sets a tone of urgency for imparting true knowledge to a wide audience. The author calls on his hearers to listen closely to his "song," which will help them to cope knowingly with this world and prepare for the next. At the same time, he condemns the competing secular epics, which offer no such help. To give his words greater authority, he claims to refer to a previously written book as their source.

In the love of Almighty God, I shall begin this song, which you should pay decent attention to. You really would do well to listen and learn about all great and true deeds. Ignorant people think it is hard labor whenever they are to learn anything to broaden their knowledge. Unwilling to hear things to help them gain wisdom and honor—things that would help save their souls as well—they are useless and show their lack of good sense.

A book has been written in German that tells us all about the Roman Empire. It is called *Cronica,* and it tells us about the popes and the kings—both good and bad—who lived before us and guided the Roman Empire down to this very day. I shall tell you what it says just as well as I can. Anyone who wants to hear it may do so.

Unfortunately, nowadays a bad habit has taken root far and wide. Many men think up lies and fit them together with poetic words. I sadly fear their souls will burn for this. What they do is done without the love of God. This way lies are being taught to children who will come after us, clinging to them and insisting on telling them instead of the truth. Lying with proud arrogance does no one any good. Those who can tell what is really true do not like to hear any such made-up things, so now let us get started with this good song!

I

Rome's Founding:
Gods for Each Day of the Week and the Bells that Warned of Revolt

In his opening chapter, the author establishes pagan worship as reflecting the woefully inadequate religion that Christianity would replace. Medieval Christians did not altogether deny the existence of the deities worshipped by pagans in ancient times, but they reduced them to the status of devils or demons, reserving the term "god" for the one true God. No written sources survive with anything like the author's details of Roman worship. Probably he is elaborating on material from early Christian attacks on Rome's pagan gods passed down in sermons. What he calls the Rotunda is the Pantheon with its large dome, where the Romans kept statues of gods worshiped throughout their empire. In 609, Pope Boniface IV purified and consecrated it as the Rotunda of Saint Mary and the Martyrs. The Venerable Bede's eighth-century "Sermon for All Saints' Day," which contains a full account of this consecration, was frequently copied in its original Latin. An Old Saxon translation of it survives from the ninth century, and it was easily accessible to interested clerics throughout Europe. The *Mirabilia Romae*, collections of past and present wonders in Rome, which contain the story of the statues and warning bells, circulated widely in many versions in the twelfth century.

Long ago in heathen times, people everywhere worshipped unclean idols. With no exceptions the heathens had to honor them and pray to them exactly as their kings decreed. Rome with its magnificent buildings and displays was already exalted in the eyes of the world back then. Two powerful brothers were the founders: one was named Romulus, the other Remus, and eventually all the lands came to serve them in awe. Three hundred Senators rendered them service in council and spread their fame. They saw to it that everything decided on at Rome was proclaimed throughout the lands. Roman power grew to be really great.

Since the ancient Romans had no fear of the true God, they wrought seven idols—I am telling you this exactly as it was—to honor the seven days of the week. If a man broke any of their laws of worship, they would throw him into the river and let it carry him away, or they would burn him to death at the stake. Laws like this spread from Rome to govern all the peoples of the earth. They knew nothing of the true God.

When Sunday came the whole city of Rome would do everything you can think of to honor that day's god. The ones they considered wisest of their leading men would carry a thing made like a wheel with burning lights all around the city. Owî! How greatly they glorified that god! Nobody among them dared to wish that he might see that god with mortal eyes. In this way, they honored the Sun, that he might grant light and joy to them.

After this, on Monday, they would all hurry to bring offerings for the love of the Moon with vessels of burning oil. They would light up their vessels in all the streets of Rome. The Romans did this in hopes that the Moon would be merciful to them and give them nights to their liking. In all the city of Rome, no noble youth or maiden over seven years of age was excused from making offerings there. If people found out that some of the maidens were no longer virgins, they sacrificed them to Apollo. They never returned. This was the way they had to honor the Moon.

Then after Monday, just like I am telling you, over the whole city of Rome all the knights would arm themselves with helmets and hauberks. With swords and shields in their hands they put on magnificent tournaments in honor of Tuesday's god and rode their horses in races. The ladies would gather to watch the splendid games that they put on in honor of the god of war. The Romans believed that if this god favored them they would be sure of victory. They were also convinced that no one in this world could injure them as long as they had this god's protection.

Wednesday they established as their market day, and very early in the morning people from the countryside streamed into the city. On a very high pedestal stood a monstrous idol, which they called their Merchant. According to their custom, Romans would sacrifice to him a part of whatever they should buy or sell from each other, so that he would cause them and their trade to prosper.

On Thursday, as I will tell you now, they had their greatest celebration of all, and men and women alike would hurry to it. It was held in a most magnificent temple, from which gold gleamed everywhere. [Its roof was a complete artificial heaven, with][1] rain flowing in pipes through its nine choir galleries. Around the temple stood one hundred archers, just to add to the splendor of the place. Thursday's god was named Jupiter and he was supposed to be highly exalted. I want to tell you of a great wonder. In front of his statue incense burned with no fire and gave off smoke and fragrance, but it was never consumed, and there was always as much of it as there had been at the beginning. The Romans set this up to present a great wonder in his honor.

One temple at Rome, which made the whole city more magnificent, was built to honor Lady Venus, so that praise of her would be greater. All those who lived unchastely or were habitual fornicators were received there with honor, whether they were rich or poor. But if pure maidens or young men came along, they dared not pray there if they valued their lives, lest all sorts of evil things befall them, for the goddess had no love for them.

Then for Saturday, there was a lordly temple called the Rotunda. Its god was named Saturn, and it eventually served to honor all the devils. Whenever the Romans had finished praying in it to their hearts' content, they would hurry out into the open fields. Their shouts would echo loudly as they jousted on their horses and jumped or danced or sang. The man who won more praise and honors there than the rest had all the more reason to worship at that temple. The Book tells us that good Saint Boniface, a most great and holy man, consecrated that same temple to Almighty God, and then also to honor Saint Mary and all God's saints.

---

1. Clause in brackets added: the author has in mind the legendary heaven-like ceiling wrought by King Cosdras (Khosrau II) of Persia with its sun, moon, stars, clouds, and "rain running in pipes through its nine choir galleries," which he includes later (lines 11154-11155) in the reign of Emperor Heraclius.

At the time when that most holy man ascended the throne at Rome as the fourth pope after Saint Gregory, he was plagued with worry that such impiety still remained under him. He sent for all the good Christians he knew everywhere in Rome. They clothed themselves in sackcloth and came barefoot to join him in large numbers. At the head of the procession, he approached the temple door and began the service of consecration. As he dedicated the house to the true God, the devils burst out of the building from above, some of them plunging into the abyss below. There is still a record of all this today at Rome.

Now let us pick up again where we left the story before. The Romans enjoyed the greatest respect, for neither on land nor sea could any people defend themselves against them and avoid becoming obedient to them and thus subjects of Rome.

The Romans commanded the people of all lands they had conquered to cast bronze statues for them. Above these statues representing all their territories, the ingenious Romans hung golden bells. As a result, the Romans were able to keep just as close a check on dangerous activities in their provinces as if every deed were done in Rome itself. Whenever any land would do the least thing opposing Roman interests, its bell would ring on the spot without the touch of any human hand. Quickly, through drawing lots, the Romans would choose a noble lord and give him the honor of reconquering the rebellious territory, to win it back for them.

It happened one day that the Senate was sitting in session when suddenly the members looked up, for a bell was ringing. They jumped from their seats and rushed over to where they could read the letters on the bell. Then they stared at each other, greatly surprised at what had happened, for they saw clearly that the German people had risen against them!

II

Julius Caesar

In modern times no Romans are counted as emperors before Augustus Caesar, in whose name the Roman Senate put an end to the old Republic's checks on monarchical power in 27 *BC*, thus inaugurating the Empire; however, a medieval historian did not feel similarly bound. Finding in ancient chronicles several early military commanders with broad political powers who were called imperator, he might introduce Lucullus and Pompey as the first emperors, as did the *Chronicle of Fredegar*, a seventh-century Frankish work, on the basis of the 300-years-older *Chronicle* by Eusebius and Jerome. More likely, however, if interested in Roman antiquities he would be decisively influenced to begin the succession of emperors with Julius Caesar by the widely available work of Orosius, possibly influenced by Suetonius, who in the early fifth century had presented Julius as a particularly capable and heroic figure.

As a committed partisan protagonist of the Holy Roman Empire, our author doubtless desired to begin his stories of emperors with a dramatic and imposing subject. It is not that he would have found Augustus Caesar lacking in this respect, but the general tendency of medieval writers to begin with Julius was reinforced for him by the ease with which Julius could be credibly related to German history. Two of his sources had already pointed in this direction. He derives a section of his account of Julius Caesar's exploits in Germany from distinctly feudal references to one of the Gallic Wars in a local Latin history of Trier or Trèves. This city had been an important Roman outpost, and its surviving Roman ruins, such as the Black Arch *(Porta Nigra)* and the ancient amphitheater, which remain even to this day, reminded medieval

Germans of the past history of Roman power in Germany. Our author's story of Julius Caesar is the first of only two parts in the *Book of Emperors* in which sequences of more than a few lines are taken from a surviving German-language source. By far the largest sections of Caesar's struggles with the German tribes, almost the whole lengthy episode of his battle against Pompey (historically the Battle of Pharsalus in southwestern Thessaly) and all but a fraction of Daniel's vision with its interpretation come from the *Annolied*, a poetical presentation of the life of Bishop Anno of Cologne, which antedates the *Book of Emperors* by roughly half a century. In the *Annolied*, a long sketch of Julius Caesar and a very short one of Augustus are part of a summation of world history since the Creation, which gradually narrows its focus to Cologne and Bishop Anno. Where the *Annolied*, naturally enough, discusses Daniel and his prediction of a succession of world empires before proceeding to Roman history, our author presents the prophet's vision as a flashback, to show its fulfillment under Julius Caesar. In so doing, he tampers more than a little with the symbolic animals. The *Annolied* had made the dreadful beast with ten horns (Dan. 7:7–8) into a boar, signifying the fierce freedom of the Roman Empire, out of which the eleventh horn was to grow. The *Annolied*, however, was faithful to the tradition of Christian scholarship since Saint Jerome, which had seen the eleventh horn as the antichrist, while our author has no intention of letting the antichrist spring from his beloved Roman Empire. He thus grafts the evil eleventh horn onto a different beast, and the unencumbered boar, symbolizing Julius, will appear on the Roman banner in several later chapters to inspire fighters for the empire.

In recording Caesar's death, the author notes the number of years he reigned. Possibly he relied on a list of rulers with their dates of the type sometimes copied in the introductory part of monastery annals. In any event, he continues to make the same kind of note as he records each emperor's death with only two exceptions. Individually his reign dates are often reasonably accurate: the five years that Caesar ruled would have been reckoned originally from 49 *BC*, when he crossed the Rubicon in order to claim sole political power, to his murder in 44 *BC*. The idea that Caesar's remains were buried at the top of a high column is probably based on a *Mirabilia* account that Caesar's ashes were buried in the great obelisk now outside Saint Peter's Cathedral.

For their leader the bold Romans chose a daring hero, whose many good claims to fame are in the Book. Chanting songs of highest praise for the young hero, they sent him to Germany. They clearly saw in him a man of steadfast mind and a true warrior in every way.

The Romans entrusted thirty thousand well-equipped warriors to the leadership of Julius. Besides these, Julius the commander engaged thirty thousand more at his own expense, because he had learned to know the Germans' strength in battle in his earlier experience in their country, for his home had been in Germany before. Thus he realized that he had no hope of victory with the forces originally given him.

Julius was a resourceful knight. In no time at all he prepared himself and the forces that were to follow him. He turned toward the Swabians and showed them no mercy. Swabia was then the domain of a very daring hero named Brennus, who rode against him with an army.[1]

The Book tells us that Brennus fought three hours with Julius in battle in the open. They slashed wounds in all directions and bloodied many a shield rim. The Swabians defended their land well until kind-hearted Julius offered to negotiate with them. They yielded their land to his gracious suzerainty. He then ordered his tent pitched on a mountain called

---

1. Brennus is the recurring name in medieval Germany and England of a legendary opponent of foreign conquerors, possibly a memory of the chieftain of that name who led a successful Gallic attack on Rome in the fourth century *BC*. Boimund and Ingram in the following sections, however, do not appear elsewhere in analogous surviving legends.

Swevo;[2] it is from Mount Swevo that the inhabitants are called Swabians. They are a people whose advice is good, and they understand a great deal of the art of speaking. They frequently set out to distinguish themselves as warriors, ever ready and eager for battle, but Julius conquered them even in their full force.

The Swabians advised Julius to invade the Bavarians, within whose land lived many a warrior. Boimund was their Duke, and his brother's name was Ingram. Very quickly they summoned their men. Many young knights lost no time in joining them, wearing helmets and coats of mail. They defended themselves furiously and fought a full-scale battle with Julius. Neither before nor since have so many fine heroes fallen, or else the heathen books are lying to us. Owî! What good fighters the Bavarians were! A marvel that can be read about in the heathen books is the *Noricus ensis*—which means "Bavarian sword." The strength of this sword stood the Bavarians in good stead, for they could strike it all the way through an enemy's helmet.[3]

The Bavarian people came from Armenia, where Noah left the Ark and received the olive branch from the dove. Signs of the Ark still remain in the mountains there, which are called Ararat. Julius had to pay a high price in blood for the victory he won from the Bavarians.

The fury of the Saxons caused him grief aplenty. One reads that they were originally the men of the fabled Alexander, who met his end in Babylonia. Afterwards four of his men who wanted to become kings divided his lands and treasure. The others lost themselves sailing for distant lands, until part of them landed with their fleet near the Elbe River, where the

---

2. Swevo is similar to Ptolemy's name for a river, possibly the Oder, in the ancient homeland of the Suevi, ancestors of the Swabians, in northeastern Germany. By the seventh century, the name had become attached to a mountain instead, and Saint Isidore then included it as such in his encyclopedia, which made it sound etymology for medieval writers.

3. Surviving "heathen books," to use this phrase, are Horace's *Odes*, in I, xvi, 9-10, and his *Epodes*, xvii, 71. Ovid's *Metamorphoses*, XIV, 712, and at least four other ancient works allude to iron foundries in Noricum (Austria and Rhaetia Bavaria) and their products. Noricum's iron was indeed famous. Here the phrase is simply taken from the *Annolied*.

Chapter Two

long knives that many of the warriors there carried and with which they defeated the Thuringians were called "sahs" in the local language. The Saxons entered negotiations with those natives in bad faith and then broke the peace they had agreed to. They are still called Saxons—*Sahsen*—from their sharp knives.[4]

After this Caesar approached his old kinsmen, the noble Franks. Their able forefathers came from that ancient Troy that the Greeks destroyed.

Whether you want to believe it or not, I will tell you exactly what happened when a Cyclops devoured Duke Ulysses' men in Sicily. With his spear Ulysses exacted full vengeance as he gouged the Cyclops's eye out while he was sleeping. That race towered as high in the forest as the fir trees themselves. They had one eye in front on their foreheads. Now God has driven them away from us to the forests inside India.

The Trojans journeyed far through the world without a destination, but then Helenus took brave Hector's widow after the destruction of the war made him leave his own lands, and with her he besieged his powerful enemies in Greece. Antenor also set out from Troy, of which nothing remained, and founded Mantua and another city called Padua.[5] Aeneas conquered the lands of the Romans, where he found a sow with thirty white piglets. Thinking the Rhine to be the sea, Franko settled with his people in the Lower Rhine Valley, where the Franks grew in strength and number. Although Caesar did subdue them, he had great trouble in doing so.

Julius established his seats on the Rhine: Deutz, a fine city, with Boppard to defend it; Andernach, a fine city, with Ingelheim to defend it; and Mainz, a fine city, with Oppenheim to defend it. That ambitious knight built a castle near Mainz. He also built a bridge across the Rhine. What better way could there have been to add to the splendor of the city? Later,

---

4. According to their historian, Widukind of Corvey, who wrote about the year 1000, this was the Saxons' own explanation of how they received their name. In spite of the fanciful context, the etymology is defensible in the light of modern research.

5. Antenor figures in Livy's *Roman History*, I, i, and Virgil's *Aeneid*, I, 235-249. Here our author appears to correct a small error in the *Annolied*, which had Atenor depart Troy before its destruction. 114.258

however, this bridge sank to the bottom of the Rhine as punishment for the Mainzers' repeated sin of never serving any of their rulers faithfully.

Even in those days Trier was a highly regarded city, situated at one end of the land of the Franks in the Belgian part of Gaul. Its inhabitants were very bold and defended their land well until Julius, that heroic commander, gained victory over their fortified city by cunning. Prince Labienus was responsible for this.

Now I will tell you now how Julius was able to take Trier. The people there—this is the truth—defended themselves against him more than four years. Within the walled city were two powerful lords, one named Induciomarus, the other Vercingetorix.[6] The two of them began to quarrel over the wealth and power that were to be had as ruler of Trier. Vercingetorix and his brother, Labienus, became Caesar's vassals. As a result of their plans Induciomarus was killed and Julius took over Trier. Within the walls he found many an able warrior.

Even while the lords of Trier were bound by oaths of fidelity, how often did they discuss how they were going to resist the Emperor with a furious full-scale battle! Then they fell victims to their own wavering. Many people meet with shame when wavering overtakes them, while those who are of one mind often are victorious. As a result of wavering, all the Trier lords' former honors fell to Julius.

When Julius entered Trier, the inhabitants all thought their lives were lost. But Caesar was noble as well as bold, and the fortified city seemed both secure and magnificent to him. Because of this he subsequently left the lords with the same honors he had found them with before. He entrusted the walled city to all of them to protect. On the highest-ranking lords he bestowed valuable fiefs, and to the boldest he gave gold. They all developed loyalty and willingness to serve him. He showed he was not haughty by

---

6.   During the Gallic Wars, Induciomarus, Chief of the Treviri, instigated a rebellion against the Romans in 54 *BC* and defeated them severely before Labienus, Roman Legate sent to Gaul by Caesar, overcame his forces and killed him. Vercingetorix commanded a great coalition of Gallic tribes against Rome. Caesar defeated him in 52 *BC* and held him until 46 *BC*, when he exhibited him in his triumphal procession in Rome and then executed him.

Chapter Two

bestowing fine gifts on the very poorest people there. Caesar was generous and kind as well as very intelligent, and so he stayed among the German lords until they willingly helped increase his fame.

When Julius thought of returning home, however, the Romans did not want to receive him. They thought his recklessness had cost them a great part of their army, and that he had remained too long in Germany without their permission. But then he sent for all the lords who lived in the German Empire. He spoke to them of his troubles and offered them his red gold, saying that he wanted to make good any injuries he had done to them.

When those eager warriors learned of his will, they all gathered in a force. From Gaul and from Germany came many bands with shining helmets and solid hauberks. Brandishing the rim of many a fine shield, they invaded the Roman lands like a river in flood. How terrified the Romans were when they saw them! Huge numbers of Romans were seized by fear when Julius came riding so magnificently with his knightly German cavalry, and they saw the steel of his broad host gleaming amidst banners and galoons. They were sore afraid for their lives. Rigidus, Cato, and Pompey left all the Roman buildings vacant, and the whole Senate fled in fear.[7] Julius chased after them, slashing blows far and wide. Pompey fled to the sea and gathered the mightiest army that any man ever assembled.

Julius carried the war to his enemies, although with smaller forces. With what power from the Germans' support he pursued them! There followed the most savage battle, as the Book reveals, ever fought on this earth. Owî! How the armored plates rang out when the battle-horses sprang toward each other! Bugles sounded and blood flowed in brooks. Many a large squadron lay there covered all over with blood. Julius won the victory and Pompey barely escaped. He fled into the land of Egypt, from whence he never returned. There Pompey was slain when Julius Caesar later took vengeance on him.

---

7.   Rigidus appears as a man in his own right (clearly discernible from the fact that *only* proper names are capitalized in the manuscripts, even sentence beginnings being in lowercase letters), but is probably derived from a reading of *rigidus Cato* (inflexible Cato), as Boethius calls him, for example, in *On the Consolation of Philosophy*.

It pleased the young man that he had succeeded in bringing all the dominions under his rule. He returned to Rome with a mighty force, free to act just as he desired. The Romans gave him a fine reception; it was then that they began to say "ir" to him.[8] They invented this form of address to honor him, since he was the first man to hold alone all those powers which had been divided among so many before him. And for the honor it betokened, he ordered the custom taught to all German men.

In those days was fulfilled that which the Prophet Daniel foretold when King Nabuchodonosor told him what he had seen in his dreams: how four winds contended in the sea, and from the sea emerged four wild animals.[9] These symbolize four mighty kings, who were to hold all of this world in their grasp.

The first animal was a leopard, which had four eagle's wings, symbolizing the Greek Alexander, who led four armies across the lands until he found himself at the end of the world. He once used two griffins to carry him up into the air, and then in a glass vessel he had himself lowered by chains into the sea. His unfaithful men wickedly threw the chains after him, saying, "Since you like to see wonders so much, you can now watch them forever on the bottom of the sea."

Then this man whose life was so filled with marvels saw an animal walking along from one day at prime until the third day at nones.[10] This was a great wonder indeed: the animal swerved around constantly. Then the clever man thought of a way of saving his life. He saluted the salty sea with his own blood, and when the tide received his blood it threw him back onto land again. He returned to his empire again, and the Greeks gave him a fine welcome. This same man encountered a great many wonders, and he brought a third of the world under his rule.

---

8. That is, to use as a sign of respect the plural "you" (later spelling: "Ihr"), instead of the singular "thou."
9. This would be Dan. 2:27–47; actually, most of the vision discussed is recorded as Daniel's own in the time of Belshazzer (7:1–28).
10. Ninth hour of the day or noon, according to canonical hours in which 3:00 a.m. is the first hour.

The second animal Daniel saw was a wild bear that had three rows of teeth, symbolizing three kingdoms that were to wage war against one another. The bear was so fierce that no art of man could ever hope to tame him.

The third animal was a ferocious boar, symbolizing noble Julius. The same boar carried ten horns, with which he struck down all his enemies. Julius conquered all the lands, and they all served at his beck and call. The wild boar is a telling symbol of the fact that the Roman Empire shall always be free.

The fourth animal was a lioness with human understanding as well as human eyes and mouth: such an animal was entirely unknown to us before. One of its horns grew up towards heaven and the stars fought against it. This signified the antichrist, who is yet to come into the world; God with His power will then send him down into hell. Thus the dream was fulfilled just as the Prophet Daniel had interpreted it.

Julius broke open the treasure chambers and found great wealth inside. He rewarded his German followers with silver and gold. As a result, German men have been full of love and praise for Rome ever since. He ruled the dominions with great authority as long as he lived. The Book tells us truly that it was only five more years before the Romans treacherously slew him; they buried his remains on top of a high column.

III

Augustus Caesar

Augustus Caesar, son of a niece of Julius Caesar, is normally called the first Roman emperor since he effectively established his one-man rule between 31 and 27 *BC* and occasionally used the title "imperator," governing Roman territories with little challenge until his death in *AD* 14.

Our author's very brief account of Augustus fits together some familiar fragments of the Christmas story. "And there went forth from Caesar Augustus a decree that all the world should be taxed." For him the great peace associated with Augustus parallels the great peace brought by Christianity. He pursues this association of the early Roman Empire with the birth of Christianity more fervently in his story of Tiberius, which follows. He passes on without judgmental comment the story of the massacre of runaway slaves under Augustus. The fifth-century Christian historian, Orosius, had explained that the deed was important for its symbolism, a warning that those who do not recognize their heavenly master are lost.

When Julius was slain, Augustus, who was his sister's son, took over the Empire after him. Although he never knew the fear of God, he still established, after he was chosen judge, a peace in all his dominions, the likes of which they had never known before. And then the king decreed an amnesty for all men throughout the Empire who were captive, or in chains, or had been thrown into a dungeon. This exalted king then went on to decree that over this earth all people—mothers with children and husbands with wives—had to return to the place of their birth. This song tells us, too, that he would not allow any slaves who had run away from their masters in the Empire. One day, so we hear the book say, he had more than thirty thousand runaway slaves slain, men and women alike.

Caesar Augustus went on to establish a coin of standard weight called the "drachma," and decreed under pain of hanging that the people in his Empire, whether they were poor or rich, should pay him four pennies of this weight. This tax remained until the day when the true Savior, who was sent from heaven with the promise of help for us, freed us from this tax.

Agrippa was then sent to govern the Rhineland, where he added to the Romans' fame by building a fortified city. He gave it its name, calling it Agrippina, but now it is called Köln [Cologne][1], and it is the just pride of all the Frankish lands. One of his men named Metius founded Metz. From Trier, an old fortified city that adorned Roman authority, the Romans sent wine a long distance under the earth in stone pipes to please all the lords who settled around Cologne. Great was the Romans' might!

Augustus, that man of whom there is so much to tell, established order at Rome with great authority. Augsburg still bears his name. Indeed, he wore the crown—as the Book tells us truly—fifty-six years and three months. Finally, the Romans plotted foully against his life and succeeded in poisoning him.

---

1.   Agrippina, granddaughter of Agrippa, Augustus' commander in Germany, named her native town "Colonia Agrippina" after her mother, the daughter of Agrippa and Augustus' daughter Julia, who was also named Agrippina.

IV

Tiberius

Very soon after the conversion of Emperor Constantine to Christianity in 312, Christian writers began to treat the past relationship of the Roman Empire to their religion much less critically than before. Constantine's own historian, Eusebius, went to some length to divorce the empire from the Crucifixion of Christ by blaming the Jews almost entirely for it. To the extent that Roman authority was of necessity connected with the event, early Christian historians presented Pontius Pilate as having acted arbitrarily and independently.

The *Book of Emperors* portrayal of Tiberius shows the way that narratives in a popular vein supported the development of this tradition over eight centuries. The episode in which the pagan emperor is miraculously cured of disease and becomes convinced of the healing power of Christ comes up more often in stories of Constantine than of Tiberius, although frequently enough with the latter and occasionally with Vespasian. The author uses this story with variations for both Tiberius and Constantine. His authority for telling it in his Tiberius story is a legend of Saint Veronica, on whose veil Christ is said to have wiped his face on the way to the Crucifixion. His face left an image on the veil, and with it Saint Veronica subsequently worked miracles.

The siege and destruction of Jerusalem has, except for its timing and the motive for it, a factual basis. Vespasian, a Roman general sent to suppress a revolt of the Jews, began the siege of Jerusalem in *AD* 66. Before the city was taken four years later, Vespasian had set out for Rome in his quest for the imperial title, but his son, Titus, breached the walls, destroyed the city, and killed or enslaved most of the inhabitants he found. The *Book of Emperors* account, however, telescopes more than thirty-five years of history in turning Vespasian and Titus into generals of Tiberius shortly after the Crucifixion, now generally dated in *AD* 29 but never dated later than 33. The point, of course, is to give a good and Christian reason by the standards of the Crusading Age for the Roman destruction of Jerusalem and heighten the identification of the Roman Empire with Christianity.

Much of the siege and destruction of Jerusalem is ultimately based on *The Jewish War* by Josephus, who plays a part himself in the author's account. As a Jew whose writings lent themselves to Christian apologetic purposes, Josephus is favored by the author as an ancient historian of most useful authority. He later seems to reason that because Josephus was Jewish, all Jews are bound to accept Josephus' word. In a debate between Pope Sylvester and the wisest of the Jews during the reign of Constantine, testimony from Josephus is to carry the day for the Christians.

The Book tells us that Tiberius ruled the Empire next. He won great honor for the Romans, and learned men say he kept his soul.

He set out over the sea to lead an army to Jerusalem. You can be sure he won a land called Tiberias in battle.[1] He slew the King of Persia—I am telling you the truth about this—and divided his kingdom into four parts. After subduing all the heathens he went to Germany. When he came to the river called the Danube, he capably took up the task of building and established a city there called Tyburnia. Now, however, it is called Ratisbon.[2]

---

1.   Tiberias was a fortified city in what is now northeastern Israel, founded south of the modern town in lower Galilee by Herod Antipas in *AD* 20 and named for Tiberius, then emperor.

2.   Regensburg, home of the author. "Tiburnia" was the name of a different town mentioned in a sixth-century life of Saint Severin. It was adopted by Regensburg monks retroactively as the ancient name of their town possibly because of the name's imperial associations. The name "Ratisbon," on the other hand, is from the older Celtic "Rataspona."

Then, at God's bidding, the king fell ill. Let me describe his sickness to you. Ferocious worms grew in his head, and no one could get rid of them for him. No medicine helped at all. In fact, no one could do anything worth anything for him. But then he was brought great tidings, how in Jerusalem there was the wisest man ever born into this world, how he bade the dead arise and leprosy depart! The king learned of his many powers and was told that if he were to reach him in time, he would cure his affliction with a single word. The king greatly rejoiced and commanded that with riches or whatever it took, fiefs or estates as gifts, the physician should be brought to him, with the promise that if he could heal him, he would have his devotion for evermore and any reward for which he might wish.

The messenger chosen embarked on his journey with his instructions. His name was Volusianus. That is what the Book calls him. When he entered Jerusalem and began riding and walking around the city, he asked people where he might find Jesus, that most excellent physician, whether he was in the city, and whether he was still living or what had happened to him.

In those days a lady lived there named Veronica, whom God in his goodness had healed of violent hemorrhaging, from which she had suffered for just two years less than thirty. When the lady understood from Volusianus that he was asking about God, she burst into bitter tears and said, "Now tell me, dear sir, whether you acknowledge Jesus, since you call him by his right name?"

He answered, "My lady, Emperor Tiberius bade me as I value my neck never to return until I had found the physician. If he can heal his disease, the emperor will divide his Empire with him."

The good Veronica gave him this answer: "It is now in the third year since the Jews took him prisoner. They hanged him although he had done no crime. On the third day he arose from the grave. Before our eyes he ascended to heaven. In his mercy he gave me a magnificent picture that helps me recall his likeness. I would never part with it—as though I could go for even a day without being so reminded by it of his suffering! Then the messenger asked the lady to let him see the picture, and she was sorry she had ever told him about it.

The messenger was capable and intelligent. He softly asked the lady for the sake of God's own honor to send the picture to his lord that he might see it himself: "And if mercy is granted to him, you will have both valuable rewards and honor."

The lady called for her picture to be brought out. No one can tell you the amazing number of times the lady fell on her knees and prayed in her heart and aloud. She spoke: "You who here hast healed my body, mercy there for my soul! You who art Lord of all the angels."

The messenger kept imploring her to send her picture to his lord. Finally, after much persuading, she said she would never agree unless she could go with it herself, so that she could guard it with the honor it was due.

Owî! How joyful the messenger was that the lady promised this! He did himself great honor by quickly ordering Count Pilate seized and bound, hand and foot. He then ordered him thrown on a ship—no one was permitted to help him—and soldiers led him back to his lord.

When the emperor first saw his messenger, he said full of anger, "I am very eager to know why your journey took so long. You well know that I cannot help myself at all. I have been waiting many a day for you to bring him for whom I sent you, for I am suffering with a dreadful disease."

The messenger answered, "Sire, do not be angry that I was gone for so long. The Jews have hanged the physician, and thus your wish was cruelly thwarted. They do say that on the third day he rose living from the grave, and they all say that he ascended in plain sight to heaven. This lady has brought you this magnificent picture in her devotion. I firmly believe that you will be helped, for this good woman assures you that wherever you reverently stroke the picture with any part of your body your afflictions, however many, must depart from you. The Lord has great power."

Then the praiseworthy king commanded the picture to be raised before him. He cast his eyes back and forth over it, and deep in his heart he said, "That was in truth a real man of healing." He made a deep bow before the picture. Then he stroked his head against it and kissed it with his mouth. The king was cured of all his afflictions. The worms fell down dead to the ground, and up sprang the ruler hale and hearty. All the Romans rejoiced together when they heard these good tidings.

When the king fully realized he had been cured, he swore upon the Lord's picture that before he should lie dead he would order the city where the Lord had been martyred—it had earned this well indeed—ravaged with fire and sword: "Filthy people that they are, none of them shall survive, for they must go to their death. That is how they are to be rewarded for taking the Lord from us. They will pay a painful price with their bodies for him."

Then he sent Vespasian with his son Titus to sail over the sea with a truly mighty army. There the power of the Romans shone around over the whole land of the Jerusalemites. All the people from the countryside, including women and children, fled before them into that one city. It was then that the time was approaching for them, which had been foretold to them. The Gospel tells us this: When Our Lord entered the city of Jerusalem at the time he was to go to his martyrdom, those who were so dear and true to him and wanted to follow him, the most noble ladies, lamented faithfully for him and wrang their hands. Then Our Lord turned around again. He looked at the city and, weeping, spoke these words:

"O woe, children of Jerusalem, what evil must befall you! Do not weep over my death, for my father has ordained it thus from heaven. But you may well weep about those things that will happen in time to come. The day will come upon you when no one will be able to help the other. This walled city will fall to your enemies, and its bottommost stone will be its topmost one. Here great calamities will overtake you, for everything here will be violently destroyed and your people will be scattered. Your own seed will never again be gathered together in Israel, for you did not accept the time when God sent peace to your home. You act without mercy, and surely no mercy will be shown to you. The father will be parted from his child. Very soon you must lament and bewail all these things."[3]

These words of God came true as the lordly army arrived full of wrath. Titus set up a strong camp before the eastern gate of the walls. Then such hunger began to take hold inside the city that the young men would gather in bands and rush to any house from which they saw smoke coming and

---

3.   Luke, 19:41-44, very roughly.

break down the doors. Once inside they would leave nothing at all to eat. That was how they kept themselves alive.

It happened one day that a woman whose husband had been killed was sitting in her house, when full bitterly she began to weep and complain. Wringing her hands she said, "Where should I, poor woman, turn in my sore afflictions? My misfortune is such that I can live no longer. Today is the fourth day I have had nothing to eat, and my body is failing me. Soon I can no longer speak a word. I am near death. The heathen Romans are taking my life. O woe, dear child, we will not be able to survive this! In the end we must perish at the heathens' hands! Sustain me for a while with your own body. Let me eat you. To do so does seem better to me than letting the raging heathens kill us both." As soon as she had finished speaking these words, she stabbed her child, scalded it, and roasted it, just as the devil told her.

In a very short time word spread within the city about a rich house from which a great deal of smoke was rising. And immediately the rabble hurried there and tore down the walls. Unable to believe the woman's frightful tale, the hateful robbers ordered her to feed them. The woman hurried to fetch the child and set it before the men, saying, "Here you see a wondrous meal. Would God that there were something better than this for you! Our Lord knows well that I would give it to you most gladly. Unfortunately I have nothing more to eat. This was my only child."

Those who heard these words were so shocked that soon a great mourning spread over the whole city, as men and women lamented the hapless lot that was to come upon them, and they all wished quick death for themselves. The most learned men known among them gathered in a scriptorium and, drawing their knives, they said it seemed better to them to kill themselves before the heathens compelled them to say any prayers before their idols.

Josephus was the name of one wise man there who, as soon as he had heard the conclusion they had reached, realized he would have to use great cleverness to save himself. "He who puts himself to death is eternally damned," he said. "Now listen all together, Jews. If the heathens martyr us or burn us in here, we still have the hope that on the Last Day we will preserve our souls. Now listen to something else. It is justifiable and necessary if each one of you is to be helped—listen all around, learned and unlearned alike—that you understand whose advice pleases you best, so that we can all follow it, and I will gladly accept it, too. But if you are willing to follow my advice, then without discussing it any further let our comrades determine by lot who shall kill the other, so that we will have the lesser sin."

Then the people assembled sat down and cast lots until they had all stabbed one another. Thus God's vengeance fell upon the whole Hebrew people. Before this they had been pleasing to God and were his chosen people, but because of their wanton lust and depravity they justly lost the protection of their Lord. They are driven asunder forevermore.

When Josephus saw the last of that wondrous turn of events, he rushed to the top of the fortress of David, from where he wanted to look at the fearsome enemies from abroad. And, sure enough, he saw Titus, determined and bold, riding searchingly around the wall. He spoke, "I ask you, sir, for the honor of the Roman king, spare for him the most learned man of all, who understands how to tell the king of the beginning of the world—how God created it at the very first—and, after this, of all mankind. He will always find me very rewarding."

"If you have any shields up there," said magnanimous Titus, "use them to get down here. You are too far away from me there in the fortress, but I would be glad to have you out here with me." Josephus took two shields, putting one under each arm, and he did use them to get down from the heights.

His descent was not a graceful one, and he survived only because God willed it. He flew down among the soldiers. Titus commanded that he be taken care of. Afterwards he wrote a very useful and excellent book, as all those who have read it will readily testify.

Then Vespasian and his son, Titus, commanded all their men to storm the fortress, and they did so with great ferocity. No one inside the walls even lifted a hand in defense, regardless of how they were tortured and killed, for they had no will to resist in the face of what had been prophesied. The people who had once been bold had turned weak, and they who had once been victorious heroes were turned into exiles. They who had once been feared had to pursue humble occupations. Those who had been chosen as princes on the basis of noble birth and law were turned into serving men. For Our Lord was angry with them then. And so they who had had their home there before were expelled. Surrounded by honors, their ancestors Saul and Jonathan had ruled there. Owî! What a kingdom they had! David and Solomon had their thrones there, and we should always thank God that they did, for Christendom still reaps joy from their wisdom. Here Lord Mattathias[4] and his son Judas reigned. Herod, who bore God no love at all, lived his hard-hearted life here. God caused his fame to be extinguished. The city of Jerusalem stood crowned with many honors until its people martyred Our Lord. After that their dominion could remain no longer, as *that* day was to reveal.

The Roman lords took the walled city then and immediately had it set on fire on all four sides. Thus they burned women and children in a really tragic happening! They had the foundations uprooted from the earth, just as we hear the Book tell us. The might of the Romans shone round about them, and indeed the very bottommost stone lay there as the very topmost. Nor was that the greatest harm they inflicted, for the Romans had the survivors bound in chains and ropes and led off to be sold. They offered thirty of them for a penny to their dishonor and shame. How could anything worse happen to them? They are so dispersed in foreign lands until the Last Day that they are beyond anyone's help.

Then the Roman lords rejoiced in the manifold honors that had been bestowed on them. The king himself praised their victory when they returned to Rome. They received a magnificent welcome. Tiberius ruled the Empire for exactly thirty-three years and one month more. Then the Romans poisoned that ruler, too.

---

4.   Mattathias was the founder of the Maccabee family. His son, Judas, began a revolt, which lasted, off and on, from 167 to 142 *BC*, against the Seleucid kings Antiochus IV (175-163 *BC*), Antiochus V (163-162 *BC*), Demetrius I (162-150 *BC*), Alexander Balas (150-145 *BC*), and Demetrius II (145-138; 129-125 *BC*).

V

Caius Caligula
(Jovinus Legend)

Gaius or Caius Caligula (r. 37–41) presided over a short reign increasingly characterized by decadence and a display of arbitrary power, exemplified in his making his horse a consul. He plays no meaningful part in our author's version of the legend of the unquenchable fiery abyss in Rome's early days.

The story of a hero riding his horse into a fiery hole as a sacrifice to save Rome belongs to the legendary Marcus Curtius. Our author combines the basic plot with the story of a man destined for future sacrifice being given women aplenty in the time leading up to his death. The story has different roots. In ancient Roman legend, Marcus Curtius was simply a model hero, offering his life for the common good. In this version his heroism is offset by his bargaining to have carnal access to all the women who strike his fancy, and our author notes that he is burning in hell because of that. In general the church in the Middle Ages did not condemn heroes and heroines for making great sacrifices for Rome or to preserve their honors. The point, as articulated by Saint Augustine, is this: if benighted pagans were willing to make great sacrifices for false gods and worldly fame, how much more should Christians cheerfully sacrifice themselves with the knowledge that they will obtain eternal life?

This is probably one of our author's reasons for including this story among his imperial biographies. Another likely motive is to highlight the miserable relationship between god and man that prevailed in pagan times, in contrast with Christian ones.

he Book tells us that now Caius held the Empire. In his reign great misery plagued Rome, as an abyss opened and hellfire broke out. Neither water nor wine was any good in fighting it, nor could any of it be stamped out. In the city, from which constant cries of anguish rose, there was great suffering. Many died in the stench of its fumes. The Romans had no idea how to cope with it, although they asked the advice of many men known for their wisdom.

Finally they brought their sacrifices to a temple for prayer. Its god was Jupiter, whose power controlled the weather, and they prayed to him very fervently that he would save them from the fire. They promised him that they would heighten and spread his reputation with outpourings of public praise for his help.

Jupiter answered them then, and this cheered the Romans greatly. "Make haste, now," he said, "to meet and decide among yourselves whom you would choose as a noble knight for me. Deck him out with gold and precious stones. Make every effort to see that he has the finest cloth to cover his horse and then tell him to take the flag and ride into the fire. No one is to force him to do this. Only if this be of his own free will shall I accept him as your sacrifice and forgive you your guilt. I was about to condemn all of you to be lost, but in this way I will quell my anger. The moment this sacrifice will be brought to me you will not need to worry about the fire anymore."

The Romans asked all around from man to man, each one individually. They consulted with one another about who would be both worthy enough for the sacrifice and willing to be persuaded to carry it out, saying that if he redeemed them from their misery then all his family should be rewarded magnificently. Together throughout the day they tried to come to some decision.

Finally a man named Jovinus stepped from the crowd and went to stand on higher ground. Then he asked for silence and said, "If you will do as I want you to do, I am ready and willing to take on the feat and take care of the threatening fire for all of you."

The Romans raised high their hands, telling him that whatever his will might be, there would be no Roman who would object to his having what he wanted. If there were, that man would be thrown into that very fire.

"Then let there be no woman in Rome, either maid or married woman, that you will not allow me to have as a lover, just as I please." The Romans all promised to accept his demand.

Jovinus got himself a black hat. Wherever his desire took him, he would put the black hat in front of the door, and the man of the house would have to come out. As long as the hat lay in front of the door, that man had to stay outside his own house. Jovinus did just what he pleased—the song tells us that—and he got everything he wanted, although unfortunately his soul must burn as a result of what he did.

And so when the time that he himself had asked for was up, the Romans decorated him with gold and precious stones, as he wanted them to do, and with a fine silk cloth for his horse. They saw to it that he was magnificently decked out and mounted on a magnificent warhorse. Then he raised his flag, and his end approached. He rode back and forth, bowing towards the women. Then he turned across the courtyard, and the flaming hole received him. No one can tell you whatever became of either horse or man. The fire subsided, and the hole closed right then and there, as though it were stamped shut.

The Romans sang praise to their god who had redeemed them, but then a bolt of lightening came and struck the king so that he lay dead on the ground in front of his seat after controlling the Empire for three years and ten months. The Romans were very much afraid of their god.

VI

Faustinian

This story has roots in possibly the oldest surviving novel with Christian themes, *The Recognitions of Saint Clement*, written in Syria in the early third century. The title reflects the climax of the original story near the end, when young Clement in separate scenes recognizes his brothers, mother and finally his father after long separations. In medieval Europe it became the basis for a shorter *Life of Saint Clement*. Both works were found in monastery libraries with some frequency, and our author appears to have drawn primarily upon the *Life* but occasionally upon the older *Recognitions*. The Clement in question is Pope Clement I, a martyr from the last decade of the first century. Very little is known about him, although from a letter attributed to him, he appears to have been a sophisticated theologian, reflected perhaps in the lengthy disputations of the *Recognitions*, shortened somewhat in the *Life*.

The name "Faustinian" appears in the *Life* but not the *Recognitions* as a relative of Augustus Caesar, but not a brother of Claudius nor an emperor himself. The version of the story below highlights differences between the just ruler, Faustinian, and the tyrant, Claudius. It gives a good indication of our author's idea of proper education for a young ruler-to-be, a combination of Spartan-like physical discipline and "learning the books." Finally, it dramatizes the early spread of Christianity under Saint Peter's guidance and the triumph of the Christian faith over astrology and pagan philosophy, both through rational debate and miracles.

One book tells us that Faustinian then held the Empire. Claudius was his brother, and he did him plenty of harm. Faustinian took a lady named Mähtilt for his wife, who was as dear to him as life itself. She was extremely true to him. In fact, she came by many virtues naturally. Like him, she came of imperial lineage. The love of the two for each other gave them great joy. Hail to the moment in which they were born into this world! What a great harvest of good deeds they offered God!

Not much time passed before the mother was carrying children; yes, she delivered twin sons. Owî! How glad the father was at this! One son was named Faustin, the other Faust. As the boys grew, the Romans busied themselves, each trying to outdo the other, to see what could be done to keep the boys raised in a way that did credit to their lineage. They were to become the worthiest lords of all, coming as they did from the highest-ranking families, although as children they were to suffer deprivation and weary suffering, which afterwards they overcame very well, as they earned eternal life for themselves.

Faustinian had one brother named Claudius, and the devil put him up to going to the queen. He put his arms around her and squeezed her to his chest, making her aware of his evil lust. He said that he really wanted to make love to her—he could not conceal it any longer—and that if she would not help him out of his suffering he would have to give up living, for he was miserable enough to be ready to die. He insisted that what would become of him depended on her grace. All this greatly troubled the lady.

"I will tell you, milord, what you should do," said the lady. "Spare me such words as these, for they frighten me. My husband is very dear to me, and you should stop talking to me this way. It will not do you any good. I do not have that sort of feeling for you. I shall never turn to fill your desires, for to do so would also bring shame upon my noble house. Also if my lord should find out about this, we would pay for it dearly."

Claudius responded that he could not live without the fulfillment of his wishes. His burden was so great that he was prepared to die or accept whatever was to become of him. He said he could not go on living the way he was, and that he was in such agony in striving for her love that he had begun to doubt whether he was still completely sane.

The good lady gathered her thoughts together in a virtuous way. She decided not to tell anyone of the anguish she suffered from him. At the same time she addressed him with threats and pleas: "If our relatives find out about this, we will lose our lives. The other Romans will be appalled at this and will call for us to be stoned." She began to cry bitter tears.

That lord would not give up talking to her as he was doing. "My good and true brother-in-law, do as I tell you to do," said the queen. "Wait for the time when my husband has traveled away, and everything at court has quieted down, for I do have a liking for you. That will not be long at all. Then, too, right now I am in a late stage of pregnancy, so that what you ask is out of the question. Dear and good brother-in-law, give me a length of time, and I will do everything you want me to."

Claudius granted her request, and his passion quickly subsided for the moment. The lady thought up all sorts of cunning ways for maintaining her honor and for dissuading that evil brute from making good on what had been said. When she gave birth to the baby she was carrying, all her friends and relations rejoiced with her. They agreed that the most beautiful name they had ever heard of was "Clement," and they gave it to him. He was to become pope at Rome, and he is a wonderful martyr who can help us out here with our lives and there with our souls.

One night after the lady had regained her strength and was lying beside the king, just when he dozed off she cried out ever so loudly, "Help me, milord, while there is still time, before my life is taken away in a terrible fashion!"

He sat up and jumped to his feet, saying, "God grant me that I may keep you, my whole happiness! What has happened to you? I would rather give up life itself than see anything bad happen to you. What did you see in your dream?"

The lady answered him like this: "Milord, I can never be happy again. I saw such a terrible thing that I have no desire to live longer. I must tell you that our children will not live one year more unless you have them taught the books."

The lord comforted her well. "My dear," he said, "let that dream serve to restore your happiness! Take charge of the two boys and find out from men loyal to me where there are good masters. Then set out with your boys to where the wisest men of all are. They will learn knowledge and virtues early, and I can see great honor returning to me because of this. They will be a great credit to us; my only regret is the strain this will be for you, but I am glad to follow your advice." That is what the worthy lord said.

The lady ordered a ship to be made ready in every way, but when preparations were complete and people heard that the royal pair wanted to send off both young lords faraway overseas, they began to weep bitterly. His chief counselor began urging the king to reconsider this, but the marvelous king told him, "Understand how I am thinking: he who spares the rod really hates and envies his son. Discipline and respect are good. If someone disagrees and gives his boy a soft upbringing, he will raise a faint-hearted man who will never be able to decide what he should do or not do, so that his childhood will have led him into deep trouble when he takes over his inheritance without having learned to fend for himself. You know, I used to hear my father say that a lord's son and a vassal's son live under the same law. A boy will take over what his father leaves him after he grows up, and if he has acquired wisdom beforehand it will make him capable and honorable. My boys will have to be forced to undergo hardships by facing frost, hunger, doing without things and hard work, so that they will live ever afterwards with honor." All of the nobles there agreed that this was in accordance with their will and that it was a quite appropriate way to bring the boys up.

When everything had been made ready the boys set off on their journey over the wide, wide sea, where they came into great danger. The mast of the ship wobbled loose, and the sailors were unable to do anything about it. Strong winds came up, and the ship sank to the bottom. Everyone on board drowned except for the two noble boys, who were the only survivors, but God came to their rescue and the waves carried them up against a stone wall [jutting into the sea], where a fisherman found them. He pulled them out with a net and took them home with him to his own house. The boys decided between them not to tell anyone where they were from. They kept this a total secret, and they also cleverly decided that one of them would go by the name of Niceta and the other by Aquila.

One day it happened that a great market was held nearby. The fisherman took the children there by the hand. After tying them to a post he offered them for sale. All the inhabitants of the town rushed there to have a look at them, and they were very curious about where they were born and where they might have come from on their journey, but they could not find that out from the boys.

In that same town was *quedam matrona* [a certain lady] whose only son had died. That had caused her great pain and suffering, but now tidings were brought to her that the two most handsome boys who had ever lived in the world were for sale at the market. Since she had lost her own son she bought the noble boys. Soon she dressed them in clean clothes and began making every effort to raise them well.

The lady treated those boys just as though they were her own sons. They called her "Mother," and she looked after their needs early and late, just the same as if she had carried them under her breasts. She took one of them aside and pleaded with him until he began to tell her a little bit about the two of them. She wanted to adopt them and was determined to set aside what had been her own inheritance for their future needs, the sort of thing that is often done among the Greeks. "Mother," the young boys said, "we should not go on much longer so free. Now you heard yourself that we set out on our journey for the sake of the books."

This made the foster-mother happy, and she sent them to the noble Zacheus, for he was the same Zacheus in the tree to whom Our Lord spoke. Saint Peter, that warrior of God, had sent him for the aid and comfort of Christendom to that place, where he founded a monastery dedicated to the Holy Ghost. Thirty men were there, never any more nor fewer of the brothers, and they gave the boys some wonderful learning.

When the messengers [who had left with the ship] did not return to Rome and the mother had waited a long time, she was desperate with grief. She would often stand alone and weep bitterly. She lamented sorely to her lord, saying, "My dearest lord, my life will be worth nothing unless you give me leave to journey forth and see for myself if my children are alive anywhere in the world."

This greatly disturbed the king, and he asked, "Why are you talking like this, milady? I have many men indeed who can find out for me where they landed. You should not risk bringing shame upon yourself and your noble kin. I have neither comfort nor joy except with you. The misery that is mine from what happened to the children cannot be helped, but if anything bad happened to you I would be ready for death. I will need to be buried in the earth if I can no longer have you with me."

"What you command, milord," said the queen, "I must accept as just. O woe is me, poor, helpless woman! I am thinking of living no longer, for there is nothing for me to live for. O woe, you Romans, why do you let me keep on living? Such misery has overtaken me that sadly I am unable to bear it any longer. When, milord, will you order that I be buried in the earth?"

She beat her breast and tore her fine purple garment. She ripped her hair from her head with her hands and soon spoke these words: "O woe, that I ever bore children into this world! Having them has brought me more than enough misery."

"Milady," said the king sadly, "I can't stand to see you suffer such agony any longer, but to spare me the disaster [of losing you] if you are determined to embark upon a pilgrimage, choose some of my men to accompany you and keep you safe and sound. If you have any success on your journey, don't wait long before returning to me. If you don't come back soon [and I believe I have become a widower], I will never take a woman to love again."

His men diligently got to work outfitting a ship the very best they could. It was well furnished. On it hung silks and fine cloths embroidered with gold, and there were many other kinds of fine decorations worthy of the noble queen. The lady hurried to the harbor with many noble ladies-in-waiting to serve her. With many laments from those left behind they departed. No one had ever heard such grieving before. If they had to get along without her they would never cease their lamenting. That is what men and women alike were saying. They all agreed that no one worthier than she had ever been born in Rome, and they took up fervent praise of her excellent qualities.

And so the lady set out upon the sea, and a veritable army of both men and women from Rome all wept bitter tears at her departure. The sailors hoisted the sail, but disaster overtook them. The size and strength of the waves burst apart the rigging, and everyone on board drowned; that is, there were no survivors except for the lady alone. God saved her by letting the waves throw her up on the beach, and Our Lord allowed her to recover. She stayed there overnight in a fearfully weak condition.

At dawn the lady arose and walked down by the seaside until she came to a fine town. She came upon a poor widow and asked her if she could stay with her. The woman replied that she would be glad to take her in but that poverty oppressed her so that she was hardly able to provide her with much of anything. "You seem very frail and weak," said the noble queen. "I would be glad to help you with what I can earn with my hands or beg from the people who live around here."

"You seem to have a good, healthy body," said the ailing woman. "If your hands and feet serve you well, and if you don't think you would be stooping too low to decide to stay with me, I would be more than happy to turn the care of my household over to you." The lady replied that she very much wanted to do that.

The lady then served the woman with great trustworthiness—truly, just as I am telling you—in the same way as if she had been her serving woman. She worked at things she was unaccustomed to and pleased the woman more and more, putting whatever she earned at the widow's disposal. She had a virtuous way of living that was chaste and pure. There was never her equal in bravely bearing her sorrow with such composure so that no one was aware of it. And so the lady served the widow for over thirteen years, as the book tells us with certainty.

Her husband was waiting in Rome in hopes that a messenger would arrive with news about his wife and children or others from the large number he had sent out with them. He hoped the messengers would recognize them from earlier. His heart was heavy-laden and grief caused him much suffering; indeed, no man was ever heard to lament so despairingly. It did not take long before the king was overcome with despair, so that he summoned his men together and told them: "I wish to take leave of you to search and see if I can find my wife and children alive anywhere. My wife is so dear to me that if I do not find her I will remain a pilgrim the rest of my life. I entrust the boy Clement, my youngest son, to your care. Have him taught the books and raise him so as to do yourselves honor. As long as he is a child, do not let him have too much free time. Youthful leisure and laziness often lead to grief in maturity. Wisdom furthers ability and reliability; immorality threatens them. When the young man can speak as is fitting and knows when to keep silent, things will go well for him! A good upbringing and faithfulness go hand in hand. Whoever tries to separate them will damage both of them. The man who is to sit in the midst of senators in Rome must have his wits about him and be able to make the best decisions and govern many lands. If my son then speaks words of wisdom it will redound to your great honor. And so, I entrust all my property and concerns to you along with the youth Clement." A great wail of lament arose.

There was still time for the lord to speak some pleasing words. He took his child by the hand and commended him to the power of all of them that they might defend him and maintain their honor in doing so. All his men wished him well as he turned to sail out over the sea. He searched through Sicily and then through Calabria. Then since he did not find them there he sailed for the land of Africa. Then he went through Alexandria and from there to desolate Romania. Then one midnight it happened that, according to God's will, the boat was struck and burst apart so that no one on board survived except the worthy lord. He was thrown to the stern of the ship, where he grabbed a large piece of wood with his hands. The waves threw him up on land. He was badly beaten and bruised from being tossed around, but still God's power kept him alive.

The lord began to doubt sorely whether there was any hope for him and to despair of living, as he stood there almost naked. He who had been the lord of the Empire, standing there in nothing but a wet shirt, had lost all his worldly goods. I am telling you the truth. He was completely convinced that everything was ending for him. From what happened to him no one could fail to recognize that evil and good came to him only in accordance with God's providence. The man whom Rome had served was calling upon death to take him. Cold and hunger were now oppressing the man whom, in fact, all the lands had served. For three days and three nights he tramped over rocks and through woods—crossing whatever he came to—without having anything to eat.

And yet, God chose to save him. He then saw a man driving a donkey cart and called out loudly to him. The driver heard him and turned the cart in his direction; when he reached him he asked what had happened, what calamity had overtaken him. Faustinian did not want to tell him the whole story and simply said, "Some other merchants and I wanted to sail to a market, but the ship sank and all the men traveling with me drowned. Tell me now, are there some dwellings anywhere close by? It has been four days since I ate or drank anything. I am at the point that I would like to die."

"Good man, why are you talking that way?" said the donkey-cart driver. "You ought to be praising God forever that you escaped from the sea. Dismiss the loss of your goods as unimportant. It was an evil stroke of fate determined by the stars. Standing there almost naked as you are, you still have your life, and you may well find help. There is a goodly town not far from here, where rich and powerful lords live and where you may recover and forget your sorrow." He took off his own tunic of humble making and slipped it on the lord. He gave him wine and bread, saying, "I have been through the same kind of suffering many times. You are not familiar with the customs of this land, but if you make the right choices you may find that you have done well for yourself."

Very early the next morning the pair took themselves to Laodicea, where the noble lord stayed. He took on plenty of grueling work, carrying wood for poor and rich alike for a little money, and every day he turned the crank of a hand-mill to grind grain. All the while he kept to the ways of truth, hating lies and other evils, which made him beloved among all the people there. He possessed very little, but his speech was full of wisdom; in fact, he spoke so wonderfully that everyone said there had never been a man wiser than he.

Now we hear the books tell us that merchants from Rome had traveled to Jerusalem. Every effort had been made to receive them well in all sorts of countries. How well they were received wherever they headed! Once they reached Jerusalem they quickly found out that a child had come into this world born of a virgin. They were told of each of his miracles individually: how he had turned water into wine; how he bade lepers to be cleansed; how he bade the blind to see; and how he had bade the dead to rise up living.

The merchants had said they did not want to believe any of this unless they could see proof of some of the miracles with their own eyes. A blind man was there in the city to whose eyes Our Lord had restored light. In search of evidence for another miracle they journeyed to find Lazarus in Bethany. They found him, and as soon as they did he taught them about God's goodness, making the faith so firm in their minds that ever afterwards those merchants loved all godly teaching.

When the rich merchants were preparing to return to Rome, they encountered a stalwart of God named Barnabas. Saint Peter, the Holy Apostle, had instructed him to go with the merchants into the city of Rome, foretelling great success for him there; he told him to reveal the holy gospel there. Barnabas was strongly moved to carry out his master's instructions, for he had no fear of worldly tortures; he thought only of the Kingdom of God.

When they arrived at the harbor a man afflicted with dropsy came up and complained about his suffering. Good Saint Barnabas offered him his hand and said, "If you will believe in Christ, who is your savior and who has no beginning, you will be made whole in body and soul."

"I believe that very gladly," said the sick man without hesitation. The holy man blessed him, and when he finished making the sign of the cross the sick man was healthy once again. The Romans remarked that he would make a valued companion of theirs.

When the merchants arrived in Rome they went to the city hall, followed by the Holy Apostle. They brought out some gifts for the princes, all of whom asked them, if they had heard any really wondrous news in Jerusalem, would they tell them about it?

"We would like to tell you of a miracle the likes of which the world has never known: a child was born unto a maiden."

To this the Romans replied that this must have been some deception.

But then the merchants went on, "He heals all the crooked and the lame. There is no one with any sickness or affliction but what he will tell him to depart in full health. We left behind us in the city of Jerusalem a man who had been blind since his mother bore him, but he gave light to his eyes. You can believe us without hesitation since we saw him every day as long as we were there." The Romans responded that he must have been a great physician.

"We can tell you great wonders of him," the merchants went on. "How could he be any more powerful? He turned water into wine. He bade a man who had lain buried for three days to arise on the fourth. We were determined not to return until we found that very man, and we stood and sat by him. Everyone there confirms this to be true."

The Romans said that he must be like a god and that, if he asked them to, they would receive him as another god.

When Saint Barnabas perceived that the message was pleasing to them, he stood up right away and made God's son known to them, saying, "May all be well with you, Romans. Acknowledge your Creator. Abandon these evil deceptions, and pray to the one true God who has saved you from hell. Let my message reach you. I will tell you about eternal life. The time we spend here is short, and at the end of it the soul must separate from the body."

"You seem to me to be a wise man," said one of the Romans. "Can you tell me just why a grasshopper, who jumps up and down all the time, has wings on both sides and yet stands on six legs, while an elephant, that huge animal, makes do with four? He really has more of a need for wings."

"Our Lord, Jesus Christ," said good Saint Barnabas, "did not send us out for the sake of birds or beasts, but rather so that we might drive out devils and harvest souls for him." That angered the Romans, who told him to clear out of their city hall. Then they mocked him and threw him out.

The young lord Clement retained what he had just learned well because—so we hear read from the books—he had been fasting. He had eaten nothing for three days and three nights. He was more concerned with his soul than any sort of worldly honor. The holy man's words had enlightened him, and he was sorry that they had been cut off.

What the good man had said about God was pleasing and consoling to the boy. "Let me tell you truly," said good Saint Barnabas, "that I have a master whose name is Peter: if you could have heard him speak you would have everything you want."

"My dear friend," said Clement, "where might I find this good man?"

"If you would come to Judea, I will introduce him to you."

Without hesitation Clement promised him, giving him his hand on it, that he would follow him to that land.

Barnabas departed—I am telling you the truth about that—and Clement lost little time in getting himself ready for the journey. He journeyed full of purpose, leaving all his people behind. He arrived in Caesarea, where the holy man, good Saint Barnabas, who had been with him in Rome, rejoiced at his arrival. When Saint Barnabas saw him he raised a prayer to heaven: O God *admirabilis* [worthy of admiration]! How wonderful you are in all your works! I pray that it be your will to strengthen this man to serve your praise and your honor." He brought Clement to his own master.

Saint Peter then greeted him. "Hail, our good host who received the blessed messenger with singleness of purpose. May God reward you by receiving you with a heavenly crown into the choir of martyrs when you are serving as a prince in this world. May Holy Christ summon you with the martyrs into his kingdom, where you shall dwell forever with the angels."

Clement began to speak. "Master, you should now tell me with what you are attempting to console me? Is the soul mortal? Is it supposed to die and become living a second time? Or is it to burn in fire when it departs from here? Or is it to live forever? Or is it to come before a judgment? Or is it to be transformed at some time into something better? Is it to dissolve into nothing or to remain eternally? Or is it to return to the body? I have heard many people claim such wondrous things as these, but I can scarcely believe in such wonders, even those about which I have heard so frequently. Here with your guidance I would like to reach a conclusion. Hardly anyone knows that I have made my way to you. If you are willing, I will not depart from here until you have answered these questions for me. I would really like to be under your guidance."

"God knows, young man," the Holy Apostle responded, "you are asking for great things. This subject is not one that arises among simple people. Let us now pray to God that he might somehow reveal to us to what end he created man and what just desserts the soul will receive when it leaves the body.

"My dear friend, Clement," he went on, "do not let this grieve you, but for a little while you must stand in the doorway of this room. We dare not include you in our circle of prayer yet." He looked toward heaven and said to his disciples, "My dearest brothers, let us pray to God, for this young man has come from Rome, and he has come for the sake of great things. He is close to the faith, and if he sees some wonders he will become obedient to God." Thirty-six men were there.

Saint Peter fell upon his knees three times with the others assembled there. As he finished his prayer, he saw an angel descending from heaven in human form, who gathered up Peter and Clement from the others, who could not see them and did not know where they had gone.

At that very moment a woman by the name of Rachel died in Gethsemane. Devils who had gathered there in such a mighty army that no one could count them came for her soul; indeed, it was impossible to tell how many devils came to take her soul away. They soon took her to the deep bottom of hell, singing their song of triumph as if they had just taken a fortress.

The three of them left that place. Something over ten miles from there a holy priest of God named Vedastus had been living, but now at that very same time he departed this life with his soul forever loved by God. A huge gathering of angels came to meet him, and with shouts of praise and with song they brought his soul as the Heavens opened to place it before the face of the Lord. "Clement, my dear friend," said the angel to the young man, "here is where you will spend eternity. With your martyrdom you will receive your crown and dwell in your heavenly home after your death."

The angel returned to heaven, and the two men returned to the place from which the angel had taken them. God was doing great things for them.

The two of them rejoiced, but then when they reached home they were faced with a most remarkable turn of events: a sorcerer had arrived to challenge God. His name was Simon, and he was twisting everything the Christians were teaching into error. Niceta and his brother Aquila also came out to join them: "Welcome back, Lord Peter, our dear master! Our hearts rejoice when we see you, just as children feel when they see their father. Now that you are back with us we would like to ask God's help in combating the evil we face: A magician has overcome us with deception, and we had to swear to render him obedience."

"I release you from any such pledge of obedience," said the holy man. "It is best to stay away from vain oath-taking, but you need not follow him any longer."

"Master," said both brothers, "he killed an innocent child and buried it under his bed. With it he can work whatever magic he wants to work, and he performs many wonders. He says that if we follow him we will be able to turn lead into gold. He says that anyone who wants to capture him will never be able to get near him. When he wants to become invisible no one can see him. He can die and return to life again. He can be in hell whenever he wants to be there, or up in heaven and then back here below. If his hands and feet are bound, he can loosen the ropes. He can command locks to open, for no iron can resist his will. He puts a spirit into wooden statues so that people think they are alive. Trunks from trees long cut down he bids bear leaves. He can become a child if he wants to, but then when he chooses he can become old. His father is named Antonius, and his home is at Gethsemane. His mother is named Rachel, and she taught him how to cut grain or hay without using his hand. His sickle cuts more than that of any other four men. When he wants to go through a mountain, the mountain will open up a way through it."

"My dear people," responded the Holy Apostle to them, "no man can serve two masters. Simon was born to have error come from him, and we should be willing for our part to suffer persecution. I have complete faith in my master against whom no power can prevail."

Then the wondrous messenger asked where the magician was, and when he was told that he was at the city hall, he began to make his way there, followed by Zacheus and good Nicodemus. Sophonias came also, as did Joseph and the good Lazarus. Helyseus was there, as was Onesimus, together with Eliosdros. Clement and Arinthos were there, as were Niceta and his brother Aquila. Saint Peter turned his eyes towards Heaven as he spoke to his disciples: "I wish you well, my dear brothers. Pray now to Our

Lord that the people may become aware that we love the truth and that what I say to them this day may be worthy of his name."

When he completed his prayer, they all fell to their knees, and, looking up at heaven, they all said "Amen."

Saint Peter entered the hall and began to speak: "Peace be to all who love God! He to whom peace is dear loves Holy Christ. Because his peace is the most sublime we will take pains to devote our words to God's kingdom, beginning with his peace."

"People can hardly say we have come here for the sake of peace," Simon replied, "even wishing peace to highway robbers and thieves and all sorts of evildoers. The two of us really do not need peace. In fact, people everywhere should kill one another and welcome strife among themselves. One land should conquer the other, and fighting is better than peace, as I will prove to you. Without conflict there would be too many people, and they would become filled with false pride. Peter, do you want to dispute any of this?"

"I will maintain today," said the wondrous messenger, "that God knows no sin is punished with such heat in hell as the grim slaughter of people, as is set forth in songs and writings. For God himself has forbidden it, and in the Covenant it is written: 'Do not kill anyone, or you will be found guilty on the Day of Judgment.'"[1]

"What makes you want to rush so, Peter?" asked Simon. "You want to raise a question, but then you want to answer it yourself."

"Now tell me loud and clear," said God's stalwart, "do you want to confirm the peace of God? If you do, I will gladly let you speak."

The magician felt severely threatened when he heard Saint Peter speak continually of peace because peace was his [Simon's] own undoing. "Peter," he said, "you are really a remarkable man, for you do not seem to understand that the Word contradicts you. Christ, your master, states, 'I have not come to earth to bring peace, but rather the sword shall conquer.' How can you reconcile these things? You have distorted what your master taught. You turned his statement about sending a sword into one of peace.

---

1. In this chapter, scripture is cited directly from the *Recognitions of Clement*; citations like this one differ somewhat from those in modern texts.

Those two words just do not go together. Now say whatever else you want to say to the contrary—that is, if you can think of anything to say."

"You have failed to understand the books correctly," the holy apostolus answered him. "Your knowledge and wisdom let you down here. You want to bring in the worldly sword, which deals injuries to the body, but keep silent about the eternal one that relates to eternal life. I will show you what is written: '*Beati pacifici* [How happy are the peacemakers:'] How blessedly they live who make and preserve peace, for they are called the children of the living God."

"I understood those words perfectly well," said Simon, "and I will tell you the truth, Peter: they contradict your master's teachings. In truth, you may claim he is your master, but you want to put yourself above him. For your master says, 'The disciple should be content to equal what his master has been,' but now you are trying to put yourself over your master. Just tell me how you can bring those different statements into agreement with each other."

"I will explain the statement more clearly for you," said the pure-hearted apostolus. "Our Lord, the Savior, sent his disciples into the world to baptize, and to instruct, and to convert the heathen. We are told to offer peace to those in any house we enter. God's peace is to be proclaimed to all inside who fear and love God, and the Holy Ghost will light a spark within them. That is the way the father-in-law is separated from his son-in-law, the father from his son, the mother-in-law from her son's wife, brother from brother and daughter from mother."

"Peter," said Simon, "your master never had all his faculties; parts of his mind were missing. I can refute him in many areas, and I certainly would not consider him a true prophet. Whoever separates a wife from her husband is acting immorally. What good could possibly come of separating a father from his son, brother from brother, or daughter from mother? Anyone responsible for such separations cannot be acting well, for doing so goes against the Covenant. Now, Peter, please respond to what I have just said."

"Separations are good," the holy apostolus answered, "if they are done for the sake of God. We are told to make his name known and to take and strengthen his Word over all the earth to all who will desire and cherish it. If one brother scorns it another may receive it well. If a son receives it, the father may fail to do so, and a daughter may accept it while her mother hates it. If a son-in-law accepts it, his father-in-law may want to have nothing to do with him. God's word will endure forever and will prevail over the devil's kingdom. God will reward anyone who leaves behind child or wife, lands of his own or fiefs, or anything else he has during his lifetime a hundredfold and open his kingdom of heaven to him. Simon, now get the answer into your mind: is separation good or evil? I would really like to hear you try to refute what I have just said."

"I have no desire to put up with such talk as this any longer," said Simon. "I just want to demonstrate to all who are content to be sitting or standing here that I am telling the truth. Since you don't seem to have any answers to what I have been saying, you must put your hands over your ears and turn your back to flee, recognizing that you have been disgraced and that never again will people listen to your teaching. Listening to me will quickly destroy the impression your errors may have made."

"Simon, go ahead and say whatever you want as loudly as you want," said God's stalwart. "Then let all the hearers decide for themselves whether I know how to refute what you have said."

"Peter, today I intend to demonstrate that there are many gods and assert at the same time that they are subject to one god but one that you do not understand, for he is unknown to you. He is god over all the others together, the lord of all gods. He is the one I want to teach you, for he is still unknown among all the gods. Now tell me whether you like what I am saying."

"That is certainly a strange thing to say," said the wondrous messenger. "Tell me from where you learned to know this god who is over all the gods, and, while you are at it, please tell us how you are going to prove the existence of such a wondrous god. Did you find him in the Hebrew Scriptures? Or in the works of creation? Or in the writings of the Greeks? Or in what other sorts of books? Or do the prophets reveal him to us? Or can we have no certain knowledge of him, this god about whom silence has prevailed throughout the earth for so long?"

"Peter, what happened to your own wisdom and knowledge?" asked Simon. "You seem unable to continue, so I will teach you. You will also find it written that the gods said: 'Let us make a man,' and in the same line it is written: 'Now Adam is made like one of us.' I can cite plenty of other passages to support this. The Jews were in haste to select one god in Israel, but he no longer wields power. [The god I spoke of] is lord of all gods. What do you have to say to that, Peter?"

A smile began to come over the lips of God's messenger as he said, "Simon, Simon, we really have not heard anything to cause us to clap our hands over our ears or turn our backs to flee, nor anything in your sort of talk to cause us to do so much as turn a foot around. You presented an idea that I could explain to you better than you could understand. Let our audience confirm: God rules alone over the whole world at the same time. He gives life without death, and he grants mercy without affliction. Everything is within his power, and no one can remove anything from his hand. The prophet Moses writes about him: *'Deus deorum, dominus dominorum* [God of gods and lord of lords], you are Lord and true God. Everything that exists does so in obedience to your command.' The prophet David addresses him like this: 'Lord God, you are wonderful, and nothing compares with you. Everything that ever was or ever will be is subject to your grace and judgment. You are a true God; any other is a deception.'

"Simon, how dare you raise your voice in asserting that there was any God except one in Israel?" God's stalwart continued. "An angel once said he wanted to be a god, which angered my Lord. For that reason he must remain suffering in hell forevermore. Do you know how God avenged what the serpent said? For what he did he must creep on his breasts forevermore. God created the angels out of nothing that they might acknowledge and praise him, and he made man out of the dust of the earth, to which, however, he must return. The angel continues moving as God sends him, while the man is mortal. Now tell me: what can be compared with God? Please respond to what I have just said."

"Peter, you don't know how all that came to pass," said Simon. "I know it better than you do because I was there at the time. Since you are only human and make yourself subject to the will of heaven, you cannot measure the earth. You have five senses. Everything that ever was, everything knowable to art or reason and all the possible achievements of man, is reached by you only through your five senses."

"Your master taught you very badly, however much of a god he may be," said Saint Peter, "but I will teach you better. The sublime prophets must have had a sixth sense, which the Holy Ghost lit within them so that they could foretell what would happen in the future of the world. Simon, when will you be able to tell me how we are supposed to serve your god? No one can recognize him yet, so how can we ever recognize him? Or can you name him for us?"

"Peter, you are quickly losing yourself on that path," said Simon. "No human ear shall ever hear his name. There has never been an angel so sublime as to be able to recognize him better than I alone or the man to whom I have chosen to reveal him. Even the God who created heaven and earth does not really know anything about him. I am telling you, Peter, teachers of the Covenant taught me about him. However, those who taught me about him really know nothing about him themselves."

The foundation stone of Christianity was quick to answer him: "Simon, were you born of humankind? When did you come into the world, if you were there when our Creator first made heaven and earth? Did God take you into his confidence? And that a god who did not understand the Covenant himself taught it to you—let our audience pass judgment on that assertion."

"Peter, I will tell you just how things are," the devil's man went on. "I am not human myself, even though I am here speaking with you. Neither water nor earth went into my creation: my strength comes from fire and air. I know very well what is in heaven, but I am not mortal as you are. I am very well aware of what is at the bottom of the sea, and I know all the forests and caves. There has never been a soul, nor will there ever be one, whose origin and end—where it would end up—I did not know."

"Then tell me about your mother, Rachel," said the sublime messenger. "Where has her soul gone? I would like to bring this discussion to a conclusion."

"Where is a soul that is still in the body supposed to have gone?" retorted Simon. "You don't know what you are asking."

Then the holy apostolus spoke: "Your father was named Antonius. Your mother was named Rachel. The devils took her soul, and that was three days ago. How does it happen that you could not help her at all? Her soul is entombed in hell. You should have released her from there."

Then the devil's vassal spoke: "I never had a father or mother. Although my name is Simon, I was not born of humankind. Heaven and earth cannot restrain me, and angels must carry me about on their hands. I am the lord of all the gods. Now, Peter, don't ask any more questions. If I had wanted to be rid of you, I would already have avenged my wrath quickly."

Then spoke the man beloved of God: "You gave us a lot of very loud talk before about how neither men nor angels were ever to call your god by name, while right now you are claiming to be this god yourself. Since you have such great power and obviously do not enjoy standing here next to me, why don't you journey away from us to Heaven?" At this the whole crowd laughed.

Saint Peter, the holy man, asked that bread be brought to him without anyone seeing it, and he blessed it in the name of the Father, and of the Son, and of the Holy Ghost. Holding up his hands, he said, "Simon, are you the true God? Well, tell me, you sublime prophet, what I have in my hand or what I was thinking just now. If you cannot tell me this correctly, then you are an unworthy god and justly the laughing stock of these people. That you dare assert yourself to be God shows that you are a man forgotten of God and are possessed of the devil. You are a sorcerer. The devils assist you when you want to do magic and deceive the people with it. You speak about how you will fly. That's not the same as making the blind see or the dead rise up. No leper is cleansed that way. You are condemned before God!"

Then Simon said, "Peter, whatever became of that 'peace' of yours? No one has ever been able to recover from 'your 'peace' yet. Well, is it a warrior you want to be? You are charging at me with such force. I have a feeling you want to make yourself my equal. You are too skilled in speaking. If only you were a poor fisherman."

The holy apostolus responded to him like this: "Now choose the twelve most learned from the company and let us go home to your house. Take out your corpse there, the innocent child with which you have been working magic and have kept hidden under your bed. With this we shall put an end to the disputation."

That enemy of God was badly shaken by this revelation, and all the color drained from his face. Many fearful thoughts passed through his mind. He was so uneasy he could barely keep his seat upon the bench. He was afraid that if he would lie about the dead child in his house people would come and find it. Then they would hang him or burn him at the stake. Overcome with shame he left the building with a crowd of people following him who would have liked to stone him; however, the holy man protected him, and he made a narrow escape after nightfall.

Saint Peter then consecrated Zacheus, entrusting the bishopric to him. When he did so, men and women alike affirmed that God had indeed done well by them. All the townspeople rejoiced and praised God, shouting, "*Deo gracias*! [Thanks be to God!]."

Now we continue to read that there was a nearby island in the sea with a town on it called Arantum, where the lady who had once been queen of Rome begged for alms. There were glass columns there to which many wonders were attributed. Each and every one of Saint Peter's disciples desired to go see those columns, and asked Saint Peter if it were all right. "I will go there with you myself," said the holy man.

The men were overjoyed to hear this and boarded a ship. When they saw the columns I know that they all confirmed that they had never seen a work so skillfully made by human hands; it had become famous throughout the lands. Saint Peter turned at a corner away from the crowd and fell in prayer on his bare knees. A lady went up to him there and said to him, "Milord, let your kindness lead you to help me with my need. I am such a very poor woman, and everybody says you are such a good man. Food is too expensive for me to buy. Can't you spare me something? Help me out today, and God will reward you for it."

When the lord heard her request, he stood up right away and looked the lady over. "Tell me, good woman," he said, "if you are sound of body, why are you acting like a cripple? God gave you serviceable hands, and if you are able to work, you are committing a grave sin to go stay idle. Why don't you heed the words of the sage who said how blessed a person is who lives by the work of his hands?"

"If I really were sound of body, and if I could still use my hands well," said the lady, "I would feel stupid to be idle and would think of myself as no good, but I have neither health nor decent eyesight. I am a poor lame woman in need. If you would consider giving me a little something in my need, God Almighty will more than make it up to you."

"You are about to receive some real help," said the holy man. "Since you are physically disabled, I will not reproach you. How would it be if you told me how all this came about? Then I might have a cure that would work for you."

"Stop talking like that, milord!" said the lady. "No one can do anything for me. Owî! I wish that I had either stabbed myself or let myself drown when my terrible troubles first began before I became such an invalid that my poor bones know nothing but regret! I can't imagine that any woman ever suffered what I have."

The holy apostolus then answered her: "Stop thinking that way, milady; it will not help you at all. Anybody who kills himself will be punished with his soul burning in hell forevermore."

"Owî!" she said, "my dear lord, I would not be so very concerned about my soul burning in hell if it would only help me to see my children once again who have been gone so long from me and for whom I sacrificed my health—or even just to be able to bury their bones."

The lord comforted her well, saying, "Milady, do not lament so bitterly. God Almighty forbids all weeping except for sins alone, when the tears are pure. Tell me what happened to you that brought you such suffering. Tell me what caused your miseries, which have left you with such bodily afflictions, and tell me also about your family. I intend to do well by you. If you will believe in my Lord, who created you, you will be healed."

"Don't ask about my kinsmen," she said, "but I will tell you part of the things that led to my being disabled for so long. Both my father and my mother came of good families. They had plenty of wealth, and they raised me with great care. They gave me to a nobleman in marriage, and by him

I had two sons at the same time. My husband had a brother who caused me no end of grief. He was a fearsome man who came after me with his unchaste desires, wanting to make love to me. I had an idea about putting him off with a ruse that would do no dishonor to my family. My thoughts convinced me that I must run away from him. When I had my third child— I had been pregnant at the time—I complained to my husband that in a dream I had seen that my boys would never live to bring us any honor unless I had them taught the books. And so—this is exactly what happened— I took fine silk cloth and money and sent them off to school, but I never found out where they ended up. No man ever came to me who could tell me anything more about them.

"After that," milord, "she went on, "I was left at home with my great sorrow, but then the thought came to me that I might find relief from my sorrow. I complained to my husband that I was ready to die unless I could see my children again, and I asked him if I could leave in search of them. He hated to do this, but he agreed to let me go. He entrusted me to his men and we set sail, but everyone on board was to drown except—unfortunately, milord—for me as sole survivor. To my misfortune I ended up on some rocks by the water. I came to the house of a poor widow, and I served her early and late as long as I was sound enough of body to do so. Now it has gotten to the point that gout has crippled me badly, and neither of us can do much, but whatever we get from begging we share in common. You have heard now, milord, how I came to be in the state I am now in. Please, do not wait any longer but let me receive some of your mercy. Do give me something because my fate depends on your grace."

Right then when they were talking, and Saint Peter wanted to question her further, young Clement came running up to him. "Master," he cried. "I just saw a wonder the like of which, I must tell you truly, is not to be found throughout the whole Empire!"

"You should go to the ship," said the holy man. "You go ahead and I will soon come after you."

The sublime messenger of God asked the lady something more: "What were the names of your boys who have been separated from you for so long?"

The lady did not want to tell him so for a while she deceived the lord by saying, "The one was called Sisinnius, the other Eliosdros."

"Owî!" said the holy man. "I think we will soon have something to celebrate. A young man has arrived here from Rome, and I learned how his brothers were shipped off to school, how later their mother journeyed after them, and how she escaped unharmed [from a shipwreck]. Finally, since they were gone so long, the husband set out himself. The boy whom they left at home told me all this himself. It looks like they are still separated from one another and the lost ones will never be found." While he was speaking, the lady turned blood red with her face inflamed as if from a fire, but then for moments she turned pale and her body felt faint. Seeing this, the holy man blessed her and bade her straighten up in good health.

When the lady realized that her body had been restored to good health, she fell on her knees at his feet and said, "I must see that child, milord," she said! "He is truly my son."

"Now tell me his name first," he said.

"My dear lord," she said, "I really did not want to tell you, but Clement is the name of my youngest son, the one I left in Rome."

"Then be of good cheer, dear lady," he said. "I will show him to you very soon." He took the lady by the hand and led her to the place where she could see Clement.

Clement saw his master leading the woman towards him, but he thought it was some sort of joke. "Master, what is this, for God's sake?" The lady went to her child, and she embraced him in her arms, but Clement jerked away from her, feeling no love for her at all. He thought this was all nonsense and really wanted to run away from her.

"Son, you should love her," said the holy man. "She is your good and noble mother, who carried you into this world." The young man was excited, and great joy abounded in all of them. My Lord brought this about with the help of his appointed master, good Saint Peter. When the townspeople heard what had happened, they all rushed to the scene. Everyone there was filled with joy and joined in praising God.

"Hail to you, my dear master!" said the good mother of Saint Clement. "If you would not have any objection I would like to take leave of you and visit a good woman who has long suffered bodily affliction. Her condition is very poor now, but—hai!—how well she took care of me!"

"We would be glad to learn to know her before we depart from here. Have her brought here to us." When the woman was presented to him, the holy messenger asked her, "Do you believe in God the Good with all your heart and mind?"

"How gladly I believe in him," said the lady.

"Do you believe that Christ, his son, is our redeemer?"

"I gladly believe that," she said.

Then the lord blessed her, he raised his hand, the shadow of the savior spread over her, and she was healed. All those who were there became obedient to God when they saw this great miracle. Saint Peter had her given ten pounds of gold and entrusted to a good husband.

Telling the lady to come along with him, the holy man departed. Niceta and his brother, Aquila, came to meet them, but when they saw the lady they started asking each other who this lady might be that they did not know. The holy apostolus began to speak with these words: "I will tell you, Christ knows, who this very woman is and what all she has been through. She is of Roman birth and—I am telling you this as a fact—descends from the best families there. Her relatives gave her to a husband, by whom she had two sons at the same time. Her husband had a brother who troubled the lady greatly. He wanted her to fulfill his unchaste desires very much against her will. She was hard pressed to cope with him and told her husband that she had had a dream in which it was foretold to her that their boys would never grow up to bring them honor unless they had them taught the books. Her husband allowed her to send the boys off to Athens, where they were to go to school. That devil's man brought her no end of misery. She escaped upon the sea, but in a shipwreck all others on board were pulled to the bottom of the sea. The waves cast the lady out on land, and she came to the house of a widow. I found her in the midst of great sorrow, wailing over and over, 'Dear son, Faustin! Dear son, Faust! Where do I have any hope of searching for my dear children?'"

Niceta and his brother, Aquila, jumped up at hearing this and looked at each other. "Hail to you, Lord God! But what should these words mean?

Hail to you, Lord Peter! Are we being troubled by an illusion or should we believe that story?"

"Unless we do not know what we are talking about," said Saint Peter, "as sure as we are sitting here you can consider everything I just told you to be true."

"Then *we* are the ones, Faustin and Faust!" they exclaimed.

The holy apostolus fell on his knees and prayed with his eyes towards heaven: "Hail to you, Lord Christ! Three kings—who had never known you before and had to follow a star—brought their offerings to you from their lands. In such a way it pleased you to preserve these children far away from their homes. You are the beginning and the end of everything that is, and the earth is filled with your mercies.

"Greet your family!" he said to the children. "Clement is your brother, and the lady is your mother. From what has happened you can see that God performed such miracles here as people will write about until the Last Day."

The brothers came together. Hai! With what joy in God they received each other and exclaimed, *"Gloria tibi deo!* [Glory be to you o Lord!]"

The mother was exhausted and asleep. In their joy the brothers wanted to wake her up, but the holy man spoke to them. "She is frail in body. Let me wake her up for you. I have a good reason for that."

When the lady looked up, Saint Peter spoke to her: "If you want to complete your commitment to God, you should ask to be baptized. Then when you fully accept the faith you may go to the Lord's Table with us."

"How gladly I believe," said the lady, "that the one true God formed me out of nothing! I believe that his son, Christ, is my redeemer. It was in his name that you healed me, and I was not so simpleminded but what I rejected those false, deceiving idols that were in Rome."

"Since you left the city of Rome, your noble kin and all your worldly possessions," said the pious messenger of God, "for the sake of your purity and chastity and kept yourself free of sin, God will open his kingdom to you where you shall live eternally as a reward for your holy life. I will now let you see your sons. Here is Faustin and his brother, Faust. God preserved them for you so that you may be surrounded by great joy as you age. My Lord himself ordains this for you."

When the holy apostolus finished naming Faustin and Faust, the lady was rejuvenated on the spot. Yes, her old age turned into youth. No human tongue will ever be able to tell you or sing to you adequately of the ecstatic joy they had in finding each other. Those boys told their mother what miseries they had undergone: how their ship had sunk, how they had been tied to a post at auction, how they had first come to a magician, and how he had deceived them until that true prophet had redeemed them; finally how they had come to know God. With hands raised high they praised Saint Peter, who had brought them all together.

"God Himself did this," said the holy man. "It was holy Christ who is a gatherer of bodies and souls, and to him we give all praise and honor." Very early the next morning, Saint Peter went to the harbor. His disciples raised their hands and pressed them together. Falling on their knees, they looked towards heaven. For a very long time they reminded God of his wounds. A poor man became aware of them and inconspicuously crept along the water's edge toward them. He was now a poor porter, although he had once been king at Rome. He had wanted to go to his work but then he saw the holy man. He devised things so he could stay within earshot of Saint Peter and his followers and never attended to any real work that day. Finally the old man mustered some courage and addressed the group with these words: "You are obviously rich and powerful lords, but, if you would not think that I am stepping over the proper bounds, I would like to salute you and discuss some things with you. To be sure I am afraid—I am after all a poor man—you may think I am acting presumptuously."

"Your greeting is very welcome to us," said the holy apostolus. "We do not look down on you because of your poverty. Our Lord has commanded us to be poor and gladly so for his sake. He who desires to serve him looks down on no one but accepts all people, rich and poor, as equal."

Then the old man said, "Peter, I would gladly have a discussion with your group. If you are confounded by any argument among you, I would be glad to settle it for you quite well. I am a well-educated man, and I know my way around in many worthwhile studies. But suppose I had a problem myself; then I would very much like to hear how you would solve it for me;

for, if you find what I have to say interesting, then by rights it would be yours to discuss. But if this is not the case—that is, if you do not like what I have to say—then I will go about my work again and talk no more with you. For I do fear that my words will bring you much grief."

"You shall have our permission to speak," said the holy man. "If you have heard or seen anything that seems to contradict what we say, then take us to account for it in whatever way you choose. If you have something useful to say—how welcome you are to us. If it turns out not to be useful, we will still not scoff at your good sense but shall be your good friends. Treat us just as you would your own sons."

Then the old man said, "Peter, as for why I have been going all day today without working, I want to tell you the true reason I have been doing this. I really feel sorry for you, now that I have seen how you are praying here. There are no gods or holy places here, nor can there be here any real worship of the divine, so if you want anything more than you can have from fate, you are a strange man indeed. If you suppose that something may ever happen to you other than what fate wants to give you—the whole time I have been forced to realize that prayer is of no use, nor can human wiles ever keep fate from having its way. This I will surely prove," said the old man.

Clement spoke: "Lord Plato says: 'Whatever springs from God seldom indeed runs out.' Father, may I ask you where your homeland is or what country you were born in? You seem to be well up in years."

The old man responded, "Why should I tell you of my homeland or of anything about my birth? My words should be answered first. If we have any time afterwards, then we can talk about ourselves to each other."

The holy apostolus of God answered him pleasantly, "We want to receive you well. Draw closer—you seem to have a good mind—and sit down here by me. You are a well educated man"—this was the way he began the discussion—"and whoever teaches the truth, spreads it, and increases it, and thus harvests the souls of men, shines more than does the light of the sun, for he has harvested and won God, to the end that he will live undying evermore in God's kingdom. We have evidence to show this. Indeed, the prophets write for us: 'When a man has built a great city upon a high mountain, he should not hide it but let it be seen afar; nor should he light a lamp to hide it under a bushel, but let him set it upon a high stand, that it may shine forth everywhere.'"

Then the old man spoke: "Such talk is beyond me. I am not familiar with anything of your prophets, and I would rather discuss something else I found in those books I studied earnestly and understand on the basis of high scholarship. This is what I want to present to you. Peter, do you know how to solve this problem I raise? Or do you want to give me something to solve? I will answer you gladly."

To this God's stalwart replied, "Say good and loud whatever you want. Someone will gladly give you an answer then."

"Peter, I tell you that no god rules the world nor ever gave it order, and that he who longs for anything in this world except what fate gives him struggles vainly. Whatever hour a man is born in must always decide what happens to him; it fixes the bounds of what he can do for as long as he shall live. He cannot go any further. And if you contradict this, then I will answer you as soon as I recognize the argument."

Niceta then stepped forward and asked his teacher for permission to dispute, saying, "Master, I desire to serve always with devotion. His words are so striking that I must answer them."

"How gladly I grant you this!" said the holy man. "Answer him just at the moment the Holy Ghost put words in your mouth."

Niceta then turned to the old man and said, "Father, you should not take it as rudeness if a simple youth dares such a great thing against an old scholar. Don't let this disturb you. I am not moved to do this by an excess of high spirits, but like a son speaking to his father. If you overcome me in the argument, I will gladly be at your disposal."

Then the old man said, "Child, choose whichever one of the seven liberal arts you know best of all how to present. That's what I want. But if you should feel uncertain yourself about some point and you have any companions who can help you with it, they will find me ready, too. I do not want to contend against truth, but only to observe all the rules of propriety. Let us designate one of the company as mediator, to regulate our discussion acceptably to both sides."

Then Niceta spoke: "Father, I will first reveal to you that I was educated on Epicurus, as was one of my brothers standing here. The third one of us was educated on Plato and Aristotle. Now select something for yourself out of the whole works of these three, whatever you like—in whatever direction your thoughts lead you—and you will find us ready. Let the listeners judge whether we have anything to answer you with. We should feel no disgrace if a man so much older defeats us in argument."

To this, Saint Peter, the holy man, replied, "He began the discussion about fate. I think it would be all to the good to bring that subject to a conclusion first."

The people all began to praise Saint Peter. When they recognized that stalwart of God they all shouted loudly, "Welcome are you, master! Praise and honor must be yours forever for coming to Judea!"

It was Niceta who took up the discussion thus: "Whatever endures eternally is certainly a unity; whatever must have composite parts must surely fall apart. Whatever is made up of many parts must surely fall apart, for everything that can be divided has no eternal strength. No man can divide nor turn from its course anything which is a unity and alone, for it has neither a beginning nor an end. If you want to be a truly learned man, then accept the fact that no human power can shake anything that is a unity. How can a man turn from its course something of which no one knows the end, which has no beginning and which exists without having had a creator? Such a thing is all-marvelous. Suppose it has a creator. If it does, then it must finally run its course. That is why angels are imbued with motion and why man is mortal. Everything that stays as it is eternally has neither beginning nor end. Father please give me an answer, if you want to dispute this."

Then the old man spoke: "Son, you proceeded masterfully. As long as I have been living, I have never heard a better talk from any youth before. You are revealing great intelligence. Still, I can't understand what you are saying about that unity. I'd want to have a discussion about fate."

"If you want to have a discussion about fate," said the young man, "we must distinguish three separate aspects of the subject: whether it always was, or if it had a creator, or how else it might be created. That, Father, I can sufficiently explain to you."

"Son, let the discourse proceed!" said the old man.

Then the young man said, "I want to tell you with certainty that the world has one creator—about the other two points I want to hold off for the moment—from whom it has its beginning and in whose care it remains. In his omnipotence, he is Creator of all forces. He is Father of all the Good. He holds in his protection everything that is in this world. Now reply, if you want to."

Then the old man spoke: "You can keep that argument for yourself alone. If the world had a Creator, and if I knew who he might be, even now I would want to come to him. But your assertion that the world must have a creator is unacceptable. For I tell you with certainty, nor will I let anyone persuade me otherwise, that a human being cannot preserve himself against whatever is supposed to happen to him. That is something that I am going to prove and insist on. From my own experience I am familiar with many things that are ordained unjustly, things that never could happen if there were a creator. If a Creator were in fact protecting me, what could injure me then? But good cannot sustain me nor evil hinder me, except as fate will. People aplenty fall over dead, or drown, or are struck down. I could tell you of many things, which, if your argument were valid, their likes would never be, for the Creator would not have let them happen. If you have anything to say to this, I would like to hear it."

Then Niceta spoke: "I can prove this point another way. If I might dare do so without offending you, I shall refute your argument so thoroughly that everyone here today will agree that although you say fate exists, it has no power whatsoever, but rather all this world stands under one Creator. That I will insist on and prove true."

Then the old gentleman said, "This argument I would like to hear."

"Father, you have undoubtedly seen enough to know how helpless all human beings are at birth. As long as one is a child, he can have no real understanding. Then he is brought up and prepared for manhood. If you want to provide for him well, then set him to learn from the books or teach him whatever you want to. The beginning means a great deal. If he acquires the right habits of mind in childhood, then he will strive for excellence in manhood. If he wants to give free rein to evil, then you say fate is to blame.

Children are given a good education so that they may profit from it when they are of age. A man must learn to excel in whatever he is to increase his accomplishments. The result is that when he makes himself useful and does well by people, he is treated the same way. If, however, he turns toward evil ways, he shall be judged by all the same standards. Man is left the responsibility to his Creator for his soul. If a man does not want to recognize this, then hell will have to burn his soul in it forever. These are wholly man's decisions. What has become of that fate of yours now? In truth, it has been quite disproven. But, since you insist it is real, go on and answer what I have now said."

Then the old gentleman spoke: "Son, you have appealing theories. Your argument is pleasing enough, but it does not shed any light on what I have been talking about. Nor will it do you any good at all, for I can refute your speech entirely. Earlier I heard you claim that all of this world stood under one authority. Tell me now, boy, isn't it true that if this authority of yours is just and good he should prevent any man from doing harm to another—any man from slaying another or from committing any crime at all. What good can I say I find in him? What kind of an authority is he now if he must allow all these evils? If I had a serving-man working under me who was obliged to perform whatever service I assigned him, how could he dare neglect it? You say glibly that the world has a creator, but if he did create the world, then he could also have made people equal, each just as rich as the rest. But many a man suffers poverty, and, as things are, this man is evil while another is good. Each one of them leads his life just as fate assigns it to him. Unless you want to advance a different argument, fate can still be considered not even touched."

To this, Niceta said, "I will clarify that now for you in this way: God is the creator of Heaven and earth and all that they contain; nothing exists without him. But it is the situation he has arranged for his creatures that I want to set forth for you here and now. All the children of man are given the same freedom, for God has bestowed free will on them. One man resolves to live in goodness, attempting many a good deed with heart and mind, keeping God before his eyes, recognizing his hidden power and rejoicing in good things. He has used the greatest prudence, and since the Creator is a just judge, he will keep him in his presence and he shall become like the angels and shall rejoice forever. By contrast, a second man will devote himself to evil pursuits, trying to see what excesses of lust and haughtiness he can reach, while plotting how he can murder this man, take that man's belongings from him, and betray the other man, rejoicing in his wickedness and committing mortal sins all the while. We have true prophets among us, and we must have false ones, too. Among the heathens are true philosophers; there are also false ones among them. Among the true messengers of God, deceiving men crept in, as did lying deceivers among the teachers of God's word. There are hypocrites among the recipients of divine baptism. One man wants to assert a lie, and another insists on the truth. No, Father, do like a wise man who knows well what distinctions must be made: choose the best part and regain your salvation. Hurry along the right way, build yourself bridges and clear yourself paths. Then you shall draw nearer to the kingdom of God, where you shall rejoice eternally. I ask your permission to bring my speech to a close." Most courteously he bowed to the old man.

Aquila then stepped forward and took up the discussion with these words: "Father, if it wouldn't be too painful for you, I will correct your idea about fate."

To this, the old gentleman said, "I have already experienced so much that never has a man known how to tell me more about this than what I read in the books: that fate must ever prevail. But if you can convince me better with your ideas and if you can recognize the truth in your words, then I will follow you."

"Father," he said, "listen carefully to what I have to say. Here on earth it has often happened that two mighty kings have led very evil lives, delighting in doing harm to each other by plundering and burning. Finally, they have gathered great forces and marched on each other to fight their huge battles in which many men lost their lives. Easily ten thousand have been killed in such cases. How can one fate-determining hour serve to explain this with all of them born in the same hour, while they really did lose their lives all in the same hour? And now, dear sir, listen to something else: where there is a public harbor, people are gathered together, and after assembling from afar all different kinds of men and women must board a single ship.

Then a savage wind arises and drowns all on board. Sir, as well educated as you are, to think that you refuse to understand this except as caused by one fatal hour; They could hardly have all been born during a single hour, and still they did have to die together in a single hour! If I am allowed to recall them for you, I can point out many things to you that would all contradict your notion of fate, and even if afterwards you insisted on it, you could not contradict my point with the truth."

Then the old man said, "Dear friend: I can surely explain this better to you than you could understand it yourself. Fate must prevail. You are still a young boy. There are twenty-four hours in a day and night. Each of them has its own power. They never increase or decrease, nor shall they ever undergo change, but they are all equally long. Son, just consider: how can men fail themselves of their arts to extend their course, once determined? Pythagoras will confirm this for you. Take the hour that passed one thousand years ago and, if you want to study its course, you will find ready evidence of it even today. I am sure of this when I tell you that if you had only been a bit more diligent in your studies you would be familiar with astronomia [astronomy]. You also mention how old and young have proceeded to a great battle. Now, let one hundred thousand be killed: whoever ended up dead there, well, it was his hour and his day and he couldn't survive beyond it. Whatever death he was destined to die, whether he was to drown or be struck down, his fatal hour had to lead him there exactly according to what it had in store for him. This is controlled by all septem [seven] planets, who rule the heavens and determine fatal hours. Each one rolls upon its separate orbit and must pass through its appointed time. You can't tell me anything about this. I was educated on the books, and it is a fact that fate must always overtake man with whatever it determines should happen to him. Boy, do you want to tell me something different?"

The boy looked at the old man and said, "How would it be if I point out a number of things to you, if it is agreeable to you, which will make you abandon the notion of fate you are so firmly attached to today?"

"Such a speech I would like to hear," replied the old man.

"Our ancestors studied diligently long ago and brought to light many wonderful things that will always be remembered. Certain philosophers discovered the laws of hours and time when the great Pythagoras measured the heavens' heights for them. Those were great achievements of the mind, and men will find no better. Such men were all wise enough, but we ought to believe more in him who bore within himself the wisdom through which heaven and earth were created, who holds the world firmly in the palm of his hand, who is praised by the angels in Heaven and who is feared and honored by all his creatures here below, as we should support and spread the teachings of those men he himself then taught while he revealed his mysteries to them. I want to say more about this notion of fate. I want to put an end to what you first began talking about:

"Father, will you tell me whether a woman can carry two burdens together? Have you read about that anywhere? Can she be delivered of two children at the same time?"

The old man replied, "She can carry seven burdens but cannot survive any more than that, or else the books have lied to us."

Then the young man said, "I am glad to hear you agree with me that there is truth in this. So then the woman's time comes, and she has two babies, who can be either brothers or sisters. When one of them grows up to be a good man, dear to the people and praiseworthy, while the other turns into a robber or a thief, his hour of birth is certainly not to blame. When that one is hanged for a crime, this happens as a result of his own guilt, as is the case when the other turns out to be moral and upright. Father, how are you going to conclude that this comes from their hour of birth, when really they were born in one single hour? If you want my advice, you might as well abandon your argument. You started out on the wrong path, and you have been fooled in your belief."

Then the old man said, "I know how to answer that argument all right. When a woman is to give birth to two babies, there must be some time in between. What about the fact that as soon as she has brought forth one child, *that* time is entirely superseded before the second is born. It can easily happen that the fatal hour changes faster than your eye can blink. Let's leave the discussion at that. The men who measured the heavens long ago were wise philosophers. I don't know whether there is a man living whose mind could produce any such accomplishment as they left for us. You thought about this all wrong in wanting to contradict the books. You can't put an end to the disputation."

Then the young man said, "Owî! Father, how I wish for you that you would accept truth as oneness and would believe in one teller of truth. Hours and time roll past all around, and they glide away from us easily. If you wanted to win your soul an eternal home, which would be of greatest benefit to you, if you chose the best for yourself and acquired a firm foundation for yourself that would never weaken from under you, only then would you be acting wisely."

Then the old man spoke, staring at him with eyes ablaze: "How am I to use my mind now to gain the best portion for myself? If you are convinced about this, it doesn't seem good to me, and you probably feel the same way about my viewpoint: fate must prevail over all people. The world today remains the same as it came to be at the very beginning. Man has to live in it, and he won't be able to get away in valleys, or in mountains, or using any kind of defense, from whatever fate wants to give him. If he takes refuge on the sea, then whenever the time of apportionment comes, the waves will drown him: fate must prevail over him. I still intend to assert the truth of this," said the old man.

Then Clement arose and asked permission of his teacher to enter the disputation. He turned to the old man and said, "Father, if it would not be irksome to you, I would like to ask you a few questions."

"By all means, son," said the old man. "Feel free to do so."

"Do you recognize any of the many gods among the heathens?"

"I recognize many of them, and I could tell you plenty about them," he replied.

"Did you ever have occasion to make sacrifices to them?" asked Clement.

The old man replied, "I have done that very often, any time fate left something unfinished. If I can be helped no other way I am glad to satisfy them with sacrifices, for I have great faith in them."

Then Clement said, "It puzzles me greatly that you would go before your gods and prostrate yourself before them. You brought your offerings to their house, and then—by Heaven!—how did things turn out for you when you left? Were they ever kind to you? Dare I ask you that?"

"Sometimes," said the old man, "they did evil to me, sometimes good, just as it happened to come. Our law requires us to sacrifice both oil and wine to Luna; in return she protects us during the night. *Ad templum Martis* [to the temple of Mars], who most certainly is a great god, we bring offerings of swords and shields. He is due great honor, for no human can do any harm to any man he wishes to protect. Fabulous Mercury—now there is a remarkable god—wants the merchants to venerate him before other gods. To Jove, the Ruler, great honor is due: we sacrifice bows and arrows to him. When he releases his anger no living thing can survive him. To Lady Venus we must show all faith and honor. We sacrifice flowers and rings to her. I am eager to stand in her favor. Our lot greatly depends on her mercy, for she commands us as goddess of marriage. To wild Saturn we sacrifice vessels of silver. If he alone wants to harm us, all the other gods cannot save us. The Lord [Apollo the sun god] wants his worshippers to offer him gold. In return he gives us sunlight and all kinds of blessings. There are many more gods worshipped by us at Rome that I don't want to name now. I couldn't recite all their powers for you in a year."

To this the youthful Clement replied, "These are strange things indeed, and with words out of your own mouth I shall lead you to reject this strange custom of yours here and now. What did you achieve by going before your gods and falling down in front of them? What could your gods have granted you if fate controlled everything that happened to you? Either fate must lie or your gods are deceiving you. If you attribute anything to them, that must go against fate; however, if you want to insist on the notion of fate, you must let the gods go. You are deceived on one side or the other, for you cannot completely insist on both."

The old man fell silent and did not answer him anymore. Anger made him want to leave. Saint Peter, that holy man, held him back, saying, "Let your mind be at ease. You should sit down a while. Don't be upset, for I shall pursue this topic of fate through to the end for you."

Then the old man said, "I would like to hear the end of this disputation, but I can't be happy about it. My wits have so failed me that I have been beaten by such an inexperienced boy. I will never be able to get over it or to regain my self-respect."

To this, Saint Peter, that holy man, said, "I want to assure you that any man who relies on fate will often suffer misfortune, and I shall prove this to you right here on this spot. My dear friend, do as I instruct you: Select two of the very best scholars in the whole Empire, take one of them secretly to a room where you will not be disturbed, and say you have suffered such great hardships in your time that you would gladly die: your life is worthless to you. Ask him whether this is the fault of your fatal hour, acting as if you want to have a final answer from him. Then, having called for his book, he will point out many extraordinary stars to you and will confront you with terrible confusion. He will trace the path of the stars back and forth, his head will move like the balancing pan on a scales, and he will say that the hour of your birth was so full of misfortune that no man could bear it. And so naturally you have had to suffer.

"Then, dear friend, after this is done, let him go on his way! But then seize the opportunity of querying the second one, this time wearing a happy expression. Tell him the same time allotted to you has been so full of success that nothing more desirable could have happened to you in this world. Very quickly he will call for his book, and in it he will point out to you extraordinary stars. Then, most impressively, he will calculate that your hour of birth was of such manifold felicity that it could yield no harm to any man living under it. And so naturally you have had happiness as a result."

Then the old man said, "Peter, I feel compelled now to tell you what fate sent my way. Even though I have now been deprived permanently of all honors, I was once nonetheless a man of great standing in Rome. I took a wife who was most suited to me, and it was not long before she bore me three sons of whom I could be proud. Two of these I sent off to Athens. It was only a short time until I found their mother in despair, beating her breast, weeping and wailing, suffering dreadfully. Over and over she would cry out: "Dear son Faustin! Dear son Faust!" Their mother set out for foreign lands in search of the children, and I could neither search out nor hear word of where any of them ended up, dead or alive. I gave all my riches to my youngest son and went after my wife and children, but I was never able to find any of them again. And so it is a fact that I am still on my way after more than fourteen years, during which I have been cooking and scrubbing for people. Here I have been earning money by carrying wood and grinding grain with a hand-mill. Peter, don't you believe in fate yet?" The boys heard this and knew that the gentleman was their father. They wanted to reveal themselves to him; however, the holy man forbade them to do so and told them to keep silent as long as he wished.

Then the holy man said, "Tell me now the name of your youngest son!"

"I am glad to tell you that name," said the old man, "for no man in the world ever had children dearer to him than I did, as long as my fatal hour permitted me to keep them. The oldest was named Faustin, the one after him was named Faust; my youngest son, to whom I left my whole inheritance, was named Clement."

The holy apostolus responded thus to his words: "Suppose it came to pass that I might show you your wife, entirely chaste and pure, untouched by any evil, with your three sons? What will you do about fate then?"

"Peter, let the discussion stop there It is just as likely that something can happen without the influence of star-determined fate as that I can ever see my children or wife again."

The holy apostolus answered him like this: "Are you willing to renounce your faith in fate as determined by the stars? If you will, I will turn your wife, whom you have been missing for many years, over to you."

"I will renounce my belief in star-determined fate," said the old man, "if you will let me see any of my sons; if, in addition, I am able to see my wife again, then Peter I will confess that everything you have said is true."

That true warrior of God took the lady by the hand, telling his youngest son, Clement, to go ahead of them. Standing in the midst of them, Saint Peter made known to the people what a powerful judge the poor man whom they saw there had been at Rome. He recounted his whole story of his wife and children, and he told about all the calamities that had beset him. "Here are Faustin and Faust!" said the holy apostolus. He told the boys to come up in front of the crowd. The old man turned pale, his legs began to give way, his breath was very short and there was doubt about his very life. The holy man blessed him and told him that his strength had returned to him and that he should stand up straight in good health. He had undergone such a change that many of those there thought him dead. He could not bear his own weight, and he seemed to be hovering in a dream-state, but when Saint Peter spoke to him, how joyfully he saw himself surrounded by his family, wife and children, and others from his household! They came together and received each other with such delight that human tongues cannot do justice to it. That was the happiest day that any of them had ever experienced. God wanted to grant them that.

When their joy was at its greatest height and they confirmed their faith, asked to be baptized and so entered Christendom, Simon the Magician was very much saddened by their happiness. He took two of his disciples, one named Agon, the other Anubion, and sent them on a mission. They came to old Faustinian and told him: "Cornelius has come from Rome. He heard about how joyfully your problems were solved. In his faraway home he now worships holy Christ. He would very much like to talk to you now when he is close by, but please don't tell your sons about this."

"Yes, I would very much like to do that," said the old gentleman. Without telling anyone else at all, he hurried to Saint Peter and asked: "Master, would you grant me leave to go and see an old friend of mine? Cornelius has come to this land and sent me messengers. Unless my bodily strength lets me down, I will be back before nightfall."

"How happy I am to approve what you ask!" said the holy man. "We should always maintain contact with good, old friends. Go now, and God be with you, but do not stray from the path you have chosen; stay where you can keep your wits about you and can understand what is going on."

When the old gentleman arrived at his destination, Simon greeted him enthusiastically. All the while Faustinian thought his host was Cornelius, who invited him to come in and sit down, because Simon had transformed his face. When they got through talking all they wanted, the magician took leave, and the lord happily departed, but he had been tricked. When he came home to his family and sat down in his chair, his wife looked at him and spoke to him in a very angry voice: "I am not going to let you sit there because I have a very dear husband. How dare you take the seat next to me? You are acting in a stupid way as if you thought I had unfaithful habits. Get out of here right away!" All those in the household who had ever seen Simon thought that Faustinian was Simon the Magician, while whoever looked at that moment at the real Simon would have confirmed that it was Faustinian the Roman.

"This really is your husband, milady," said Saint Peter, the holy man. You can recognize him by his voice! I have reached the conclusion that he visited the magician, and he took his face away from him. The man he thought was Cornelius was really Simon the Magician; that man would do anything to spoil our celebration."

The children heard how their father had been tricked. They fell at their master's feet, pleading with him to let them be joyful again. They asked him to be mindful of how he had brought them together, weeping, wailing and suffering great need. The holy man stood up, and he asked the old gentleman to stand in front of them. He made the sign of the cross over him, and immediately he was made whole again: his face turned back as it had always been. He showed Faustinian to his old seat, and put his hand in his lady's hand. All who were there praised the Savior, for they had seen His great miracles.

Afterwards, Faustinian and his wife were often struck by the idea of asking their teacher, who had given them their happiness and honor, to accompany them. And so they invited the great man to come to Rome. The divine apostolus of God granted them their wish, at which everyone rejoiced. When they arrived in the city of Rome, Faustinian gave Saint Peter all his property. Then he and his wife took holy orders, and Claudius ruled the Empire.

VII

Claudius

Claudius (r. 41–54), Caligula's successor, enjoyed a certain reputation as a good emperor in the Middle Ages because of his supposed attempt to punish the Jews for harassment of Christians by expelling them from Rome and, in Christian legend, for proposing to put a statue of Christ in the Pantheon along with the other gods from all parts of the Empire.

The historic Claudius had an odd mixture of personal traits. He was easily the most scholarly of the early emperors and wrote several histories, including an autobiography, all of which are lost. His early reign achieved some military successes, particularly the addition of Mauretania to the empire. He personally took part in a Roman invasion of Britain, which solidified Roman rule in the southern part of the island. On the other hand, he allowed his favorites too much independence in making governmental decisions and led a disastrous family life. He married his own niece, Agrippina, which in itself shocked contemporaries. She persuaded him to set aside his own son, Britannicus, from possible succession and to adopt her son by a previous marriage, Nero. Claudius died unexpectedly in 54, thought to have been poisoned by Agrippina to make way for Nero (see next chapter).

Faustinian became a monk and his wife a nun, leaving Claudius to rule the Empire.

Simon the Magician found out what had happened, and quickly betook himself to court, where he became a secret, close friend of the king. They both suffered greatly from his doing so.

Saint Peter preached God's word, which angered the emperor greatly. Saint Peter instructed many people so that they turned to God. He would bid the dead arise and lepers be cleansed. His power would let those who lay stricken with gout get up. People learned about Saint Peter and how, if people came where he cast his shadow, they would all be cured of their afflictions immediately.

Simon, that enemy of God, nursed a deep grudge against Saint Peter. He would often lie to the nobles and just as often deceive the king. He would fly up to the sky and transform his image while the king was looking on. The people began to affirm that they had never seen any deity so marvelous or who pleased them so well, but God was to change that in a hurry.

When Lord Faustinian passed away, Simon the Magician advised Emperor Claudius to ban the Holy Apostle from the city of Rome. It angered the Romans that the emperor was following the magician so far. He also abused their women, and so they plotted against his life.

He definitely held the Empire for thirteen years and eight months before the Romans poisoned him.

VIII

Nero

Nero (r. 54–68) has served from his own century to our own as the embodiment of evil in a ruler. Claudius, who adopted Nero as a son, had died in 54, poisoned on the orders of Agrippina, his wife of five years and Nero's mother. She had helped arrange her son's acclamation as emperor by soldiers, to which the Senate gave its approval. Several years later, Nero saw to it that his mother boarded a boat that had been constructed so that it would fall apart. She saved herself by swimming, but was later killed by soldiers loyal to Nero.

As emperor, Nero persecuted Christians, subjecting them to in-human tortures, although he did not organize a campaign to eliminate them altogether as Diocletian later attempted to do. Both Saint Peter and Saint Paul are thought to have been executed in Rome during Nero's reign, which was more than enough to make Nero the symbol of evil for the Christian world. An aspect of Nero's evil personality that loomed large in late-ancient Christian writings was his boundless curiosity, which led him to reveal forbidden secrets of nature and defy divine sovereignty by toying with God's handiwork.

The story of Nero's having burned Rome to satisfy his morbid curiosity—one ancient version has him seeking inspiration to write a new epic about it—was widespread following the great fire, but, according to the usually reliable Tacitus, there was no solid evidence to back up the rumors. Nero's suspicions led him to have many prominent Romans, including the philosopher, Seneca, seized and executed. He was also generally inept in military affairs. When Galba was hailed as emperor, Nero's shaky support dwindled. On hearing that the senate had recognized Galba and sentenced Nero to death, he committed suicide to avoid a public execution.

The Book goes on to tell us that Nero held the Empire. That was absolutely the worst man that a mother ever bore into this world. Once he had Rome set ablaze by having fires started at twelve places at once; that seemed a fine amusement to him. He ordered knights to take up weapons and ride into the middle of the fire; they were all supposed to kill each other. They suffered greatly from the fire and the sword blows, but the king said he wanted to see the marvel of how things went for the brave Trojans when the Greeks inflicted misery on them with fire and sword. If any man escaped the fire Nero ordered him to be killed and fed to the dogs. King Nero busied himself with thinking up more and more evil things to do, so that he would be talked about forever.

One day it happened—there were many of the higher nobility sitting before him—he called for his mother to be brought in speedily and ordered her stomach to be slit open. He explained that he wanted to see where he had lain in her womb.

Those were really strange things to tell of, but now listen to more about the evil King Nero. He called for wise and knowing physicians to be brought to him, saying he wanted to bear a child himself—he would not settle for anything else. He said he would torture and then behead them if they failed to make him conceive and become pregnant with a child.

One of the wisest doctors softly objected. "Sire, we will carry out your orders. However, we fear that you will undergo pain in the process. In fact, you must put up with great suffering. How is the baby ever supposed to get out of you?"

"If I experience any pain, it will mean death for all of you: you will burn to death in a fire. That is the way I will have all of you rewarded."

The doctors had many a fearful thought, but, putting their heads together, they thought up a most wonder-producing drink and brought it to the king. The king took the drink from them and drank it. Inside him, against the nature of man, a monstrous worm began to grow. When the time arrived when he was to go to the chambers, he ordered a feasting celebration that went on for seven days and seven nights. Finally, sitting at the table, the king leaned over it, and a huge toad emerged upwards from his throat and out—I am telling you the truth about this. The Italians there all jumped up and shouted, "*Lata rana*! [wide toad]," and from that the palace got its name, so that still today it is called the Lateran.

It was not long afterwards that Saint Paul was captured and taken in shackles to Rome, where Saint Peter, that blessed messenger of God, received him very lovingly. News about this reached the court, and Simon the Magician told King Nero, "Those men are two heretics, and I hate to see them around here. If they do stay here in Rome, you will not be able to have my services any longer. I will fly to the heavens and down here you will never see me again."

That aroused King Nero's anger. In a fury he ordered the men brought before him. They were among God's chosen people and had no intention of trying to get away. They feared neither fire, nor death, nor any worldly suffering. They went before King Nero, who said to them, "You are heretics, which I resent very much. I have chosen a god to be my own. He dispenses life and death and performs many miracles. When he wants to be there, he is in the heavens, and then he comes down here again. He is full of grace, he is good, and he can read the minds of all men. This being the case, I will give you the period of three days, and if you refuse to show obedience to him, both of you will have lost your lives."

"That would make us happy," answered Saint Peter. "If we would be hanged on a gallows, it would be in accordance with our desires. Since the reigning God suffered for us a death of torture and carried His own gallows [cross], we should be glad to follow him, and we are perfectly well prepared for martyrdom. Now you tell that god of yours to fly up to the sky before our eyes. If he prevails with us watching, then go ahead and torture us all you want to.

Very early on the third day came the people from all over the country-side, knights and ladies. There was a huge crowd of Romans who wanted to witness the promised wonders. Simon the Magician came out among them and climbed up onto a column. All the people's eyes were on him, as devils raised him with much power into the air.

Saint Paul fell to the ground and prayed sweetly and worthily. Saint Peter stood upright, but both men were willing and ready for martyrdom. With hearts and minds, they reminded God the Good what he had told his disciples when he left them greatly grieving—that whatever they would pray for in his name, he would do everything to avoid letting the devil succeed in bringing shame to Christendom.

When the two men finished praying as much as they wanted to, Saint Peter raised his hand, and he revealed Our Lord's power. "I command you black devils," he said, "in the name of Holy Christ that you stop taking care of that man and let him fall down here again. Give proof to all these people that God alone is the judge over everything together in this whole world, over land and sea and over the heavenly host."

Saint Peter made the sign of the cross, and when he was finished the devils flew away immediately. They left the magician behind, sending him crashing to the earth. He fell so hard he broke everything. How sad this made the king!

Then anger overcame King Nero, who ordered both gentlemen seized, ordering that one be hanged from a gallows, the other beheaded. The heavens then opened, and holy angels came down. The men received their crowns. God told Saint Peter that he was granting to him the power to open all the gates of heaven with his words. Both of them were to have the power to judge and give the people of Christendom what they deserved. We must all make our pleas through their power and their grace that we may be received into God's kingdom.

Nero judged over the Empire—this is true—exactly thirteen years, one and half months. Things went badly for him after these sublime martyrdoms. He began to be very sick, first with podagra—that is what is recorded—then with full-scale gout, and finally with leprosy. At the end, he ordered a hundred and three of the noblest Romans from the Senate to be brought to his chambers and—I am telling you the truth about this—he ordered all their heads struck off and then the sword brought to him. "The whole city of Rome will rejoice at my death, but tomorrow they will not be burying me alone. Everyone will be lamenting and weeping over a friend."

When he finished speaking he stabbed himself with his sword. At the same time a commotion broke out in Rome. The people wanted to drag Nero's body out, pulling him by the feet to the moat ditch surrounding the city, where they threw him in. A huge flock of devils came in the form of black birds, who carried off his soul, which is confined to hell evermore. His corpse was unclean. Wolves gnawed on his bones.

IX
Tarquin

According to Roman tradition, Tarquin the Proud was the final king of Rome from 534 to 510 *BC*. The crime of his son, Sextus Tarquin, who raped the wife of a Roman nobleman, was enough to cause Romans not only to depose the bad king, sending him and his worse son into exile, but to abolish kingship in Rome, after which Rome became a republic (509–27 *BC*). The taint left by the Tarquins on kingship made it a virtual act of treason for any man to attempt to become king during the republic.

Real and imagined attempts to become a king cost Julius Caesar his life and made Augustus very careful to use a title other than *rex* (king) to denote his own authority.

The story of Tarquin and Lucretia was passed down by the Roman poet Ovid and the Roman historian Titus Livy, among others. Shakespeare's poem, "The Rape of Lucretia" and Benjamin Britten's opera of the same name carry the tale into modern times. As we have seen, the great majority of imperial biographies in the *Book of Emperors* feature real emperors, however fancifully their stories may depart from historic fact, but several times the author includes some fast-moving action stories by making non-emperors—elsewhere a few outright fictional characters such as Faustinian—into emperors for the purpose of illustrating models of good and bad rulership.

Here and elsewhere we also find him simplifying the cast of characters in a story. He fuses King Tarquin the Proud and his son Sextus into one person. The particularly illustrative flaw of the composite Tarquin as ruler is his willingness to abuse a woman who is his subject, because of excessive pride, although our author innovates in making his queen—whose pride is more out of control than his—put him up to the crime. It is probably a bit more pointed to have the king, rather than merely his son, embody the highlighted villainy.

he Book tells us that Tarquin then held the Empire. He was the proudest man that a mother ever bore into this world. In those days there was a prince in Trier who became a dear friend of Tarquin the king, to the subsequent undoing of both of them. His name was Collatinus, and he was a brave, high-spirited knight. In retribution for great harm done him by the nobles of Trier, this worthy hero killed a prince of Trier, after which he was forced to leave his home and soon made his way to the city of Rome.

The Romans cordially receive this nobleman with great honors. Soon, wherever their military expeditions headed, this bold hero served them well enough to carve out with his sword such military fame for himself that they held him in the greatest esteem, and their eager knights chose him as one of their equals.

In the Senate, the lords would always solve their problems by enlisting the aid of this nobleman for any undertaking they felt required great ability. Finally it came about that the Senate proposed that he take a Roman wife of fitting nobility. He asked for one lady—how quickly she was given to him! Her name was Lucretia, and her story is recorded in Ovid. He came to value this woman just as dearly as his own life. The lady loved him, too, and showed him every manner of devotion. She gave the bold hero her love with charm, kindness, and all humility. Great happiness was theirs to enjoy.

Quite often the lord would be told wonderful tales about how in Viterbo there were good knights aplenty, many festive tourneys, and many charming ladies of the court. What shining excellence he could find there if he wanted to, in company worthy of his own nobility!

And finally riding to Viterbo became a frequent pursuit for him, one that he became greatly attached to. The lords of Trier, where he had come from, found out about this and paid a large sum to have him killed. How narrowly he escaped! He had to flee from the city disguised in woman's clothes provided by his female admirers.

When the bold hero had fled to Rome, he complained to the senators about what had happened to him. They rang their bells, and the eager knights assembled there. Hearing of what had happened, they all asked how the Viterbonians ever dared do it, saying that it was the greatest insult ever handed to any Roman.

They besieged the fortified town. The Romans had confidently resolved that the city must burn. They were not after any kind of treaty: they wanted lands and lives. The Romans began their attack, but the Viterbonians were also good fighters, and swore that they would never be driven away from what was theirs by ancient law, but would rather all die together. Quickly every man made himself ready. Having put on steel armor, they threw open the city gates and found themselves facing the very best warriors who had ever appeared in the whole country. The Romans, who had maintained their honor in many a huge battle with other peoples, were very resentful that the Viterbonians were such good fighters as to face them squarely with many a glittering squadron and many a proven hero, thus doing proper credit to the Viterbonian good fighting name. A violent storm of battle followed.

Collatinus took the Roman banner and headed toward the fortress moat. Rows of heroes swarmed out unwaveringly through the gates. Then spear flew against spear. Many a hero was wounded, and many a young squire lay dead from wounds, too. They were splitting many a helmet, until the dark night had to separate them. The two sides shared in the casualties.

It happened one day during the siege that the Romans were enjoying themselves greatly. Between times they had begun talking of excellent knights in the Empire who fought with daring.

With some of the knights they started finding fault, however, and these were now brought to account for their cowardice. At the same time they spoke of beautiful horses and good hounds, they spoke of falconry and other diversions, and they spoke of beautiful ladies, saying that they would like to see some in whom there was no trace of fickleness whatsoever.

Then one of the Romans said, "God desert me if I lie! Whatever be the way in which I might be separated from my wife, I would neither mourn nor weep about her."

But then another said, "So help me God Almighty! I have a fine wife who is like life itself to me. She can do everything, she is kind, and she cheers me greatly!"

Then that foreign lord who had come from Trier spoke. "By my very life! I have the finest wife that ever any man won on Roman ground."

"You are bragging entirely too much," said the mighty king. "All the time you claim more than you can prove. You have no right to praise your wife so extravagantly in my presence, because mine is of nobler birth and of much better character as well. I can prove that by many a worthy man."

"I have always heard it said," responded the foreign knight, "that a man should be willing to yield to the emperor gracefully. But if you were not lord over all the Empire, I would have quite a bit more to say about this."

"You want to go on with this, do you?" asked the mighty king. "Then I will make a wager with you here before all these people: if your wife is a better one than mine, well then, Our Lord have mercy on me, because—if you really can prove what you say—I will not take it amiss, nor ever get angry about it afterwards." Both men agreed then to this challenge.

Headstrong heroes that they were, the two of them rode away from the siege camp; they wanted no one else with them. They rode into the city of Rome shortly before midnight. The lord from Trier knocked at his own gate, and someone asked who was out there. As soon as his voice was heard, the gate was opened quickly for him. The lady was brought the news that her husband had come, and she jumped out of bed. She ran the length of the courtyard: "Welcome home, my dear lord! I have been very worried about you. So help me, God Almighty! You did a wonderful thing to come here to me! Now all my fear is gone."

Then the nobleman said, "Milady, what do you want me to have? I have not had anything to eat all day today."

"To tell the truth, milord," said the lady, "I am glad of that. May God just let me live a while, and we shall give you food aplenty!"

She called for a table to be set up[1] and she waited on them with great charm. She drew wine in golden vessels and bade the guest be merry. As soon as the lady handed her husband his quart of wine, he raised the cup

---

1.   Meals were often served in medieval castles on "tables" of heavy boards set on racks resembling sawhorses—hence the phrases "the tables were set up" and "the tables were raised."

and poured the wine down between her eyes, so that the whole measure flowed down over her clothes. She stood still a moment and bowed to him politely. At this the mighty king broke into a smile.

The lady hurried back to her chambers right away and took pains to make herself attractive again in a second white dress.

She drew wine for her husband and bade the guest be merry, taking the golden cup for him and filling it. The lady was doing all this to please her husband, so that he could entertain his guest with honor.

Then when the tables were raised[1] and it was time for them to go to bed, the lady did not wish to leave the guest alone until he had been shown to his bedroom. Then she paused and bowed politely to him, at which the king said, "May God reward you, milady! You may be credited with every honor. Your ways are good, and you have an abundance of every virtue."

When night came a second time, they carried out the agreement that they had both sworn to and hastened to the king's court. The queen was brought the news that the king had come. "He gets no thanks for that," said the queen. "Today was such a long day, but he deliberately waited to arrange it so that I was rudely woken up." The lady lay still and did not want to get out of bed for the king's sake. The guest had understood very well what she had said.

The king came and sat down on her bed. "Lady," he said, "How can you complain like that? After the long way we have come, we would be glad for something to eat."

"Would you care to consider, milord, that I am neither the lord high steward nor the cup bearer, nor do I take care of the rooms and cook for this whole court? I don't know why you are imposing on me. It is no concern of mine whether you ever get another bite to eat."

And so the headstrong heroes rode back again to the siege camp.

As soon as the nobles saw the king, they all began asking him who had won the bet. "I will gladly concede him this honor," said the mighty king, "for I assure you, milords, that truly never before nor since have I ever seen such a fine woman as his wife in every bit of her conduct. She would be well suited to being queen over all the Romans."

One day it came about that the king was in a particularly good mood, and the Romans held a great tournament. When the news came inside the town of Viterbo, all the ladies of the court hurried to look down from the castle battlements. When the Romans caught sight of the ladies, they hastened to give a better and better account of themselves, so that the ladies might judge what good knights were there from Rome.

The Romans desired a truce afterwards until they had had a chance for a chat with the ladies. When the truce took effect, many a charming lady stood there speaking with many a noble hero. A quick-tongued woman named Almenia was among them and said, "Totila, you noble man, you can come closer to the ladies. You are bold enough and from your whole appearance a proven hero. Tell me, by God, in answer to my question, whether you would rather—upon your word now—have a beautiful lady give you her love this whole night through, or go in your armor tomorrow to fight all day with a man just as bold as you consider yourself to be. What would you do if you had the choice? Which would appeal to you more?"

The hero Totila answered her like this: "I don't know whether I can give you a good answer. I will tell you the truth: no worthy man should ever shrink from any chance to increase his reputation with his sword. At the same time, he should not boast about his knightly ability ahead of time, lest he have cause to regret this afterwards. But with love, it's like this: no living thing can withstand its power. Any man who experiences the love of a fine woman, if he is sick he gets well, if he is old he gets young. Ladies will make him courteous and brave enough that nothing will turn him from his course. You are asking me too much. I am a plain man, and I just cannot give you a good answer."

Then Almenia said, "Warrior, I have this complaint to make to you: your guest, Collatinus, often used to ride up to our city, seeking honor for the Romans. Because of our respect for the Romans we received that lord well. The ladies here saved him from death. Is this the way you want to repay us? Are we supposed to starve or burn to death? For this, people would always denounce you Romans. Let the guilty ones pay the penalty; it is only right for this to happen to them. But what harm have the lovely ladies ever done you?"

In the Senate, the Romans reached the decision that for the sake of the ladies they would accept their treaty offer of surrendering the guiltiest of all the inhabitants, those who had accepted the money from the nobles of Trier. They hanged them in front of the castle. They broke down the walls and thus satisfied their thirst for vengeance. With this the score was settled, and the Romans returned home again to their city.

One night the king lay in his bed, thinking of his old wager that the queen had lost for him. He grew angry, too, as he thought of how she had received him, and began to complain sharply about it to her. Then she inquired eagerly what the wager had been—how she would like to hear about it!

The king told her exactly how he had made the bet. The queen realized that she was the one put to shame and prodded the king by admonishing him over and over that either he would gain back her honor for her—for never had she been so heartsick over anything—or she would never be in good spirits again.

"You are doing him an injustice, the king replied to her. 'He is every inch a good knight, and his lady is a fine woman. Why should I spoil her life?"

The queen started crying and said, "Then our pledge to each other is broken forever. You have lost me. Never again will I come to your bed."

The king talked to her for a very long time and finally asked, "What do you advise me to do about it?"

"Milord, if you will follow my plan, I will tell you how you can have that very woman."

"By my faith," said his royal majesty, "I would be glad to follow this plan of yours."

The queen put it to him this way: "I shall tell you, milord, what you do: wait until her husband happens to be out of the country and then go there—now listen carefully—and when the lady wants to go to bed, then you stand in front of her door and plead passionately to enjoy her body. And if she refuses you, then give the order to a man you can trust. Have one standing by you ready and shove him into her bedroom—by my faith, I will reward you well for this—and say that you are going to announce to the people publicly that you found him with her. And so, dear as you are to me, milord, by so doing you shall have everything that you desire."

The king lost no time in riding, full of anticipation, to Lucretia, who gave him a splendid reception and waited on him most attentively. When finally the tables were raised and she wanted to go to bed, the king went to her bedchamber and pleaded passionately to enjoy her body.

The lady was terrified and said, "Sire, spare me such words. If someone were to offer me this whole world, how passionately I should despise it, if it meant rejecting my dearest husband. Any other service you shall have from me as before."

The king did as he had been told. He shoved a male servant into her room and swore by his life that he would announce to the people that he had found him with her—and that as soon as they were convinced of her guilt, according to the prescribed sentence—"Then they will condemn you to be stoned."

The lady was seized by fear of death and said, "Now I am forced to suffer anything that you command me to do, since you have me within your power."

The king satisfied his will. He told the queen how it had turned out for him. She promised him that she would repay him ever after with kind affections, for he had well satisfied her will, as well.

Lucretia hesitated no longer but sent a message to the lord from Trier that if he ever wanted to see her alive again, he must come home. As soon as he heard her message, he set out for home in great haste. She gave him a splendid reception and said, "Welcome home, my dear lord! I ask you, for the sake of your own honor, to let me give a banquet. I am not doing this without a reason.

In your kindness and generosity, grant me what I ask of you. I want to have all my friends in this castle. Milord, you must grant me permission to do this."

"Do just as you like, milady. But why did you require me for this? You could have done all this without me."

She replied, "Oh, but, milord, I must have you take your place before all the rest." And so, summoning all her strength, the lady prepared a banquet, and indeed her friends and relatives did come. When the merriment was at its height, the lady took her golden pitcher and poured wine all around, bidding the nobles be merry with graceful movements and with laughing eyes. And truly, no one could have believed that all this was to take such a bitter end. Many a fine man praised the lady.

When water had been brought and the tables were about to be raised, she asked all the Romans assembled there to listen to her for a moment. The guests told one another to be quiet for her, because they very much wanted to hear her speak. Quite openly she told all the Romans what had happened to her with the king.

Just when the lady had finished speaking the last word, she ran herself through with a knife and fell down dead. A great sadness and lamenting ensued, for you can assure yourselves that all those sitting at the banquet began wailing and weeping. Never had her husband experienced such sorrow. He tore the hair from his head and grabbed for his sword, and if he had not been restrained he would have quickly killed himself. Then he spoke:

"Alas, wretched man that I am, that I ever heard of you. If someone were to offer me this whole world, how passionately I should reject it if only I might be lying here instead before you and might never have to see your death. Alas, outcast that I am," he went on, "that I ever settled in Rome! If only I had remained among my enemies in Trier, I would have lost my life at their hands quickly, but I would have been spared these sorrows that were hidden from me until now."

The news traveled in Rome throughout the city, and a great lament arose there. The senators reached the decision that Tarquin no longer should be their king or their judge, and that for his great crime he should be forever excluded from their councils.

Since Collatinus was a foreigner, he had to bear his sorrow alone. Often he would stand alone and begin crying bitterly, overcome by his great misery. And yet, it was not long before Tarquin had to depart from the city, and as soon as Collatinus found this out, he dressed in peasant's clothing and set after him stealthily across the countryside. When he caught sure sight of the king he said to himself, "Woe is me for my dear wife! Woe is you for your life! Whatever I must accept now as my lot, you shall pay for what you did with your death." He spurred his horse and gave his avenging anger full rein. Full of rage he rode up to Tarquin. No one became aware of what was happening until he had run him through, so that he never spoke a word again.

The king fell dead to the ground. His men were all in a state of confusion. Even as quickly as they rode over to their lord, no one came close to reaching Collatinus. The bold knight flew across the countryside. At Rome, no one ever again searched out or found what had become of him in life or death.

It is a fact that Tarquin held the Empire exactly four and a half years and two months. Then in this fashion the lord struck him down.

X

Galba and Piso

Servius Sulpicius Galba (3 *BC–AD* 69) enjoyed a reputation as a competent administrator who governed several of Rome's outlying provinces with integrity. He was proclaimed emperor in 68 by Gallic legions who rose in revolt against Nero, but he soon lost his popularity because of favoritism and ill-timed austerity measures, which led the Praetorian Guard to assassinate him in Rome. Galba had adopted L. Calpurnius Piso as his son and designated him as his successor, but both were murdered in mid-January, *AD* 69.

Galba and Piso now held the Empire. Treachery and strife broke out at that time in Rome. The princes decided in council that Galba should oversee things in the city of Rome, while Piso should ride around through the land. Piso lost no time in founding Pisa, while Galba founded Capua, but then both of them were murdered. The crime was Otho's beyond a doubt. They had governed the Empire for seven months.

Otho

Otho had been a friend and supporter of Nero, but he refused to divorce his wife—whom Nero had chosen as his imperial consort—and ended up in virtual exile as Roman governor in Spain. He briefly supported Galba after Nero's overthrow in 68, but had himself proclaimed emperor by the Praetorian Guard in Rome and had Galba and Piso murdered. He soon committed suicide—after his forces were defeated by those of Vitellius.

hen the reprehensible Otho, whom the hero Vitellus was to slay, took over the Empire. The Book tells us this: he had possession of the Empire but held it just three months before the Romans complained that his rule was a disgrace to them and they wanted him to pay for his crimes. Fifteen thousand Romans had been killed in the Capitol. Crowds of other Romans then hailed Vitellius to be their judge and ruler. All together they came to rue that day sorely.

Vitellius (Odnatus Legend)

A favorite of emperors from Tiberius through Nero, Vitellius was appointed by Galba to command the legions of the Lower Rhine, where he was hailed as emperor in Cologne in 69 by some commanders of his troops. He put an end to Otho's rule in Rome, but when Vespasian was acclaimed emperor in Alexandria and gained support in other parts of the empire, many of Vitellius' troops deserted to him. After losing two battles and most of his support, Vitellius was dragged through streets in Rome and murdered.

The story of the hero who burnt his hand off to intimidate a king is an adaptation of the story of Caius Mucius, as recorded by Titus Livy in his *History from the Founding of the City*. In the original version, after Rome expelled the Tarquins, King Lars Porsena of Clusium attempted to help them regain power by leading an invasion of Rome on their behalf. Mucius intended to stab Porsenna but was confused and killed his paymaster instead. Subsequently he burned his right hand off in front of Porsenna. He told him the act was a token of the indifference of many young Romans to pain when it was a matter of defending Rome from takeover by royal tyranny. He also told him there was a conspiracy of 300 men who would draw lots—as he had drawn the first one—to determine who would have a turn at assassinating the offending king. The conspiracy was a fiction, but Porsenna believed the story sufficiently to make peace with the Romans.

At the time Vitellius took over the Empire, the Book tells us that Otto had many kinsmen who were unwilling to see him running it. They really wanted to have him killed. Once he just barely escaped with his life at night.

The king had to cope with many challenges. He shared with his vassals what was weighing upon his heart. His followers all advised him to ride before [the gates of] the city of Rome. He quickly agreed and did so, winning over many headstrong heroes. Rome was occupied with a great display of force. His adversaries had many chivalrous knights among them, who defended the Roman fortress with spears and with swords. Inside was many a valiant hero who was determined that he would run a spear through anyone wanting to take his life with a sword. That is the way the Roman heroes wanted it. In whatever way a man wanted to challenge another he found a willing adversary. Owî! What lethal blows they struck! Many a helmet was split then, and those whose time to die had come fell in great numbers. The king was sorry about all the Romans killed.

With grim determination the Romans defended themselves until hunger began to take its toll among them. Those who had nothing and were just barely surviving went to the Senate, and, full of passion, they pleaded for the surrender of the fortress to the king. The rich and powerful did not like that idea, however. They did not want to yield to him ever, for they had many good knights who wanted to fight, and they thought the king must surely flee. What honors could he possibly win at Rome?

Finally one man came forward: his name was Odnatus. He asked for silence, then he spoke. "If you agree and are willing to make it worth my while, I will liberate this city of Rome. I will give you my promise that neither sword's blow nor spear's thrust will be needed to make this happen. I will see to it that you keep all your honors and that the enemy must flee."

The people answered that—by the love they had for their wives and children—whatever sort of thing he might want in return, they would see that he got it. That is just what the Romans said.

Odnatus spoke. "Hurry now and choose twelve men as my comrades, so that I may begin to put my plan into action."

As soon as they understood what he wanted, they hurried about among one another, several of them saying to him, "I pledge you all my trust. Since I am of your clan it is only right that I stand with you."

"Of course, you should have me with you," said another man. "Wherever you put me, you can rely on me without fear."

Odnatus began choosing men until he had twelve. They swore a firm oath that they would never falter in serving him in everything he commanded, wherever he wanted to send them. Odnatus, the hero, revealed his plan to them as follows: "You should carry good knives, well sharpened so that they cut as well as a pair of shears.

"It is better that twelve of us die, rather than let the city of Rome be taken. Pay attention now as I tell you my plan. I will be the first volunteer for it myself, putting my own life at risk. I am letting you lords know that I intend to kill the king. You will soon hear it shouted from a distance how I fared in the attempt. Hold back until that happens; you should not leave each other until then." All together the noble band swore agreement to this.

The hero, Odnatus, spoke further to the twelve. "You have little to fear. I really have no desire to keep on living. You may play your part confidently, for, as I am telling you, if my plan succeeds, you will soon be sitting at home in peace and quiet, absolved of your oaths to do anything more. But if I am caught and mutilated or hanged, do not be overly hasty in reacting. Only after four days have passed make good on what you intend to do." He then gave each of his comrades a time when each would risk sacrificing his life. If he let that time pass he would have defaulted on his oath. Disregarding all dangers, they all pledged sincerely to carry out this plan.

One morning it happened—Odnatus was not the least bit worried about his own life—that he went over fields until he stopped opposite the king's own tent. A duke named Riomus—that's what the Book tells us his name was—and the prince of Capua were walking on the lookout. The duke sat down in the king's chair, something that he soon had good reason to regret. Odnatus turned to confront him there, and—before anyone was aware of him—stabbed the duke through the stomach so that he never spoke a word again.

There was no way out. He was brought before the king. The king ordered many sorts of torture prepared with which to martyr him. He said that he should not remain alive one day longer. All his nobles pronounced their agreement.

Odnatus pleaded sincerely with the king that he might let him come before a fire and after that he might torture him any way he wanted. He said that it would be only right to purify himself in the fire. That puzzled all the nobles standing there.

Vitellius was a cunning man. He began to ask the guilty man, "Now for what were you seeking vengeance from this lord? Why did you stab him for no reason?"

Odnatus, guilty as he was, answered the king, "I will tell you afterwards. I am so drawn to the fire that I don't want to tell you that until I have purified myself in the fire."

The nobles commanded that a fire be made. "It's not 'for no reason'" all of them said. "We will soon find out everything he wanted to do. There is no way he can get away from us."

Listen now to a wondrous thing: the youth went over and stuck his hand in the fire. He did not move from the spot and said neither "Oh!" nor "Woe!"—you may search far and wide, but you will never find this told of any other mortal man—until his hand was completely burned off.

Odnatus told them to bring him before the king. On the way they begged him to tell them why he carried out this miraculous deed. Many of the princes asked him that, but he would not give an answer to any of them. The king stared at him for a long time. He pondered within himself what he should make of all this and do about it.

"I will let you live," he said. "You did not do this without a very strong reason. Tell me now, truthfully, why did you kill the duke? Or why did you put your hand in the fire and burn it up? I would really like to hear your explanation. It all seems very strange to me."

This is the answer Odnatus the hero gave the king: "I will tell you the truth, king. You need have no regrets about my hand. I should have killed you with it. Now, I went and did the wrong thing. My hand lied to me and thereby deceived me. My hand has committed perjury against me. The right thing was for it to have been your undoing. I will tell you something else that is true: no human cunning can protect you, nor can Jupiter, the reigning god. You are very close to death. The whole world of humans cannot protect you. In a short time you will be slain."

The king, whose arrogant high spirits had tumbled, sent him back to Rome, into the city. Odnatus told the Romans what all had happened to him. He held out his stump and said, "For the sake of all of you I suffered this to happen."

The Romans replied that they had never heard of any feat like this, nor seen any man so wonderful. From that time on, he would enjoy the right to receive praise and honor there at Rome. They told him to go ahead of them. They would give him a goodly palace like Brutus had had in days gone by, to be his very own. He became the richest man among the residents of Rome. He was well repaid for his suffering.

King Vitellius sent a message to the city, asking for a time of peace. He showered them with acts of friendship, which caused the people in the city to rejoice.

He held the Empire for nine months. When the time stipulated for the peace ran out, twelve of Vespasian's men carried him out of the fortress at night and buried him alive in the earth.

XIII

Vespasian

Vespasian (r. 69-79) was introduced in the *Book of Emperors* Tiberius story as leading—together with his son, Titus—the Roman forces that put down the Jewish rebellion in Judea. This account is more or less historically accurate except for timing. The Jewish War and destruction of Jerusalem occurred *AD* 66-70. Our author moves the events back to the early 30s, portraying them as punishment of the Jews for the Crucifixion. The historical Vespasian had a distinguished military career in Germany and Britain, making him a logical choice for Nero to appoint in 66 for directing the war effort in Palestine. After Nero's overthrow and suicide, Vespasian was proclaimed emperor, first in Egypt, then in other parts of the Empire. He returned to Rome, leaving affairs in Judea to Titus, defeated his rivals and presided over the Empire at peace during his last ten years.

This chapter also highlights an important virtue for rulers—the willingness to take good advice, even when it means suddenly reversing a course of action.

The Book tells us that Vespasian held the Empire. As soon as the Romans raised him to be their ruler, they sent messengers quickly to the Jerusalemite lands. But when Vespasian understood from them that Vitellius had been buried alive, no one could induce him with any sort of offers to accept rulership of the Empire. He said that he would not accept it and that he felt it was better for him to oversee the cultivation of the land he had conquered—won with his warshield. He had no intention of leaving that land behind, and that was his reply to the messengers.

When the Romans received his message, they hurried to assemble. They agreed that Vespasian should be forever condemned, deprived of all rights due a Roman. They persuaded Arimespus, who was his sister's son, to break into Vespasian's palace and take for himself everything there was to inherit. City and countryside swore loyalty to this nephew of his, and thus they rejected the noble Vespasian.

Vespasian learned that he had been condemned at Rome. He then consulted with the one dearest to him. He complained about what had been done to him—he had never suffered such injury. Noble Titus answered him, "Father, I was there taking part in the discussion when the Senate with all the people of Rome chose you to be their leader, so that you would take charge of their army and take vengeance upon their enemies. Then they wanted to honor you. Now I cannot see the reason you want to struggle against the Romans. How should we oppose them and come to any good end? They will come after us with their army. There is no way we can defend ourselves against them. Father, I advise you to change your mind. I value the honor you have earned. I am faithful and committed to you whether things go well or badly. I am willing to die for you or to take whatever comes out of this, but, if you do not renew your loyalty to them, their anger will surely roll over us."

Vespasian commanded that haste be made in writing a letter to the Romans, telling them how he wanted to carry out their will and was prepared to do so forever. He had not intended to do anything against them. He mentioned that he was lacking in troop numbers, complaining to them that many of his men had been killed in Babylonia and that he could not return to Rome before taking vengeance and redeeming their honor. He would rather lose his own life before seeing the Romans lose their honor.

The Romans now said how willing they were to support him.

Before, when the noble Vespasian had won the fortified city of Jerusalem, he had the Jews sold, and nothing left there that was good for or worth anything. The song tells us, and it is surely true, that he directed his army against Babylonia, which was ruled by the most powerful king that ever lived in this world under this heaven.

King Milian commanded his army to come out and meet the Romans. He rode against him with a huge crowd of soldiers. He had many a brave hero, many green flags and many white and red ones. They were to come into great danger. There one could see many a white hauberk glittering and many a golden shield rim. There was many an excellent warrior, many a squadron with weapons gleaming, and many a hero through and through.

Titus took the Romans' flag and with great speed charged the Babylonian flag-bearer; he brought him real trouble as he plunged his spear into him. His high spirits led him to shout these words: "Your fiefs are forfeited! Never again will your lord hear any more news about you. You found that things were not so soft." He raised up the shield and stretched out the flag—it was all the color of blood now—and headed toward King Milian's troops. How solidly the young heroes closed in combat with one another! How well they ran their spears through each other! How well they broke through the lines! Many a white flag lay red, and many a hero lay dead there. The Romans sustained many casualties. They hewed through their enemies' chain mail. Those hard rings of steel could not protect them. They hewed their way through the battlefield, subjecting the enemy to great losses.

Owî! What massive slaughter they carried out! Many a helmet was split then, as the Babylonians could not hold their ground against the Romans. King Milian was slain, and the heathens fled from there back to Babylonia. Their condition was a sorry one.

Vespasian and his son, Titus, cheered their men on in a way no one can accurately repeat. Titus stood up in his saddle and spoke to the heroes. "Well, now, you Romans, just think of the great honor that our forefathers let us inherit! There is no way around it. If we don't follow them home there will soon be trouble. When we were in Jerusalem they killed many of our relatives, and for that reason I would rather die than let our kinfolk go unavenged with losses of their wives and children. We should see them home—these most unwelcome guests. Be firm now and do honor to all the Roman lands!" The heroes all raised up a hand and swore that whoever fled from the fight would never again have lands of his own or fiefs and he should be cut off from all Roman honors. All the nobles swore to this.

When Titus saw what their will was, the young man was filled with joy. Full of energy, he rode before the troops waving a green flag with a wild boar embroidered on it in gold in a wonderful picture. The same boar had ten horns with which he struck down the enemies. That wild boar symbolizes for us very well that the Empire of Rome has primacy over the others.

Each hero took his place in his squadron and followed King Vespasian to Babylonia. There, right in front of the fortress moat they found something no tongue can ever describe—the books would not want to lie to us about this. The ashen spearshafts of the enemy stood so close together that no bird could fly through the mass of them. They were so thick that no human eye could see through them.

Titus took up the Roman flag and turned toward the fortress moat. Spears flew back and forth in such a hail that blood was flowing everywhere. So many men were killed that their bodies filled up the moat. Swords clanged loudly against each other as Titus pushed through the fortress gate. Titus the hero slashed many a wide wound and left many a shield rim bloody. Within the walls many warriors lay with many a good hero covered with his blood. They had defended themselves well so long as they lived.

When they won the fortress, Vespasian and his son, Titus, sang their victory song and ordered their tents set up on the fields of Babylonia. They occupied the city that had fallen to them. For seven days and seven nights they gave vent to their anger in vengeance; they broke down the walls. Then they furled their flags and with great joy rode away.

Let us now hear how the Book tells us about a king named Hylas *ad Affricanum* [in Africa]. He was Milian's brother, and, when he was told the shocking news that his brother had been slain, he quickly dispatched word to all his lands. That king did show some signs of wavering, and some of his vassals were unwilling to come; however, he soon commanded twenty-four squadrons. The brave Romans found out that this king was assembling his forces, and they prepared a defensive position. Full of joyful anticipation they took themselves to the appointed spot.

When they came close enough that they could see one another, the Romans, burning with hatred, charged the enemy ferociously from all four directions. With sword blows and spear thrusts they forced their way through the enemy forces and drove them to flight. Their king was captured with his highest-ranking men. They trampled and captured the men they came to. They struck and brought disgrace to the enemy lands, all of which they burned. Then, full of high and wild spirits, they turned toward the Roman Empire.

When the lordly army arrived back in Rome, the Romans came on foot and rode from the city: Owî! How well they received their king! For a fact, I am telling you that King Hylas was thrown into the dungeon. They said that his guilt deserved death. He had fiercely violated Roman rights; however, Titus, that man of noble spirit, saved him from death and sent him from Rome back home to his Empire.

Vespasian lived the royal life—the book tells us for a fact—eight years and ten months until he died of a hemorrhage.

XIV

Titus

Titus (r. 70–81), Vespasian's son, served with his father and took command of Roman forces in Judea when Vespasian returned to Rome upon being chosen emperor. As emperor in his own right following Vespasian's death, Titus became famous for moderation and clemency. He put a stop to frequent indictments for treason and did not exact vengeance when he learned that his brother, Domitian, was plotting against him. It was clemency—in spite of holding nearly absolute power—that marked Titus' reputation through the Middle Ages. Our author is aware of clemency as a major element in the image of Titus and praises it, but with his own propensity to extol law and order he lets his Titus learn the lesson that too much clemency is badly misplaced. He admires Titus more for his commitment to rule by the Imperial Law.

$\mathcal{S}$ince the Empire was without a head, the Romans said that Titus was compassionate and brave, fully noble enough that it would be well fitting to make him ruler and judge. They hesitated no longer and elected Titus. They wanted their will carried out through him. Titus called for the Imperial Law to be brought out. He never wanted to hand down judgments except according to the Imperial Law.

There were some foolish lords at Rome who were supposed to give privy advice to the king for maintaining his honor; however, they really wanted to assassinate him. The king was warned about them, and they were in grave peril.

Mighty Titus displayed great wisdom. He sent word to them quickly that he was coming to his chamber. When he saw their leader, he spoke to him in a very conciliatory way. "From the moment I took over the Empire, I relied on you as a man loyal to me. What have I ever done to hurt you? Or what are you accusing me of doing? Tell me now upon your honor—you will never have cause to regret it—what would you want to do if you wielded over me the power I now have over you? Reveal to me what you would have wanted to do. Would you have wanted to let me live? You should confess the real truth."

Then Ariolus, the guilty man, answered him, "I will tell you the truth. If I had your power and you came to me in secret, you would have lost your life. You would not have been able to survive, for you would have lost your life at my hands. You are too strict as a judge, we have no love for you, and for that reason we want to kill you. The judgments that you make injure us."

Mighty Titus then spoke with great wisdom. "If I judge the people rightly by the Imperial Law in a way that makes you want to kill me, the guilt cannot be great. If you want to take my life, I will give you my gold." He ordered that he be given without delay as much red gold—he did not even weigh it—as he could carry. He told him to leave the chamber and had him escorted home to his own house.

Soon after that he sent for the others and treated these conspirators the same way until he found out the truth from them. He gave his gold to all of them, asking each one individually to choose how he wanted to relate to him—that they could be friends or enemies, whichever suited him better.

The twelve conspirators met together with one another after that and said they had been greatly insulted in a way their forefathers never put up with. What the king had said went beyond all boundaries. They got their daggers so sharp they could cut as surely as a shears. If they could not gain vengeance publicly, they were going to stab him in secret.

Compassionate Titus, lying one night in his bed, had a dream in which he experienced a calamity. As he was riding through a forest he saw wild lions, who wanted to pull him down off his horse. He fled before them, barely reaching a dried-up tree, which had no branches that were the least bit strong. Whatever branch he put his foot on—how quickly it broke off! Then he would grab another one, and it would vanish in his hands. Titus felt he was in great trouble, but soon he came to another tree, and it had green branches and a top that drooped over near the ground. Then the king was able to save himself. He swung himself up as the tree straightened itself, and he woke from sleep in a fright.

He pondered the dream as to what it might foretell. He used great wisdom in doing this. The good king stationed his guard, who watched over him day and night, in a way that made sure no one could do him any harm, neither by stabbing nor otherwise murdering him.

In those days there was a public hall sometimes used as a theater in Rome called Asilus [the Gadfly]. The lords made a regular practice of going there—always at nones. They would tell one another what they had heard about who was gaining a great reputation, and this would keep them occupied.

Powerful Titus came up with a very cunning plan. He sent agents over the whole city of Rome to make it known that he would be going to that hall with his privy councilors. At one point he did enter the hall, but then he soon stole away from it after coming out the other side. He ordered all his men armed, but he would not tell any of them the details of his plan. He told them only that he was sorely in need of their aid, and the heroes readied themselves quickly.

Then word spread throughout the fortified city that the king had gone to the Asilus. His enemies were very happy about this, and very quickly they gathered there. Their daggers were well sharpened and ready. Joyfully they crowded in at the site where they searched for people they never did find, although they looked everywhere through the hall. The king came up with his men and cunningly surprised them. He ordered the hall surrounded, letting no one in or out, and commanded that the conspirators and everyone who had anything to do with their plot be seized. He had them led across the courtyard—the order is contained in a document still in Rome—and with lawful consent of all the Romans commanded that their heads be chopped off. He had their bodies thrown into the city moat for birds and dogs to feed upon. That is the way he made an example for people who could learn no other way

Then the far-famed king ordered his master craftsmen to pour bronze and make a statue, which you can see to this day in Rome. He ordered that the twelve conspirators be portrayed on it; their names were written in gold, so that you can read them to this day. Until Judgment Day this will provide evidence of what happened.

Well-beloved Titus sits atop the column. In his hand he holds a sword, the gleam of which can be seen far and wide across the land. This was done for the reason—according to what we hear the Book tell us—that whoever sees the scene portrayed there may take its lesson to heart.

The king inspired proper fear throughout the whole Empire. At the same time people praised his kindness: he was full of compassion and humility. He was an unwavering hero in every kind of crisis. The book tells us for a fact that he lived only a year and fifteen days [as ruler]; then he departed from this world.

XV

Domitian

Domitian (r. 81–96) presented an image of faulty rulership in contrast with the good model of his brother, Titus. He had a well-deserved reputation for cowardice. When Vespasian was first hailed as emperor in Alexandria, Domitian went into hiding until forces loyal to Vespasian had defeated those of Vitellius. Domitian remained under some suspicion of complicity in the early death of Titus, although there is no hard evidence to support this. As emperor, his military accomplishments were slight. He attempted to oversee governors of the provinces to lessen corrupt and harsh rule there, but in Rome and the rest of Italy his government practiced arbitrary arrests and extortions.

He succeeded in suppressing the one serious revolt against him, but Domitian showed a paranoid fear of being assassinated, particularly in the last three years of his reign. He sentenced Flavius Clemens, his cousin, to death for allegedly conspiring against him, having exiled Clemens' wife for alleged support of Christianity. Stephanus, a freeman loyal to Clemens, eventually stabbed him in his bedroom.

In Domitian's reign, Saint John was exiled to Patmos, where he wrote the book of Revelation. There is considerable debate today over whether that John was the same as John the Apostle, who wrote the gospel that bears his name. The apostle would necessarily have been in his eighties at that point, which in itself does not rule him out.

The Book reveals to us that his brother, Domitian, then controlled the Empire. He was an enemy of God and a persecutor of Christians. He rode off to Benevento with an army and destroyed the fortress there. Aiming to crush Christianity, he ordered that all who believed in the true God were to be tortured and then beheaded.

The book goes on to tell us that meanwhile John the Evangelist had come to Rome. He was a true messenger of God, who had known God's Son. He publicly stirred up the people, urging them to turn to God, teaching large numbers of them to become obedient to God.

Then the evil man found out that Saint John was in Rome, which made him very angry. He demanded that this great man appear before him. He urged him and threatened him, but he would not obey him. He revealed to him the Father and the Son and that the Holy Ghost completed those two—the three names should be recognized as referring to one God.

That made the king, who wanted to hear nothing of these sweet teachings, very angry. He ordered him taken away and a vat filled with hot oil. He wanted to bring him to total shame. He tied his hands and feet and ordered him thrown into the boiling oil. That, however, did not do Domitian any good. He could not injure this man. Our Lord sent a lordly angel who relieved him of any pain, and John came from the intended ordeal unblemished as a virgin. The flaming oil had done him no injury at all. He told all the Romans that it had felt like he had been resting in a meadow of dewy clover.

But even though the king had witnessed the miraculous signs, they could not dissuade him from his wrongdoing. He accused the holy man of using magic. Even though the Romans had seen what happened, no one was allowed to stand by him or give him any kind of help. He commanded that John be thrown aboard a ship and sent into exile far away.

These orders were carried out quickly. The holy man was seized and taken across the sea to an island. That little land is called Patmos. There John strained with determination to write his great work, Apocalypse [book of Revelation]. In it one can surely learn about many of God's wonders, which God let him see in heaven. This is Lord John the Apostle to whom Our Lord Jesus Christ commended his Mother, when he saw him there at the time he was being tortured to death. It is John the Evangelist who wrote the Gospel of Our Lord Jesus Christ, which begins, "*In principio erat verbum* [In the beginning was the Word]." The great man wrote it because dissension had broken out among his followers. His book settled that dispute so that they never doubted him any more. This is the same John the Apostle who is called *"Dei electus* [Chosen of God]." He is the lordly man, pure as a virgin, who is to guide us until the Final Day. May he help us attain the eternal grace of salvation then. Let everyone say to that, "Amen."

Now let us take up the story of the misbegotten Domitian—who had no fear of God at all—where we left it. He was so severely accursed that God did not choose to spare him. His body became weak and he was afflicted with leprosy.

At Rome the custom prevailed that, no matter how high in honors a man stood, if people became aware that he had leprosy, nothing would change the fact that he must leave the city after such a sentence was handed down in the senate. When King Domitian realized the state he was in, it still did not dissuade him from his most evil ways. The Romans all took an oath that they would strike him dead or else bury him alive.

Then when King Domitian found out that the Romans wanted to assassinate him, he had to flee. He ordered a horse tacked up for him and rode it to the bridge, but when he came to the middle—the song tells us beyond any doubt—his horse threw him into the Tiber, and no one ever saw him again. The devils are torturing his soul.

He judged the Empire two years and two months. Devils had brought him to the Romans and devils took him away again for themselves. From his evil example let all kings learn the lesson of saving their souls and retaining worldly honors as well.

XVI

Nerva

In his short reign, Marcus Cocceius Nerva (r. 96–98) contributed to the model of good rulership acknowledged by Romans of his own day. When Domitian was murdered in September 96, crowds of Roman soldiers and civilians hailed Nerva as emperor. He reversed Domitian's harsh policies in Italy, recalling men Domitian sent into exile and restoring much of their confiscated property to them. He adopted Trajan as his son and choice to succeed him, thus beginning the century of the "five good emperors" under whom talented successors were chosen by ruling emperors: the sequence of Nerva, Trajan, Hadrian, Antoninus Pius and Marcus Aurelius gave the Roman Empire some of its best years before Marcus Aurelius failed to install a talented successor, allowing his worthless biological son, Commodus to succeed him.

The story of the bronze horse designed for fiery executions has a long history as far back as the tyrant Phalaris, ruler of Agrigentum in Sicily in the fifth century *BC*, whose master craftsman designed a bronze bull for that purpose. For the rest of Greek and Roman antiquity the story illustrated either the evil in a cruel ruler or in his unscrupulous master craftsman. The *Book of Emperors* version departs in three main ways from other sources of the legend: (1) It makes the story show poetic justice that reflects well on the ruler. (2) It introduces Nerva as the ruler in the story for the first time. (3) It also substitutes a horse for the bull, possibly because the statue is introduced as providing a monument for the emperor, for which a horse, rather than a bull, might have seemed more appropriate.

he Book informs us that Nerva then held the Empire. He became a marvelous king. A master craftsman once came to him and said, "Sire, to please a king as mighty as you are, I know a wondrous art. If you will follow my advice, then so long as this world lasts and if it is in accordance with your will, you will have to be remembered at Rome for all time."

"I would really like to see that," replied the noble king, "and, if you fulfill my wishes, you will enjoy my favor forever."

"Sire, command that I be given the site that I will need, and your will shall reach fulfillment," the master craftsman told him. "I will see to it that my pledge is fulfilled, but if I do not succeed in pleasing you and all your companions with what I do—why then—pronounce any judgment over my life that you wish."

"I will be glad to follow your advice," said the noble king. He instructed his chamberlains to give the man everything that he himself asked for—everything that he needed; whatever his work required—and that they should be eager to help him in whatever he asked of them to carry out his plan. They were to carry out his every request.

Further, Nerva told his chamberlains to show the man every courtesy. He showed them an extraordinarily large room and said the craftsman should have full use of it. Indeed, everything the cunning craftsman asked for was immediately given to him. The king himself looked in all the time, admonishing the craftsman; "Owî! I can hardly wait to see it! Now, my well-beloved man, do hurry along quickly with your work. I will make it very much worth your while." The craftsman, who was to die very soon, was greatly cheered to hear this. He told his workers to go to that room, but he chose for himself a secret spot. The master craftsman then asked that no one disturb him until he was finished his work.

He hastened night and day with his work, taking very little rest, until in the middle of the king's courtyard he poured an image in the form of a horse. All those who ever saw it confirmed that never under this heaven was there ever such a statue of a horse made that impressed them so much with being lifelike. All the Romans agreed.

So when the master worked everything into the statue that he needed until it was completely finished, he asked the king to come where it was and look inside. "I want to show you its cunning complexity," said that man who was about to die, "but I want to do it this way. I ask you upon your royal honor that no earthly man who may enjoy your grace shall ever again know how this device works."

The noble King Nerva answered him like this: "This device came into being through you, and I will tell you with certainty—since you are its master—with you the device will also come to an end. From this day forward no man will ever learn about it. This very day will see its end." The Book goes on to tell us that everyone who was anyone in Rome, knights and ladies, came to have a look at what was happening in the king's courtyard. There they found a wondrously pleasing bronze image of a horse, and the whole crowd marveled at it.

"Good health to you, you rich and lordly king!" said the statue's master. "If you want to see the culmination, sire, then turn a strong man over to me. He shall burn to death. That will make the horse jump the length of your courtyard, and then you will see that my art is a true one."

So that the whole crowd gathered there could hear him, the noble King Nerva answered him in a way that reflected his noble thoughts. "Those devoted to me warn me against that sort of thing. I am not willing to follow you so far. Who is supposed to be giving you permission to burn people to death? If you want to be a good master of your art, go in yourself as the first one. If you can keep asserting real mastery of your trade, it won't harm you."

The master fell at his feet and said, "By your royal honor, please excuse me from doing that. Now I regret serving you with my work."

"A great crowd has come to watch," noble King Nerva answered him. "You must show them your performance. You know well how this thing works. No one else can play with life and death so well as you. Beyond a doubt, you must get inside." He told his men to shove the man inside and to close the little outside door, fastening it shut tightly, and right after that to light the fire under it.

Owî! How that horse jumped! The master screamed very loudly as the horse sprang around. Nothing could be done for him; no one could come to his aid. All over the wide courtyard the jumps were so terrifying no one wanted to stand in their way. The whole crowd, men and women, looked out for themselves by getting out of the way until the master was burnt up.

When the man was dead and the horse no longer jumped, the king told his men to take the mechanism out of the horse and ordered that valuable creation burnt in the fire, so that its wondrous power has not been rediscovered to this very day; nor has human knowledge been able to find out how the master made it work. That was the end of the great trouble it threatened to bring. Everyone praised the king's wisdom.

King Nerva judged the Empire until podagra struck him down. He did not rule more than one year; that is the truth. He was a well-loved and fabled king; the Romans lamented his passing.

XVII

Trajan

Modern accounts of Trajan (r. 98–117), whom Nerva adopted and named as his successor, are full of praise for his military genius and administrative talents. They retain the ancient enthusiasm for the fairness of his rule of Rome and the provinces. In non-Christian Roman histories, Trajan's record as a just ruler is unchallenged. His uncertain pursuit of a policy of persecuting Christians, who were, as he advised Pliny the Younger, not to be sought out by the state but were nonetheless to be condemned if denounced,[1] earned him the contempt of the Christian polemicist Tertullian, writing at the end of the third century. Eusebius of Caesarea, however, in the glow of excellent church-empire relations under Constantine, "rehabilitated" many of the pagan emperors to respectability from

---

1. Letters on Christians: Pliny, X. 96. Trajan's reply, X. 97.

a Christian standpoint in his *Church History* and professed to see in Trajan's wavering a policy of quasi-toleration. Orosius, like Trajan of Spanish provincial origin, heightened that ruler's reputation for justice, and he rapidly grew into the medieval prototype for good rulership.

The story of the emperor's stopping to hand down justice to a widow who approached him as he rode off to war was originally attached to Hadrian, also an ancient epitome of excellent rulership but much less favored in the Middle Ages. The episode's connection with Trajan was suggested by a stone relief in the Forum of Trajan, symbolically depicting a conquered province as a female suppliant before that emperor. The story of Pope Gregory the Great's successful attempt to have Trajan's soul released from hell goes back to an early eighth-century *Life of Gregory* of Anglo-Saxon origin, which found its way to the continent with Irish missionaries to Germany. Since Trajan's redemption was linked with Pope Gregory the Great, who died in 604, this legend would seem to have grown up rapidly in the century after the latter's death; however, the author's phrase "over two hundred years" in fixing Gregory after Trajan may point to a fusion with the legend of Saint (but not Pope) Gregory, traditionally dated 257-337, whose own great suffering and healing of the King of Armenia may have lent material to the growing legend of Gregory the Great.

The author's account is significant for reducing the role of Gregory and magnifying that of Trajan to the point that the emperor is the main figure. The depiction of Trajan was one of the elements in his work most widely borrowed by later German histories. Where contemporary sermons and Gregory legends left the details of Trajan's campaign vague, the author imparts vividness to his story by sending Trajan's second-century expedition in an arc over time to meet the Normans, who had wrought havoc on the ninth-century Carolingian Empire and who remained potentially formidable enemies of German rulers in the twelfth century.

The Book goes on to tell us that Trajan held the Empire. He conducted his royal court very wisely, and all the Romans were bound to show him every earthly honor. When the Romans sought justice from him, he was painstaking in observing the laws; and he judged the lord and serving man alike, taking no fees at all from poor people. Nor did any man ever attain such great wealth as to be of any avail to him in dealing with Trajan. Neither their silver nor their red gold could help those miswrought and criminal rogues who deserved to be mutilated and hanged—death was always awaiting them. No one dared to stand by guilty men or offer Trajan any payment on their behalf.

Trajan was unflinchingly bold, but generous too. He treated the princes of his dominion with great respect, letting them enjoy all their rights, and he did so willingly. Nor was there any individual so insignificant that Trajan would deprive him of any of his rights, and yet he kept his judgments such that the whole population received its due. He was objective in deciding all cases, and the Romans came to love him for this. He became an awe-inspiring king with many a land subject to him. It happened one day as the king sat at a banquet that messengers arrived in haste. They told him the sad news that the savage Normans had killed many of his people and were laying waste his lands, plundering, and burning. They were sailing the sea in their ships and inflicting great injuries upon his people. They were seizing many captives on their raids ashore.

The king called his army together and prepared for the journey across the sea. When his forces were assembled and he already had one foot in the stirrup, a widow came running up to him and loudly called to him: "Hail, thou worthy King! Hear now of my distress, for I would make a complaint to you about great harm done to me. Just now my son has been slain, and my heart is heavy with anguish. Give judgment now, sire, as your custom has been of old."

"Milady," said Emperor Trajan then, "I have no time to spare for giving you judgment now. Right now I am on my way to rescue widows and orphans who have been taken captive within my Empire, to relieve them from their terrible afflictions. I intend to liberate them, but as soon as I return I will gladly judge this case for you."

The lady looked at him resentfully. "Now you tell me this, Emperor Trajan," said that good woman. "Who has revealed to you the time you have yet to live and to take care of rendering justice here at Rome? You are not so mighty but that you too must surely die, the same as the very poorest man in Rome. What is the reason you are giving me such a long time—until you come back again—to wait? What will happen if you end up dead out there? Then you will have completely deceived me, and you will be eternally lost."

"Milady," answered King Trajan, "what you are saying goes too far. If I die or am slain, the Romans must still have a judge. Make your same complaint to him who shall administer justice after me, and he will gladly give you judgment. But now, I must ride off on a far journey, for many a man is waiting for me. Milady, let me take leave of you and depart."

With both hands the lady grasped him by his garment. "But sire, if any other man gives me judgment, how do you expect God to reward you for it? What will have become of your good administration of justice? Never again will I praise your wisdom, and truly, if you leave me like this, you will have lost God's love forever."

"Owî!" said Emperor Trajan, "In all my life I never before heard such knowing words. As I live, I shall right the wrong done you." Dismounting from his horse to the ground, the ruler said with tears in his eyes, "Milady, I shall not depart from here without fulfilling your wish for judgment."

Then Emperor Trajan had the guilty man sought out. He dispatched competent men to hurry into the city of Rome, where they thoroughly searched both Rome and the Lateran until they finally found the man and led him before the emperor, grim in his determination. As soon as the emperor saw him, he addressed him angrily. "Now tell me, doomed wretch, how did the man you struck dead injure you? What crime did he commit against you?"

"Sire," he said, "it was a great wrong he did me, as I have firm evidence to prove. I ask you to consider well, sire, that he was the rightful object of my vengeance because he had killed my brother. By your grace, this should rightly pass without judgment."

Then said Emperor Trajan, "That is not at all the way things go. When your brother was killed, you should have made complaint to me. Since it was me the Romans acclaimed as judge, you were made subject to my judgment." Immediately after this—the lords concurring in the just sentence—he ordered the man's head cut off and presented to the lady.

When the lady saw the head she addressed the king. "Ah you, Emperor Trajan, you have done magnificently! May God now increase your strength and grant you victory, and may all your enemies be brought to shame evermore. Since this city of Rome was first raised, never have the Romans been blessed with such a noble judge as you, nor will they ever be again until mankind dies out. You have well avenged my son. Depart now, and may Our Lord watch over you." The emperor and his army eagerly betook themselves over the sea to confront the hostile Normans. There he won great fame as he destroyed their fortresses and led the people away. He and his army slew or captured all of the Normans they encountered. The enemy king was captured, and they led him away with them.

Then Emperor Trajan joyfully returned to the Lateran. He was accorded a magnificent triumph and was received there at Rome with loud shouts from men and women: "Praise and honor, Sire, be yours evermore!" Afterwards, the emperor continued to give righteous judgments in his whole Empire, establishing a peace that could not have been any better. As for the man who broke the peace—how harshly he took vengeance upon him! In time to come, his righteousness earned great mercy for him, for a most holy man by the name of Saint Gregory released him from his torments. This the book tells us as a fact: it happened over two hundred years later, when he held Saint Peter's throne and—reading of Trajan's excellence—was overcome with pity that this extraordinary ruler was suffering the pains of hell. How the thought of this tortured him!

One night as he was about to begin his prayers and was walking past Trajan's grave, he recalled his great sense of justice. Raising his eyes toward heaven, he sat down on the ground, considering whether or not Trajan could ever be redeemed. Then he knelt in prayer, and from heaven came an angel of God, who, appearing before Saint Gregory, said to him, "It should be enough for you that Our Lord hears you when you ask greater mercy for the Christians in your prayers. But the heathens have been cut off from the Christians, and now you have done wrong." At this the holy man wept.

But then the angel spoke to him. "Gregory, I'll tell you what to do. You are a trusty servant of God. Now receive from God the power to choose whether you will let this heathen suffer what he earned with his life or whether you will take care of his soul from now on—and in so doing accept seven sicknesses for yourself that you can never be healed of until you shall die. If this is your will, then take his soul out of hell and keep it until Judgment Day." Then the grave opened. The soul came back to the corpse, after which the angels took it and entrusted it to the holy man. The devil was forced to flee from there, and loudly did he cry, "Woe!" You never heard such distress before or since. He broke down all the doors, smashed out all the lights, and burst the shingles into pieces. Then the devil departed in God's hate. The angel told Saint Gregory that he was to suffer seven sicknesses and keep Trajan's soul with him until the Day of Judgment; then at the place where all the world is gathered together, he should present it. Now, let us all keep our hopes in God, in order that this may stand the man who now does so in good stead at the end of time. Let all kings of the world now heed the example of noble Emperor Trajan, how he gained this mercy from God for having persevered in righteous judgments while he lived in this world. They will be sure of the same mercy, if they keep Our Lord in their administration of justice.

The emperor lived a good life in this world, and the people feared his justice as he ruled—the Book gives us this as a fact—exactly two months more than nineteen years. The Romans sorely lamented his death.

XVIII

Philip

Marcus Julius Philippus (r. 244–249), came from Bostra in Arabia Trachonitis and is often called "Philip the Arab" because of that, although he enlisted in the Roman army at an early age. He rose through the ranks, and when the young emperor, Gordian III, embarked on a campaign against Persia, soldiers loyal to Philip assassinated him and hailed Philip as emperor. Five years later a rebellion broke out among the legions of Moesia. Philip sent Decius to put it down, but Decius ended up taking control of those troops for his own ends, marching with them into Italy, and killing Philip after defeating him in a battle near Verona. Decius then became emperor himself.

Very little is known about Philip as emperor except that he held elaborate celebrations for the thousandth-year anniversary of the founding of Rome. Early Christian historians called him the first emperor to become a Christian. This made him a model of good rulership for the Middle Ages and Decius a correspondingly bad one.

The Book tells us that Philip then held the Empire. He was the first of our Christian faith to have won that power and honor. He made a praiseworthy king. The king became the father of a son and named him Philip also: good Saint Sixtus baptized him. The two of them, pope and king, made every effort eagerly to see who among the heathens could be converted, baptized, and instructed in the faith. In bringing this about they were tireless. Their spirits never faltered, and their minds were completely devoted to God. The two of them let earthly treasure and gain slip away from them for the sake of the heavenly kingdom.

Decius was a terrible man. As quickly as he learned that King Philip had become a Christian, he turned violently resentful, for he was determined that no sort of Christian should judge over the Empire. He ordered his vassals to appear before him, and to them he passionately complained about what had happened and commanded them to set up ambushes and lie in wait for Philip at all times. Wherever they heard he might be they were to surprise and capture him.

One day, spies arrived and told Decius that the king was staying at a palace familiar to him. Decius was delighted to hear this and speedily made preparations and arrived at that palace:

Decius with a horde of men; the king kneeling in prayer;

Decius with weapons; the king with alms;

Decius with armed force; the king with faithful simplicity;

Decius seething with anger; the king with goodly love;

Decius bringing destruction; the king concerned with saving his soul;

Decius found the king true to his faith. With his own hand he sent father and son and others of the royal household altogether into God's kingdom to receive abundant honors. Seven and a half years they had ruled.

XIX

Decius

Sources friendly to Decius (r. 249-251) claim that he was proclaimed emperor against his will (see introduction to preceding chapter). After disposing of Philip, Decius was occupied mostly with fighting off the Goths, a conflict that put an end to his short reign when both he and his son were killed in battle. Decius was the first emperor to undertake a widespread and systematic persecution of Christians, hoping thereby to revitalize the ancient Roman religion.

Because he had killed the king, Decius—that violent and angry man—was able to call the heathens together and address them, saying that he would be most fitting to hold the Empire; which they would surely want to let him do, since he would make a good judge.

When Decius held the Empire—the Book tells us this—he did not want to tolerate any Christians living in Rome under him any longer. He pronounced his ban over all of them, demanding that they be brought before him quickly and that whoever would hide them out of his sight would be guilty of a capital offense.

Very soon then Decius understood that good Saint Sixtus was converting, baptizing, and instructing the heathens. He heard that he was the foremost teacher of Christianity and had no intention of hiding himself.

The overly vicious man, Decius—*furore repletus* [full of fury]—ordered that good Saint Sixtus be seized at Saint Peter's throne. He ordered him brought before him very quickly and said, "You deceitful old man, how dare you flaunt your power so openly before me in Rome? Without delay begin praying to my god, or you will lose your life."

Good Saint Sixtus lost no time in answering him, saying "Our Lord Jesus Christ was born to a virgin, in order that with his sublime death he might redeem back the otherwise lost numbers of mankind. I would be a very happy man if I were worthy to be called a martyr. Then I would live splendidly and receive my promised crown. It is certainly right and proper for a vassal to follow in the squadron of his lord. I am willing and eager to die for the sake of my dear Lord that I might escape the pains of hell."

These words enraged the king further. He ordered Saint Sixtus and two of his chaplains, one named Felicissimus, the other Agapitus, who had been seized with him, to have their heads chopped off. Then, when they were about to be led off to their martyrdom, Saint Laurence realized what was happening and spoke. "Hail to you, sublime father! What could I ever have done to offend you? Remember I was your private chaplain and was very accustomed to doing things together with you always and wherever we should be able to perform God's services. Why are you letting me down now? Let me partake of your sublime martyrdom since you promised me I would never be separated from you. I plan to divide your earthly treasures among widows and orphans. Do not let me remain tormented, but let me go with you."

The holy man answered him. "My dear son, I never will abandon you, but listen to what I have to tell you. Three days from now, Our Lord will reward you with so many honors that eyes of the flesh can never see them, nor human ears ever hear tell of them. I am an old man. All the tortures will pass over me lightly, and I will be killed quickly. Your flesh and bones will be tortured much longer. Your soul is holy and pure. After these three days have passed, you will journey after me. All the heavenly hosts will rejoice over your sacrifice of your youth."

The three men were slain very quickly. At the court the remaining chaplain was subjected to interrogation. His accusers charged that he was actually the chamberlain who had control over all the treasures [of Sixtus]. The furious king ordered that he be summoned before him. When he saw him he spoke to him with grim threats. "Show me the treasure and all the things your master used, or you will not survive this very day."

"I lost my master today when he was killed, and I am willing to tell you what you are asking about. But give me three days' time, and I assure you truthfully I will direct that all the treasures I have then be brought out for you."

The king granted him this request. Saint Laurence sent word through the whole city, asking that the poor be brought to him in the love of the true God. He distributed the treasure among them until there was nothing more in the chamber. Whether a man was naked or sickly, he did not leave until Saint Laurence had helped him in his distress with clothes or with money. He washed their feet and kissed them gently for the sake of Our Lord. He commended his soul to all of them, asking that early and late they pray for him to Our Lord that he might be merciful to Sixtus, his master, and might also forgive his own sins. In doing so he was preparing himself for his own long journey.

Very early on the third morning, the king addressed him threateningly, asking whether he wanted to bargain for his life—that he should bring out the treasure.

"You cannot have any treasure from me," said the holy man. "I gave it away for the sake of eternal life. After these tribulations it will pave for me the way into the heavenly kingdom before God. There I will certainly receive a good bargain. The time has come for me to have my body transfigured. You may well tear up my flesh, but you cannot injure my soul, which is to return to its creator. Your earthly tortures don't really interest me."

The king's anger was great. Upon hearing these words he sentenced him to be roasted upon a grill, which [in spite of his intent] would bring great comfort to Christendom. The grill was of iron—Laurence praised Our Lord for sending him to such a martyrdom full of suffering. When everyone around thought that he was dying from such tortures, he saw angels from heaven, and he said to his tormentors, "Well, now, you silly men, why don't you turn me over. Sitting here, you have not paid good attention. You might be able to eat half of me, where I am cooked through like a fish worthy of being set on the king's table. This torture is not hurting me at all. Angels from heaven have made me feel like I am lying on a bed of dewy clover." That was enough to convert many women and men there.

Then Laurence spoke out to Count Hypolite, who was assigned to torture him. "Hypolite, believe in the God who suffered torture and death upon the Cross for our sins, as he wanted to do. He sent angels to protect me so that this glowing fire cannot hurt me. Why are you demanding my treasure? I distributed it for the sake of eternal life, for I have total trust in God. You are truly a debtor, and you cannot go on without him. For the sake of God you shall die, undergoing a great martyrdom. You are chosen to share the heavenly home. I am telling you in truth—through great tortures as a martyr you will gain God's kingdom."

At that, good Saint Hypolite had himself baptized. Then King Decius ordered Valerian, who was the Roman seneschal, that he should think up tortures that would bring this man around. And so Count Valerian called his men together. He discussed this with the knowledgeable ones among them, and those cowards advised him to have his servants tie Saint Hypolite to the tails of wild horses. They dragged that stalwart of God through briars and hawthorns, tearing his skin and flesh off. Suffering this great martyrdom, he prayed to God that all his family would be converted, men and women alike. As if to answer that great man, Count Valerian ordered that his family be tortured to death with swords.

When King Decius finally saw that nothing was of any use in keeping the teachings of God from starting to multiply in his land, he commanded his chamberlains that, as they valued their own lives, they should bring him all the Christians they knew to be in his Empire. He swore by his crown that at Rome there was no prince so rich, so mighty, so sublime, or so strong—who because of his favor held fiefs or lands of his own—whose life would not be forfeited and whose holdings he would not distribute among the heathens, [if he did not comply]. Every man should accept the torturing of Christians. This could not be put off any longer.

The king's ban spread through the land. It flew everywhere. The search was a very wide one. The king ordered men and women seized—some of them hanged, some sunk to drown in the waves, some to have their skin flayed off, some thrown in dungeons, and some cast into pits full of serpents. No one dared help them. Some of God's servants were martyred with boiling quicklime until their bodies became corpses. Martyrdom was widespread and thorough for all those who affirmed their faith in God. Blood flowed from them through the whole city of Rome. Owî! How great were the sounds of torment that rose there! At that time, the Holy Scriptures were fulfilled in that the lordly David foretold what was to come: In the Psalms it is written about the *mors sanctorum preciosa* [the precious death of the saints]. Those who suffered a grim death are now among the judges of the world. Those who suffered tortures now have their crowns, but those who martyred them went to evil destinations; they are condemned to eternal sufferings and deprivations.

Decius took himself away to the fortified city of Ephesus. He ordered all there who believed in God tortured and beheaded. Seven brothers there were Christians who wanted to save their lives from him. They took refuge in a cave, which the king sealed off with a wall built inside the entrance. They remained alive in there—that is true—more than two hundred years and two less than fifty more, until the lordly Theodosius became judge there, a well-beloved king and a marvelous one. A great church council was held there. Heretics came there who said that our resurrection was not possible, nor that body and soul of the dead would ever be joined together again.

Indeed, Christendom suffered great trials and tribulations, until Our Lord opened the wall for his very dear servants. They became living proof of sublime resurrection.

Decius had Christendom's people slain—we can have no idea about the total number—until devils broke up his rule, avenging the sublime martyrs. He held the Empire, it is true, no longer than a year and two months more. Devils are torturing his soul.

XX

Diocletian and Maximian

Following Decius by a little more than thirty years, Diocletian (r. 284–305) outdid him in launching the most widespread and systematic of all the Roman imperial persecutions of Christians. In other ways, Diocletian was an efficient and successful administrator. He divided up the Empire into four more easily governable units and devised a much more rational succession system than what passed for one in the third century—one of free-for-alls among military contenders, producing a sequence of "soldier emperors." As the instigator of what Christian writers soon called "the Great Persecution," however, Diocletian vied with Nero in the Middle Ages for being the worst Roman emperor of all.

Diocletian's succession system provided for two senior emperors, each called an augustus, and two junior emperors, each called a caesar. Maximian had risen through the military ranks—and after being named a caesar by Diocletian in 485—became an augustus the following year. Since Diocletian was the other augustus himself, it is correct enough to say they ruled jointly. Both

Diocletian and Maximian stepped down from the emperorship in 305—Diocletian's system set limited terms for emperors—but Maximian ended up taking part in the succession struggles eventually won by Constantine. Maximian first allied with Constantine, then opposed him. Soon after losing to Constantine, Maximian was found dead.

When Diocletian and his companion, Maximian, those evil and fiercely angry men, held the Empire. They turned all their thoughts to discovering how to persecute those faithful to Our Lord. All the same, believers began to multiply. The rulers' bans flew through all the land. Wherever any Christian was found who stood by his faith, for him much suffering was in store. At that time they martyred good Saint Vitus. They also martyred Saint Pancratius and good Saint Maurice.

We ought to include here some of the special blessings we receive through these gentlemen. Vitus was only a small child, but as he was being tortured he asked Our Lord that whoever was beset by epilepsy might all turn to him for a cure. Our Lord himself granted him this, so that now afflicted persons are freed from the disease after one year.

But now let us hear about the blessing we have from Saint Pancratius, that holy man: whoever swears a false oath by his holy bones will live with pain and suffering for ever after that; and if he dies without doing penance for it, he will remain beyond help evermore.

The third one I will tell you about from whom Christendom may enjoy great blessings is Saint Maurice, who drives out devils and to the blind restores sight. He has that power from heaven—Our Lord bestowed it on him. I have other things to tell you about him. He especially heals sinners, and he cleanses lepers. He is a very valuable martyr. All sinners should show him the love due a father, for they may very well want to flee to him.

Now we will tell you about how this highly honored duke came to his martyrdom. He was, in fact, duke of the Moors, when he heard startling tales of how the Christians had been placed under the king's ban, and that holy man was sorry for them. He then admonished his loyal followers who wanted to earn eternal life through God that they should come quickly to him [for] he had great need of them.

In a short time the lord gained the support of six thousand, six hundred and six men—they all formed one huge royal army. The duke told them what he wanted—to lead a military expedition to carry out God's will. They all spoke up, affirming that this was also their will; they had every desire to fight for God's cause.

Now, we hear the Book tell us, however magnificently royal this army was, its men never rode with a greater or lesser number wherever they rode on this expedition. The six hundred looked out for six thousand; sixty of the comrades looked out for six hundred, and then six specially chosen men had command over all of them. Saint Maurice set off from there with his army so dear to him. Soon they were headed for the fortress-city of Rome.

Meanwhile Maximian commanded his own expedition. When Saint Maurice arrived at the city of Rome, the king gave him a magnificent welcome, saying that he wanted to make every effort to include him among his privy councilors [for] their military order seemed to him to be of the very best.

Saint Maurice and his army did not want to remain there. They took everything along with them. They followed virtuous customs, and they lived according to Christian rules. They wanted to serve God. They were sure to have sung matins and the mass. They gave alms and performed good works. They fell on their knees in prayer. They prayed to heaven, and their hearts took up the love of God. This allowed those with whom they were lodging to see quickly that they were practicing Christians. Then they hurried to the king, saying, "Sire, our guests here are all an evil company. Now you are trying to suppress Christianity in Kerlingen [home of the Ripuarian Franks], but an astonishing thing is happening, and the Christians are here among us. We don't hear anything but Christian talk from those black Moors. They all name one God, who was martyred at Jerusalem. They take no rest by night or day; no one can adequately tell you how restless they are. Lord, have mercy upon us heathens so that we don't become contaminated by Christians."

That infuriated King Maximian, who ordered the head struck off of every tenth man in Maurice's army, so that they would properly fear him and let him convert them away from their faith. The remainder, however, devoted themselves ever more eagerly to God's service. Neither with threats nor with cunning could he win them over. Then he ordered his men to take their swords and torture and kill them, but then they received their crowns in God's kingdom, where they will live forever more. All six thousand, six hundred and sixty men were murdered in one day.

King Maximian was glad then with all the murders he had commanded, but even that evil was not enough for him. He wanted to bring back the false gods again, whose idols had earlier been smashed. New idols were poured once more, and the false gods were restored and honored. The devil showed them how to do this. They killed the pope and nine successors to him [one after the other, as quickly as each was chosen]. Very few of those serving the church survived. Throughout the whole Empire they would not tolerate any kind of churches. They destroyed them with fires to bring shame upon the Christians and went on to hunt Christians through the woods with dogs, in ravines and in mountains. All Christians had to die. Christianity was brutally suppressed, and heathendom began to revive.

Diocletian and his joint ruler, Maximian—those furious agents of destruction—handed down violent and bloody judgments. Throughout this whole earth people were deathly afraid of them. They wielded power as judges, the Book tells us for a fact, twenty years and six weeks. Diocletian was assassinated, while Maximian escaped from the Empire to England, but God made him pay for his crimes, causing him to stab himself.

Severus

Lucius Septimius Severus (r. 193–211) was one of the more effective "soldier-emperors." He introduced roughly a century of fairly overt military despotism characterizing Roman government between the death of Commodus in 192 and Diocletian's assumption of the imperial title in 284. In order to gain full power, he waged war against his rival, Albinus. Against him in 197 near Lyons, he fought the battle with the most casualties of any battle of Roman forces against other Roman forces since the great victory of Octavian (the future Augustus Caesar) over the forces of Brutus and Cassius in 42 *BC*. He led extensive military campaigns against the Parthians and, much later, to pacify Britain. In the *Book of Emperors* he presides over a vast conflict within the empire, ending in huge numbers of casualties, his own defeat, and suicide. The massive slaughter scenes may reflect the reputation attached to him from the battle at Lyons, but this is probably the only—and rather tenuous—link to factual history; otherwise he provides simply a convenient imperial name for the story of a heroic Bavarian duke offering justified resistance to the Roman Empire.

While our author is full of praise for the Roman Empire from it earliest days, it is clear that he thinks more highly of Germans than of inhabitants of the city of Rome and gives Bavarians a certain preference among Germans. The story of Adelger, the legendary Bavarian duke who defended Bavarian independence within the empire, has its roots in a story attached to Theodoric the Ostrogoth, which also features a similar animal fable. The fable itself makes sense only if it is kept in mind that for medieval people the heart was the seat of reasoning power or intelligence as well as of the emotions.

The Book tells us that Severus then held the Empire. In his reign there was a highly respected duke in Bavaria whose name was Adelger, and often he would take actions against the Roman Empire. The king came to realize that that within his empire there was no other man of this world who more frequently rebelled against his grace, and that if he kept putting up with him much longer it would undermine his own honorable reputation.

One day royal messengers reached Adelger and summoned him to appear in Rome, since he had committed acts against the ruler in spite of the latter's grace. The duke had a vassal whom he often took aside for counsel. He asked him to come to his chamber and said, "Your thoughts have often been good in the past, and I would like you to be the first to advise me about this: the Romans have sent for me, which gives me grave misgivings. I fear that they will do me some shameful harm—they are hard-hearted people. My feelings tell me not to go there. It may be that I will get over such feelings, but right now I would hate to go there."

"By my very life," his old counselor told him, "I will advise you in a way that increases your honor. Do not be afraid of all of this. My advice to you is: send men there who are loyal to you. See that they are dressed in the finest clothing that can be found in your whole land. You may not fight against established Roman rights, but go with these men to Rome yourself. Pay homage to the crown, appease the king in whatever he is doing that annoys you, pledge to support him in his wishes if they are reasonable; but let him know that if he goes beyond that he will easily have trouble on this hands."

The duke then made preparations and set off for the king's court, but when he arrived there he was not treated well at all. When the king saw him he turned angry and said to him, "How dare you come directly before me. According to law you forfeited your life with all the misery you caused me, and I will take vengeance on you today."

"Your messenger conducted me here, sire," said Duke Adelger. "I hope to win your approval and protection with the approval of all Romans by negotiating with Your Majesty, full of grace as you are.

"I don't know what grace you are talking about," King Severus replied. "Your head should be struck off and your lands should be given to another man." Some Romans came to Adelger's defense, saying that in all the Empire there was no man to be found so reasonable as Adelger, and that the king should extend his grace to him.

In the Senate, it was decided to cut off Adelger's clothing, so that what was left crept back up around his knees—that was to make him the object of ridicule—and to cut off his hair in front. That is how they wanted to treat the most praiseworthy lord who ever won lands in Bavaria as a means of disgracing him. Everything turned out later in a way exactly opposite from what they intended.

When the noble duke returned to his quarters he was sorely distressed, and all his men shared his sorrow. "My Lord," said his old adviser, "may God come to your aid. You should stop grieving. If you follow my instructions it will all turn out in a way which reflects well on your honor. All the great houses of Rome will show you respect."

"Your advice brought me here," said Duke Adelger. If you restore me with your good ideas to the way I was before, then I will trust in you more than ever, but if I do not regain my honor here, I will never return to the Bavarians again."

Then the old man said to him, "Milord, have me treated the same way they treated you. You should then send word to all your vassals that you will bestow fiefs and outright gifts of land to them if they all let their clothes and hair be shorn. Well, what more do you want? I will agree to restore your honor, milord, or forfeit my life. Let me accept death if I am wrong about this."

The duke then summoned his men, and, taking each one aside individually, he said to him, "Whoever stands firmly beside me in my present distress—for me there is no question about this—I will grant him both fiefs and lands of his own. I mean the man who for my sake lets himself be sheared as was done to me."

"Yes," said all his men. They were ready to follow him until death. They would never let him down when he was threatened. They were completely committed to carrying out his will. Very quickly, all those who had come with him took shears to themselves and cut off their clothing, so that the remaining cloth crawled up around their knees. Those heroes were of tall stature, each one with a fine build. They were so good-looking that there never was a king so rich and powerful, but what he would have wanted to have them in his own retinue. Those heroes were so capable-looking as well as handsome that everyone was amazed who saw them—so much so that they all shouted their approval, confirming that these men gave evidence of such high and bold spirits that they deserved love and honor from the Empire. That is what the noblest lords all said.

First thing the next morning, the duke came to the court. The emperor felt uncertain when he saw him and asked him, "When did you decide to do that, my dear fellow, and whose advice did you take?"

"When I came here," said Duke Adelger, "I brought along many of my vassals, who have shown me great loyalty. Now at home our custom is that when any one of us—be he rich or poor—suffers an insult or injury we must all bear it together, as if though it had happened to all of us. And so we have come here, but we brought our custom with us."

"Give me the man who advised you. I want to keep him at my court," said King Severus. "You should know that when you depart from here you will have my friendship and support forever more."

The duke really did not want to do this, but he felt that he must grant this request. He took his vassal by the hand and commended him to the service of the king. Then the duke and the rest of his men took leave of the king. All the Romans confirmed how devoted they were to him.

The duke then set off. He enjoyed more respect and praise from the Romans than any German before him had ever won among them. When they were under way, his advisers met and counseled him to send word ahead to Bavaria, commanding all his men there to swear by their right hands that whoever wanted to hold fiefs from him or bear the title of knight should cut off their clothes at the knees and their hair in front as a sign of respect to the duke and that whoever refused would lose his hand. Word spread that the men of Bavaria were cutting off their clothing at the knees and their hair in front. Soon the custom caught on and all men throughout the German dominions sheared themselves as the duke had been shorn.

It was not long after this friendship had been sealed between the Roman king and the duke that people at the Roman court started to regret it, and the Romans spread all sorts of evil rumors, making up misdeeds and then asking, "How does the duke dare to commit such crimes?" Adelger was commanded, on pain of life and honor, to come to the Lateran immediately. The emperor wanted to speak to him.

This made the good duke a bit uneasy, and he secretly sent a messenger into Italy to his old vassal, requesting that he be reminded of old pledges of loyalty and to reveal quietly what the king really wanted, and whether he should come to the King's court or stay at home.

"You did the wrong thing by coming here to me," said the old man to the messenger. "Once the duke was my liege lord, and I counseled him as well as I could, but then he gave me away to the king, unfortunately making a big mistake. If I were to reveal a secret of the Empire, I would be acting faithlessly. Still, I will tell the king a fable. Pay attention and remember it, and if you re-tell it to your lord correctly, it will serve his honor very well.

First thing the next morning the old man went to the royal court. "Are you listening, my dear lord? I have been thinking about things far away in olden times, and if you would want to hear it, sire, I will tell you a great fable."

"I would like to hear it very much," answered King Severus.

"There was once a man—my father told me this—who cultivated a good garden for himself. He worked at it very hard and grew herbs and cabbages in it. His garden was very close to his heart. A stag became aware of it, and at night he went there stealthily, and jumped right over a low stile. The man's good herbs were sweet to his taste, and he ate what was growing there until the garden was on the way to ruin. He continued this for many days.

"Then the gardener became aware of him, and he got ready for him when he came again. The poor man took vengeance as he cut off one of his ears. The stag wanted to run away, but the gardener was quick and before the stag had escaped the man succeeded in chopping off half his tail. 'Take those marks with you as a reminder of what happened to you here,' he said. 'If they hurt you enough, you won't come back here anymore.'"

"It did not take long for the stag's wounds to heal. He slipped through the woods again to the old stile. He destroyed beds of herbs and the cabbage patch. Aware that the stag had returned, and, thinking clearly about what

Chapter Twenty-one

to do, the man surrounded the garden on all sides with nets. When the stag wanted to leave by way of the old stile, the man picked up his spear and, running at the stag, ran him through the stomach and shouted, 'Sweets have turned sour for you. You paid dearly for my herbs.' He cut up the deer, as was his right, but a sly vixen lay close by in a furrow. When the man left for a while, she crept over to the carcass, took out the heart, and carried it with her back to her den.

"The man was very pleased with his hunting results, but when he returned and could not find the heart anywhere he struck his two hands together and hurried back to his wife [saying] 'I want to tell you something really strange. The stag that I killed is big, and he is good except there was no heart to be found inside him.'

"'I already figured that out,' said his wife. 'The stag suffered pain when he lost his ear and tail, and that shows that he did not have any heart, because if he had had one, he would never have come back to the garden again.'"

This whole fascinating tale was lost on the messenger since he understood it only in a simple, word-for-word way. Feeling some anger, he headed back to Bavaria, where he found his lord. When he saw his lord, the duke, he shouted at him, "No matter how much trouble I went through, I was not able to find out anything that would help you worth a bean. What was the point of sending me to Rome? That old man offered nothing to tell you except for a fable that he told his lord. He asked me to come along to the court with him and listen closely to the fable, then to repeat the fable to you back home—I hope his years are miserable ones from now on."

When the duke heard the parable, he called for his men to come to him and said, "Well, now, you bold and swift heroes, I will interpret this fable for you. The Romans want to trap my body in nets, but you should know now that they will not succeed in trapping me in Rome at the stile. On the other hand—I will interpret more of the fable for you—the Romans may well come looking for me in Bavaria. If I have a heart of my own and my men choose to support me, the Romans will find that they made a bad bargain. Their reward will be to have their stomachs run through. Even King Severus will not gain anything useful to him or that does him any honor."

It was announced at the Roman court that the duke had no intention of ever coming there, and this made King Severus more and more angry. He said he would take charge of the matter himself—that he would have a look and see in what land Adelger was now.

Supported by his whole council, the king quickly summoned his men, and in a short time thirty thousand came to serve him. They were all well equipped with helmets and with hauberks. The army made a turn at Verona, and, following him, they rode through the Trent Valley. Those who were soon to die were happy when they came to the land of Bavaria.

The duke was informed that the Romans were searching for him with a very well equipped army, thinking he would not be able to withstand it. But then that good hero displayed a brave spirit. He sought help from both kinsmen and allies, asking them to aid him. They all came to a river called the Inn with many a bold hero and many a young knight in their massed army.

The duke strode to some high ground and spoke to the Bavarians. "Hail to you, high-spirited heroes! You will surely not forget that you have often assured me of your support. Now you will have a chance to put those words into action. A great injustice has been done to me. I was abiding by law and custom when I went to Rome, but there the king shamed me by cutting my hair and clothing. Nonetheless, I was obedient to him and earned his loyalty. He is after me now for no guilt on my part. I would not really be sorry to see that man lying dead. The Romans want to throw us into their dungeons; they will torture us and shamefully abuse the women who are so dear to us. They will kill our children, set fire to our homes, and plunder our lands. They would like to conquer Bavaria that way—and gone forever will be the power and glory that I was accustomed to providing here. But now, heroes, knowing this, defend your lives and lands all the better!" They each stretched high a hand, swearing that if anyone deserted he would never again have a fief or land of his own anywhere on Bavarian soil.

He sent Margrave Herold off to the Swabians, so that he could provide defense of the borderland, which invading Romans had put under heavy attack. He fought a stormy battle with them, and God let him be victorious. He caught Duke Prennus and hanged him from a gallows.

Chapter Twenty-one

He sent Count Rudolf, his two brothers, and others loyal to him off to Bohemia. The Bohemian King Osmig was in Sallern, ravaging Bavaria with a mighty army. When Count Rudolf located him, he raised his flag and charged him with great daring. He slew Osmig, whose men deserted him. What they had gained by robbery Rudolf won back again. Then at Kampach he furled his flag.

Wirnt was lord of the castle [at Regensburg]. Adelger sent him against the hordes of Huns. No one can tell how many Huns lay dead after he attacked them. They hunted them down all one long summer day as far as a river called the Trune, and hardly any of them survived the Bavarian onslaught.

The noble Duke Adelger then led his army into the field at Brixen, where they set up their tents. Some Roman sentries saw them. They raised their own flag and charged the Bavarians. Those whose lot it was to die then fell, as many an ashen spearshaft splintered. Volkwin was stronger than the king's flag bearer and ran him through, piercing right through his armor where he struck him. Then he spoke these fierce words: "I am bringing this as debt-interest for your lord, and tell King Severus that although he may have put my lord to shame with his hair and with his clothing, things have come to the place where he will more than even the score." He jerked his flag upright again, and, spurring his horse, he broke through the enemy ranks. Nearly all the enemy troops were to stay there. Whatever land they came from they did not want to retreat, but how few of them escaped who would be good for anything afterwards!

The battle had subsided at the end of that summer-long day. The ever-so-brave Roman soldiers had their green flags all turned the color of blood. So much blood of battle flowed over the squadrons, which had been so bright and gleaming, that it showed that never before did so many heroes lie fallen on a single battlefield. No one can adequately describe the horror of the sight where the daring young heroes lay hacked to pieces. Man had fallen over man, as the battle's blood ran from them for over a mile—and then some. The only thing to be heard were shouts of "Oh!" and "Woe!" You have never heard anything like this before, where all the heroes so brave struck each other down. They still did not want to be taken from the raging battle by death or any other earthly cause. They also did not want to leave their lords there. They sought vainly to bring their wounded lords away with honor. Only death and destruction remained.

The day began to sink, and the Romans began to show desperation. They were badly beaten. Volkwin, the flagbearer, became aware of this, and he began to point his flag in the direction of King Severus. Those hardened Bavarians pressed towards the king with their sharp swords, singing their battle song. The Italians serving Severus were unable to flee or to fight any longer. Severus realized that nothing was of any use now that all his men were either wounded or dead, and that they could no longer hold out in the battle.

He threw his sword from his hand and said, "Rome, Bavaria has wrought a terrible shame upon you. I do not care about living any longer." Volkwin slew him then truly; he held the Empire for seven years and a half.

XXII

Helvius (Helius) Pertinax

Publius Helvius Pertinax (r. 193) was of humble family background. His father was a freed slave who had become a charcoal burner. After teaching grammar, Pertinax rose through political and military ranks, twice becoming a consul. Soldiers who assassinated Commodus pressured Pertinax into agreeing to be proclaimed emperor, but three months later other soldiers came to resent his alleged stinginess with public funds and in a mutiny assassinated him.

It seems most unlikely that Pertinax ever engaged in wrestling matches. The spectacle of an emperor in a sport with a life-or-death outcome may have been suggested by the lasting image of Commodus as gladiator. Julian (Marcus Didius Julianus) did not kill Pertinax, but, soon after his death, he bid highest in an auction for the emperorship held by the Praetorian Guard and became emperor himself. He was also assassinated after serving a few months in 193.

To he Book tells us that Helvius Pertinax[1] then took over the Empire. Something very remarkable happened in his time: in Rome there was scarcely any man of the nobility who did not want to leave a legacy by doing something that would make people talk about him forever—that had become a custom among them.

And so it came about that King Helius had a stadium constructed with an arena. It was built as well as it could be built with good blocks of marble and gold finely inlaid for decoration, just as I am now telling you. Roman nobles soon became accustomed to going there every Saturday. Women came as well as men, and there they went naked with no clothes at all—just as people are born into this world. In this way they gathered inside the stadium—only members of the nobility—and rubbed themselves with oil, so that when they grabbed each other their hands would slip off. Their skin would be so slippery that it would be impossible for them to get a firm grip on one another. That would make everyone laugh who was there. Whoever was strong enough to throw another man down would be honored by the women, who would sing him a song of praise.

It happened one day that King Helius also wrestled in that arena. He displayed good skills, and he was so bold and strong that he threw down *all* of the Romans he wrestled with, showing that no one could resist him successfully—although his display was to become the cause of his undoing.

Now, we hear the Book tell us, a prince by the name of Julian had maintained the title of best wrestler ever since he was quite young. It had been said of him that there was no man in Rome who could stand up against him. Hai! How he hated to see how well the king was doing. He took off his clothes and jumped into the arena, where he began to wrestle. Everyone there thought he would quickly defeat the king, but soon the

---

1. While our author calls him Helius Pertinax, common English usage is Helvius Pertinax.

king caught him around the chest and squeezed him so hard that blood spurted out from his eyes. He raised him high in the air and, with a mighty swing, sent him crashing to the ground, where he lay dead, which made the king laugh.

Julian had a brother, who secretly sent for his men. Very soon five thousand of them and more answered his call. The king knew nothing about this—until the unwelcome guests came crashing into his tower singing their battle song.

King Helius defended himself until all his men had fallen. Nothing was of any use. He could no longer offer resistance. They cut off his head, and other Romans carried him to his grave. He judged over the Empire seven months and five days more.

XXIII

Helius Adrianus (Hadrian)

Hadrian (r. 117–138) was Trajan's adopted son and designated successor. He is ranked with the "five good emperors," who headed honest and efficient governments for most of the second century. In early Christian history, Hadrian's fame was linked to his rebuilding of Jerusalem far more than to his building his namesake Hadrian's Wall, more or less between England and Scotland.

He renamed Jerusalem "Aelia Capitolina" after his own name, Aelius (modified to "Helius" by our author). He adopted Lucius Ceionius Commodus, probably the inspiration for our author's "Lucius Accommodus," whose story follows in the next chapter. This successor-designate, however, died shortly before Hadrian himself. Hadrian then adopted the man who succeeded him—Antoninus Pius.

elius Adrianus then judged over the Roman dominions. Jerusalem, that city of marvels, was lying wasted and empty. The heathens had destroyed it, tearing down every bit of its walls. King Cosdras was responsible for that, but Eraclius was to take vengeance upon him for it.

King Helius Adrianus had plans for Jerusalem. He had begun to love that city, and he restored it with magnificent buildings that may be admired to this day. He changed its name into one based on his own. According to him, it was to be called "Helia," but God soon avenged his wonton pride. He was killed at Damascus, and Jerusalem took back the same name again that it had before. Damascus paid dearly for his death. The Romans avenged the loss of their ruler. They ravaged the territories ruled from Damascus with their armies, which destroyed their crops and left their landscape desolate—so that they soon regretted that the king had been killed in their city. Then the Romans entered the city of Jerusalem.

XXIV

Lucius Accommodus

This chapter contains many historical names, sometimes with hints of their actual place in Roman history, sometimes without even those. While Hadrian had originally named Lucius Coeionius Commodus to succeed him—and that may have suggested our author's name for Hadrian's successor—it is also true that Lucius Commodus Antoninus (r. 186–192), famed for his devotion to the gladiator's art, may be intended. Antoninus Pius (r. 138–161), the grandfather of that Commodus, makes a vignette appearance in one of the battle scenes below, although not as emperor.

Alaric, king of the Visigoths, led forces that besieged and then sacked Rome much later in 410, an important episode in the beginning of the fall of the Roman Empire. Actually, as Saint Augustine was to point out soon afterwards, Alaric's destructiveness in Rome was limited. His notoriety remained, however, as an early victor over a Rome in political and military decline. Putting him nearly three centuries earlier at the head of hundreds of thousands of warriors from the "borderlands" and beyond—united in avenging the failure of Romans to name Alaric their emperor—is, of course, fiction.

After conferring together, the Romans quickly selected Lucius Accommodus. They agreed that it portended evil for the imperial throne to stay empty and that he should be their choice for Judge; however, the strife that began with choosing him lasted a long time.

Alaric and his men—so we hear the Book tell us—really wanted to leave for home. They thought that what had been done was scandalously against their interests. They requested their king to ride to Apulia, which was what he intended to do. But then when two factions—that of people from the borderlands and those from the interior of the empire—discussed the election with their allies, they discovered that those from outlying areas wanted to replace Lucius Accommodus with Alaric, which was unacceptable to those from the interior territories. Lucius Accommodus continued to judge the Roman dominions, but later the Romans suffered greatly for that. Many of them were destined to die when Alaric would take his vengeance and rip the foundations of Roman fortifications out of the ground.

When the nobles returned to the city of Rome they were well received by friends and relations, young and old, who sang songs of praise to them and rejoiced at their arrival, expressing thanks to them for the triumph they brought them when they achieved victory in their invasion of Damascus.

Not long after the nobles had been well received, the Senate decided that they should all swear their allegiance to Lucius Accommodus. These lords began to separate into groups. Some among them [who had sworn allegiance to Alaric] said they would rather die than break their oaths. These nobles suggested putting the decision off until the next day, but when night came they used cunning to get out of the city, leaving wives and others of their households behind.

When those heroes arrived at the camp of Alaric, their lord, and told him what had happened to them and what they had suffered, he sought massive assistance from many kinds of countries. The brave Medes—I am fairly sure that is what is recorded here— brought him sixty thousand fine knights, while the Saracens and the Moors quickly brought a hundred thousand and more for the aid of their lord. The King of Parthia made every effort to find troops for him and furnished him fifty thousand well-armed heroes. In a little while the King of the Jacobites furnished him with fifty thousand men wearing chain-mail armor. It is known with certainty that the King of the Greeks brought him eighty thousand men, and the Duke of Poland seventy thousand men with bows of horn. Another hundred thousand came to him from Russia, while the king of Arabia lost no time in sending him thirty thousand of his heroes. The rulers of Calabria and Sicily led eighty thousand firmly committed to helping him. The rulers of Apulia did the same. They led twelve thousand good soldiers well prepared for battle. The prince whose name was Willehalm committed his flag to King Alaric.

The Romans soon found out that this king was mobilizing forces, and they sent messengers from land to land. They were told to make requests of the king of the Britons, reminding him of all the things the Romans had done for him earlier. He then furnished them with many a fine man. The king of Italy—yes, and the one of Burgundy, too—made every effort to collect and mobilize forces; these displayed many a white hauberk. The rulers of Lombardy and Tuscany led many a handsome hero. The Duke of Merano and his vassal, Sclavus, led many a fine hero. They arrived, all of one mind, in the city of Rome. People counted three hundred thousand men serving the [Roman] king's crown. Even though they were to stand their ground loyally in battle for the brave Romans, in my opinion they never before experienced such a disaster as was to befall them.

Alaric and his army moved inland from the sea and camped before the city of Rome. I think that neither before nor afterwards was there ever such a ferocious battle storm. Willehalm led with the king's [Alaric's] flag almost up to the castle gate. Pius Antoninus took his stand there [for the Romans] with a golden-boar flag, which many a noble hero defended with a determined spirit. Squadron crashed against squadron with the heroes fighting recklessly until they were all mixed up with one another.

Alaric put a cunning plan into action. He told all the men from twelve of his squadrons to wear some red markings so that they could be recognized in the welter of battle and not confused with the enemy. Those were truly young heroes and they secured victory for their lord. There was such a massive slaughter that it will be told of forever as an event of great interest. They filled the ditches with the dead, while the Tiber almost overflowed its banks from the stream of blood flowing into it—enough to make it possible to float ships on it. So many men were killed that the Book has no number for them. The Romans were defending their city with determination.

When the sun started fading with the onset of evening there was not a man left who was able to help another. Willehalm seized the fallen flag with the boar on it and stuck it, point first, into the ground. He soon broke through the Roman lines, and, when the soldiers with the red markings saw what he had done, they roused themselves to action once again. No one can tell you what slaughter was unleashed then. Alaric pushed into the city with all of his forces, and the Romans were unable to resist any longer. They had to flee, and very few of them survived.

Extraordinary happenings followed then. Alaric's army struck down women and children, and they set fire to the buildings. They rammed their way into armories and towers, tearing down their walls—Hai! How they were avenging the injuries that had been committed against them in the past and that remained always on their minds. They were all avenging their kinfolk, those from Calabria and from Africa who had been slain in earlier times. Now Rome sustained such a remarkable disaster that it will be told of with great interest until the Last Day.

Lucius Accommodus was slain, but Alaric directed that he be given a fitting burial with high solemnity, which improved his reputation among the Romans as an honorable man. [Alaric] ruled his people five and a half years, until men he trusted killed him with poison.

Chapter Twenty-four

Achilleus

Achilleus is briefly mentioned by some early Christian historians, including Orosius (VII, 25), as a rival, would-be emperor, who gathered forces together in Alexandria during Diocletian's reign. These references put him in the last part of the third century or the first years of the fourth. Diocletian besieged Alexandria for eight months before taking it and killing Achilleus, who is not recorded as ever having reached Rome.

The Book tells us that Achilleus then held the Empire. He was eager to make Rome beautiful. That noble king had costly palaces built of the whitest marble, and he required the people of the land to pay him taxes, with which he completed fine walls and moats, just as he directed.

After some time it came to pass that Romans sent after the worthiest nobleman of whom they had knowledge. Right away Posthumus came to the group who had sent for him. When he learned from them that it had been Achilleus who had killed his father, his revenge was ferocious, and he stabbed the king all the way through. Posthumus also lay there dead. Achilleus ruled the Empire for nine months.

All the followers of Posthumus were taken prisoner. They suffered great pain from torture before being mutilated and hanged. That is how the Romans avenged the death of their lord.

Gallienus

The historical Emperor Gallienus (r. 260–268) had been joint emperor with his father, Valerian, beginning in 255. But when Valerian was taken prisoner by Shapur of Persia in 260, Gallienus did nothing to get him back and seemed quite content to rule as sole emperor. Shapur was reported to have killed Valerian, stuffed his skin, and displayed it in a temple. While Gallienus had shown some military talent as a young man, as emperor he did very little to halt invaders who threatened the Empire from several sides. Constant revolts broke out against him, and he was never really in charge of the whole Empire at one time. His reign became known afterwards as the "Time of the Thirty Tyrants"—although, as Gibbon notes, there were no more than eighteen by the most all-inclusive count.

Our author's Gallienus shares only the name with the historical Emperor Gallienus. The real Gallienus was much less fervent in persecuting Christians than his father, Valerian. The link with medical experiments and poisonings may derive from supposed memories of the great Greek physician, Galen (ca. *AD* 130–ca. 201), whose work contributed heavily to the medieval study of medicine. There is certainly no factual basis for linking Galen—if, in fact, it was his name that suggested "Gallienus" to our author—with anything like mass poisonings or sadistic medical experiments. The Gallienus chapter illustrates instead one of the many faces of evil in the author's mind, made all the more threatening by the power of a ruler. It also illustrates, as does the Nero story, the ambivalence of many medieval people toward any art that seeks to probe too deeply into secrets of nature.

he Book now lets us know that Gallienus held the Empire. He was the wisest physician ever to be born in Rome; however, his great knowledge was to cause frequent suffering. He greatly hated Christians and with them he revealed himself to be a cruel ruler. Any Christian who came to the attention of Gallienus had to pay for being one with his life. After sentencing Christians to be led out of the city, he would practice his medical arts on them. He would order that their hands and feet be cut to pieces, and he searched for every means of abusing them further both on their limbs and in their veins. The first man to introduce the practice of gouging out people's eyes, he would never believe himself to be finished with them until he had exhausted his medical knowledge on them. This made the heathens take up the praise of his wisdom.

King Gallienus was also a wise philosopher. One night he read in the stars what a future day would bring—that his chamberlains would try to poison him. The king could not allow that to happen, but even though he knew their intentions, he remained silent until the next day when he was sitting at his table and many princes were sitting with him. The lord high steward brought in the meal and served it, but Gallienus did not eat or drink anything himself. He cunningly held back from everything, knowing that he was intended to be an innocent victim. When the steward came before him, Gallienus let his head hang low and began to gather his thoughts of distrust. After what seemed like a long time, he straightened up and said, "Bring that closer, over here, my dear steward. You shall take a drink, and the princes may all well observe, what you were planning to give me. Let us see what happens to you, and I will drink the same thing afterwards."

The steward saw that he could do nothing to help himself, and so he said, "Sire, I beg you upon your royal honor to change your mind about this and to show me your royal goodness."

King Gallienus answered him like this: "By my health, which I value, you will drink this to the very bottom. You set a trap for me, and now you must suffer the injury it will cause."

The steward had no choice but to do what the mighty king commanded him to do. As he drank from the cup his eyes jumped out of his head, and he fell to the floor dead. "I take real pleasure in seeing you lie there that way," said the mighty king. "I must say this now about what you have done: Many men who had nothing to do with it will pay the price for what happened to you."

The king hesitated no longer but rode out of Rome. He stopped to take a look at the city and uttered these evil words: "Woe to you, Rome, you accursed city! How frightened of you I have been the whole time I lived inside you, but you will pay dearly for that!

"Woe to you, Romans," he continued. "You never could keep any one of your rulers for long before putting him to death. I will never let my anger subside until you have been well paid back in kind. What you did to injure me will now be visited upon your wives and children."

The king rode to Boimund's Castle, where he wanted to stay until the words he had spoken were proven true and there would be no recovery for the Romans. Without losing any time he ordered a big and strong ark to be poured of bronze; then he ordered poison to be brought to the ark and the ark filled with it just as he wanted it done. Then—there is no doubt about this—he ordered the ark sunk in the Tiber. As soon as the river's current flowed over the poison, whoever drank downstream of it, God knows, died. All the people in Rome thought this must come from a plague. Day and night they kept dying until there were thirteen thousand deaths.

The ark was located upstream from the city, sunk in a way that no one was aware of it until a wise physician appeared, who was very learned. When he noticed a strange scent in the air, it was very clear to him that it came from the water. He lost no time in ordering the Romans to stay away from the Tiber.

That physician was a resourceful man. He took his hounds along the river in the direction of the scent. He came to the place where the ark had been sunk. With one hound he confirmed that the water upstream was good, but a second hound died quickly when the physician threw him in the water downstream from the ark. That let people know of the king's evil intentions and implacable anger.

As soon as news of this reached the Romans, they hurried to the site and began setting up a great and strong device of pulleys with which they raised up the ark—and I know that they all confirmed they had never seen such a strange form of vengeance, which they denounced as diabolical. They all agreed that this vengeance must come from the king, who would now be visited by evil himself—he deserved to die a bitter death. All of them swore they would make this happen, since so many of their kinsmen now lay dead. The king was warned and escaped to Syria, where afterwards he was killed as an act of respect for the Romans. He ruled for four years.

Constantius Chlorus

The story of Constantine I, "the Great," who became the first Roman emperor to tolerate Christianity and who favored it in a way that led to mass conversions of Romans, is predictably one of the high points in the *Book of Emperors*. What follows is the story of Constantine's father, Constantius Chlorus—a caesar or junior emperor in Diocletian's system of plural rulers, 293–305, and augustus or senior emperor from 305 until his death in 306—told in a way that focuses upon young Constantine. Many biographies of Constantine, both long and short, were transmitted through the Middle Ages, with the fictional story of Constantius' affair with Helena, as well as Constantine's illegitimate birth and need to overcome that taint. These elements survived in a Byzantine version written around 900 and probably used in Latin translation as one of our author's sources. His own innovations include a Western Roman and German setting for the events, with the substitution of Trier for Drepanum in the Byzantine Empire as Helena's home.

The story of overcoming the seven usurpers historically belongs to Constantine's son, Constantius II, but is assigned here to Constantine's father.

The Book tells us that Constantius held the Empire. You probably heard before that by the Bodensee [Lake Constance] there is a city named Constance, which was built in his honor. He took a lady of Trier for himself, and she bore him a fine son named Constantine, but then Constantius decided to keep this lady only as his concubine. As a boy, Constantine developed great courage and many other excellent traits. He [later] loved the holy faith and added something specially his own to holy baptism.[1] Sparing no labors, he gave firm support to Christianity as no other earthly lord has ever done since in this world.

As soon as Constantius found out that his son was so capable, he placed his subjects in the Trier region under Constantine's authority, in spite of the fact that he was not yet of age, for he was turning into a bold hero.

King Constantius sent his messengers to the land of Trier and offered the [future] queen devotion and love, as well as an honorable marriage. Helena swore that she would rather die than ever consent to see him again, but the worthy Constantine spoke to his mother: "My dearest lady, please hasten to change your mind about my father, now that he is offering you an honorable marriage. Even if no one else should advise you to do so, I am your only son, and you should accept for my sake. It would be a shameful thing to have the princes refer to me as 'the concubine's son.' All of Rome's dominions serve my father in awe. You, too, milady, are descended from kings and dukes, and such noble birth is ill-suited to being a concubine. You should make every effort to come into your rightful happiness, respected by people all over the world. Bring great honor to your family, and help me establish mine as well. Then I can take much more pleasure in fulfilling my duty."

To this Lady Helen replied, "My son, for the sake of your honor, I will do as you ask since you are indeed my only son. Now send the messengers on their way and have the Romans come to escort me with royal honors. Yes, I will be glad to do as you ask."

---

1.   This probably refers to Constantine's reported introduction of a substantial monetary gift to poor people upon their baptism, which comes up in the next chapter.

When the king heard this message from her, he bade his men hurry with preparations for having the queen shown great honors as she was escorted to the city of Rome. She was given such a magnificent welcome that neither before nor afterwards was any earthly woman received so well at Rome by its men and women

But just when the king had the most to rejoice over, the Book tells us that seven savage usurpers wrought destruction within the Empire. They had been plotting against his honor and his life, and it was not long before they dared to bring him shame through robbing and burning.

The king's thoughts turned very grave, and, when the Romans saw this, all of one accord they pledged to him that they would never relax in fighting for him until all those who rode against him with banners aloft should lose their lives. They were to pay very dearly for their crimes.

The bold Romans then sent scouts to Apulia, where they located two of the tyrants, one named Gallus, the other Sylvanus. The Romans moved in on them stealthily, keeping their forces concealed. One morning when dawn was first breaking they surrounded a mountain, and on this mountain called Gargano both usurpers were killed. How few of those who had come to support them escaped!

When the expeditionary forces returned to Rome, messengers in the imperial service arrived with the startling news that Capua was being besieged. Milius, the count who held the fort there, reminded the Romans of the relief they had promised to send him when he should need it, pointing out that the siege was an act of defiance against the king, and all his men were doing their best as defenders.

The fabled Constantius challenged the Romans, "Hail you heroes so quick to respond! Remember what eagerness for battle our forefathers displayed for us to imitate. We have no choice now but to even the score a bit with our enemies. Either I shall lie dead under my flag, or I shall redeem my honor!" To this the Romans answered that they would never desert the king, but would bring him through the battle with honors. This the heroes swore to, one and all!

Without delay they mounted their banners and rode off with unbridled spirits. Then the mighty king rode to the land around Capua, where he found his enemies. They were besieging that fortified city, but soon the bold Romans charged them from all sides. Then the enemy forces began to weaken. It was time to flee, and many did save their lives. Magnentius could see that nothing was of any use and that he could not survive. Seizing his sword, he himself avenged the injury done the king by plunging the blade through himself. He had a brother, Decentius by name, who hanged himself on an olive tree as soon as he saw what happened to his brother. Duke Veterion [Vetranio] fell at the king's feet, and the Romans let him enjoy their clemency. Constantius pardoned him for his great crime, and he served him ever afterwards. Thus the Romans confirmed their honor.

One of the usurpers named Nepotianus still remained at large and continued to incite violence against the king as long as he was able. When he could hold out no longer, he left the country and sought refuge in a commercial city—Mainz, that city of solid fortifications—which seemed to him to offer the most security. Very quickly news of this reached young Constantine, who did not hesitate but set after him in secret. When he located him in Mainz, he would have preferred to kill him, but the townspeople would not allow this. Then he sent his messengers from land to land, and his friends and relations came to aid him. Owî! What an army that was that besieged Mainz! Time passed slowly for the inhabitants. Hunger pressed them hard until the doomed defenders gave way. The survivors among them had to agree to terms that were limited only by his mercy, in order to restore themselves to his good graces. They turned Nepotainus over to the young king, who led him back to the Roman lands.

That fabled Constantine, however, was afraid that this man might somehow survive if he reached the city of Rome—he had received more than enough good advice at that point—and ordered him thrown into the city moat after his men had cut off his nose and gouged out his eyes to satisfy the youth's wrath.

Constantius held the Empire very solidly in his power, the Book tells us for a fact, exactly seventeen years and five months. Then the Romans buried their ruler.

Constantine I, "the

The fame of Constantine I (r. 312–337) re
as the first emperor—rather than the semi-legendary figure or
Philip—to espouse Christianity. After winning a key battle in 312
with a monotheistic symbol painted on the shields of his soldiers
against a rival for imperial power, he introduced toleration of
Christian and all other monotheistic worship. The shield-painting
episode was recorded by Lactantius—an eyewitness to the event—
in his book, *How the Persecutors Died*. The more familiar story of
Constantine's vision of a cross in the sky was not told until nearly a
quarter-century later. By appointing Christians as his advisers and
allocating imperial funds for Church projects, he made significant
moves toward establishing Christianity as the Roman state religion,
although the final step of making the Empire a Christian one was
not taken until Theodosius did so in the 380s.

Constantine at least furthered the fusion of church and state by
intervening in church controversies at the urging of factional leaders of the Christian faith. He used some military force to suppress
the activities of Donatists in North Africa. Their leader, Donatus,
personified strictness in the faith. He taught, for example, that the
sin of having cooperated with persecutors who had served Diocletian in his "Great Persecution"—particularly in the act of handing
over Christian Scriptures to them—was too grave to permit a former
priest from reassuming his duties. Constantine supported the less
strict, majority faction within the church, who believed that while
such a sin was indeed grave, it could be forgiven through repentance.

Constantine convoked and presided over the Council of Nicaea,
the first Christian ecumenical council held anywhere. He favored
what became the Catholic Trinitarian position against that of the

These were followers of Arius, a priest in Alexandria, who
[re]used to accept the idea of the Trinity, insisting that the use of
"God the Father" and "God the Son" meant that there must have
been a time when there was no God the son, so that that the powers
of Jesus were derivative. Critics of the Arians extended this notion
to accuse them of believing that Jesus was a separate deity.

Emperor Constantine's influence in church affairs obviously
helped to push church and state together. In doing so, it also served
to lessen the essentially negative view of the state often held by early
Christians, who believed that "our kingdom is not of this world."
Both church and state in Constantine's Roman Empire were very
much concerned with things of this world. Constantine and his
supporters attributed his long and successful reign to his support
of Christianity. The association of Christianity with victory and
prosperity became part of the medieval European tradition and remained an important one for centuries to come, particularly the
centuries of the Crusades. The author of the *Book of Emperors* emphasizes this connection repeatedly as his good Christian emperors
win their wars and his bad pagan rulers lose them.

Constantine's mother, Helena, provided the original inspiration
for his interest in Christianity, rather than first playing an adversar-
ial role in the story of Constantine's conversion, as in this chapter.
It is historically correct that she accumulated relics considered very
valuable by the faithful.

The Empire stood without a head, and the brave Romans elected
Saint Helena's son, the worthy Constantine. To be sure, that lord
was still a pagan; however, he was intelligent and level-headed. God made
it happen that he began to fall ill, and his sickness was such a terrible one
that no worldly man could be of any help to him, and the princes began to
withdraw from him.

One wise man, however, came to him and said, "Sire, if you want your
health returned to you, you should do as I tell you. Tell men you trust to
take for me little children two years old or less. I must bathe you in their

blood and that way you will recover your health. If I fail to make you hale and hearty again, have me hanged or stoned."

The king quickly ordered the little children seized and brought before him, but when he saw their mothers' terrible grief he spoke in lordly fashion: "You gave me bad advice. I do not want to order the children killed. I will forego my own life before I will take the lives of so many children. My Lord forbids me to do that. It is better that I, one man, die before I should take responsibility for the death of so many human beings. I have no further use for your medical advice." Those were the words of that worthy lord.

One night the king lay weak and miserable in his bed. When he fell asleep, the noble Peter and Paul, God's holy apostles, appeared to him—Saint Sylvester was pope at that time—and Constantine saw them very clearly. "You have been sick a very long time," Saint Peter said to him kindly, "and you are beset by great troubles. You are looking for good medical advice. Listen now to what I tell you. There is one man here at Rome to whom you should render obedience. His name is Sylvester, and he shall become your spiritual father. Do as he instructs you. Follow that holy lord, and I assure you your afflictions will depart from you. In a very short time your whole body will recover its health."

The king could hardly wait for the morning star to betoken the coming break of day. He sent a messenger, and I will tell you what that man said when he saw the pope. "Milord, for the sake of love and compassion, please come quickly to King Constantine. He is suffering greatly. You dare not delay or you will hardly find him alive."

The pope was quite ready for the occasion and joyfully betook himself to the palace. He was thinking that he was about to die, that he would suffer martyrdom for God's sake. That, however, did not reflect the king's will. Instead he said to the holy man, "Sylvester, my dear man, you dealt very badly with me in concealing from me the fact that you are such a good physician and that you took so long in coming to me to help my body get cured."

The holy pope responded immediately. "Who told you that I was a physician? My Lord in heaven knows that I am no physician. I never practiced earthly medicine down to this very day."

"Those words of yours simply cannot be true," said King Constantine.

"This past night I saw two men, handsome and distinguished-looking, who comforted me by letting me know that if you wanted to bring it about you could restore health to my whole body in a very short time."

The holy man understood very well that this was the result of God's will. He had his chaplain bring out portraits of Saint Peter and Saint Paul. Then he asked the king to take a look and confirm that these were portraits of those same men. "Those are the very same men," said the fabled king, "whom I saw last night. It was as if they were alive again and speaking to me. The one was gray-haired, as he is in the picture; the other was bald. I am sure that I am recognizing them."

The pope fell to his knees in prayer and addressed the king again. "God made that happen because of his love for you. Render yourself obedient to God and follow his teachings. Those are the holy lords who healed your body and released you from your sins. And so, I *am* after all the doctor who tells you God's word. It was God who made this happen because of his love for you. He wants to gain you for his own service."

"All my concerns must be directed toward God, master," said King Constantine. "I have complete trust in you, and I want to make a new beginning. Everything I do shall be according to your will."

Saint Sylvester blessed the font, and what followed became the greatest blessing ever bestowed upon Rome. He spoke words of the faith before Constantine and immersed him three times. The king was completely restored to good health. When he stepped out of the baptismal font all his old skin fell off, and, yes, his new skin was as smooth as a newborn baby's. He was hale and hearty. On the spot he cried out that God in heaven was a true healer. The wolf became a sheep, and the Romans had to abandon their worship of terribly wicked idols that were found throughout the city. Much joy and praise abounded over what had been brought about by the ruling God.

And so the sublime king came to love the true God, making himself obedient to every divine teaching. His works were all praiseworthy, and he went about performing them early and late, whether he was disbursing alms or bringing things about through prayer. He was well disposed to the poor, giving them silver, gold, and much of his fine royal clothing. Pope Saint Sylvester taught him to do all this.

On the second day, just as I am telling you, the pope readied himself with everything he needed for the mass in Saint Peter's cathedral. He sang a mass about the holy wisdom known well to God in heaven, and King Constantine prayed these words:

"Hail to you, reigning God, who saved me from heathendom, I now entrust myself both in body and soul to you, O Lord." His thoughts were simple and pure as he received God's body and his blood.

When the final blessing was said the holy man took the king by the hand, leading him towards his court chamber. There they set down the Imperial Law with the king writing down his edicts just as they can still be seen in writing in Rome—that no one should worship idols but should pray to the one true God who commanded that heaven and earth be made from nothing. He was their true Creator. This made many Romans rejoice.

On the third day, as I will now tell you, they praised the Holy Ghost and prayed that he would support the king in his works according to what Christendom might need. When the final blessing was said, he led the king by the hand. Soon they were sitting in the court chamber, and he decreed that whoever believed in the true God, had himself baptized in the water *in nomine patri et filii et spiritus sancti* [in the name of the Father, the Son, and the Holy Ghost], and was found to be the least bit poor, should be given a love-donation of a hundred shillings by royal command so that he could better maintain himself. I am telling you truly that news of all this reached wondrously many: They believed in the son of the true God and the love of the Holy Ghost, recognizing that they had been deceived for a long time. Yes, many of them took up the praise of God.

Early on the fourth day the pope began the service, and they praised all of God's angels, recognizing the help they supplied when Christendom was in need. His efforts had sweet results. When he finished singing the mass, he took the pope by the hand and led him again to his magnificent throne. That day the king ordered the temples of all false gods destroyed, as Christendom required. Some people failed to do so, since the devil was prompting them not to take revenge [for the deceit they had suffered], but throughout Rome God's teachings spread, and their hearers multiplied.

On the fifth day, the pope began the holy service chanting a mass in honor of the twelve apostles. On the same day it happened that all the pagans, both men and women, were celebrating a great festivity. The king sat upon his seat of judgment, and the pope told him to write as a decree in his name—Constantine Augustus was his title—that whoever worshipped in pagan rites from then on was an enemy of the king and all Romans. He took the pope by the hand and entrusted a great power to him, that however heinous a crime a man might commit and how certain the guilt of a captured man might be, if the pope would only look upon him he could be acquitted. If the pope gave the order, he should be allowed to live. Lord Saint Sylvester secured that privilege.

Early on the sixth day, the pope opened the service by singing a mass in honor of the Holy Cross on which God was martyred. The pope proclaimed the day to be one of fasting and giving alms for strengthening Christianity. The pope provided for his *Curia* (court)—this can still be seen in writing in Rome—and for what pertains to patriarchs and cardinals with all those who are under them, and for how bishops and priests should take care of the people; that is, for all clerical life—what the orders of obedience are and instructions concerning ordinations and tithes; further, that Rome is the head of the clerical order for all those who profess Christianity.

On the seventh day, as I am telling you, the pope addressed the king. "Now, dearly beloved, today we shall worship God and Saint Mary, our dear lady, with pledges of devotion." The fabled king responded that he found this altogether fitting and that he was happy to follow by serving according to God's will.

After the final blessing the two warriors of God hurried to the court chamber, where they completed the Imperial Law. The king provided for his court—this can still be seen in a document in Rome—establishing dukes and counts and all who were under them, as well as for all those who took the name of "knight" and how they should live their lives: how they should buckle on their sword on which they were to display a cross against the wiles of the devil, to direct and protect Christendom. Very many people were to praise his wisdom. He established laws for farmers and merchants, providing that they should be left in peace and that any man who seized their things would become the king's enemy.

When Sunday came, the pope officiated at the service as priest of God. At that time he prepared the king for his duties. He blessed the symbols of his office and set a splendid crown on his head. The whole city of Rome hastened to observe him. The longer they beheld him in his magnificence, the more it pleased them. When the pope consecrated him emperor and he spoke words of faith and repentance, I doubt that ever before had there been so much rejoicing in Rome. The pope went to the Lord's table and then, it is known with certainty, he chanted words of God's resurrection. When he ended the benediction, the emperor ascended a raised place [in the cathedral] and asked for silence.

"Hail to you, Romans," he began. "You seem to understand quite well how God took mercy upon us poor humans and sent his only son to release us from our sins. Before that, deception prompted by the devil led most of us to worship wood and stone. Now for the sake of the true God, show some remorse for what we did and become obedient to the God who created us out of nothing. Our whole lives come about through his grace.

"At his Word, heaven and earth came into being out of nothing. He is rightfully called our Father, and we are called his children. All who obey him will share in his kingdom. Let us now reach out to serve our true Creator. Reject any interest in the filthy deceivers made by the hands of our forefathers. If anybody throws them into a fire and nobody pulls them out they will burn down to powder and ashes. What do you expect to get from them? What human hands can make, human hands can also break. They have eyes that cannot see, ears that cannot hear and noses that cannot smell. They can't tell day from night. At no time can their mouths speak unless the devil is working within them. They have throats without voices. They cannot so much as move their hands or feet—yes, they do have feet, but they have no power to walk. They have neither sight nor thoughts and they remain completely unclean. I ask all of you: recognize the one true God whom Sylvester has preached. Betake yourselves to the holy Christ, who is the foundation of all good things. Show him your love, for he is the beginning and the end."

The people held up their hands and praised Our Lord for his many acts of grace that he had performed for them, according to what we have heard the books tell us. More than seven thousand of them were baptized without delay, not counting women and children. It was all a most praiseworthy turn of events.

When Helena heard about what had happened with her son, and that he had accepted Christianity, she did not hesitate, but immediately ordered a letter written in which she assured her son, the worthy Constantine *semper augusto* [emperor forever] of her motherly love and her wish for his security, success and all royal honors:

"Owî, my dear son, the son I raised to achieve honor as lord of the Romans, you seem beset by evil. Must I live with losing you? Why did you act so as to pervert my own honor? Your father, Constantius, ruled over all of the great noble houses of Rome. No one every heard of him being swayed by such foolishness as yours. What do you want from Christianity? The man the Christians worship met his end long ago outside the city of Jerusalem. Anybody who believes in him stands condemned before [our] god. Do you really imagine that he healed you? Nothing was due to him. You should understand it differently: the return of your health came as a result of the great number of your good deeds. You should return to the worship of our god and serve him faithfully. Dear son, repent the misdeed you have committed, for my heart is sorely distressed with sorrow and pain, and I shall never be happy again so long as you fail to renounce your foolishness."

That was the message she sent the noble lord. Constantine, the rich and powerful, received her message in secret so that no Romans—not even his beloved master—would be aware of what the heathen messengers were hoping to achieve. His response was well thought out, and he sent his messengers to Bithynia, where Queen Helena lived and the messengers found her. In his message, Constantine addressed his mother with filial loyalty, saying that no one in this world deserved such great honor as she did; further that all the might of Rome would stand at her disposal and that whatever her wishes might be the Romans would surely find them fitting.

"Owî! My dear mother! Do not let yourself be sad if I seem to be complaining to you, but no one could ever tell you how great my suffering was until the day came for me when my God had mercy on me. He sent his messengers to me, and I carried out their command. Right away I was cured. I accepted holy Christianity, and now I know the truth well. I have turned to him whom his father sent for the comfort and redemption of all those who desire to place their faith in him. His followers possess the light of day, and nothing can ever go amiss for them. His is the power of all the angels, and he is the light for all the just. The sun shines only as he wills and commands it. There are so many manifestations of his grace that human tongues cannot tell of all of them, nor human ears hear them, nor human hearts contemplate them. Receive the love that Our Lord now offers to you and go where he summons us to go. I promise you that [if you will do this,] I will do whatever you ask me."

How sad Helena's heart became when she read his letter, and she ordered a letter written in reply, warning Constantine that if he would not renounce his foolishness quickly she would stir up the whole city of Rome and all the dominions of the Roman Empire against him, after which he would have to eke out a meager and shameful existence.

That good Constantine could no longer keep news of all this to himself. He sent a message about it to his master, good Saint Sylvester. When the holy man received the news, he replied to Constantine, *"Te deum laudamus* [We offer praise to you, Lord God], you who promised all your followers who would rely on you forever and would choose to suffer being made outlaws in your name that they most certainly would dwell in your kingdom.

The pope spoke thus to the messenger: "Tell King Constantine that he may well rejoice, for Our Lord himself has chosen to honor his own name through him so that the Christian ranks will be multiplied. Let us convoke a council, to which we will ask the old and wise to come, those who are leaders among Jews and heathen. To counter their words we will direct those children of God in holy orders to come and speak so that everyone can hear both sides, and rely upon Our Lord's power to make clear who has prevailed over the other, so that with no delay the hearts of those who have opposed us will be won over to the teachings of the Holy Ghost. Let the queen then hold her court, but in a way that God in heaven will direct her."

This advice seemed good to the king and his deep melancholy began to slip away. He ordered some of his vassals to be summoned and sent the queen offers of service and love, everything that a son should be ready to give his mother. He asked that she let her anger subside and agree to holding a synod or council, letting the wise scribes among the heathens and those who oversaw the keeping of the Covenant among the Jews come together, so that when everyone had heard all the arguments God in his might would reveal who among the disputants was right.

When the queen received the message she called for her wisest vassals to come and attend her. With grim determination they consulted with each other for three days. The queen insisted that she would hold a council that would trap the Christians. She was firmly convinced that the Roman Christians would not come to the council without losing their lives. As soon as the pope had been overcome in the debate they would all be beheaded.

Then the queen said this to the messengers: "Tell Constantine now that my heart is very heavy because he has followed his old deceiver so far. I will be glad to attend in person such a council as he proposes to see for myself how it came about that my son became a Christian. If no powers of darkness come to Sylvester's aid and he is overcome, he must die a shameful death right there on the spot, and I will lay waste all the lands of the Roman Empire."

The queen made haste to order letters written to the Jews and to the heathens. She ordered that all those who pursued wisdom among them should come quickly to her court and all those who were entitled to bear the sword should assemble against Christendom. If it were in her power, she would see to it that Christianity was totally destroyed. Her message flew quickly to all pagan people, who were glad to hear such news. Yes, all the pagan peoples rejoiced.

The pope was not letting any distraction keep him from working early and late in the service of Christianity. His labors were very strenuous in sending messengers from land to land to summon all the great scholars, old and young, to come to the great council for the sake of the true God's honor and to advance the Christian cause.

The emperor issued a general decree throughout all his dominions that whoever was entitled to wield the sword should come to the aid of Christendom. He forbade women and children, as well as those who were very old, from coming to the conflict, instructing them to remain at home. No man need come to join the emperor's army unless he was quite sound of body and a man of sufficient means to provide enough food and arms for himself.

For his part the pope commanded the entire clerical order near and far, admonishing them for the sake of Our Lord to do penance by setting out on this mission. Their travel would be blessed and lead to joy, and, in fact, their march was soon carried out. Man for man, they all hastened to join, each taking up a red cross and carrying it before him. With hearts and mouths they offered praise and sang, praying to Our Lord that he might be merciful to them, that he would guide them and look after them on their march.

The Christians marched joyfully through French and Italian territory, advancing to the seashore, and their crusade was glorious to behold. The emperor inspected the armed forces, looking carefully at their weaponry. When he was satisfied with them he spoke joyfully. "Lord Christ, be honored and praised, for you are more than worthy of having so many Christian men assemble in your name!" He made God mindful of the need for preventing the mighty heathen armies from doing harm to them, saying, "We have sufficient armed forces ready so that—if the God of Christianity approves—should the heathens try anything with us they will not be able to make a shameful escape. If all the heathen peoples of the world attack us we shall not be found wanting in the defense of Christianity."

Lady Helena wanted to look over her armed forces that filled hill and valley. The air was laden with the sounds of warlike preparations. They were arrogant and over-confident, which is always the way with unbelievers. At that moment they are recorded to have had three hundred and thirty-six thousand men under arms. They intended to have their way throughout the lands of Rome with plundering and burning.

Constantine the Good sent messengers to his mother. For the sake of her own honor she should choose five hundred mature men who could distinguish themselves in knowing and observing the rules of a synod; they should come peacefully to the city. Urgently he pled with his mother to make sure of this, since riff-raff would be totally incapable of carrying on a debate, and it would not be possible to hold a council with them.

The queen responded that she would be very glad to do as her son requested.

The council was set to be held at Durazzo. The ruler of Rome went there as did his teacher, good Saint Sylvester. Patriarchs and cardinals came; in fact, we hear the books tell us, eleven hundred crooked staves made their way to that city. The Christians counted a hundred —I am telling you this just as it was—and thirty-three thousand of their fighting men. The queen declared her ban against a man of any description who would start any sort of fight in the synod—he would have his head cut off.

Very early the next morning the pope prepared patriarchs, cardinals and all who had come there with him for what was coming. He sang a mass about the Holy Ghost, fully aware of the enmity of the queen. He asked God the good to let her have a change of heart and to send him the Holy Ghost bringing him words for the debate which would be worthy of his name.

The queen sat holding court, and, as the book tells us, the king led the pope there with a magnificent host of many men of the spiritual calling, worthy of the service of God in heaven, following him. The queen opened the council with these words: "All those who are pledged to take part in this council, please listen, for I will tell you something you should know. I felt a strong personal need to agree to this synod and convoke it because I have lost my son. I have come here to learn well for myself just what happened to make him desert his own Covenant; in having done so, he seems to have desired to sully my honor totally. If it should turn out to be Sylvester's advice that made him lapse into this betrayal and become a Christian, I do not expect to put up with what he has done any longer. I shall confront him with his wrongdoing and insist that he do me justice for the suffering he has caused me."

The most holy pope gave her this answer: "Milady, your son has not been taken from you, but rather he is fulfilling himself now for the first time, since he recognizes the true light. I will not lie to you about him. It was my will that persuaded him to change, and I have great things in store for him and for you as well. Receive the gift of the Holy Spirit, and believe in the Christ who suffered martyrdom for your sake. If you will get wet in the baptismal font for his sake—I am telling you the truth about this—he will reward you with his kingdom, putting you in such a state of ecstasy that no human tongue would ever be able to describe it for you and one which will never subside. Milady, heed my advice: believe in the one true God who formed you out of nothing. Of what use are 'gods' made of silver and gold? They are all unclean spirits, and whoever follows them with the most devotion they reward with the pains of hell forever welling up around them. Give honor to the God who created you!"

The queen commanded her wise debaters to answer what the holy man had said, and with that the council began.

Quickly the queen selected twelve of the very best scholars among Jews and heathens who were confident of being able to overcome the stalwarts of the true God in debate. An oath was taken to allow only two philosophers the right to preside over the synod with its opposing speakers. Any man who had come there and spoke out of turn would be sacrificing his neck. Crato and Zenophilus—that is what the Book tells us their names were—were the judges at the synod, and they could analyze and explain arguments coming from both sides. Neither love nor hate influenced their decisions, which were made strictly on the basis of what they saw and heard. When it would happen that a man misspoke or was refuted, they would judge him fairly on the spot and announce jointly that he should not have any more hearers; in that way the judges would dismiss him from the synod.

The *archsynagogus* [synagogue ruler] named Abiathar stood up and began the debate with these words: "Sylvester, are the words true? See how it is written here—you can read it yourself now in the Book of the Covenant—what God out of his very own mouth proclaimed to Moses: 'Let Israel hold me in honor, for I am one God and one Lord, a true God, and if you obey my commandments, I will give you my kingdom.' You are contradicting that here, Sylvester. If you insist on having three gods, anyone who affirms that teaching is breaking the Covenant and God's commandment, dooming himself to eternal death. As you also may very well read for yourself, he shall not survive God's final judgment."

The mighty pope stood up, stately and dignified with his handsome face—he really benefited Christendom—and spoke. "You are a well educated man. Why do you refuse to understand the books correctly? When the hand of the true God released you Jews from slavery and dread in the land of Egypt, he wrought many miracles for your sake. He gave you everything you needed, so that you wanted for nothing, but then you poured an evil deception over what He had given you and prayed to an idol in the form of a calf. You forgot Our Lord quickly enough. That angered God greatly until the holy lord, Moses, prayed to God with great sincerity, mindful of having received the Covenant from him, and this assuaged God's great wrath. Because they had great need of correction, God warned the faithless people who had been so dear to him before. That is the reason he said, 'Israel, hold me in honor, for I am one God and one Lord. I alone am one true God.' God's name is distinguished, as he is called Father, he is called Son, and he is called the Holy Ghost. Because of our weakness he took flesh and bone upon himself, but the three names refer to one true God. He who refuses to believe this—that there is one God alone with three names—will be interred forever with the devil in hell."

"Sylvester," said Abiathar, "I will tell you with certainty that we had lordly men among us who successfully pursued truth and wisdom. From God they had the power to awaken the dead. Fire from heaven burnt up their enemies. When they asked that they might go to the depths of the sea, they went there without delay. When they were determined to rise to the hights of heaven, nothing stood in their way. They bade the sun to keep shining over forty-seven hours without moving from one spot. No one has ever heard of any Christian causing wonders like this; certainly no one could ever prove it."

"I will tell you truly," said the holy man, "about one of your princes by the name of Jairus, who was *archsynagogus* of the Jews, just like you are today. According to what is sung and read today Our Lord commanded his daughter to arise from the dead in the middle of Jerusalem. He returned her to her father, after which she lived many a year and day."

"Sylvester, you are telling me a story," said the Hebrew man, "on a level with something seen in a dream. Can you support what you are saying from the books?"

"Let the book be brought out," said the holy man, "written by the worthy Josephus, your own historian, and I will agree to lose my life if I cannot show you where he records this."

This made the queen furious, but she directed that the book should be brought out. When the book was opened, Sylvester proved his point immediately. That angered the queen even more, but it made Christendom rejoice.

"Abiathar, now listen to something else," said the wonderful pope. "Our Lord journeyed to Naim, and his disciples followed him. A dead man was carried towards him, and a crowd of people stood by. Moved by the grief of the man's mother, he revealed his grace and beneath the city-gate arch he restored him living to his mother."

A third time he showed him what was written: "Our Lord bade Lazarus from Bethania to arise from the dead before the fortress of Jerusalem on the forth day after he was buried. The whole city of Jerusalem could testify to this, and I will show you still something else which is written: Kaiphas, your bishop, at one point was enflamed by the Holy Spirit, and although he had no desire to be obedient to God he nonetheless prophesied through him, saying, 'It is better that one should die than that the whole world should be lost.'"

"If he told the dead to rise," responded the Hebrew man, "that meant he could prove what a great physician he was, but that is no reason to proclaim him a god or even a true prophet. In Israel we have *one* God, and I do not want to hear about any more gods. If you want to speak about the God, I am prepared to answer what you say."

"If you want to discuss the one God, I do not intend to bring in any other god than the One of Israel, who ordained that Saul should lie dead and his son Jonathan be slain and whose power made this happen," said the holy man. "Is what I have said true?"

"I will not deny it," said Abiathar.

"Then you undoubtedly have heard of Dathan and Abyron. They took the field against God with great forces, but the earth opened her mouth and swallowed them in no time. Is it true what I am saying?"

"I will not deny it," said Abiathar.

"Then look and see what is written about your great evildoer, Korep, and how he met such a miserable end with many thousand men."

"But now you are presenting two gods," said the Hebrew man, "one who ordained among us that King Saul should lie dead and the other among the Christians in Jerusalem, who told that dead man of yours to arise. Now look where this discussion is leading us: today we have three gods. Yes, look where this debate is ending up."

"Sylvester has not named any more gods than the one in Israel," said Crato, the synod judge. Abiathar was forced to withdraw, at which the mighty Constantine rejoiced.

Up stood Jonas, who had been an archbishop, and said, "Sylvester, we just heard from your own mouth that one god came down from heaven, and here on earth he was martyred and died like any other human being, but that he is also a true god in heaven. Tell me now: How did the Son suffer death then? Were the Father and the Holy Ghost not around at the time? I will tell you the truth about this: if they were of the same substance and glory in heaven, it would have been impossible for the godhead to separate as you say." He made his point only briefly.

The holy pope, Saint Sylvester, quickly answered him. "Since you have read the prophets it surprises me that you do not understand how through weakness and sin mankind was left in dire straits. God the Father of heaven and earth created the angels with powers stronger than those men were to receive for his own praise and honor, that they might sing his praises day and night. The lordliest angel among them—his name signifies "vessel of light"—had to fall because of his pride, as did all his followers, who also made themselves guilty of boundless pride. They inhabit hell with him in wretchedness and fury. Because of their weakness the angels lost their bliss. Isn't this in the Scriptures of the Jews?"

"I will not deny that what you say here is true," said Jonas, "for we must believe the Scriptures."

"Then listen some more," said the marvelous pope. "To fulfill his plan he created man in his image as part of his handiwork, which made the [fallen] angel wild with anger. Since then he has been condemned to occupy his throne in the fiery heat of hell forever, which he greatly regretted. His envy led him to wage war against mankind. With great cunning he enticed the first man into violating God's command, so that he was condemned to die and go to hell along with all his kin forever, but Our Lord from heaven later had mercy on mankind. Can you tell me how God redeemed mankind?"

That angered Jonas, who asked him, "Sylvester, why are you doing this? Do you imagine that this synod assembled, in order to have you read Genesis to it? You cannot tell me yourself why you held that long speech."

"Since you cannot tell me why, I will explain the matter to you," answered the lordly pope, "so that you will come to the end of your debate with me. Neither man nor angel could do anything useful in overcoming human weakness, and so God sent his Son. He took the part of humankind on this earth, and with his martyrdom he redeemed man from his weakness and brought him back to the throne that had been his before. As Our Lord the Savior, he took up his divine power again, equal to that of the Father and the Holy Ghost. That is the reason that the three names signify one God. Anyone who recognizes things as they really are and has sufficient faith will possess the bliss that never fades."

"Well, now," said Jonas. "As long as he was such a god that he could win back a man from hell, was it really his will that he let himself be given a terrible fate, his hands tied, his skin flayed with whipping--the same sort of shameful torture a thief undergoes—and finally subjected to a slow death upon a cross? Who is supposed to believe in your god? Or who will so much as say that he is a god at all?"

"I will prove that to you from the prophets," said Saint Sylvester, that holy man. "If I confront you with their books, you will find that I have made my point beyond any doubt, since I am confirming what I have said through your own prophets. Tell me now if you have anything against my doing so."

"If you find it," said the Hebrew man, "said by any prophet on this earth who foretold us of things to come that God should die—yes, if you find it in his book, then I will have to yield to you."

Saint Sylvester, the holy man, then called for Jeremiah to be brought out. On the very same page where the book was opened, he pointed out to Jonas, *"sicut ovis ad occisionem ducetur* [thus a sheep is led to the slaughter]." He directed that this passage be shown to everyone, and, speaking to all of them with the same humility, had the words that gain eternal life for us translated into their languages: the One who gives us life will be handed over to death, just like an unblemished lamb who has not done so much as open its mouth. Since they saw it written in the books—and from this confirmation were convinced that Jonas was in error—the judges told Jonas to depart, at which many a Christian rejoiced.

Up stood Godolias, at that time a noble prince, and spoke to the worthy man. "Sylvester, is it your teaching that a woman was a virgin and yet bore a child, and that we should consider this same man to be a god? Are you attempting to prove that by citing the prophets? I would like to get to the end of this talk."

"Now listen closely to my teaching and answer me with the words God will direct you to speak," said the worthy pope.

"Our Lord the Savior was sent by his Father to comfort us. He arrived from heaven upon this earth and was born of a virgin who recovered from childbirth as a virgin, remained a virgin after giving birth, and remains a virgin eternally. Her son, the holy Christ, saved us through his martyrdom. Now we are blessed and cleansed of the sin of old Adam's fall—we are all summoned to eternal life. You may now contradict what I have said if you wish to do so, or say whatever you are able to say."

Godolias raised his hand high and said, "Listen well, all you gentlemen of the synod. Sylvester says he wants to prove that a virgin bore a child and that we should worship as a god the child that virgin bore—he is supposed to be the redeemer. Then listen also to what I maintain today. Whether a maiden or a woman bore him, that was his beginning and he did not exist before that time. [If he existed before that time] he must have had a[nother] beginning. On the other hand, I can tell you about his end upon a cross. Now tell me, all of you scholars, how does this 'god' strike you?"

The pope displayed wisdom in answering him. "Those words will prove very useful today, and I will be glad to use them to reach a conclusion, which I will prove to be true on the basis of what your prophets say. Let the two of us together search in your books and see if we do not agree that I have not been lying about anything at all, that I have proven my words to be true, and that this should be enough on this topic for the synod. Why should I be worried about your accusations?"

Sylvester's words daring to rely on the Hebrew prophets made the Jew furious, and he addressed the judges. "You gentlemen should not allow that kind of talk. Sylvester is guilty of blasphemy as he stands here before the Empire and asserts that a virgin bore a child whom we should worship as a god. You should ask him how he intends to prove the existence of this god as you prepare to render judgment on this matter."

The judge, Zenophilus, gave him this answer: "My friend, I am really surprised at what you are saying. It would seem that every time you Jews speak you lose an argument. Do you really think that we should dismiss Sylvester in violation of the rules agreed to and before considering evidence for a decision simply because he is using the prophets to substantiate his points? If he succeeds in showing that something is written in your books that shows his assertions to be correct, then he is dealing fairly with you. Many a good knight here has heard and can confirm—and I heard the synod agree—that our rules permit the introduction of evidence from the prophets. It was you Jews who insisted on that stipulation. Apart from that, it is the better course of wisdom to allow evidence to be presented fully from all sides." The Jews and heathens agreed then to treat evidence from the prophets as admissible.

Saint Sylvester, the holy man, called for the book to be brought out. Isaiah was brought out, and in it they found written that the marvelous prophet foretold of God: "A virgin shall bring forth a son; the angels from heaven will proclaim his name, and the child shall be called Jesus Emmanuel, 'God with us.' He is a most wonderful God, there has never been the equal of his powers, and he is a prince of peace. With his coming no one need fear any harm. All God's creatures make way for him, and none can resist his might." The judges ordered that a true and faithful interpretation be made of these words, and when the truth was revealed how joyful the Christians were!

But then the holy man went on to have the books of Moses brought out, to show what that prophet had foretold of him. There they found written: "God will choose a prophet for himself, and from his seat in heaven he will send him to the nations. Be mindful of everything he will teach you, and be fully obedient to him until you have received my commandments from him."

Once again the holy man called for a book and had Habakkuk brought out. Quickly the wisest men at the synod located and read, "The One whom the angels with all their power day and night praise and call by name will be recognized as the holy child when he is found between two beasts, a donkey and a cow, who are looking at him in his crib." That passage was the third Sylvester offered for evidence, and the judges announced that now the evidence was sufficient; no more would be needed. The lordly Constantine rejoiced to hear this.

Doech then came up and began to present his argument. "Sylvester, you let us hear much idle talk here before the Empire. You were saying that God came down to earth where human eyes saw him, but we will show you how it is written: 'Moses was the dearest of all men in the sight of God. He asked Our Lord many times that he be allowed to see the very face of the godhead; however, God would not grant his wish, nor have eyes of the flesh in this world ever been allowed to see the face of God.' Now you are saying that even sinners in this world saw him, and that they sat, stood, ate, and drank with him. That is blasphemous talk. Sinners could surely never have such contact with God."

"'*Dixit dominus domino meo* [the Lord said to my Lord],'" the pope answered him. "Now bring out the Psalms. There you will find it written, '*sede a dextris* [seated at the right hand].' These words were spoken by David, your prophet, and were fulfilled at the time when God's Son journeyed from heaven to earth. Here the human nature he took upon himself concealed his sublime divinity until he died for the sake of man, having brought his divine message to earth. Then he journeyed back again to sit at the right hand of his Father, equal to him in power and possessions. I will explain this to you with an analogy:

"Regard now the sun, from which we have warmth and blessings as it shines pure and bright over all the earth without ever moving from its fixed position. The sun is nothing but a creation of God. The Creator has indeed the greater power that, when he chose to become human for the sake of mankind, he appeared here in human form, but that provides no grounds for lessening his divinity. He is so pure and perfect that he never could be separated from his divinity. Nothing is impossible for God." The Jew felt weak and turned around; he departed without taking leave, at which many a Christian man rejoiced.

Aunan then stood up and spoke to the holy man. "Sylvester, whether you love it or hate it, today I shall demonstrate the truth of my words."

A smile began to creep over the face of the holy man, and he said, "I certainly would not mind if you would substantiate the truth, for truth is dear to God. I will not contradict the truth since Our Lord Jesus Christ is both the way and the truth, and all those devoted to him gladly follow the truth."

The Jew wanted to get the best of him with cunning and said, "You said with some assurance that Christ's mother was a virgin when she bore him, and then you went on to say that she remained eternally a virgin."

"I intend to bear witness to the truth and defend it," said the holy man.

"One thing you said may well be true: that Mary was a virgin," Aunan went on, "but that she was supposed to remain a virgin after she recovered from the birth of her first son—I can show that statement of yours to be false."

God's pious messenger gave Aunan a fitting response. "If you have the ability to prove your words so that I can find nothing with which to contradict them, go ahead then, and let the outcome for both of us be according to God's will."

"I will show you," Aunan continued, "and reveal to this whole synod how you have exaggerated your claims by pointing out how it is written in your own books that after recovering from the birth of her first son—how could I prove this to you any better?—Maria knew her husband, Joseph, by whom she bore Jacobus (James), the brother of your god, and other sons and daughters. In doing so, I will prove the truth of my words. Let me hear you confirm now that she is always supposed to have remained a virgin!"

The pope answered him: "You are prematurely claiming that you have bested me by presenting the truth. Soon you will be leaving the debate, having gotten the worst of it, since you will not be able to demonstrate truth on your side; however, if you insist on sticking with your assertions then show us the exact source. You are standing here before the Empire—speak up so all can hear, naming your source or telling us what book contains what you are claiming to be true."

"Suppose I can produce a good witness whose testimony you could never reject," Aunun the Jew continued, "and he affirms that that what I have said is true?"

"This council was convoked," said the holy man, "with the understanding that questions in the debates should be answered by the lordly prophets or what is found in approved books."

"How could anyone bring out all those books?" asked Aunan. "The question should well be decided by what I confirm authoritative people to have said."

"These rules under which this synod is convoked," said Crato the judge, "prohibit the introduction of statements that cannot be substantiated in approved sources."

This made Aunan the Jew furious. He uttered strong words of denunciation, waved his arms, shook his head wildly and acted like a man set on fire until the judges rebuked him.

"My dear man," said Saint Sylvester, the holy man, "why will you not believe the prophets? They have indeed written it down for you, so you can see that I am not making it up. The prophets predicted and made known the truth of what I have said. You might as well stop making your claims."

"I never read in any of the prophets," said the Jew Aunan, "any statement confirming that she remained a virgin ever afterwards."

"Then let me offer testimony from the book," said the holy man. "Ezechiel, who was a prophet of the Jews, wrote that for us." He called for that book to be brought out, and he showed him where it was written: "Queen of heaven, emblem of virginity, you are chaste and pure, you have never thought of knowing any man. Your gates are sealed shut by the Word of God, you are the source of all springs, and you carried God's son as a virgin. You were still a virgin after his birth. He was conceived in you by the Holy

Ghost, and you will remain a virgin forever." After that the Jew was compelled to withdraw.

There was a bishop in attendance named Kusi who went up to the great man and with his words stirred up confusion and conflict. "Sylvester, even though we have it in writing, I would like to hear it from you. Lucifer and all his followers have fallen."

"What you say is true," said the pope.

"Our father, Adam," the Hebrew man continued, "fell because of disobedience and went down into hell with all his descendants."

"What you say is true," said the pope.

"Well, now, if those things are true," the Jew Kusi went on, "and humans had to remain in hell until your god came to earth and wanted to die for the sake of mankind, so that he brought people back to their original state, what sort of thing must that angel have done to keep your god from ever redeeming him back? Is he supposed to burn in hell forever? Is perhaps some time set for him to be allowed to return? In that case your god should die once again, this time martyred in space above the earth, so that old Lucifer may return with all those who fell because of him and take up his old power again; that is, if your god were fair in his judging."

"Kusi, can you tell me what God does in heaven?" asked Saint Sylvester, the holy man. "What things make up his activity there?"

"In pursuing my study to be a master, I learned that he judges the measure of all things and people," said the Hebrew man. "He holds the scales of judgment and assures that everything is in proportion, diminishing what proud and arrogant people have and adding to the lot of the downtrodden, so that they no longer need seek to assuage their needs. He summons the humble to their ordained inheritance, and they will possess his kingdom. That is what God does in heaven every day."

"Let the two of us pursue your statements further," said Saint Sylvester, the holy man.

Meanwhile Kusi was turning things over in his mind, and he said, "Let me go from the debate. I am telling you, Sylvester, an apprentice asks his master many things, but I have done all the asking I want to do, and would like to take leave from the debate."

"I will tell you with certainty," said the holy man, "that if you really were under my teaching authority, I would have severe words for you; however, since you are not, may Holy Christ know, he who has given me the world, how unwillingly I would stop here without answering you before the Empire. Your talk sounds most discourteous.

"There have never been any more angels than the ones created at the beginning," the worthy pope continued. "Part of them joined in rebellion; however, God gave his kingdom to those who displayed a fitting humility and remained loyal to him. He showed them such honor that they were never moved to fall away at any later time. The one who led the rebellion had said he wanted become God's equal. You learned yourself that no one can approach God with arrogant pride, and places in hell are prepared for all those who follow that path, where they shall burn forever without ever being able to regain God's mercy. Even today they oppose God, rejecting Him with mockery, contempt, arrogance and perjury. Following the devil's lead, they employ their cunning against all things that come from God, hoping to weaken all good souls and make them fall into eternal perdition.

"At the devil's prompting, Adam and Eve fell into a great misdeed. For his disobedience in taking the forbidden apple Adam was condemned to hell after death with all of his descendants forevermore. Our Lord in heaven then had mercy upon mortals in hell: through the lordly prophets he made it known beyond any sort of doubt that he intended to be martyred himself on this earth for the sake of mankind in defiance of the devil. His martyrdom freed us if we are willing to be loyal to God, our Creator."

The judges announced that Sylvester had sufficiently explained and proven the points he was making in the debate, and everyone there agreed.

Kusi departed then and Didascali stood up and took his place, beginning his remarks with a description of Lord Abraham, saying that he was the very first man to be completely obedient to God. All people descended from Adam and Eve, men and women alike, had been ordained to be dishonored and lost until the time of Lord Abraham.

"I will give you evidence which puts that matter in a better light," said the pope, pure of heart. "You must have read of Abel. He is a worthy martyr who was killed by his brother because of jealousy. For the sake of what was good and right that gentleman lost his life. His offering was pure and clean, and for that reason his soul is well blessed before God. Regard now what is written about our father, Noah, whose memory is surely hallowed since God himself chose to save him from the great flood. Finally, I may point to Enoch whose soul remained in the shadow of God's might as proof that the righteous were saved even back then. You should have thought your words through better."

"You should also understand my speech better," said the Hebrew man. "First of all, I began speaking of Abraham. He was the very first man to render God complete obedience when, following God's command, he instituted the custom of circumcision. Isaac and Jacob all held to that commandment. Moses, that holy messenger, told us all to be circumcised for God's sake. Besides, I can tell you that your Lord Jesus was circumcised according to Hebrew custom. Anyone who avoids being circumcised according to the Covenant shall not be among those saved by God, as you can read for yourself, and if you make a decision to avoid carrying out God's command the result will be that you are cast out of the community of the faithful. You will have no share in God's blessing. There is no hope for you if you die in a state of such great sin."

"You should also understand my speech better," said the holy man. "Abraham was certainly just and good. Chastity was no doubt among his virtues, and he carried out the custom according to which people circumcised themselves in the flesh. From that beginning the custom spread from man to man, including all the prophets—Moses and Isaiah, David and Jeremiah, as well as good Daniel, and many other worthy prophets all knew the terms of the Covenant and how it was put into practice until God's Son came to earth. He was born to a virgin to bring us consolation. He is whiter than snow, and he brought us a new Covenant after being born under the old one. I will tell you how it really was: He was circumcised according to Hebrew custom, but then the time came when he no longer wished to hide who he was and chose to reveal his divine powers according to the purpose that God the Father had in sending him here. That brought about the end of the old Covenant. There came to us the *sanctus sanctorum* [the holy of holies] to your own ancestors in Israel and gathered together for all eternity those who became Christians and who were then called the children of God. Consequently, those loyal to him should follow him in the marvelous sacrament of baptism. He who has complete faith shall possess the bliss that will never fade."

"Do we really want to enter into a new Covenant?" asked the Hebrew man. "Are we supposed to abandon the one with which our ancestors gained God's kingdom—that is the sublime custom of circumcision through which both old and young who came before us were saved?"

"Didascali, can you tell me," the Pope began to ask him, "was circumcision introduced before [the coming birth of] Isaac was made known to Abraham, or was it begun after that?"

"Circumcision was introduced after that . . ." the Jew started to answer him.

"If circumcision was introduced after that," said the holy man, "it follows then that Abraham was beloved of God before that, too, something that could not have come from circumcision. The wise men and prophets, including Enoch and Noah, came long before Abraham. See in Scripture if any of them observed that practice. They were all beloved of God, although they knew nothing about circumcision. I will show you where it is written: '*circumcidite corda* [circumcise your hearts]' to rid yourselves of mortal sin, to show good will toward God, and to love him with all your hearts and all your minds. Circumcision of the flesh is worthless unless it is also done in the spirit. Man should approach God with purity of heart."

The synod participants all agreed with him, saying that they had never heard tell of any worldly man whom God had inspired with such a speech and that God himself was surely with him.

Up stood Aroel and began a long speech. "Sylvester, did I understand correctly? Did God come down from heaven to earth?"

"It is as you say," answered the pope.

"Please tell me more then," said the Hebrew man. "Did he suffer martyrdom because mankind had been lost?"

"It is as you say," answered the pope.

"Please tell me the whole story then," said the Hebrew man. "Did he redeem from hell everyone in all the five worlds?"

"All who honored his name, believed in him, and had praised him while they lived."

"Well then," said the Jew, "we can be happy, for paradise is open to all of us. Now we may be confident of going there. No one has any more reason to worry or to go to any great trouble about his soul. Let it be known beyond any doubt that we will be conducted to paradise without any strain on our part."

"It is my opinion," said the holy man, "that we should be discussing useful things, but now I have become aware that you understand how to use God's word the same way an adder uses the cover of grass to crawl towards a man and bite him. You should keep God before your eyes. He gave you five senses, but commands you to be guided by your spirit, obeying the Ten Commandments that Our Lord gave us through Moses, as you have read yourself in Scripture. No man can be saved without doing so."

"I am quite familiar with the Ten Commandments," said the Jew. "You are referring me to what is in the Old Covenant, but now can you tell me on the basis of your New Covenant what your god gained with his martyrdom? If people are still condemned to go to hell, what made him submit to being nailed to his cross and suffer all those torments? Tell me now how you like your god [as] you cannot point out any comfort or salvation coming from him." With those words the Jew wanted to conclude his part of the debate.

"You should follow your arguments to their destination," said the holy man. "I will explain what you have been citing and reveal solid reasons for comfort from it. The five worlds had to pay dearly for Adam's disobedience in being condemned to hell. No one, good or evil, could escape condemnation but had to suffer punishment until the fullness of time when the blessed hostage arrived. He released the righteous ones, leaving the evil ones to burn in hell, for they would not put their trust in him. He made the devil an outlaw and barred the gates of hell. He opened paradise to those who wanted to serve him and would be obedient to him, but those who oppose him are called children of the devil, and he rewards their sin with sulfur and pitch. My Lord himself rewards the good and the just who rejoice ever more with him. That is what his wonderful martyrdom gained for us poor mortals. You were about to leave this debate prematurely."

Benjamin arose and began his speech. "Sylvester, do you support the institution of lawful marriage that Moses commanded that we uphold? Or do you want to destroy it? We would like to hear your answer."

"Surely lawful marriage should endure," said the holy man, "as God has ordained that man and wife shall be as one flesh, conceive and bear children without sinning, and both fear and love God. If they do that their marriage will be stable, hallowed, and eternal."

"Milord, how is that possible?" asked the Jew. "If lawful marriage is good and just, how did it happen that one chosen maiden bore a child into this world? Further, how was it that God did not want his son to have a lawfully married father and mother? Please explain this matter clearly to me."

"I am very glad to clear that up for you," said the worthy pope. "All the prophets foretold that Our Lady would be both virgin and mother, that her gates would nevermore be opened. Your prophet Ezechiel foresaw them remaining shut. Moses saw smoke rising while the fire beneath it was not consuming anything. It is also true that our father Adam was born from the virgin earth. In that fashion the Lord of the New Covenant chose to be born of a virgin that our sins might be expunged in the way the prophets all foretold a virgin birth."

"Are you really trying to prove with that comparison that Adam was born of a virgin? Your talk is more like a lie than anything else, and a peculiar one at that," said Benjamin.

"I intend to derive from it the proof of a great truth," said the holy man. "The earth was as pure as a virgin, never having taken any dead bodies to herself or having been stained with any human blood, until Cain murdered his brother, whose blood ran from his body onto the earth and took away the earth's virginity. That was the first instance of human death, and all mankind was forced to go to hell until the Virgin brought forth the One who redeemed us from that bondage. Do you want proof of that from the books?" At that the Jew departed without taking leave.

Then a Jew named Thara stepped up before the assemblage and said: "You were born among the heathens, and no one has ever heard of any prophet sent to them. The Covenant was given to us: should we now live in the fashion of heathens who were never given any Covenant and act like the

Scriptures have lost their validity? You want to discredit our Covenant for us, and we will certainly get even with you for doing that. You choose not to observe the chosen day of Saturday as one of rest, nor do you observe the other laws, nor to you really want to let us answer your questions."

"Our Lord was not sent from heaven except for the sake of sinners," God's warrior answered him, "and so that we might fulfill the law according to God's will where it had been abandoned. Job was a heathen, but how dare you condemn him, for he was very dear to God, and we should count him among the just? There was a king long ago named Nabuchodonosor during whose reign three children of God were cast into a fiery furnace. Our Lord himself came to help them, and when the king beheld the work of Our Lord, he converted to his service in good faith. Sybil and Balaam were also prophets, and there were plenty of others whom you Jews did not wish to recognize. Our Covenant is a one of the true spirit, and before God it will last forever. Your Covenant has been badly broken, and you spoke too fast in belittling our birth. It is not a matter of your being required to answer to us. You have run away from God. We have won God's favor, and God has healed us. You refuse to convert, and so you are condemned before God. It was on a Sunday that the coming of our good Lord was announced to his mother; on a Sunday Our Lord, from whom all salvation comes, was born; on a Sunday he rose from his grave; and on a Sunday he sent the Holy Spirit to us. We prefer to worship on Sunday, to rest and to honor that day for the sake of Our Lord. I will tell you truly, Thara, Sunday is the true octave of the week, and signifies that we should commit ourselves to believing that righteous souls shall settle in the Kingdom of Heaven for evermore."

Jubal was the next to step before the assemblage, and he began his speech by asking, "Could he be a true God? How did it happen that he was so poor and lay naked in his crib? Was he not rich and powerful? Did he not enter the world with a display of power? Did he not attract kings to come to him? Did he not perform many miracles? That was so that people might understand really divine things and the world might trust him all the better—was it not?"

"I will tell you great things that attest to his divinity," said the holy man. "When Our Lord was born into this world a great host of angels came down from heaven, rejoicing at what was happening. The angels brought tidings to shepherds, who found him lying in his crib. Three mighty kings brought him gifts from afar—myrrh, frankincense, and gold—evidence of the great honor they were showing him. It all signified that he was king of kings. He received the very poorest unto himself, proving that he will turn no one down who wants to follow him because of wealth or poverty. He treats them all as equal to one another. Later the noble king would ride a donkey into Jerusalem. Jews went to meet him and welcomed him with song. Very young children joined in praising him. As he passed by, it is known with certainty that they sang 'Hosanna in excelsis! [Glory in the highest!]' Every sort of person worshipped him mightily: maidens praised his power, widows desired to follow him day and night, and married women did much the same. They had difficulty realizing that they were finally able to see him. Very aged persons, those who were worthy to have been preserved long enough to be able to see and touch him, expressed their joy the same way. He bade the dead rise up and the blind to see. In the fullness of time when it was ordained that he should die on the cross for the sake of mankind, he descended into hell and redeemed those of his own who were there."

"All you men of the synod, listen to this," said Jubal. "He just said that his god descended into hell. How would the devils have dared to touch him? Pay attention to what I tell you now: no one goes to hell except those alone who have deservedly lost their souls for having failed to fear God and so forfeited any possibility of heaven when they depart his world. Devils are ready for the lost souls and take them there. If your god had to descend into hell he must have served the devil obediently. Consider how he stood for it when the devils tormented him in the pitch and sulfur. Now see if you can refute this: If he were a true god, the Creator of all things, he would not have arranged things so that he would burn in the pitch. That argument of yours should never again be raised before so many learned men."

"If I began an argument," said the holy man, "without being able to substantiate it, I would be forced to leave here in disgrace. Let us come to some conclusion."

That made the Jew very happy indeed and he addressed the pope. "We Jews place no confidence in those books of your New Testament, but if you can show me proof in the words of an Old Testament prophet I will acknowledge your assertions to be true and will never show my face before this synod again."

"You are making a very heavy wager indeed," said the holy man: "It is like you are betting against the loss of a hand or foot." He called for the book of David's Psalms to be brought out and showed him where it was written: *"Tollite portas principes vestras!* [Lift up your gates, you princes]." The Jew turned pale and sat down.

The pope turned and faced the heathens, saying, "We will explain these words to you. When, in the fullness of time, Our Lord died for the sake of mankind and he was to descend into hell, many choirs of angels came and flew towards him. They offered their service to their Lord and praised his holy name. It was his will that they descended before him into hell, and with one voice they all cried, 'Those who are princes among you, open your gates! Here comes my Lord himself!' In greater numbers the devils shouted back, 'Who is this Lord of whom we should be so sore afraid that we would open the gates for him?' The angels addressed them a second time: 'Be quick to raise the gate. He is Lord of all kings, the mighty God in the cradle. Today he desires to redeem his own. He is true God and true Lord: you must be sore afraid of him.'

"When the worthy prophets within heard his name spoken they raised their voices tearfully, saying, *'Advenisti desiderabilis, quem expectabamus in tenebris*—that is, come to our aid, O Lord, release us from this great torment, from this fiery dungeon where we are confined and from the shadow of eternal death, since you are our Redeemer!'

"And so he descended into hell, where he freed all those who were his. On the third day he arose as God from the grave, and ate and drank with his disciples. He did this in order that they might recognize all the more clearly that he was true God and true man. Then he ascended into heaven, but he will come again on the Last Day—I am telling you the truth about this—to render judgment in the sight of man. He will bless the good on his right hand and let the evil on his left hand be damned. They will inhabit the darkness and live in pain and suffering." The Jew had nothing more to say.

Zeleon stood up and without the slightest display of humility strode forward and spoke in a hostile manner. "Sylvester, what is all this supposed to mean? You preach Jesus to us: he was Mary's son: was he not a man of flesh and blood, as was evident to anyone looking at him. He was arrested for a crime and hung upon a cross and then was buried in the earth. What divine power could he possibly have had? His disciples stole his body away at night and the next morning they asserted that he had risen from the dead. Those same heretics made their way throughout the lands, telling people that he was a true god and leading people to believe in him and let themselves be baptized in water. I can prove that I am telling the truth in what I say through the testimony of many men. At night he was stolen from his grave, and you really are one of his disciples."

"You said one thing that really is true," said the holy man, "for I am very glad to be his disciple; I understood very well what you meant to say. Will you confirm those words? Or do you want to raise some other issue?"

"We wish to have those words set down now, to be proven later," said Lady Helena, "that he was taken at night from his grave, just as Zeleon said in contradicting you."

Daylight was beginning to fade, and the pope had the last statements written down and sealed authoritatively so that no evil cunning on the part of any of Zeleon's colleagues could tamper with them in any way.

The queen returned to her quarters for the night, where she began to weave a scheme for disgracing the Christians the following day. All the Hebrew people there gave her advice; they held nothing back in their support of her.

"Owî, my good master!" said King Constantine, "why did you say what you said? You went way too far in accommodating the Jews. If they can produce evidence to refute our claims then we will really have come here for a lost cause, and we may easily lose all our honor in failing to win the debate."

"You know now, milord," the pope responded, "that you should be very happy! I tell you, my dear son, that Our Lord himself will help us. We could not accomplish anything without him. He must send us the Holy Ghost for us to succeed. They are full of deceit with their false evidence. They lied to the queen, but that will cost them all their honor."

That made the noble lord laugh to himself. "May mighty Christ help us in this hour!" said the worthy emperor. "I will gladly serve him forever."

Very early the next morning the queen summoned Saint Sylvester, the holy man, and ordered witnesses to go to the circle in front of the crowd. The names of the witnesses were announced; then they were officially introduced.

"Milady," said the worthy pope, "we would really like to know what evidence these fellows intend to present against Christianity or how much of their testimony will be admissible under the rules."

Overly confident, the queen replied, "I intend to have sixty approved men give testimony to confirm that they all heard and saw how his disciples stole him away at night."

"Either I will have this testimony refuted once and for all and thrown out by judgment under the rules before all these good knights in a fashion which respects the honors due Your Majesty, or I will accept it," said Saint Sylvester, the holy nobleman.

The pope began his skillful interrogation with the most senior among the sixty, asking him how old he thought he was at the time and whether he could lawfully testify concerning the matter at hand.

"Lord have mercy upon me," said the Jew, "my companions have confirmed for me that I am ninety years old."

Right after that he asked the next one, and the Jew responded: "I am eighty years old." And so he asked all the Jews one after the other until he was told how old all of them were.

The pope returned to the most senior among them and most skillfully continued his line of questioning. "I beseech you, so help you Almighty God under his law, which Moses received from him when he went to Mount Sinai and brought to you to save you, when God freed you from bondage in Egypt, tell me the absolute truth." This elicited many perjured oaths.

The Jew was happy to hear this and spoke to the pope. "By God's Covenant I will tell you that I heard and saw that his disciples stole him away by night and the next morning claimed that he was risen from the dead.

This caused me no end of misery. I was severely persecuted and all of my kin were wiped out."

The pope addressed the next man: "What do you have to say now about this?"

That Jew answered: "That I heard and saw how it happened just as he described."

All sixty swore upon the Covenant that they wanted to confirm the truth of this testimony, insisting that they had all heard and seen themselves what had happened.

"Woe to you for the oaths you swore!" said the holy pope. "Let the judges ask: How could these good gentlemen all have heard and seen the theft of the body which they allege?"

His question gave the queen the first inkling that she had been deceived by the testimony. With what sadness the whole group of Israelite witnesses returned to their seats!

"Milady," said the holy man, "let the book now be brought forth: [it will show that] this year it has now been fully two hundred and thirty-six years since Our Lord went up to heaven. None of these men who has sworn his oath today can begin to support his testimony by claiming to be even one hundred years old. That proves their testimony to be perjury, nothing but shame and sin."

There was another Jew who had sat through the debates there from the beginning. He was so versed in a sort of learning that nothing that was said had any influence on him. Up to that point he had not responded to anything said in the synod. It had all seemed very childish to him, but now he was roused to insist that he could preserve the honor of the Jews. He went over to the holy man of God and said, "Sylvester, please tell me now: what power could your god possibly have? My God is so wonderful that there has never been his equal. No one can ever hear or say his name without losing his life right there on the spot. My God's name is so sublime that I will assure you that if it is your desire I will let you see what great miracles he can perform. That will put an end to your teaching and expose it to shame as deception. Sylvester, what is making you twitch now?"

"Zambri, you tell me," said the holy man, "how you were able to learn the name which no mortal could see or hear? You have been speaking of miraculous things, but if you want to bring your speech to a conclusion favorable to you—if your god is so good that he will work miracles for you as signs, let him kill a man or woman for your sake and afterwards bid that person rise up again as full of life as before. Then this whole synod will have every reason to put all the more faith in what you say."

Once again the Jew addressed him. "Sylvester, do you really think that God would ever consider being tested or tempted to make something miraculous happen and then reverse it. That would contradict how he works in the world, and it would be an unbearable fellow who asked him to do it. You will not find anything like that in the Scriptures."

"Yes, and now I will show you where it is written," said the holy man. "Duke Gideon tested Our Lord as he spread out a lamb's skin. At one point it was wet where the earth was completely dry. At another point the whole earth around was covered with dew. God's worthy follower asked that it remain dry, and it did so. That is very damaging evidence against your argument. God's customary ways are well known to me: we should pray seven times seventy to God that he will honor his name through us. He works many great miracles. He kills any man he wants to kill, but if that man has done something really pleasing to him, he may bid him to rise up again."

"Milady," said Zambri, "have these points made in the debate recorded [where we will break off for the day]. Sylvester has publicly vaunted that he can recall the dead to life. We all heard those words come out of his mouth. That will be as far as the Christians get with their deceptions."

The debate between the two had been going on until the evening sunlight began to fade. Both men were still going strong, but the judges postponed the debate until the third day of the council.

Very early on the third day, the Jew Zambri ordered a hundred men to lead a huge and ferocious animal with chains and ropes into the courtyard, a fantastic living image of a wild bull, and no one at the synod could claim ever to have seen anything like it before. The bull had been raised to be so fierce that no human dared come close to him for fear of being killed. The Hebrew man then went out to him and told the bull to stand still, which he did. Then he told everyone to step away from him far back so that no one could hear him: he whispered something into the beast's ear, and when he finished speaking his word, the bull fell down dead. At this all the Jews and heathens rejoiced together. They yelped loudly, claiming that the god who gave such a sign of his power as this had no equal, and they intended to revere him forever as their god.

Huge was the number of heathens there, as they set up their tents to camp on hills and valleys. The Jews also raised loud yells and blew their war-horns. This made the Christians very angry. They hoisted many white flags and many green and red ones until the queen forbade them [to prepare for conflict] as they valued their necks and feared willow noos-es. She swore that whoever broke her peace would be beheaded before the synod, however much she would have enjoyed seeing the heathens triumph over the Christians, so that they could find out how the debate would end.

Saint Sylvester ordered all the priests who had come to the synod to prepare themselves for what was coming by having no one among them neglect to sing a mass telling of God's resurrection. He told the laymen to be sure to make their confessions and recite the creed with tear-filled eyes, with fasting and with falling on their knees in prayer. The crowd wor-shipped Our Lord barefoot and wearing coarse woolen garments. The hea-thens conferred with each other in a council about whether they should seek vengeance; they really wanted to fight with the Christians, but the judges said to both the Jews and the heathens: "You really should not do what you want to now. Just wait for the day and the hour when Sylvester is defeated and as part of the judgment he is handed over to you, but in the meantime we should hear what he has to say."

On the fifth day the queen ordered an announcement made to all the forces gathered there that the people should not take matters into their own hands but should wait for the conclusion of the debate.

The emperor led the pope into the courtyard. [What was left of] the body of the bull lay there for all to see how it had been torn up with pieces and scraps taken by dogs and vultures. It was plain to see that it had not taken very long before they had left nothing of it but hide and bones; they did not leave any edible parts.

"Hail, you Roman Christians," said Saint Sylvester, the holy man, after he had obtained quiet with much difficulty. "Do you imagine that this is God's doing? I assure you truly that it is the work of the devil. He wants to bring shame and sadness to you any way that he can; however, I admonish you Christians who have not forgotten or failed to consider the way your true Creator works in the world, that he has not been set back at all. The devil has never won a test of strength when he has fought with God, and this will not have an evil outcome; the devil is always the one put to shame. Ask the Son of the true God to reverse this, which he can easily do. We seek the outcome which his grace will provide."

All the Christians said, "Amen."

The pope went on to address the heathens. "Listen to me, all you people: Zambri has made a bargain with the devil, and you will see the outcome of the debate in this way: if the devil helps him refute me, then you will have to believe in him all the more, but I tell you truly that he will not be able to reverse what he has done, and all of you will observe that no power can prevail against God. What Zambri did is no more from God than murder, as when a man slays another and buries his body in the ground, but now listen, all of you, and I will explain the contest: if Zambri did this with God's help, let him ask the beast to arise again with God's help. If he gets nowhere with doing that, it will be a sign that his work should not be praised." The judges agreed that this seemed like the way to bring out the truth.

Abiathar came forth and said, "Sylvester, I will tell you truly that I saw many eye-witnesses observe the wonder that Zambri performed, and we must judge the truth accordingly. Sylvester, if you will let me hear and see that you reverse what Zambri did with God's help and invoke his name as you do it—just let me hear the words and I will follow you and live the rest of my life according to your teachings."

"We have no previous knowledge about [restoring] animals [to life]," said Sylvester; "however, since you seem to be speaking in good faith and it is a matter of necessity for Christendom, we will put our heart into attempting it." The Jew only shook his head.

Jonas stood up, followed by Godolias, and they said, "We promise you before this great crowd that if you will restore this dead bull and we see him walk off, we will follow your instructions and become obedient to you."

Kusi arose, followed by [the heretical] Bishop Didascali, and they said, "These dead bones can no more stand up than this whole earth can turn to gold or the sea flood the heavens, but, Sylvester, if you should succeed we will become obedient to you."

Aroel and Benjamin stood up and addressed him. "Sylvester, if you call upon the god who was martyred at Jerusalem, and if he helps you in front of all these people by calling the dead beast back to life, we will carry out your orders, too."

Jubal and Thara went before the crowd and said, "These dry bones can no more be brought back to life upon this earth than the highest mountain can turn to water or all the forests to stone; however, if we do observe that you can make your words come true as you tell the beast to arise by the will of God we will gladly render you obedience."

Doech and Aunan said to the holy man, "Your teachings are gentle and good; our thoughts are leading us to agree that if we see the bull walk off healthy, we will gladly take you for our master. We will then have ourselves baptized and believe firmly in your God according to your will." That is what this pair promised.

Zeleon then stood up and said, "I have come here for the sake of justice, and I do not want to stray from what my comrades have agreed to. Never has there been a king so sublime, so powerful or so rich that he could bring back the dead with cunning or intelligence without relying on the help of God—doing it through God, in fact. That is why I will be glad to render Sylvester obedience if he successfully calls the beast to stand up."

Zambri stepped out in front of the crowd and spoke earnestly to the pope. "Sylvester, the bull is still lying here dead. Where is your great God now? Those three gods of yours are taking a very long time. How is it that your god, Jesus, is leaving you in the lurch today? I guess your Lord Christ is far, far away from you now and will not get here in time to help you today. The contest is over for you, and your life is given to us to dispose of as we see fit. The bull lies scattered in so many pieces so many different places that no one can restore him back to the way he was three days ago, and this should put an end to your deception."

"Lazarus was buried for three days in the earth," said the holy man, "until God bade him arise on the fourth day and go on his way. He escorted the Jews on a path through the Red Sea in a way that let the army of their enemies be drowned on the floor of the sea. He took care to keep his own people healthy with his manna for forty years. He relieved Daniel from the pangs of hunger and protected Susanna from wicked men. Our blessed Father Abraham saw the three names to which we pray as one true God. Zambri, if you are threatening me with death, death for the sake of God is what I have wanted for a long time: Owî, if only I could be granted my wish to be hanged on a gallows for his sake and receive my reward in the choir of martyrs! How glad my soul would be if that could only happen!"

Saint Sylvester, the holy man, fell to the ground on his knees and said: "Lord God, Father, hear me. I call to mind all your miracles. You sent that wonderful angel, Gabriel, from heaven to earth, and to redeem us from our sins you were born into mankind, Lord, taking flesh and bones upon yourself. You were conceived by the Holy Ghost and born of Saint Mary, a true virgin."

Zambri and the other Hebrew people laughed at this; however, Sylvester's prayer worried them.

God's sublime messenger fell again to the ground on his knees and said: "Hail to you, gracious and good Lord! For our consolation your Mother carried you and bore you into this world, and yet she remained a virgin forever, as the prophets foretold. Lord, you were baptized in the River Jordan, washing away all the misdeeds of those who believe in you. It was your Father's plan that in your human nature you should die upon the cross and descend into hell in your divine nature. On the third day you rose again from the grave and on the fortieth day ascended into heaven, sending us the Holy Ghost, who offers us the greatest assurance today. Free us now from the results of this great misdeed."

"Amen," said all the Christians.

The pope fell to his knees a third time before the whole crowd. He lifted up his hands and proved Our Lord's power as he spoke: "I command you, wild beast, arise quickly from lying there as the veritable image of death and walk away fully restored and healthy in your whole body, better-looking than anyone ever saw you before but tame and never doing harm to people again."

When Sylvester finished making the sign of the cross, large and small dogs ran to the spot and the birds returned with the whole crowd watching; with what they brought the skeleton was reassembled. The Jews were stricken with grief as never before when very soon the bull jumped up healthy and shook himself. Master Zambri was forced to admit that he had never seen anything so splendid before.

Owî! How miserable all the Jews were when they saw the miracle! Sounds of great praise arose from the heathens, who said that it must be a reigning God who caused such a miracle to be worked through his people.

The pope fell to the earth, with his body in the shape of a cross, and all the other Christians did the same thing. They cried tears of great joy and raised shouts of "*Gloria in excelsis deo* [Glory to God in the highest]!"

The pope told the synod to be silent, and he asked, "Milady, what is now your will? Will you now become obedient to God or what else would you care to hear debated?"

"Zambri, can you do anything more?" asked the noble queen.

"Milady, why are you talking like that," said the Jew. "You saw very well for yourself what miracles took place here. Milady, as much as I value your protection, I must say that our guilt is great, and we may deceive you no longer. I certainly do not want to lie anymore as we have been doing up to now." He hurried over to the holy man and fell right at his feet. "Milord," he said, "before sudden death overtakes me I must receive baptism from you! Now that I know with certainty that you are a true servant of God, I will gladly pledge my obedience to you forever."

The holy man then baptized him and did the same with the twelve speakers and then the two judges. He led them into the faith with tear-filled eyes and great humility. God revealed his compassion—84,500 were baptized then and there. As for those, however, who were not destined to receive baptism, every man among them ran away in shame.

Lady Helena in good faith desired and requested baptism; she was filled with the Holy Spirit. Sylvester baptized her *in nomine patris et filii et spiritus sancti* [in the name of the Father, the Son and the Holy Ghost]. He set the hat of the newly baptized on her head and gave her God's body and his blood.

That noble queen came to love all divine teaching: she was ever mindful of the three names and became obedient to the pope. She journeyed to the land of Jerusalem, where she found the True Cross. She had the seamless robe which God himself wore at his martyrdom sent to honor the ancient and wonderful city of Trier, along with the nail which had been driven through both his feet; also the head of saint Cornelius, the sandals of Saint Andrew, a tooth of Saint Peter, the chain with which he let himself be bound, and the bones of Saint Matthias. She also sent gold and precious stones along with many other splendid things for the adornment of churches in the city of Trier. The queen did this because she was a native of Trier.

XXIX

Sylvester

Sylvester I (bishop of Rome 314-335) never served as anything like emperor, although it is easy to see why he became a quasi-emperor in medieval legend. He was pope during the period of Constantine's gradual conversion to Christianity from generic monotheism, but he did not baptize him. Like many Christians of his day, Constantine chose to wait until he sensed approaching death before being baptized, so that all his significant sins would be absolved in the rite and he would not be burdened with many more. Bishop Eusebius of Nicomedia baptized Constantine several years after Sylvester's death.

As discussed in the general introduction, the image of Sylvester as ruler was much strengthened by the forged eighth-century Donation of Constantine (as discussed at some length in the general Introduction), which leaves Sylvester in charge of much of the former Western Empire with its revenues. While the historical Constantine did found Constantinople as a capital in the East, he did not relinquish Rome itself or western territories to anyone else during his lifetime.

The year was a very difficult one, filled with suffering for the people, as hunger spread throughout the lands of Rome. The emperor viewed it with a ruler's responsibility and said to Saint Sylvester, "Dear father and master, the people are looking to us. Now must be the right time for me to leave you. I entrust my Empire here to you until I shall return. Master, I have complete trust in you. Grain will be expensive for you to buy, but I am placing all the revenues of the Empire at your disposal for the love of the true God. This will enable you to take care of my people well."

God's stalwart promised to do as he was asked.

Constantine then asked some Romans to come along with him for one year. It was part of a cunning plan for him to tell them that. The Romans affirmed how willingly they would serve him in everything to maintain his honors. They readied themselves for departure and accompanied the mighty emperor through the lands to Greece. Constantine wanted to rebuild Troy, but an angel from heaven appeared to him and showed him Constantinople in a way that he could see it through and through.

"Here you are to settle," said the angel, "and build your capital, which shall be your legacy until Judgment Day. Our Lord commands you to do this." The emperor was very happy. He understood the heavenly message very well, and went about expanding the capital and measuring off the foundations of buildings. He was well assisted by those who came with him. The city was formerly called Byzantia; however, the name was changed in honor of the noble king, and today it is called Constantinople.

Very early one morning the Romans reminded the emperor to let the promise come true which he had made almost a year before, for they wanted to see their wives and children again. The emperor took each one aside by himself. He asked each of the princes of his Empire who had come with him from Rome to give him his seal-ring and insisted that every last one of them should give him his wife's name.

The Romans gladly complied with the emperor's request. Then, quickly and secretly the emperor ordered letters to be written containing messages for the women of Rome, each sealed in a way to make it look as if it had come from her husband. The letters told them to be mindful of the faith they had pledged and that they should now come and be reunited with their husbands, who did not want to farm and build on foreign soil without them. The women responded by making themselves ready for the journey, which they made very willingly. It was touching to see the crowd of them emerge, each one showing how dear her husband was to her.

The fabled Constantine then summoned his chamberlains and told them to go out on the peninsula and strew it with soil from Rome, so that they would be able to swear later that the good heroes had been standing on Roman earth.

It happened one Saturday morning that the emperor asked the brave Romans to accompany him to an assembly. The noblemen were pleased with this announcement, thinking it meant their return to Rome, and gladly agreed to go.

"You can't just go home like that," said the noble Constantine. "Whether you like it or not, I have kept my promise. You are standing here on Roman earth, and you will never see Rome again. Whatever happens to us, we shall die here together."

The Romans were greatly saddened by his words, but meanwhile the women arrived, and joyfully the men took up the work of construction.

The emperor provided for Constantinople to be expanded and for the founding of many other cities, too. He served God with energy and good will. He headed the Roman Empire, the book tells us truly, for exactly thirty years and six months. Angels from heaven summoned his soul.

The Book goes on to tell us that while Saint Sylvester was pope at Rome he converted the heathens and gave good instruction to Christians, but then one day a marauding dragon appeared who brought misery to the Christians. No one dared leave the city of Rome for fear of losing his life on the spot. Great lamentations arose through the whole city of Rome. Some Christians whose faith in God was less than firm asked where their great God was and how it fit in with his reputation to tolerate the way Christians were being subjected to such a death.

Saint Sylvester, that stalwart of God, told the people to gather together. In response to the widespread suffering he proclaimed a fast for three days and three nights—also the carrying of the cross in processions. He told them to give alms to the poor and to live chastely. Owî! How the people complied with his instructions all over the city of Rome!

On the fourth day—I am telling you the truth about this—good Saint Sylvester offered God's body and his blood. That true messenger of God fell on his knees before Saint Peter's altar and said, "Lord Saint Peter, God's stalwart, all the people are calling upon you. They are holding me responsible since I received authority from you and have been seated upon your throne. Now milord, you should not forget what God himself told you when he left you in great sorrow. Christendom is now widespread and holds to your name. You are to conduct us before God. Now do some honor to your name and grant us mercy. Otherwise we sinners will never find cause to be happy."

There is no doubt about what happened next. Saint Peter appeared to him so that all could see. He looked at him and spoke to him kindly. "Sylvester, true stalwart of God, you have the power from God to bind and to loosen from bodily afflictions and sins. What you command on earth is done, but now, since you want to have my help with this, take your key in hand and lock that devil up. Address him this way: *'Haec dicet apostolus* [Thus speaks the apostle]: with these words you shall be locked up until the Last Day, by order of my master, Saint Peter.' And as truly as I am speaking to you now, that dragon will never again disturb mankind." Sylvester broke out in tears of joy.

Saint Sylvester, that holy man, ordered the sacred object to be carried with him. No women or men from Rome were allowed to go with him except for two of his chaplains. Then that worthy man of God turned toward *Mons Gaudii*. The dragon flew up before him, and Saint Sylvester followed him back to the far end of his cave, where the dragon was unable to turn in any direction. "You filthy dog," said good Saint Sylvester. "Now you will receive your reward for all the injuries you brought upon people in this world." He raised his key and turned it with these words: "You are herewith bound until the Last Day!"

The dragon was thus confined there with no door and no lock. God's wonders are great. The cave was barred and the dragon sealed in with the holy cross, so that he was never able to do mankind any further harm, and Saint Sylvester returned to the city.

When the Romans saw that their lord was in good health, they rushed out to meet him. "Praise and honor you must have forever!" they shouted. They praised our Lord for such a patron and for looking after them by sending them such a teacher to their home. The Romans rejoiced forever over what had happened.

Saint Sylvester converted the heathens and taught Christendom well, the book tells us truly, twenty-four years, six months and five days.

Let everyone who listens to this song chant a *pater noster* in the love of the Holy Ghost to praise Saint Sylvester, the holy lord, and for the help of the poor soul who was the first to begin this song. Saint Sylvester, that holy man, is standing by him full of grace *ante tronum dei* [before the throne of God] and may he help all those who listen to it politely, both the living and the dead. Let God the good show them his grace, here for the body, there for the soul!

XXX

Julian

Julian (r. 361–363), who was often called "Julian the Apostate," was a nephew of Constantine I, "the Great." After Constantine's death, however, Julian was thoroughly alienated from the family by the murders among them committed by those who thought they had a claim to more of Constantine's territory and authority than they had received. His suspicions in the case of Constantius II seem likely enough; however, he blamed Christianity with much less justification for the massacre. An avid student of the arts and humanities, Julian came to admire both pagan philosophy and the ancient Greco-Roman culture with its traditional gods. When Constantius was killed in battle in 361, Julian, already holding power in the Western Empire, became sole emperor.

Julian was the last pagan emperor of Rome. He did not actively seek Christians out for persecution, but he had some of them executed for physical destruction of statues in pagan temples and made it difficult for them to teach publicly.

Sources for some of the legendary material incorporated here include a Syrian novel about Julian from around 600, a biography of Saint Basil, translated from Greek to Latin around 900, and the legend of Saint Mercurius, who was originally recorded as a victim of Decius. The *Book of Emperors* shares with other medieval works—such as *Policraticus* (*The Statesman's Book*) by John of Salisbury—the role of Saint Mercurius as killer of tyrants.

The point for medieval political theory is that tyrants deserve to be killed, but not by ordinary people. God will execute tyrants in his own good way by having the Virgin Mary rouse Saint Mercurius from his grave to carry out the divine sentence.

The Book tells us that Julian held the Empire, and now we will tell you how that enemy of God actually took it over.

In those days there was a lady in Rome who was a model of good conduct. She raised this same Julian as if he were her own son for the honor of God and the salvation of her soul.

Later, when her husband died and she became a widow, she took all her money—that is what the book tells us—and entrusted it to Julian for safekeeping, so that he would hold it for her and let her have it whenever she might need it.

This lady was a good woman. She never missed matins or a mass wherever she knew of a worship service being held. She did many good works, and when these began to require money she asked to have her property back again. The devil put the idea in Julian's head of swearing that he never saw her money or other valuables and that she had certainly not entrusted them to him.

Filled with regrets the poor lady went quickly to the pope and fell at his feet. "Milord," she said. "I seek your grace. Judge for me what Julian has done. I entrusted all my gold to him, thinking that he was true and loyal to me and would keep it for me with devotion. Unfortunately, now I can't get it back again."

Julian swore with increasing fervor that he did not know what all this talk was about. Spending the widow's money at the court freely, he had become a favorite there, and the lady had to leave without a judgment and without her money. Bitterly she complained of this to Our Lord.

Since the woman no longer had anything of value, she soon became poor and needy. She washed people's clothes, cooked and baked. Yes, she did laundry for the Romans, letting her noble hands do work she was not accustomed to do. Faithlessly, Julian held on to her money.

Late one evening the lady gathered up her laundry, planning to wash clothes in the Tiber. She found a statue in the water and hung some of the clothes on it. Some heathens had hidden the statue there and came to pray to it every morning. They wanted to keep it safe from the Christians, who would have smashed it.

The lady raised a cloth and struck the statue around the ears with it, which it found very painful. The devil spoke to her from the statue. "Woman, for the sake of kindness, spare me those blows. Please, don't do that any more, for I am a very sublime god."

"Then why are you putting up with your pain and suffering?" asked the lady. "What evidence can you give that you are a god? You can't even defend yourself from me; you can't spare yourself these blows. You are lying in the water colder and wetter than you would be if you were a great god. If you were one you would walk away from here and warm yourself at some fire. Now, however, my blows are hurting you, and I will give you more than enough of them." She raised the cloth again, striking the statue around the ears with it, and kept giving it blows.

"Spare me this shame," said the devil, "and I will get back for you all the treasure that belonged to you and your husband."

"What good can you do me where my money and valuables are concerned?" said the lady. "You can't even help yourself out of your predicament. You are an unclean fraud, lying there in the water like a lump of stone."

"Woman," said the devil, don't misbehave like that! I am the god, Mercury. Go back to your house and spend the night there. Then, in the morning, go and lodge a complaint against Julian, and he will be required to swear an oath before you by what is holy to him. You can then point the way to the Tiber and announce that you want to have him answer questions concerning the judgment before me. The Romans want to hold me in contempt. Julian will swear an oath by me, but I will require him to agree to give you all your gold back again. Woman, let me live honorably tonight!"

"I can't imagine that anyone ever obtained anything honorable from *you*," said the lady, and, by my poor soul, you will receive still more blows from me. I can see that you are lying to me about everything, and, if you are deceiving me tonight and if I don't get my gold back very soon, then—unless I am lying there dead—many an evil day will be in store for you. You have no idea how many blows around the ears I will give you."

The next day when mass was sung the lady pressed forward through the whole crowd and fell on her knees at the pope's feet. "I ask you to grant me grace," she began, "Judge for me what your chaplain did in faithlessly taking my gold from me! Have mercy upon me, very poor woman that I am. I have nowhere else to turn for help."

That angered the Romans, and they asked that justice be done for the lady. The pope ordered, as Christendom authorized him to do, that an oath be taken from the lady. The lady began, "Give me a judgment against the god Mercury! That is an unclean deceiver lying in the river like a block of stone. I want to receive your judgment against him, and then, after receiving your gracious decision, I will not trouble you again." Many people cast doubts on what she had said, but the Roman princes all said they wanted to come along. When they saw the idol, all the Romans showed their contempt for it. Julian was worried and clapped his hand over the idol's mouth, but the devil, acting inside the idol, bit down on his hand and held it so firmly that he could not escape, and, no matter what all the Romans tried, they could not get him away from there.

"Woe! Woe!" Julian screamed. "What have I gotten myself into? I wish you well, Lord God, just let me live! I will give all the lady's gold back to her." And so he agreed to restore the lady's treasure. All the people of Rome who amounted to anything hurried to the spot, to behold the great wonder that could be seen there.

When evening began to advance, the people had to go home. Although no one else could hear or see anything, the devil spoke again to him. "Julian, now listen to me. I caused you a great deal of grief today. Standing before me you received only great shame. By yourself, without my advice, you can never recover, but do as I say and I will make you a great lord, so great that you will rule the whole Roman Empire."

And so Julian then became the hateful devil's man and did everything the devil told him to do. He turned away from God and renounced his baptism. He welcomed the devil, and he chose to be the vassal of Mercury, losing both his body and his soul.

Now listen to what else I have to tell you. Fourteen days after that when the marvelous emperor died, the evil devil advised the Romans—he flew from man to man among them—saying, "Hesitate no longer, but elect Julian to be your ruler. He can teach you many things and will make a fitting ruler for the Roman Empire." All the Romans thought they must be hearing the voice of an angel. They began to like what they heard very much and to be convinced that it was coming from the Holy Ghost, which was the greatest mistake they could make.

The Romans hesitated no longer before electing Julian. They chose him to be their judge, which they would greatly regret afterwards.

Julian instructed his stewards to take the idol from the Tiber and to raise it again in the temple which heathendom had made for it. He would leave neither man nor woman alone: they all had to go there to sacrifice and to pray to the devil. Great suffering and need became common in Rome; many of the high nobility were martyred.

There were two rich and powerful dukes in Rome, [Paul and John], who did not like the evil Julian, nor could he force them to bring any sacrifices to the idol. He then sent one of his men, named Terentian, to the two lords, telling him to ask and to plead with them to worship Mercury. He was to assure them that, if they did this, as long as he lived he would hold them in the highest honor, even naming them to follow him as rulers upon the throne. He promised them that they would lead a fine life with land and treasure at their command, but that if they refused to agree he would deprive them of life and honor. That was his message to those lords.

Paul and John were quite happy to hear this. "We tell you, Terentian, we will never serve your Lord Julian with obedience. We wish to serve him above, who has heaven and earth in his hand, for life and death are in his power to determine. He suffered martyrdom and death that he might redeem us; therefore, it is only right that those devoted to him follow him in suffering violence, torture, and martyrdom. If God should will it, we wish only that martyrdom would be ours!"

Paul and John knew very well that they were about to make the journey to God's kingdom. Therefore they told the many holy men who were their companions to divide their earthly goods among the common people whom no one else wanted to help because of their faith and who for that reason were suffering need.

With great anger the king ordered them brought before him. At first he started to plead with those noblemen, saying to them, "Keep your lives and your honor. Leave this evil strife behind. Pray to Mercury, and I will give you great riches and maintain you with the highest honors."

The noble Paul and John answered him, "We are very surprised that you are worshipping a devil that human hands can break or burn. You know you will have to accept the fact that, if someone throws your god onto a manure pile, his cunning will not help him ever to come out of it without human help. That is what you have chosen for your lord. What shall become of you in the hereafter, when your soul is burning in hell? Satan will give you what you have chosen as your lot forever. In hell he has plenty of misery to bestow on you who served him so well: to your sorrow you will be there eternally. We believe in the Father, Son and *spiritum sanctum* [Holy Ghost] and that together they form the true godhead. For you to carry out your threat is the thing we would welcome most."

When they spoke these last words, the king's anger became ferocious. He commanded that the holy men be whipped with hawthorn and other thorn branches and that their flesh be torn off with very sharp crowels [instruments of torture: forks with sharpened tines bent forward like hooks]. Their martyrdom was great. They have become comrades of the angels and are called "two candelabra," as they light the way everywhere for the angels. The Book tells us about them that they can control the weather, and they may even release us from our sins, saving us in body and soul.

But then Our Lord avenged the stalwarts so dear to him. Julian, that enemy of God, commanded an expedition to sail against the Greeks. He crossed the sea with a mighty army, and when he arrived in Greece he found a monastery by the wayside. Hunger was pressing the Romans and the king sent word to the man in charge of the monastery, asking him to supply them with food without delay. The holy man was named Basil, and he could not come up with what the king asked for except to furnish him with five loaves of barley bread, but over these he said his blessing. He told one of the brothers to take them and bring them before the king. He commanded him by his oath of obedience not to return until he found the king himself.

Under this compulsion the brother did what his master ordered: holding the bread high he took it before the king. "Sire, accept this sign of affection from our master! In receiving it, please take into account that our master would like you to know that, if he had the means, he would treat you with the royal honors you deserve; but unfortunately we do not have any more food in this monastery."

The king ordered the brother removed from his presence, warning him, "Now tell your master to count on this: when I return I will make the earth around here so barren that it will not grow anything. That is the love I will show him. I will satisfy my anger with revenge: All of you have already lost your lives. This whole landscape will never bear anything again." He directed that the grain all be cut down and salt sown in the furrows. His gestures reflected convulsions of rage, for he was a fierce enemy of Christendom.

When the brother repeated to the others everything as he had heard it—the king's rage and his threats—they were greatly distressed and fearful. They fully believed that they were waiting for death to come soon. Throughout the whole monastery the brothers were saddened beyond consolation. They were thinking they would not be alive much longer, and they commended their souls to God in heaven.

Good Saint Basil hurried to the chapel of Our Lady, Saint Mary. His thoughts were heavy ones as he fell upon his knees before her altar. "Hail to you, Queen of Heaven," he began. "We will never stand well with God or be worthy in his sight, but we pray that you will lighten our burden of sin and grant us more time to live in spite of God's enemy, whose mind is made up too harshly against us. For us you bore into this world the One who consoles us and redeems us from hell. He is sweet and kind; he loves all humility; he is holy and full of grace; and he loves all that is just. The sinner finds him when he searches. How quickly he will take care of him!

Chapter Thirty

No matter how deeply the man has fallen into sin, his grace will tell him to stand upright again. He is the origin of all that is holy; he is both Father and Child with the Holy Ghost in between them; he is the true divine love; he is our refuge; he is what we believe in; to all who trust in him, he is the beginning and the end. Heaven and earth are in his power, and no one can resist him. Now save us from that vicious man. Do not let him destroy any of us or disturb any services we offer you. We are relying on you for this. Holy Maiden, save us now!"

Some time before that, the same King Julian had ordered a duke who was a man beloved of God beheaded. When he had heard that the king was there with his assembled forces, he had ridden to meet him, desiring to gain his favor with treasure or an offer of vassalage. The king, however, would not accept him as a vassal unless he would agree to serve his god.

The duke said that he would never want to do that. He believed in the Father and the Son, and he wanted to revere the Holy Ghost. The king gave the order for that lord to be martyred with diligence and with many kinds of tortures, but they could not force him to recant no matter what they did to him—no matter what agony he suffered—to deny God. Finally Julian ordered that his head be struck off, and Saint Basil, who had become its master by then, had him buried in the cathedral there. With weeping and prayers they had commended his soul to God. He is a worthy martyr, whose name is Mercurius. His shield and spear have been kept in that same cathedral. That holy man was a prince of the land and was martyred for the honor of God.

There is no doubt about what happened next. The Heavenly Maiden appeared to good Saint Basil and spoke so that everyone could hear. "Your prayer has been heard in heaven, and I have come here to bring you comfort. You may well be joyful for today My Lord himself provides you with relief. You are entangled in fears, but God does not choose to put up with that any longer." The holy man burst out in tears of joy.

Right then Our Lady, Saint Mary, turned around and said, "Mercurius, dear man, you are to stand up and get out of your grave. Take vengeance for defying God upon that enemy of God. He is the one who owes you a debt. My Lord himself ordains that you do this. Yes, Holy Christ, for whose aid all Christendom has need, commands you to do it."

When the slain man understood what Our Lady was telling him to do, he stood up and climbed out of his sarcophagus and hurried to grasp his shield and spear. Mounted on a horse, he rode into the countryside, where he found King Julian. When the king saw him for the first time he said to the Romans, "There I see Mercury riding towards us. I am sure that he would like to strike me dead."

Each of his men marveled at him, not understanding what he was talking about. It seemed like a strange state of affairs to them. They took up their weapons and all of them hurried to the king's side. Very bad things were in store for the king. Mercurius turned towards him and ran the king through the stomach although no one could tell the exact moment when it happened.

Julian fell down there dead, which evoked cries of lamentation. The Romans fled all together, leaving the king to lie there alone. His corpse— the Book is quite clear about this—is burning in pitch and sulfur in Constantinople. He will stay there until the Last Day. No one should or could change the state he is in.

Mercurius returned again to the city to enter his own grave again, and the grave closed itself again. Very early the next morning the abbot was taken by surprise when he learned of Julian's death. No one could tell him with any certainty when or how he had been killed until it was revealed to him by God. He went to look at the grave and saw blood running down all over the spear. They sang great praises to God that they had been saved from the evil Julian. They had suffered deprivation and misery from him, and all Christendom rejoiced at his death.

Now who could have worked all these wonders except he who created the first man from dry earth and determined that he will return again to nothing?

Julian had the Empire for exactly two years and five months more. Devils are torturing his soul.

XXXI

Heraclius

Heraclius (r. as Eastern emperor 610–642) led a successful rebellion against the usurper, Phocas, and was proclaimed emperor in 610. He defeated the Persian armies, which, after conquering Egypt and Syria, were camping opposite Constantinople. From 619 to 626 most of his military operations were conducted against the Avars, who had invaded the Byzantine Empire. In 627, however, he returned to the conflict with Persia and personally led his armies against those of the Persian King Chosroes II (Cosdras for our author) to a victory that led to the overthrow of Chosroes by his son, Kavadh II, who executed his father and made peace with the Byzantine emperor. In 629 Heraclius was given a hero's welcome for bringing the True Cross from Jerusalem to Constantinople. For many years afterwards, September 14—the day on which he did this—was celebrated in the church as the "Feast of the Exaltation of the Cross."

The Book now tells us that Heraclius held the Empire. He won great honor for the Romans and also saved his soul at the same time. While he served as the Roman ruler, the devil advised a heathen king named Cosdras to have a heaven of brass constructed over his land [as] he very much wanted to be a god himself. On the inside he had the sun and moon painted. On the outside it was covered with carbuncles, its clouds were made of lead and tiny stars were made out of well-carved, precious stones. In between were nine balconies for choirs [to sing accompanied by music made by] rain descending through pipes. Now the Book goes on to tell us how powerful he was among the heathens. He brought the Christians grave suffering. He rode off to Jerusalem with an army and took the Holy Cross—the one on which God himself was martyred—away with him.

He also intended to break up the Holy Sepulcher, although he was never able to touch it, since one of God's angels guarded it himself. He thoroughly ravaged the city with his army, leaving very little of it that had any use or value. Great lamentations arose, but the survivors all called upon heaven, taking the great calamity to God in prayer.

When the Romans heard that Jerusalem had been sacked—Owî!— what cries of despair rose throughout all the city of Rome.

Heraclius had great love for God. From heaven a fear-inspiring voice spoke to him: "I will tell you, King, what you should do. Hurry straight to Jerusalem, where you must fight a mighty battle with that King Cosdras. You shall win back the Holy Cross that he robbed from God. The ruling God in heaven commands that you do this."

That mighty lord, Heraclius, dallied there no longer. Because of the great and pressing need he ordered a military expedition into the heathens' land. He took the green and white flag in his own hand. He was a very bold hero, as would be shown one day soon after that. When he first saw his enemies riding at a great distance, he shouted to the Romans, "Grasp your weapons firmly! I am convinced that today the devil wants to take a vast army with him to hell. Here today you will see both life and death. If we are threatened with destruction, I feel that he who commanded us to set out on this expedition will not let us down."

The king strode to higher ground and asked for silence. "Hail, you eager heroes! I will tell you a parable. It is about a people called the Hebrews, and you should see it as an example to follow: God showed them a wonderful land, since he found them in need, and he told them to forget their sorrows in it after they had taken it away from his enemies. The Hebrews had no knowledge of the land, and they sent two scouts ahead of them so that they should bring back a report of what the interior of the land was like. When the scouts returned they brought with them a huge wine-grape hanging from a staff. The whole army marveled at this. The scouts also reported that in this country there were three crops of grain in a single year and there were crops of cane like pipes with honey in them. They would be able to see and hear all kinds of wonders there.

"The very first things the scouts told them were a great consolation to the nobles—that there was great food there, as in paradise. The inhabitants, however, were ferocious, huge and ugly. Their crossbow bolts and their arrows were actually able to pierce through steel. When the scouts had completed their report, the people felt hesitant and abandoned the land that Our Lord had told them to occupy, and so—now that they sorely doubted his goodness—they surely will never enjoy his peace again.

"Well, when they failed to obey God's command to them through their hesitation, they fell upon hard times. Roman heroes, think of the fact that God himself has willed for you to serve him now. If you are eager to serve him, he will reward you with his kingdom." The Romans all raised their right hands and promised that no one should share in taking the land with them who fled from battle or failed to support them when they needed it. Many a good hero rejoiced at this.

Having assured themselves of victory, the Christians charged the heathens. They struck them down in the battle like dogs in a valley. Heraclius saw young Cosdras, who looked pale and sickly; blood was running all over him, and his men had all been slain or had deserted.

A clash in single combat was agreed to—the Roman ruler should fight with the heathen ruler. The king was well prepared to welcome whatever God might decree for him. The two met in the middle of a bridge. Each one pronounced a ban on violence from his men—any man who committed an act of violence before the outcome would have his head cut off on the spot.

Heraclius addressed the heathen king. "Hurry to have yourself baptized, and believe in the true God. Believe firmly. You have great need of doing so, for otherwise death is very close to you now. But if you are sincere in having yourself baptized, your soul will never go to hell."

"No, I will never do that," the heathen answered. "I would rather suffer death from you before I believe in your God, and I would rather allow my soul to go to hell before I would consent to baptism in the water."

For the king, that was not a worthy answer. He drew his sword and in a moment he cut through Cosdras' neck. Our Lord himself was helping him.

When the king overcame the heathens and found the Holy Cross where they were, he ordered the great hall broken up and all torn down—

that heaven fell to the earth. He took the cross, showing great reverence for it.

Heraclius was quite a good hero. He killed the elder Cosdras, but he caught his son up in the brass heaven, so that things afterwards went very well for him. When Heraclius raised him from the baptismal font in Rome, he became a very good Christian. Cyril was his new name, and the Book contains many stories of virtues he showed.

Then the Roman army returned, rejoicing to the sea. They displayed an excess of high spirits, which they were soon to regret gravely.

When they first came close enough to Jerusalem to see the temple, each one of them wanted to ride in front of the others to that *speciosam portam* [bright and shining gate]. There is no doubt about what happened next: God's angel appeared at the shining gate and barred his way. The king was sore afraid and lost no time in asking the angel, "Since this expedition was commanded to me by God—down here from heaven—and I won back the Holy Cross, what might I have done against God's grace?"

"Will you listen to something more," said the sublime angel, "about how God himself because of his humility rode a donkey here through this gate?"

The king was still sore afraid. He went barefoot and put on a coarse wool garment. With true devotion he prayed to Our Lord. He took up the cross on his shoulder and walked, rejoicing, through the gate. That is told to us poor sinners *ad exemplum* [as an example to follow]. It will teach us to fear and obey Our Lord with discipline and compassion. Arrogance is of such a nature that it always brings shame to a man.

Heraclius ruled the Roman Empire for thirty-two years and sixteen days more, and, I will tell you truly that he died of dropsy. His soul is dear to God.

Chapter Thirty-one

XXXII

Narcissus
(Legend of the Two Theodorics)

The theme of a chaste wife pursued by an evil brother-in-law, followed by her trials, tribulations, and eventual vindication, emerges in a large number of stories that reached medieval Europe in various adaptations, probably from an Indian original. In Europe it quickly acquired a Christian context. The version probably used by our author was contained in a collection of miracle stories originally centering around the Virgin Mary, although he or an intermediary source substituted Saint Peter as the major worker of miracles in the story. The names "Narcissus" and "Theodoric" appear to be the invention of our author; there is no historic connection with any Roman emperor. His rendition of the story is less about rulership than the rewards of Christian virtue.

The book reveals that his brother Narcissus now held the Empire. He was an old man, too old to expect to father children. When he took over the Empire, he asked the people every day to pray to God—for his own divine honor—to send him an heir who would take care of the Empire after him.

The people sought this in their prayers, and his wife, Lady Elizabeth, became pregnant and bore two fine sons in a single night. According to heathen custom both twins were given the name "Theodoric." In the sixth year after that, it came to pass—just as I am telling you—that both the emperor and his queen died, and much unrest broke out in the territories that had been under them. Rulership was to be given to the brother who married first, as the Imperial Law at Rome prescribed.

The boys were raised with great care, and they matured quickly. At the time they were coming of age there was a king *ad Affricanam* [toward Africa] who had a most attractive daughter named Crescentia, and the young lords separately sought her hand in marriage, each trying to outdo his brother. Her father, the king, was puzzled as to what he should do and consulted with the princes, not wanting to assign her to one of the brothers as long as the other might object to it.

The Senate offered this proposal: "To decide the matter let a circle be drawn [and let the two men stand inside it]. Whichever one the lady chooses, let him also have the Empire," and everyone agreed to this outcome.

One of the Theodorics was a hero in good looks as well as deeds, the sort who could be expected to be favored by the princes. He was called "the handsome Theodoric." By way of contrast, the twin who shared his name was of blacker hair and paler skin. Throughout the Empire, people called him "the homely Theodoric." When they went to stand in the ring, the good lady chose the one less well favored; his spirit appealed to her more than his brother's did. Her choice was to lead her into great misery afterwards.

And so he became judge and ruler, and his use of power gained him a fine reputation. Rome and the Lateran pledged him their allegiance, and he subdued the Normans, for which the Romans were very thankful. Then he led a huge army overseas, intending to defeat a rich and powerful king, but before he left he asked his trusted advisors how they thought he should maintain his beautiful wife, who was as dear to him as life itself, until he should return. They advised him to take her and send her back over the sea to her worthy father and kindly mother. They would make every effort to maintain and protect her, so that she would not have any reason to regret the ruler's expedition.

The king soon regretted the advice his men had given him, but he went ahead and shared it with the queen. He embraced her and said, "Having to send you home to your own country grieves me sorely. I am afraid that if I am killed on this expedition, others may want to ban you from the Empire—yes, I am really afraid that could happen. But now, my dear, give me your own advice as to how I should have you looked after in a way worthy of my honor."

"If I am to play the part of your counselor, then let me say that, if there were no way for me to remain on Roman soil, I would be most unwilling to return to my father. People would have reason to say they thought I had disgraced you by committing adultery, and I would prefer death to that. If God will guide you, you should not act on any such advice to send me back overseas. Before you do so, you should really think it all over."

"May Christ know that I love to hear those sweet words from you," said the king, "but tell me now what advice you would give me—you who are so close and dear to me—and I will be glad to follow it."

"You have a wonderful brother, named Theodoric," Lady Crescentia replied. "The lands of the Empire are well known to him, and while you are gone he should rule and judge them. Tell him to protect me also. I can recognize goodness in him. He will treat me in a way that adds to his own honor, and you should not worry about me any longer."

Very early one morning in the presence of many princes, the king entrusted the lady to his brother's keeping with the heartfelt request that he protect her well. The king took her hand and placed it in his brother's hand; then he departed with his men for foreign lands. But then the hate-filled devil began to tempt that lord into wanting to sin with his own body upon his brother's wife. Then when that terribly faithless man began putting these feelings into words it greatly distressed the lady. "Where have you let your senses go to?" she asked in a tear-filled voice. "You know full well that I am your brother's wife, and if people find out about this we are lost. I want to warn you about this while there is still time."

"Since I have no control over these feelings of mine, I intend to break my faith and let my body avenge my suffering. I no longer have any thought of making you my wife since you treated me shamefully when you rejected me and took my brother instead, even though I would have been more of a credit to you with my accomplishments and abilities. That insult will always rankle inside me. If you won't atone for what you did to me, you will be the one who suffers most."

Lady Crescentia quickly thought over many cunning ruses to put off this evil. "If you really want to make love to me," she said, "first see to gathering together fine marble building stones and gems. Listen carefully to what I tell you: summon together highly skilled craftsmen, and have them build a tall and finely decorated tower. Then I will do what you desire me to do. We shall take ourselves high up and far away, leaving behind all concerns of the world. Then people will not be able to catch us. If the Romans should find out about our crime, my good knight, they will stone us by rights."

Her brother-in-law called for craftsmen until he had assembled as many as he needed, and there in Rome he had a tower constructed—which angered the burgesses of the city—out of stones and lead. He asked his sister-in-law to come and see it; then he asked her how she liked it. "You know," he said, "all these marble stones were brought here from over the sea. Now the structure is complete, even the topmost pinnacle. Now you are to let me have my will of you."

"But now summon some smiths, and have them make the tower secure with many solid locks that will keep us safe from our enemies," said the lovely woman. "If you fail to do this you will cause our bodies and souls to be lost."

And so he put smiths to work, making the structure secure with locks. He informed the lady when the work was done, saying, "The building is now secure with locks. You should not forget what you promised me. The heroes will soon be returning, worn out from battle."

"Before anything else happens, you should furnish our chamber with food and drink," she said. "I am not insisting on that without thinking it over carefully. If we don't have bread and wine, we will be lying dead up there." He then had twelve men sworn to secrecy bring meat, bread and other good things to eat high up in the tower, where they would have all they could need for thirty nights.

"Now I am finished," he said. "There is a plentiful store of provisions—no matter how long we want to be up there, we will have bread and wine."

"Why are you telling me about bread and wine?" she asked. "You should be more worried about having forgotten our God than about drinking and eating. Send some of your chaplains to the Lateran in Rome and bring us a holy relic before anyone misses it. You should install it in the chamber before I would be willing to embrace you there. Do that, milord, and I will be quick to submit to your will. Then before the holy relic we should fall to our knees and repent our misdeeds; that will help us gain remission of our sin so that at the end we may enjoy the blessings of the heavenly kingdom."

By the time he had finished installing the holy relic after much difficulty, it was quite late in the evening. The lady hid the keys in the folds of her gown, and the lord led her merrily by the hand. The way did not seem long to him as he showed her all the chambers. "My dear," he said. "Now let me have my will of you. In this one chamber there are fine loaves of bread, spiced wine, and a saintly bone."

"Yes, milord," she said. "I will let you do as you wish with me. You know, I have subjected body and soul to a great strain, so I will ask you to take the first step into that chamber before me." But then, as he strode into the chamber, she slammed the door, and the latch fell with a loud clang; she gave the key a twist with her hand and took a step back, having turned the tables on that faithless man.

"Woe is me for your change of heart!" cried the lord. "If you are showing your thanks by locking me in here, I would call that a total lack of love. My dear sister-in-law, let me out of this predicament, and I will swear you a double-strength oath: I will never do anything to cause you bodily shame and suffering, and I will no longer want to have you as my woman."

The lady quickly replied that she did not intend any injury to the lord but that she could never accept his oaths. "Just look all around you! You have fine loaves of bread and wine along with a comfortable bed, plenty of clothes and many other fine things. Then, when you want to pray there is no need to delay, for the saints are close by. You will not be so rash in your actions again. Instead, you will stay in there awaiting the return of my lord. I cannot continue to oppose you out here any longer."

With these words the lady locked all the tower's doors and gates, leaving that hero sitting alone in his chamber. She gathered all the keys together and threw them in a chest, so that no one could find out about the cunning plan she had carried out, and so she kept the secret to herself. The next day when mass was chanted, none of the people knew what had become of their lord, and they all grieved for him. The lady herself began to weep just as if she were mourning a dearly beloved brother-in-law. Actually, this most lovely woman was cast down in spirit, as the heart inside her body grieved for her husband. She was determined to wait for him honorably, secure against all worldly shame until God should send him back to their own country.

Winter was approaching, and the king and his men set out happily on the journey home. A messenger ran ahead of the army and let the queen know they were coming. She arose without delay and strode across the broad courtyard. Secretly she climbed the stairs to the locked chamber in the tower where she rattled the door. The hero inside responded: "I hear someone outside the door in the tower. Who is it?"

"Do you still want to get out of here?" asked the good lady. "Or have you not been able to change your way of thinking?"

"With all my heart I would like to get out of here if I could have your protection. I am very much afraid of being beheaded unless your goodness saves me. You must completely forget what I proposed to you back then. You know, I have been sitting in here for two whole years, but go ahead and do what you like with my life. I am also afraid that the emperor will banish me."

She unlocked the door and opened it, saying, "May you have God's mercy and mine, good brother-in-law! [It is as if] I remember nothing about you since before all that happened. Prepare to go out before the people. Your brother will arrive yet today, and you should receive him well. We should hurry to meet him and gain God's blessing. I am perfectly willing to keep silent about your guilt."

He bowed to her most courteously. The lady raised his head and kissed him on the mouth; then she said, "Before any words of mine will threaten your well-being, I will let my head fall to my feet. You can trust me."

They left that chamber, came down and made their way in front of the tower, walking happily as the new day dawned. The larks began singing, and the watchman cried out the news around the whole castle that his lord was arriving. Crescentia stood next to the handsome Theodoric in front of the crowd and asked him to ride out and meet their dear lord; however, he did not really wish to change his ways. He made up a story and spread it among the soldiers—a monstrous lie that he had been captured at night down by the river after Crescentia had asked him to go there, and his knightly sense of honor required him to grant her wish. He now mounted his horse and rode, accompanied by many bold knights, but God would make the final decision as to who was in the right.

The lady, a worthy follower of God, made her appearance with a beauty unequaled in the whole Roman world. She had invited many women from Rome and the Lateran to come with her and wait in the field. Their headdresses were decorated with gold and ribbons, and the lady went among them like the moon before the stars, confident of maintaining her honor against any detractors.

The lordly ranks drew closer until they could see each other clearly. Handsome Theodoric asked a group of bold heroes to tarry a little.Then he quickly chose twelve of them to serve him in word and deed. Those noblemen were made aware that none of them would survive if they failed in any part of carrying out his plan. They all raised their right hands high and promised that they would never act against whatever he would tell them to agree to. Then he asked them to take vengeance for him against the queen.

Those heroes were very startled at his words. They all complained about the plan to get rid of the lady, as he was asking, saying that it would bring disgrace upon his honor. "It seems to me," said the wisest among them, "that the best course of action would be not to show any hatred for the queen and to avoid carrying out the plan. What she did, she did for the sake of keeping good faith, and I am afraid that if we take sides against her it will bring disaster upon us at the end. Make yourselves keep what you have just heard a secret!"

"Every one of you," said handsome Theodoric, "has promised me aid. Now do you intend to have your oaths count for nothing? My Lord! Consider that I am really forced to do this, and join my men in helping me! Yes, I was shut in there for such a long time, unable to see anything outside in the world."

The lord who had spoken against following his plan now said, "I do feel sorry for the lady, but I will be true to the oath I have sworn, and I will stand by with the knights of your household in defending you. Still, when all is said and done, this will separate us from honor."

When the king rode up over the broad field and saw his brother, he asked straightaway, "Brother, how fares my wife, of imperial kin and the very dearest one to me ever born upon this earth? May God grant her long life!"

His brother answered him as craftily as he could. "She has been behaving in a way which shows that the evil warden of hell has been guiding her. I cannot bring myself to describe what she has been doing, but ask these good knights. They will make you aware of just what her adulterous behavior has been."

"May God have mercy upon me, wretched man," said the king, "for leading her away from her kinsmen. Now, although I am loathe to turn against her, God will no longer grant her to me, to comfort me as I govern the Empire.

"You should not share in any of the shame," he went on, addressing his brother, "nor should you turn to help her avoid the consequences of her filthy acts. You should have hanged her or stoned her, but now the best course of action is to have her thrown to the bottom of the waves and let her be swept away. She shall not survive her repeated acts of whoredom. Do with her whatever you want; just never let me see her again." His brother ordered his men to tie her up and not to return until the Tiber was carrying her off to drown; she should not be alive after the evening of that very day.

The lady was walking along a slope when she saw the men dispatched to seize her riding fast towards her. "Why are you arriving with such sad faces?" she said to them. "Tell me, is my worthy husband still alive? Tell me for the sake of God the Good!"

Then they told her why they had been sent—that God was shunning her for what she had done and, although they had wanted to spare her, they had all sworn solemn oaths before the king that before the day ended they would have drowned her, sinking her to the bottom of the waves.

"Since my lord ordered you to do this, you should not sacrifice your lives [by defaulting on your oaths]," said the lovely woman. "Just let me give some of my fine clothing to the women who have served me so long and so well. I understand very well what has brought on this calamity." Then she began to untie the wraps of her headdress and motioned to one of her ladies. "You should take these wraps and other clothes and give me your dress. I will put on your things, and you put on mine—wear them in good health! You followed me from my father's land. Now death will separate us forevermore—and, yes, I do feel very sorry for my dear lord."

She wept bitter tears as the men tied her up with silk cords and hurriedly led her to the bridge in Rome. There one of the men carried her on his back and threw her into the waves. She floated and later was washed up at a sandbar where a fisherman was to pull her up on dry land.

But right then God passed judgment on the two Theodorics. They became weak and leprous just at the moment the lady was thrown from the bridge. But then a wondrously good thing happened—as a fisherman was pulling in his nets the current swept an unconscious maid in his direction. He hurried to net her and carried her up on the bank. God showed his goodness, and the lady began to breathe again. The man greatly rejoiced and turned the noble lady over to his wife so that she could help her recover her strength.

When she understood that she could stay there a while, the fisherman asked her to tell him where she had come from or of what birth she was. "I am a poor, worn-out woman," she said. "I would very much like to earn your good will, and I am hoping that you will give me shelter for the sake of a heavenly reward. Have mercy on my insignificance!"

The fisherman replied that he would be more than willing to fulfill the lady's request.

"I would like to ask you to be silent about this, so that no one knows I am here," the lady continued. "I will serve you faithfully, and you need not worry about my doing enough to earn some of your food and drink. Just let me forget my misery!"

The fisherman arrived at his lord's court almost empty-handed, for he brought very few fish. Men were about to stretch him over the table to be beaten as punishment, but just before they did this he told them what had interrupted his fishing. "A lost maid was floating in the water, and I feared

I would be committing a sin if I left her there to drown, so I hurried over to her with my nets." Upon hearing this, they poured some of their very best wine for him and told him to bring the maid with him the next day, so that he could make his case before the assembled court.

The next morning, as God knows, he brought her to the court before his master around the midday mealtime. He offered some scanty goods, which he had had great difficulty getting together for the dues he owed. All the while Crescentia's sobbing moved everyone. One of the ladies at the court comforted her: "There is no need for you to be kept down by your grief, for it seems to me that we would do best to treat you with mercy and kindness. How would you like to have some of our furs and gold?"

"What should I ever do with furs and jewelry?" she asked. "I remain beset by constant sorrows that surround me in the evening and in the morning as well. I have no desire to have furs, or fine tunics, or silver, or gold, ever again. If you will consider my distress and let me stay, I will never let you down as I serve you. Why should I ever run away from you?"

On the day when the overseer began to account for the goods and services owed to his lord and master, it was evident to the seneschal that he was short a day's worth of fish the past week, and he threatened retribution against the man who owed the fish, saying, "As long as God lets me live and I am serving my lord, I will not accept this kind of faulty service!"

"I can explain very easily what went wrong and has confused the accounting for you," said the overseer. "One of my serfs was fishing along the sandy bank when he saw a maid washed up near a meadow. She knows how to do excellent needlework with silk and make anything she wants to. She does well with ribbons and fine cloth, no matter what task you set for her. She is such a valuable asset. Why should we want to punish the fisherman?"

The seneschal lost no time in going to his lady's chamber and spoke. "The overseer told me how one of our fishermen pulled in an abandoned maid when he caught her in his nets. The water had carried her there from far away. The overseer has been praising her handiwork. She is highly skilled in fine embroidery."

"You are really telling a marvelous tale," said the duke's wife. "As my life is dear to you, do not delay but hurry back to that maid and see to it that she be brought here!" That same day at dinnertime, he brought her, as God knows, before the duchess, who received her lovingly just as if she had been her equal and a worthy companion. She ordered that Crescentia be clothed well, intending for her to be a lady-in-waiting for her in her chambers and that her clothing be ornamented with gold and precious stones. Moved by her beauty to have mercy upon her, the duchess showed the needy woman honors and kept adding to them.

When the duke returned from the court [at Rome] and before anyone else had so much as a chance to greet him, his wife said to him, "My dear Lord, why are you acting so strangely? You must be bringing us bad news from your long journey to the court."

"First I must tell you some news that is very sad, as the Lord knows," said the duke. "My two good lords are lying near death, and my lady has drowned. Who could ever see any good in what has happened? The Romans are complaining that no one is governing the Empire."

"Early the other morning I was brought a maid who had been cast out," said the duchess. "In her company you may well stop thinking about your lady. Grieving alone will not help you get over your sorrows. You should welcome her kindly. She was washed up on a sandy bank and found. I don't know, but perhaps someone ordered her to be thrown into the water."

"My dear," he said, "by your very life have this woman brought to me. I must have a look at her. God has put her into our hands for my lady's sake. Is it possible that the fisherman was unable to recognize her?"

Then they called for the woman to be brought to them. Her skin and, yes, her hair and eyes, too, were pale and faded. Nothing about her let him recognize Crescentia, regardless of how often he had seen her in days gone by. He really had no assurance that she was still alive. He told the ladies [except for the duchess] to withdraw, and he gave her a kingly welcome, telling her to sit down on a bench. "My dear," he said to the duchess, "thank you for what you have done! We will keep this woman. Let her take charge of your chamber."

Then to Crescentia he said, "*Filia naufragata* [daughter of the shipwreck], I want you to tell me now where you came from, floating to us over the sandy waves so that a fisherman found you. You may well have been in authority back at your home. My guess is that you were betrayed by ladies of the chamber."

"It is not at all the way you are guessing, milord," she replied. "I was sailing to Rome with people loyal to me when because of my sins the waves broke apart the ship, and everyone on board drowned except me alone. When the ship's deck sank from under my feet I lost all my worldly belonging, and I very nearly lost my life."

The duke told her to make herself comfortable and that he would try to console her for her losses with many honors. She appeared to be very intelligent, and so he asked her to teach his son. He named her "mistress," to oversee the boy's upbringing, and all the duke's people called her that. The lady was unassuming, kind, of a thoroughly chaste mind, honorable, and generous. The duke soon insisted on discussing matters at hand with her before transacting business at his court.

The fact that she enjoyed such a good name aroused great envy in an enemy of God, the duke's seneschal. For his very life he wanted to make love to her, and to gain his will he enlisted the help of a maid as a go-between. She spoke with the lady at all hours of the day, trying to get her to let that bold hero have his way with her. She told her how he wanted to give her many broad acres of land without delay for her very own and how he would treat her lovingly in such a way that she would never have to sacrifice any bit of her reputation.

The lady answered her cunning messages softly. "What purpose do those pretty words serve? Does this faithful man really want to inflict such a mockery of love on my body? It would be far more fitting for him to embrace his wife than to warm me in his arms. I am of too humble origin for him anyway, and he would be committing a sin in making me his concubine."

"He would make it all up to you with his kindness," said the maid, "but then, if only you would take hold of yourself and let me bring him to you in your chamber very late at night, you could have the last word so that he would not send you any more messages."

"I have already told you what is on my mind. All this talk serves no purpose. There is no reason for it. There are plenty of women he could win over. If he would be kind enough to stop these sinful approaches, he could count on my loyal service in other ways, but what he is asking would destroy me. You should stop singing his kind of wedding song for once and for all!"

The maid took note of these heated words and then went quickly to tell the man who had sent her, "Tell me what you want to do now. That woman has rejected us. I am not able to bring her around to accepting you, and I do not want to try any more."

He answered her by saying, "What did that accursed wretch have to say? She scorns my body, does she? That filthy woman, how high and mighty does she think she is! She was condemned to drown for sorcery!"

"She did not say anything really bad," said the maid, "but that you are too noble for her. She has been through terrible troubles. At night she has told me of such things as make me feel truly sorry for her. Just let that suffering woman live her own life so that we will not add any more sins to those we have already committed."

"We should all share the treasure she has," said the seneschal. "She took it all and locked it up in a chamber. Let us all pull together and see to it that she no longer enjoys my lord's protection." Deep in his own guilt, that same man did not know what he really wanted to do. "The duke should not tolerate her at his court any longer," he continued. Angrily he strode into the hall where the maids were sitting all around and shouted, "What are you hiding, you evil sorceress? You should go to the forest and gather wood instead of looking after these maids. You are a wicked witch, sitting there dripping with gold."

"God knows, good knight," she said, "that you are doing me a terrible injustice. I offered to serve you if you would not trouble me anymore. God knows, too, about any guilt I might have, if I am a wicked woman, or if I have ever practiced witchcraft."

The seneschal wanted to strike her a blow and kick her with his feet, but the maids would not let him. He was very unhappy, and he made terrible threats as he left.

"O me, miserable outcast," she said, wringing her hands. "Surviving the waves has helped me very little. Now I am having unjust accusations flung at me. Lord God, have mercy on me through your grace! My great and many sorrows still afflict me. Now he is accusing me of many wicked deeds."

Her maids then told her to stop crying but to complain to the duke, her lord. "He will render judgment and preserve your honor, for we maids will all testify for you. What do his threats mean to us? He shall pay for daring to make such accusations against our mistress."

"I have no wish to ruin him," said Crescentia. "He may well make his injuries up to me. Then I will let them go unavenged forever. He did accuse me of many dreadful things in spite of knowing my innocence."

With his hammer, a smith fashioned a very solid key to the chamber where she slept with no one knowing about it except that enemy of God. The smith swore him a double oath that he would keep it a secret if he stole into the lady's chamber.

Very late at night he went to the lady's chamber. A burst of wind blew in, and while it was so loud in the room he cut off the head of the duke's son with his sword, making it appear that she had murdered him. Then the seneschal hostile to God laid the child's body in her arms. With this wanton crime he lost any claim to nobility he might have had. Then he went quickly to his lord's bedchamber and said, "Lord, you should arise and come to the morning worship service. The morning star has risen. You have never wanted to sleep into the morning before."

"Spare me the morning service," his lord replied, "until the mistress decides it is time. It's not really very late yet. I don't think any rooster has crowed yet in the dark, and I don't know why you woke me up. Go and see why the mistress has not woken up herself."

And so the seneschal went quickly to the ladies' chamber, where he raised his foot and gave the door such a kick that it burst inwards. Right then he raised a loud cry. "Up, up, everybody in here! See how the devil woman has murdered the child who slept in her arms. God must have mercy upon us forever having seen her!" They all hurried over to see where he was standing.

The lady soon felt the blood and stretched out her hand, searching for the boy: "Merciful God!" she cried. "Of what crime have I been made to look guilty? Why didn't the fish eat me before the fisherman found me down at the sandy bank?"

"My trust has been very poorly rewarded," said the duke, full of regret. "What did you imagine I had done to make you want to kill my child—you, standing there before me all bloody as you are? If I had not rewarded you enough you still might have held back for Our Lord's sake."

"I may well appear guilty of a crime God knows I did not commit. I am only a miserable and homeless woman, and I can see that I have forfeited my life. It has been brought home to me that God is not taking my part. Still, I am not afraid of death since I have been rushed into losing my life through no guilt of my own. No one can help me if you want to hang me or cast me into the water unless Holy Christ, who is Lord of all the widows and the defenseless, decided to come to my aid."

Up spoke the man the duke trusted. "How dare she let her voice be heard! Or think up lies? You should lose no time in ordering her drowned."

"Why should we make anything out of a woman's idle talk," said the worthy duke. "If we hang her the damage will still not be undone. There is no way we can restore things. We should let her go her way and do what is hers to do, so that she will not bring about any more sinning among us."

"It would seem,' said the duke's seneschal, "that you will not let God protect either your honor or your life. You are not convinced of this woman's guilt. Yes, she has overcome you with black magic. You will suffer even greater harm from her yet."

With a downcast spirit the good duke responded. "Do with her as you like."

The seneschal hit her on the head with his fist so that her ears rang and the child's body slipped out of her arms. With both hands he grabbed her by the hair and dragged her outside the chamber door. All the ladies asked him to let her live and not to kick her with his feet.

He made every effort to torment her, as if he thought she had not suffered enough pain. He struck her mouth so hard she could not speak. "I will take my vengeance on you, filthy sorceress, so that never again will you bewitch or deceive anyone. With your crime you have chosen death at my hands."

He dragged her by one leg down over the castle moat-ditch to the bottom of the hill [by the river]. "Now it is up to me to choose," he said, "whether I let you die or live, and you cannot do anything about it."

When the lady was facing death, she raised her prayer up to God. "Lord, receive my spirit since you know very well how guilty I am!" When she finished these words, he grabbed her by the neck and pushed her into the water where she sank to the bottom of the waves. That dog of a man rejoiced at the murder [he thought he had committed].

God passed his judgment for this injustice on both lord and vassal. They became leprous and terribly weakened throughout their whole bodies. They more than earned this because of what they had done to this woman.

The lady floated downstream for two days until on the third she found herself lying on an island. She saw Saint Peter walking on the water towards her, having taking upon himself the image of an old man. "Good lady," he said, "why do you want to sit here in the sand? Why don't you go up on the dry land? You must have gone through quite an ordeal to end up in such a pitiful state."

"You are asking me to step upon the water, in order to reach the land, milord, which I dare not do. I fear that I would be committing a sin if I were to put myself to death in the waves. I would rather put up with the misery I now have."

"I command you," said the holy man, "under pain of excommunication to vacate this island—grace has been granted to you—and return to the duke's castle. Then let him swear to his sins in public confession. After that, restore health to his body." Saint Peter bestowed the power to do this on the woman.

That lordly man held out his hand to her and led her to walk over the water's current with dry feet. Her gait was so quick and firm because of the saint's good words that in two days she had traveled over the water all the way back to where she had begun her ordeal, arriving back at the castle at nones on the third day. The wonderful saint had brought her there.

The saint then took leave of the lady, who said, "Who could ever fail to trust God? He has now spared my life according to his grace, for he was watching over me while everything was happening to me according to his will. He continued to be mindful of his serving woman. Now I have enjoyed the fruit of my faithfulness to him."

When the lady came up to the castle, no one recognized her. The great suffering she had been through had drained all the color from her face. People at the castle asked where she had come from: Was she in the service of the duke, or was she on a pilgrimage? Also, had she met up with a good physician in all the lands or did she have any information about where one might be found able to take upon himself the healing of their lords? If he could cure them, they would be willing to divide their lands with him.

"Direct me now to the chamber," said the lady, "where I can see the lord and tell whether his affliction is of the sort that a physician can cure."

They soon brought her to stand over the duke's bed in the master chamber.

"This is the third day," they told her, "since this affliction came upon him. He has not been able to see or say anything, nor has he had a bite to eat. God knows we would not be able to tell whether he is dead or alive, were it not for the fact that the breath coming from his mouth is still warm. Please give us some consolation that he will be restored to health again!"

"My dear lord," said the lady to the duke, "why has this happened to you? Look up with your eyes, and show us what you are capable of doing. If you will confess your sins before us, God's wonderful grace may well come to you."

The lord looked up. "I will be glad to tell you," he said, "everything I can remember. I have no desire to conceal anything." Instructed by the lady, all the people prayed to God that he would hear their prayer and restore their lord to health.

When he had finished his confession, the lady told him to get up, but his legs would not support him. She told him he was mistaken. He seemed to want to hide something that God wanted revealed beyond what he had confessed.

"Holy Queen," he said, "My Lord did not make me aware of any other sins. I have not hidden anything from you. I have told you about everything sinful I have ever done in my life, except perhaps the time when I let my vassal kill a poor outcast woman. I felt forced to let him do that because she murdered the child I entrusted to her care. Now I sincerely regret letting him kill her, and I would be glad to do penance for this misdeed of mine forever."

When he completed his confession the man was healed of the leprosy in his body, and he lost no time in falling on his knees at the woman's feet.

"I am dust and dirt," said the woman worthy of God. "My Lord is the doctor who healed you from all your suffering. See to it that you do not forfeit his protection ever again!"

"I still have an afflicted man in my service," he said. "Would you please consider seeing him also, since you have come to us through God's grace? If you will help him overcome his disease and regain life and health I will give you his weight in gold. He has always been so true to me, serving me as a faithful vassal, that I would not regret giving you that reward."

Then the lady was taken to observe the sick seneschal. She touched him with her hand, and he turned his face from the wall. "Look up and speak!" she said. "Confess your sins openly before these people. Just think of how my Lord will accept penance and cure your sickness if you make a complete and proper confession."

"Holy serving-woman of God," said the seneschal, "just let me reveal something to you privately in two or three words before the people find out. . . ."

"It will really not accomplish anything," she said, "unless the men and women here can hear you. Otherwise no one can cure your leprosy or save you from death."

"If you don't want to spare me from having to make my whole confession so that everyone hears it," he said, "I would rather suffer my affliction alone."

"Change your mind about that," said the good duke. "You are heading towards a bitter end. Raise your hands high to the Lord, and tell him your sin and remorse before death carries you off. Let us all hear what you have to say, and leprosy will no longer afflict your body. Do just what this woman tells you to do!"

"You are giving him fatherly advice," said Lady Crescentia to the duke's words. "Now forgive him yourself for the crime he committed against you that you mentioned to me earlier. If you should not assure me that you will pardon him for it, he will probably hesitate to confess it."

"Why should he hesitate to confess before me?" asked the duke. "I am easily able to grant him pardon for anything since I never had a man so loyal to me or one whose affliction I regret so much. It would be only fitting for me to sacrifice much in the way of worldly goods for his sake."

When the seneschal confessed what he had done, confirming that he had committed the murder, his lord, the duke, stared at him—the man stood up with his health restored—and said, "What are you telling me, you worthless dog? You shall sorely regret causing me such dreadful sorrow while I trusted you completely."

"Do not let this make you so angry," said Lady Crescentia. "You agreed to forgive him for anything he did in violation of your trust. You should not be accusing him and seeking revenge now."

"I agreed to forgive him for guilt in crimes against me," said to duke, "but I intend to see that he suffers just and severe punishment for what he did to that miserable woman in defiance of God's law. I am not open to any further discussion of his case."

He ordered the seneschal thrown to the ground—no one was allowed to help him—and then bound hand and foot before being thrown off the bridge. He sank to the bottom of the river, where his sins overtook him.

"We have also suffered a grievous loss with our lord, whom we chose to be our ruler and judge," said the good duke. "He suffers from gout and is lost to the same afflictions that beset my seneschal and me. No one has been able to do anything for his leprosy or his great pain, but then I really should not be imposing on you for any further help—unless God were to put you in a mind to offer it,—but if you would like silver or gold for curing him, take any amount from me you would like to have."

"Why are you talking this way?" she asked. "My Lord is the *medicus* [physician]. Any abilities of my own fall far short of what is needed. I am reckoned a poor sinner and yet I have received from my Lord the power to obtain grace for whoever confesses his sins to me. I do not intend to bargain with you for any sort of payment. Just arrange for me to be brought to him."

The lady was escorted to Rome in a splendid procession. The duke rode with her, and great numbers accompanied them. Having heard the good news, Romans flocked to meet the lady in the field before the city, where she was given a fine reception with singing and sounds of instruments. Then she was brought to the master's chamber [in the castle] where she saw her lord. Tearfully she spoke the words that came to her mind only to herself. "Gracious and good Lord! How sorry I feel for my husband even though he is responsible for this bodily suffering I have been through." Everybody there was moved by the lady's evident grief to shed tears of their own.

"You are fearfully weak," said the good lady. "What good is your position as ruler, your red gold or your fine raiment to you? Unless my Lord withdraws his ban from you, you will not be able to speak so much as a word to any of your men, but speak your confession aloud before all of us. My Lord has no follower whose words he does not hear, and with prayer you may win God's help."

"Milady," he said, "since my Lord has sent you here, lay your hand on my bare skin, and I will say my confession out loud for you. If you touch me, desperately ill as I am, I will quickly be relieved of leprosy and pain. I will be very glad to do as you tell me."

He said his confession, but when he stopped he still could not move because he had forgotten to include one of his transgressions. "Just think some more!" said the good lady.

God sent to his mind that he should think about the queen and put into words how he had let her be drowned, which he did. Then he said, "I can think of nothing else that I have done against God's will," and the lady bade him stand up as healthy as he had ever been before. The Romans rejoiced over the good news that their lord had recovered.

"Now that you have saved us from death," he said, "there is one more thing for you to perform with your sweet instructions, doing it for the honor of God. Poor man that I am, I have a brother in the same condition I was in. Please have mercy on him, and let him enjoy your kindness the same way you have bestowed it on me, whom you bade arise in health in the face of certain death."

"Have me led to where he is," said the lady. She forgave all the injuries that this lord's scheme had brought upon her and entered his chamber where she addressed him graciously. "My dear lord, what has happened to you? Make your confession aloud before us, and you will be accepted back as a follower of God and released from your suffering."

"Saintly maid of God!" he responded. "Just let me tell you two or three words privately before they reach other people."

"I tell you truly," said the lady, "it will not do you any good unless you make a complete confession; failing to do so will leave you in your present state. If you hold anything back you will not be letting me help you. Rich and poor must hear it all."

"I will tell you the truth," he answered the lady. "If there is no other way except making a complete confession of everything I have done wrong in front of everyone, then even if it means I will never recover and I must continue to bear my afflicted state, I would prefer to choose death rather than bring such shame upon myself."

"Brother, tell us more about what sort of guilt is yours," said the worthy king. "I would rather do a forty-day fast and undergo the most severe penance before I would let you die. What is life supposed to be worth to me if I cannot have you with me, my dear brother? If I should let your life ebb away, who will there be to comfort me for the loss of my lovely wife?"

"Your brother was subject to you," said the lady. "You entrusted to him the throne and judicial power here at the Lateran. If he violated any part of the Imperial Law, sinning against God or the people, you should sincerely forgive him today for what he did." The good king assured her that he was more than willing to forgive him if he would reveal all his misdeeds.

Then he confessed his sins, including how he had falsified evidence, to which he had sworn a double oath and on the basis of which the lady had been condemned. "She told me to build a tower—which greatly angered the Romans—at the Forum, and used it to keep herself safe from whoredom. She locked me inside it—with something I call a complete lack of love—for two years and two months, which caused me no end of suffering. That is why I ordered her drowned and why I cannot bear to think how I offended against God's will." The lady told him to get up hale and hearty, but the Romans wanted to condemn him.

When the king heard the heart-rending story, he said, "What were you thinking about me, brother, when you took my wife from me? She was as dear to me as life itself. I will always be grieved by that before God, and even if I have to wear chains the rest of my life you shall not escape the results of ordering my wife cast into the water."

The woman intervened just in time to quell the strife. "I cannot call that an honorable act for a mighty king to go back so quickly on his word. I forgave the man for the [attempted] murder, but if this is how you intend to repay me for serving you so well, I am beginning to regret my service to you."

"I will be true to what I promised. For your sake I forgive him for causing me such grief as no other man has ever suffered," said the king in the midst of tears. "Just let me do something concerning you, dear woman, that I am longing to do, or I will surely die. Let me relieve the pain in my heart, milady," he went on, "and I will not put you to any more trouble."

"And what sort of request do you have?" she asked.

"I want you to let me cut a small hole in your clothes between your shoulder blades."

"I grant your wish," she said. "Since you wanted to do what I asked of you, as Christ knows, I will let you do what you want with me."

Then the fabled king called for a scissors, and, asking the ladies there to help him, cut through her fine linen dress, tunic and the garment beneath it and found a birthmark that he recognized well. He called her by her name and fell on his knees at her feet. "How happy I am to have you again, you best of all wives!" he said as he held her neck to neck and then kissed her.

They lived together quite properly, as Christ knows, for a year and eight weeks. Then an open court was announced. The king sat as if in judgment, and the lady rose in the sight of everyone there and reminded him of the pledge that he had given her that he would join the spiritual order. "And give your brother the Empire," she went on, "while you become a monk and renounce all worldly honors!"

The king was much taken aback by this, but he wanted to be true to his royal words, since he had spoken them to the assembled princes earlier. "I will do what I have promised to do," he said, "although it is the most difficult thing I have ever done in my life, for love of you."

"My heart hurts me the same way," the lady said to him. *"Portio mea sit in terra viventium* [Let my portion be in the land of the living]." God's grace is not concerned with earthly possessions.

And so he permitted her to enter a nunnery; and she likewise permitted him to become a monk. The woman became a saint, and—while the man had renounced his throne—as a reward God gave him a place in the Heavenly Kingdom, which has no end. Now let us raise up our hands and ask them not to forget us since they possess the Kingdom of Heaven.

He judged the Empire, to be exact, eight years and four and a half months, then angels summoned his soul.

XXXIII

Justinian

Justinian I, "the Great" (r. as Eastern emperor 527–565), is easily the most famous of all Byzantine emperors. He restored much of what had been lost from the Roman Empire and, for a time, united its eastern and western parts. He is best remembered for having sponsored the collection and editing of Roman laws. The resulting Justinian Code became the basic source for the study of Roman Law in Western as in Eastern Europe. Nearly all his military campaigns were successful, partly because he appointed and relied on good generals, particularly Narses and Belisarius.

Justinian was also responsible for rebuilding the Church of the Holy Wisdom, "Hagia Sophia," in Constantinople, the Eastern

Roman capital. Begun by Constantine, completed and enhanced by several successors, it had been destroyed by riots severe enough to give Justinian the idea of fleeing the city. Justinian employed 100,000 workers to rebuild it as a huge and lavishly furnished cathedral with a massive dome. It remains an architectural wonder even later as a Turkish mosque, when Constantinople became Istanbul after the Islamic conquest of the Byzantine Empire.

As an actress and prostitute, Justinian's wife, Theodora, had a dubious background for an empress. Unlike that of Tharsilla, below, Theodora's personal life as the imperial spouse was shockingly dissolute. Yet it is true that she was one of Justinian's most reliable advisors, persuading him to stay in Constantinople and ride out the savage riots mentioned above—which he did successfully—rather than flee.

Our author pays little attention to the facts of the historical Justinian's reign, preferring to dwell on him as a model of bad, then good, then bad again rulership. His wife, Tharsilla, gives him good advice, but she is much more a model of godly queenship than Theodora ever thought of being. In constructing the character of Tharsilla, our author may have been influenced by the figure of Plakilla, wife of Theodosius I, whom early Christian historians, such as Cassiodorus and Theodoret, presented as a model of wifely and queenly virtue.

The Book tells us that Justinian then held the Empire. Even though he rendered good judgments as a ruler, he was too proud and arrogant. The princes thought him too aloof, wanting all the honors that should belong to all of them only for himself. The princes began to desert him. He judged too severely in a way that made everyone afraid, until the princes became hostile towards him, and no one wanted to stay around him.

He had a wife named Tharsilla, who was a very capable woman and saved his life many times. She had many good ideas—how well she got him out of difficulties through gifts and just the right words! She used her good sense and imagination to keep even the most powerful lord from ever killing the king because of what he had done. Still, the nobles starting complaining among themselves about Justinian.

The king could not escape the terrible lack of moderation he felt when anger overtook him. The whole Senate shied away from him because no one dared to give real answers to his words. It did not take much time before the king was the prisoner of hatred and jealousy, which he took out on his wife. She paid dearly for his wickedness. He took to scolding and beating her, but our Savior helped her so that she was able to prevail in her trials while maintaining her humility.

Good Tharsilla, keeping her thoughts fixed upon a solution to what confronted her, lay by the king's side. How kindly he spoke to her. "Tharsilla, my dear wife, you are to me what life itself is. If I live long enough I will gladly make good all the bad things I have done to you. What can stand in our way? You know, you never heard it said of any of my ancestors that they won more honors than I have. All my kinfolk serve me; the princes must all yield to me in everything. When was a king ever so rich and powerful? My dominions are great, and no prince has the power to avenge the effects of my wrath without losing his life, fortune and honor. You will not find that to be true of earlier kings."

To this, good Tharsilla replied, "God in heaven knows what is on my mind, milord: it brings me great sorrow that you are so all-powerful."

"What are you saying, milady?" said King Justinian. "Let the hatred of all the saints be upon you!"

"Don't be angry with me over this!" she went on. "All the Romans know that if I did not care what happened to you, then what you are doing would not be important to me, since by rights, I should bear everything with you. Now I truly wish to stand by you as long as I am able, or as long as any woman could be of use to you."

"I would like to have an end to this talk," said King Justinian. "On one hand you say that you love me and in the same breath you say you care nothing about my honors!"

The queen wept bitterly: "Milord," she said, "if you would be willing to pay some attention to my explanation, I would be glad to set forth what is really troubling you and would be equally glad to put an end to this talk."

"I would be eternally grateful to you if you would interpret those words of yours, making clear what you wanted to mean by them."

"I am counting on your grace, that you will not punish me if I do," said the queen, and the king confirmed that he would not.

"Milord," she began. "You are a rich and powerful king. There has never been your equal. The princes serve you in fear; however, I will tell you the truth: this will not come to any good end. Love is constant and good. Fear brings on a resentful state of mind, and no one can combine love and fear. Whoever must fear another will easily come to regret serving him. That is the reason I am very much afraid myself that the great fear with which the princes must behold you will lead to them turning on you. Over that I would be lamenting and weeping forever. Truly, milord, if you do not consider this in time, the unfaithful Romans will take your life."

"I will ask you now to accept my eternal thanks," said the king after a long pause, "for ever having been so faithful. This very day, I will put in order what I must do to defend myself from any man's injury to me."

"Milord," said the queen, "stop talking that way! I will tell you the truth. No one can defend himself against faithlessness. You have, milord, the greatest treasure ever assembled, but how is that helping you the least bit? It lies hidden away, and you are living with great worries. If it should come to pass that you would die, then whatever manner of death should befall you, those close to me will not rest content until they have given me to another man in marriage—whether I like it or not. He will go through all your treasure in a hurry. Think about it, milord. You will have neither material gain nor honor from what you have amassed, nothing for your body or your soul. Now, if you did not mean anything to me, I would not be concerned with what happened to you."

"As long as I live," said King Justinian, "I will reward you truly for this good advice. Now decree throughout my Empire, to the lands and to the peoples that they should render you abundant honors. That is my will. Now speak up, good Tharsilla. If you will use your good sense and wisdom to help me always return to the point where I can keep my honor, I will follow your instructions only too gladly."

"Milord," said the queen, "let your good will provide for all of that. You know, I heard my father tell how on the occasion of great feasts our ancestors would invite their vassals from far and wide to be looked after and to enjoy hospitality. Easter Sunday is approaching. Now show your own hospitality; offer to serve your vassals, showing your love for them for the first time. Summon them into your chambers, and be willing to follow the counsel they give you. That way you will gain many faithful followers who were secretly your enemies before, and they will put more and more trust in you.

"Milord, when the last day of the celebration arrives, do as I tell you: when the princes want to take leave, you should give them magnificent gifts. Call for plenty of your gold, of which we always have a good supply, to be brought out. Command that all the princes be given some; yes, to the other lords, too, their vassals and those who are simply their followers. And if you want to continue following my advice I will convert the princes for you so that they will willingly serve you once again. I will turn their hatred of you into lasting affection. That way you can easily regain your honor. Fear means making a man flee; love means keeping him. Fear chases him away; love means having him stay. Fear means having him resist everything; love means having him live with honors."

The noble king followed his wife's proposal: he offered a great feast in the city of Rome, to which princes from throughout the Empire came, and he gave them a very magnificent reception, showing them every honor that was worthy of those noble lords. When the celebration was over, the king called for the gifts to be brought out, many bracelets of red gold, many wide silk blankets, many fine vessels and high-footed goblets with cups inlaid with gems. From man to man he went, presenting gifts to all of them until all of those who were at the feast agreed with one voice that they had never seen such marvelous gifts, and each one said to him, "As long as I live I will serve you in remembrance of these gifts."

There was no one among them who did not join equally with the others in affirming that they would never fail him or leave his service. They all took up praise of the king, and fear transformed itself into love, which was all due to Tharsilla, the queen.

Then the fabled Justinian, Roman judge, increased his abilities and his successes until he was very mighty indeed. He had such willing support from all his men that no one could resist his authority. He also became quite good at playing the lyre and added many other achievements to his name. He kept this up as long as he lived.

But, finally, it happened that King Justinian seduced a lady and secretly slept with her. Her husband was named Marcellus; his brother was called Theodosius. When Marcellus found out that his wife was unfaithful to him, he spoke with great feeling. "By my love of God the Good! He will sorely regret this day what he has done!" He then crept stealthily and all alone to where the king was with his men who had arrived at his court. He approached the king, who was surrounded by his men, and ran him through with his sword, shouting defiantly, "The devil betrayed you, luring you into seducing my wife, but you will never seduce another woman! My honor was very dear to me so long as I could maintain it. [It is gone, but] this is also your last day!" For a fact, Justinian had the Empire for just seven and a half years and twelve days more, and then this lord killed him.

XXXIV

Theodosius

Early in his reign, Theodosius I, "the Great" (r. 379–395), established what became Roman Catholicism as the Roman state religion and, after some disputes with Saint Ambrose, accepted the principle that the emperor should be guided by the church in matters where church and state interests crossed. He was also a man of the utmost piety, who prayed long and fervently before battles and gave God full credit for his victories. His wife, Plakilla, as mentioned in the introduction to the previous chapter, may be the model for our author's Tharsilla.

The fact that a Council of Ephesus figures prominently in the account below, however, would point to Theodosius II as our author's subject figure, since he convoked the first Council of Ephesus in 434 and the second in 448.

Coping with heretics through councils or synods and debate—rather than simply trying to annihilate them—was part of church policy in the fourth and fifth centuries. In our author's own day the handling of heresy was heading towards the prompt, physical elimination of offenders, and it is of some interest that the *Book of Emperors* defends the earlier policy of debate with heretics against the more recent policy of wiping them out.

Arius taught, we recall, that there must have been a time when there was a God the Father but no God the Son. This teaching denies Jesus as co-eternal with God the Father and contradicts the opening passage in the book of John, which portrays Jesus as God's Word, given at the dawn of eternity, that became flesh. Arius was accused of making Jesus into a separate, lesser divinity, and the Arian controversy rocked the church during the time of Constantine, who dealt with it at the Council of Nicaea. Arius died unexpectedly of unknown causes in 336. The story below that he died in a privy was widespread by the twelfth century.

Theodosius II lived a century after Arius, and the Councils of Ephesus dealt with different questions. Debated at Ephesus was the Monophysite idea that Christ had only one (divine) nature—and not a human one—rather than the Arian heresy or the idea of the Resurrection.

Saint Eusebius of Caesarea was the foremost chaplain of Constantine I, in whose service he distinguished himself as a Christian orator and historian in the 320s and 330s. The story of the devil entrapping a young man with a beautiful statue was probably inspired by an account of Roman *mirabilia*. William of Malmesbury's *Deeds of the Kings of England* contains a more elaborate version some twenty-five years before the *Book of Emperors* was completed. The two accounts are similar enough that they may well descend from a common source that has been lost.

he Book tells us that Theodosius, born a Greek, then held the Empire. He stood completely in the fear of God when he was chosen judge. He did many good works and devoted all his thoughts to how he might serve Holy Christ. He prayed to him silently but fervently, which brought him great honor.

It came to pass that King Theodosius adopted the custom for himself—which was to benefit him greatly—of staying away from the crowd and never saying a word in the morning until he could set his eyes upon the Holy Cross, falling on his knees in prayer before it. In his prayers he was mindful of God's wounds.

At the same time there were two brothers of a distinguished family in Rome who paid no attention to matters of the soul. Instead, they struggled to find ways of showing love for idols. They became obsessed with material splendor, and did not recognize the true God.

The king frequently instructed men whom he sent to these brothers to tell them and plead with them to be aware that they should stop worshiping idols before Christianity, for the honor of the holy faith. The young nobles scorned this advice.

It happened then that one of the brothers, named Astrolabius, and some of his companions were playing with a ball. He threw the ball and it landed in an old walled-up place. I know that he just could not resist being led by pride and curiosity to climb after it, when suddenly the young man saw a beautiful statue that greatly appealed to him. He was overcome by the thought that if he could get to it he would feel better than ever before. I know that he did not turn back. He jumped down on the other side of the high stone wall and stood before the statue. The devil pursued his work within the statue and signaled with his hand for him to come closer. On the spot the youth was so fervently enraptured that it transformed all his senses. He fell in love with the statue, which had been made *in honore Veneris* [to honor Venus]. The devil then told him what to do: he took a ring from his finger and put it on the finger of the statue as a bridal gift. In an extravagant promise, he assured the image that he would love it as long as he would live.

His good friends were waiting for him nearby on the street, but he seemed to them to have been gone a long time, and they were worried that he might have fallen somewhere. They asked the heathen priests if they would open the gate for them. The priests gave all of them the same answer—that Emperor Constantine had forbidden this gate to be opened for any Christian man for all time.

The youths became angry at hearing this. They hit the priests and stabbed at them, becoming violent until they had broken open the gate. They found Astrolabius. Although things stood very badly with him, he concealed from his friends the grave misfortune that had befallen him.

His comrades led him back to where the ball lay, but they could do nothing to help him. He had fallen so deeply in love with the statue that he was possessed by the devil. He could not eat or drink anything, nor could he sleep by day or by night: he would imagine having the statue lie beside him. His body seemed very heavy to him, and his skin turned pale and sickly. He looked very close to death, as friends and relations said, as well as anyone else who saw him.

One day it happened that the boy Astrolabius was standing all by himself, when he began to cry bitterly. Then he pulled himself together and said, "This thing is not good for me in any way, and I can't stand it anymore. My life is no longer good for anything. No doctor can give me any advice about what to do. If I knew someone I could flee to, and if he could make my life worthwhile again, I would gladly become a Christian.

He had heard it said that the emperor had a chaplain named Eusebius, whose fame for knowledge and wisdom was widespread, and Astrolabius wondered if that man could tell him something to help him out of his dire straits, once he had explained his sufferings to him. When he finally convinced himself that this was what he should do, he hesitated no longer, but secretly made his way straight to Eusebius. There, falling at his feet, he said, "Milord, I seek your mercy. For a long time now I have been held by great sorrows. I call your goodness to mind. Please help me out of my misery. No one has been able to do anything for me, but I would like to have your advice about it. I will listen to you and follow whatever you tell me to do or not to do."

That same priest had a strong fear of God. When he realized what had happened to the youth, he burst into tears himself and he reminded Our

Lord that he might want to think of his own honor and restore sanity to this youth. Eusebius the priest kept the words of the Holy Apostle [Paul] in mind: "If you want to have God's protection, you should help each other carry your burdens." He was determined to help Astrolabius and promised him that he would never let him down, and that he would help him regain his strength again and return to his senses if he would only put his faith in God.

The Book goes on to tell us that when he was still a youth, good Eusebius the priest had read in the black [magic] books, from which he diligently learned much that stayed in his memory. He knew that with the devil having taken it so far, no one could restore things to the way they were without getting back the ring, which only Our Lord could do.

Very early one morning with the young man present, Eusebius read aloud from a book, and it did not take long before the devil came to them. He urgently implored the devil to clear up what was causing this; that is, who was making the youth so miserable? Could it be that he had some part in it?

"Look now, Lord Eusebius," the devil responded. "You took an oath to stick to Christian ways. You have now perjured yourself. I never felt such torment—in hell it never was so hot as I feel in your presence. Just let there be a pause in the words you are saying and let me go back to hell again; I will take care of what you want me to do."

"I command you under pain of God's ban," said God's vassal, "to bring the ring to me. There is no other possibility for you. Hurry off to where it is and return quickly to me. I am telling you as a fact: if you do not return quickly, you will have very good cause to regret it."

"See here," the devil responded to him. "Why are you talking to me like that? You would consider it very unfair if your servant or someone else of yours would be taken from you, as you are now doing to me. Look, the fact that he is in my possession proves that he is rightfully mine. My having his ring is proof of the same thing."

"You are not telling it as it was," said God's vassal. "You were after him early and late with your temptations. You trapped him into doing what he did with your evil counsel. You do not have a proper seal on your contract. You must bring me the ring, or you will never get away from me here."

"Beyond any doubt," the devil answered him, "even if I must burn here forever, I still can't bring back the ring. It was not entrusted to me alone. It is impossible for me to take back anything given to all my colleagues, and there is many a squadron of them."

"Then you can take me where they are," said God's vassal. "I command you to do that under pain of God's ban, so that I can see the ring, and do not lead me off the path that heads straight to there. Your comrades have been given no power over me." How these words were hurting the devil! "Unless you take me there, if I keep on living, things will not stay what they are for you. I shall break apart your home and drive you out of it, since your power is not all that great. Come now, I can't wait any longer. I must have that ring, and you are to serve as my companion in finding it."

The devil was sore afraid of him. In a short time he traveled with him three hundred [German] miles [approximately 1,500 English miles] down through the bottom of a swamp. That dog gnashed his teeth and shouted at Eusebius, "There are two of these rings. If you touch the wrong ring, that will make you a robber, and if you do us that injustice, my companions will tear you apart as they would a chicken."

"Tell me the name of the stone that is mounted onto the ring," said God's vassal. "I command that *in verbo domini* [by God's word]."

"Jasper is its name. You seem to want me to tell you everything there is under heaven. You make a bad traveling companion."

It was a difficult time for the devil when God's true vassal took back the ring. "Now, bring me back to the place from which you took me!" Eusebius commanded, and the devil set him down in the city of Rome, where the devil asked to take leave, saying, "Let me travel back, and you may have my willing service always."

"Don't be in any rush to go!" said God's priest. "You must still be burning here tomorrow at this time unless you tell me about the original cause of all those bad things that happened to this youth."

"Well, I am forced to tell you: the heathens fashioned a statue *in honore Veneris*. We were there when they did it. Herbs are buried under it, and—I will tell you the truth—they have such power as to make the statue irresistible so long as they stay beneath it. Whoever sees the statue above them will fall in love with it forever. That is the way they honored Venus."

"Now you may take your leave—be off in God's hate!" said God's vassal. "We will take care of things from here on. In God's love we will have another kind of house here." He asked people to move the column [on which the statue stood] just one foot away [and he removed the herbs from under it]. The youth was relieved of all his afflictions, and he believed in the true God.

Eusebius the priest brought it about that the column was dedicated to honor good Saint Michael. It towers over the city of Rome and can be seen to this day.

They baptized the young man, and even the heathens who happened to be there and had witnessed the great miracles became obedient unto God. King Theodosius rejoiced that Priest Eusebius was winning so many souls for God. Our Lord has also rewarded him, giving him the inheritance he justly deserved. He does not forget anyone who comes to him in great humility with great needs.

A heresy spread itself in Emperor Theodosius' days: Arians arose—I feel sure there is a record of this in Rome to this day—and they sought to bring shame upon Christianity. They taught that there was no resurrection and that when the body dies the spirit dissolves in the air, the body turns to earth, and no living thing ever returns from the air. With that kind of false teaching, they saddened Christendom greatly.

Those who had charge of Christendom were particularly grieved by this and complained about it to the king, saying, "It is disgraceful that throughout your lands teachers of error have arisen. Because of them we will lose God's care and protection and must be prepared to give up the worldly honor as well, which our forefathers won with their warshields in battle and bequeathed to us. They are confusing our faith. Sire, you should declare them outlaws, proclaiming your ban against them among all your peoples."

The emperor made the sign of the cross. "O Holy Ghost," he began. "Keep me from taking anyone's life before just cause has been shown. I am called the Roman ruler and because of that I am hailed as judge. It is expected that I judge justly both the lord and his serving man. Now we hear the books tell us that the sinner should be summoned and pursued with death upon the wheel, but let no one tell me to follow that advice. If he has preached mistakes, that is still no reason to kill him. We also hear the books tell us that our own forefathers proposed synods and let the arguments come to an end in them. Whether we are dealing with rich or poor, we should show patience and kindness, and—yes—God himself showed great humility; therefore, let us gain souls by harvesting them in his love."

When the bishops heard what the emperor was saying, they told their subordinates that all who were concerned with this factional teaching should come together, and they included Archbishop Arius with the rest. Emperor Theodosius chose to call the Council at Ephesus, saying that he would be glad to hear their heresy; he owed Christendom an answer to it.

Arius then sent messengers from land to land, and the Book reveals to us that more than fifty thousand responded to him. They were all set against Christianity, and they were taking advantage of the great freedom they enjoyed rather than being concerned about truth for the sake of their souls.

And so the Council was set to be held in Ephesus. The Roman ruler attended as did many a foreign guest. Most of them wanted to come in order to hear what the heresy was. Arius and those close to him had no desire to avoid conflict; they wanted to speak publicly in Ephesus, and there was a great horde of their followers. The emperor provided lodging for them, and throughout the night the Christians were worried.

Very early the next morning they all gathered at the assembly place. All those who had come rushed to be in the front of the crowd. Those from each faction consulted together about what they were going to say; however, they really had no need of preparation since the Holy Ghost was to become the comfort and the help for all of them.

Arius was still at the inn. His people missed him and were very worried. He was still not in attendance by mid-morning; the emperor thought this showed a lack of respect and ordered that he be brought before him. The men he sent went quickly. They wanted to seize Arius; however, God exacted vengeance for his Christendom: Arius was sitting dead on the inn's privy, where he had expelled his insides. That was how the synod turned out: the heretics learned that their master was sitting dead, and they fell at the emperor's feet, saying that they wanted to do penance from then on for what they had done to injure Christianity.

"Now, be obedient to God," he said. "Keep the right faith, and keep God before your eyes! This is better than having you killed and your souls go to the devil. But if I hear any more of this heresy, I will hold you responsible and punish you severely."

When the synod was ended, its members raised high their hands, saying that God in heaven was a just judge, and that he had well shown his power. It happened that on that very same day the emperor was told as a matter of greatest interest that one of the Seven Sleepers had come into the city. His name was Serapion, and he wanted to buy some bread. Everyone came walking and running so that they could see him. The fabled king asked him how he made his living—what sort of work he was looking to do.

"Great need brings me to this place," said Serapion. "It has been four days now since Decius went after us with a vengeance. He decreed that all Christians should die, and so we fled to the hills. Ever since then we have been hiding there in a cave. It seems to me, however, that I have brought about my own death. I understand now that I came out too soon. Decius surely will not let us go yet. Mighty Christ! Even if I suffer martyrdom today for your sake, help me remain among the just to the very end."

Lord Theodosius fell to the earth upon his knees. He smote his breast and prayed to Christ. "Lord God, you are worthy of all praise. With those devoted to you, you are wondrously kind, and you punish your enemies severely. To the good, you are sweet; to the evil, bitter. Coming to the aid of Christendom, you took Arius out of the world today; and now, Lord, I bring to mind your sublime resurrection. Reveal to us this hidden wonder in a way that will give people no choice but to believe. Forgive us our sins and show us the proof of the final Resurrection, for you are the beginning and the end. I am not asking this, Lord, for my own sake, but for the sake of these people unsure in their faith so that they will know truly that at the end of time you will return in a way that all will fear; then our Resurrection will take place following your mercies."

"Amen," said all the Christians there.

"I don't know how I got here," said Serapion, the holy man, astounded. "When we heard it told that bans had been proclaimed over the city of Ephesus we fled from there—I just do not know where I am now—to Mount Celeon. If you would like to see proof of that—I am assuming that you are Christians—Why don't I reveal them to you? I left them early this morning, and, if you like, I will show all of them together to you. Milord, what is this land called and how did I get here? That mountain called Celeon—is it anywhere close by? Is there anyone here who might know?"

The crowd greatly rejoiced at hearing this. The crowd was quite large, with both men and women. The people praised God [who is] from heaven, put on woolen garments and went barefoot all in the same spirit. They carried crosses, and hordes of people followed them. The emperor led the way. What was happening provided great consolation for Christendom.

When they came close enough that they could see the cave, they heard flint stones splitting apart and very soon the wall in which the men had been sealed came tumbling down. They saw six fine-looking men come out of the cave. Nothing about them had changed. Their hair was the same color. Their clothes were the same. There was no blemish upon them, and their faces shone like the morning sun. The people saw this, and Serapion spoke. "Here we are on Celeon Mountain! Now you may be convinced that I have been telling you the truth. Here you see, my brothers."

The emperor fell to his knees in prayer, and the whole crowd did the same. Malchus told them to get up again. "God made this happen for love of you. I proclaim to you the true resurrection. You see health in this body. Render praise and honor to the Heavenly Lord—that is, the Holy Christ, who is Our Redeemer. Practice goodness to the end. Judge the people fairly, taking no bribes, and have pity on the poor! Help widows and orphans get along. Strengthen the faith and keep God before your eyes. Then God will reward you with a heavenly crown and admit you into his Kingdom. You and all those dear to you should prepare for eternal life. We commend you to God and pray that you remain in good health." With that the six turned around and lay down again. God in heaven was telling them to do that.

Emperor Theodosius began to chant *Te deum laudamus* ["We praise you, Lord]." They sang and gave praise with hearts and mouths. Praise and joy abounded there. They said that no one can survive without God. This is an example of why you should always sing and read about the miracles that God himself wrought in answer to the emperor's prayers. That is what David the Psalmist spoke of in saying, "To him who desires justice, everything shall be granted."

The lordly Theodosius kept serving God more and more ever afterwards. With great commitment he judged the Empire twenty-six years and seven months, as the Book tells us truly. Angels from heaven summoned his soul.

XXXV

Constantine Leo

The Byzantine Emperor Constantine V (r. 741–755), son of Leo III (r. 717–741), is the most likely historic emperor—if indeed there is one—behind the figure of Constantine Leo, since father and son lived roughly at chronologically appropriate times and were distinguished by a desire to defend the purity of the faith in their own way. Constantine V and Leo III were heavily involved in fighting the veneration of images in the Eastern empire's "Iconoclastic Struggle;" sometimes this Constantine is surnamed "the Iconoclast."

On the other hand, Constantine V ruled as an arbitrary tyrant and, apart from trying to suppress image-worship, did not distinguish himself as a Christian emperor, so that "Constantine Leo" may simply be a made-up name for a figure whose reign covers a long period of time.[1] Our author presents only a few, somewhat

---

1. Ohly, op. cit., p.216.

randomly chosen Eastern emperors for his book and may feel the need to fill in the gaps with a composite figure or two.

We have met Saint Helena, mother of Constantine I, "the Great," in the chapters on Constantius I and Constantine I. She was credited in the Middle Ages with bringing the most important relics of Christendom to appropriate resting places, particularly the True Cross to Jerusalem and the seamless robe of Christ and the remains of Saint Matthias, the thirteenth apostle, who replaced Judas Iscariot and whose reliquary—is presented as "the only apostle's grave north of the Alps"—to Trier, where they may be seen to this day. Saint Stephen was the first Christian martyr. His story is told in Acts, 7-8, while Saint Laurence appears in the Decius chapter above. Our author appears to have used one of at least two accounts of the "translatio" ("setting over" or "transferring") of the remains of Saint Stephen—one from the seventh or eighth century, the other from the early twelfth—which are similar in many details, including that of having the body of Saint Laurence roll over in his sarcophagus to make room for his friend, Stephen.

After the noble emperor's death, the city of Rome was rife with feuds and fights. Many was the time the Romans had no judge at all. None of them wanted to give support to another—every house thought itself too mighty to be ruled by another. They thought that accepting the rule of another house would cost them all of their honor.

The Senate reached the decision that they should send out and search from land to land for the wisest lord to be found anywhere, since they did not desire to be without a judge any longer. Our Lord aided them in uniting on Constantine Leo to hold the Empire. He judged very wisely and had all the noble youths taught the books. He focused all his thoughts on being like the good judges. He came to love the princes and to force evildoers to do right. He was also generous to the poor and helpful to men of good will. He began to pray to God ever more often, and in every way he came to be highly honored.

Then it came to pass that Constantine Leo fell ill. That made the Greeks happy because they wanted control of the Empire for themselves, thinking they had a right to it. The Romans could not put up with that, and they prepared a military expedition. The news quickly spread to all parts of the Roman Empire, and the people roused themselves with fierce determination to set out for the sea.

When they all were ready, the emperor announced his personal plans, saying that he could not be talked out of being borne on a litter, to accompany the others traveling there. The Greeks soon became aware that the expedition was headed for them, and so they considered who were the very wisest men among them and then chose twelve of them. They advised persuading the king that he should turn back the expedition and that the reputation of his house would not be put to shame. They hoped to win over his good will by silver and gold.

The Romans, however, heartily approved of their expedition, and showed no intention of being turned back by such offers. The [Greek] messengers arrived secretly where the mighty Constantine Leo was staying and said to him, "Upon your royal honor, sire, please consult with us. Your family stems from Constantinople; marching against us seems like a very improper thing for you to do."

The fabled king replied, "You have a holy martyr. If you will show your devotion to me by giving him to me, I will help you obtain good terms. Saint Helena, the queen—God in heaven put her in a mind to do this—sent him to Constantinople for [her son,] Constantine the king. Now choose to help me take possession of him, for I will tell you exactly what I intend to do: I will force you to fight or to flee, but no one in the world is going to save you. The nature of the Greeks is such that they must have help from other countries where they fight, and then they give way to them. You dare not fight against the Romans; you dare not remain in the field. For that reason, depart quickly, and send me word about what the Greeks intend to do. If that nobleman [Saint Stephen] is entrusted to me, you will live evermore secure in your honors."

The messengers lost no time but hurried to where they found the Greeks. They reported the news that the brave Romans intended to plunder their land. They would not be satisfied until they destroyed Constantinople and ruined the rest of the lands held by the Greeks.

The messengers showed wisdom in quietly taking the princess aside and telling them more. "The Romans are prepared fully to unleash their forces; however, the king himself was heard to say that you have a sublime corpse—that of good Saint Stephen—and if you will send him to the king out of devotion to him, he will turn his expedition around and return home. Further, he will treat you with mercy forever." A cry of despair went up from the Greeks.

I will summarize this part of the story very briefly. The messengers brought no other conditions to be negotiated, unless the sublime saint's body were turned over to the emperor.

When the king caught sight of the holy remains, he spoke to the Romans. "This is true glory, so help me My Lord! If the Greeks have deceived me, they will have paid for it by losing all pf their honor and will always regret it. I sought to invade them in their homeland, and it was a question of life or death for them. At the end they had no choice but to give him to me."

The emperor went closer to the remains, and reverently he fell upon his knees. Looking up to heaven, he spoke in deep humility. "Hail to you, Lord Saint Stephen! God has performed many miracles through you. Milord, since you are able to do it, I pray that you will lead me today to God's grace. Give me back my bodily health, and put an end to all this strife! For that I will serve you ever more, trusted Lord."

When the emperor finished his prayer, the heavens were opened, he saw a great light, and good Saint Stephen brought about his cure. The emperor jumped up completely healthy, and all who were there gave thanks to God. The Romans took the sacred remains and joyfully bore them away with them. The Romans furled their flag, and, praising the Lord, they showed the greatest respect for what they were carrying as they took the remains back to the city of Rome. Hai! How well Saint Stephen was received!

The Romans in the Senate decided to give him the finest burial they could, laying him next to Saint Laurence as his companion. When the sarcophagus was opened, many prayers and offerings were made. After a short time, Saint Laurence turned over and welcomed his equal—Christendom rejoiced at that—and he edged over in a way to make room for Saint Stephen. Be assured that all righteous souls will follow him. His power and renown are still increasing in Rome.

Constantine Leo found his joy in God. He performed good works and never let a day go by without visiting these lords of his. He entrusted his soul to them and had a grave made for himself in the cathedral, saying that he wanted his resurrection to be in their company. He held the Empire for exactly thirty years and six weeks; then the Romans buried their lord.

XXXVI

Zeno

This chapter introduces most of the main players in the replacement of the Roman Empire in the West by the rule of Germanic or other non-Roman kings. Attila the Hun had negotiated his marriage to the sister of the feeble Western Roman Emperor Valentinian III, but before the time for the wedding elapsed, he had taken a young girl from the Balkans as a bride and died in the wedding night of a hemorrhage, so that our author's description of his death as "died in his own blood" is not far off. As far as most Europeans were concerned the Huns then settled down in what became Hungary. As we will see in future chapters, Europeans assumed that the Magyars who invaded them from bases in Hungary were latter-day Huns.

Aetius, who was the dominant personality in the Western Empire during the second quarter of the fifth century, rose in its military service under Valentinian III and his more decisive mother, Galla Placidia. He commanded the forces that defeated Attila at the battle of Chalons-sur-Marne in 451. Aetius sought to claim Valentinian's daughter in marriage, but the emperor, who suspected that Aetius might desire to be emperor himself, stabbed him fatally with his own hand at what was supposed to have been a friendly meeting.

Odoakar was king of the small Germanic Scirian tribe, significant mainly for replacing the last Roman emperor in the West in 476 with himself and thus—although this was not obvious to most contemporaries—putting an end to the Roman Empire outside of what was left in the East. After 476, he called himself simply "King Odoakar," dropping the Scirian appellation, although it was never really clear of what he was claiming to be king. In retrospect he appears to have been king of the German forces in Italy, which falls rather short of being the Roman emperor.

Theodemir ruled a portion of the Ostrogoths or East Goths and sent his son, the future Theodoric the Great (454-526), as a hostage to guarantee the good behavior of his tribesmen to the court of the Eastern emperor, where he was very well treated. He received enough Greek education to enable him partly to shed the stigma of being a barbarian, although he never did live down the rumor that his mother was one of Theodemir's concubines rather than his official queen.

Zeno (Eastern emperor 474–491; sole emperor after 476) sent Theodoric to Italy with considerable forces to conquer and rejoin it to the Eastern Empire. Theodoric took over Italy and then stabbed Odoakar with his own hand at what was supposed to be a feast of conciliation. He then took his broadsword in both hands and clove Odoakar from the shoulder to the flank. Our author mentions Theodric holding his big sword in both hands, although he provides a fictional context of a trial by combat. After that he ruled Italy and much of the remnant of the Western Empire, maintaining the fiction that he was functioning at the behest of Emperor Zeno in Constantinople. The capital of the Western Empire had been moved from Rome to Milan and then to Ravenna. Theodoric turned out to be an excellent de facto emperor, presiding from Ravenna over a period of peace and revitalized economic activity. The Ostrogoths, however, like most of the Germanic invaders, were Arians, and, as heretics, at odds with the papacy and most Italians.

In 524, Theodoric dispatched Pope John I to Constantinople to try and negotiate the emperor (Justin by then) into adopting an imperial policy that would extend basic toleration to Arians. Perhaps John's heart was not in it, but when he returned, Theodoric put him under house arrest for failure to have Justin change his religious policy. He died a few days later, which gave rise to rumors of foul play. Boethius and Symmachus were Roman intellectuals at Theodoric's court. It is a fact of history that Theodoric became suspicious of their loyalty on flimsy evidence and had them killed, as our author notes. Theodoric and his Ostrogoths or East Goths presided for three quarters of a century over a center of mixed Gothic and Roman culture, but no one in the West forgot that they were Arians. Finally, generals sent by Emperor Justinian in the East effectively defeated and destroyed the Ostrogoths in Italy.

A senator named Zeno then held the Empire. He was born a Greek and liked his own people better than the Romans, which made it very difficult for the Romans to accept him. Eventually, Zeno requested the Romans to choose a judge at Rome until he would return [from a journey he was planning to take]. Aetius was their choice. The emperor soon set out on a pilgrimage to Constantinople, but he had no intention of ever returning to Rome.

Now let us interrupt the main story. There was a prince in Merano who was called Theodoric the Elder, a hero with a keen sense of honor who never would agree to being a vassal of Aetius. He gained control of his rightful possessions, taking both people and land from Aetius, who fled to Lombardy. But then Theodoric the Elder had a fine son, brave Thietmar, whom everyone acknowledged as having excellent knightly abilities and virtues.

When Theodoric the Elder lay on his deathbed, he commended his dear sons to his vassals. Soon after that Attila hemorrhaged and drowned in his own blood. The worthy hero Thietmar rode to the lands around Merano, where the nobles were eager to become his vassals.

Attila left two sons, Plôdel and Fritel, who were unwilling for Thietmar to occupy their lands. They sent a message to Thietmar that they planned to come after him unless he would either become their vassal or agree to pay taxes to them.

Thietmar answered the messengers like this: "I am quite certain that my father never was Attila's vassal. He took Merano by force. Attila's children should learn to moderate their claims, since they seem unwilling to let me have what is mine. You tell them now: they will have to get taxes here as best they can."

Plôdel and Fritel then sent word to the Russians and Poles for their men to come and assemble for war, and they rode to Merano. Thietmar lost no time in sending word to Lombardy for his relations to join him. Hai! How willingly they came to serve him! Many valiant heroes rode to meet him. They fought decisive battles in the borderlands with much slaughter. Most of the Huns and their allies were killed, with both of Attila's sons lying dead among the rest. After that, the Huns never demanded taxes from anyone.

The victorious heroes furled their flag and joyfully began to ride home, when they were approached by messengers who told Thietmar that a son had been born to him, which made him return from battle even more joyfully. "May God bless him!" he said. "Here and now I wish to make him the heir of all my possessions. Old Zeno will have to accept him also. He shall truly possess the whole Roman Empire."

There were jealous men among them, who left in a hurry and went to tell the emperor about Thietmar, how he had defeated the Huns and wanted to have the Empire himself. They also told him about Thietmar's son, saying, "Sire, you should revoke Thietmar's decree favoring his concubine's child. He should never enjoy your favor again."

The emperor dispatched his army, which set sail upon the sea, heading for the land of Merano. Thietmar and his men hastened to prepare themselves. They would have been happy to fight, but his wise counselors advised him against warfare then, and so he gave his son, Theodoric the Younger, to be a hostage. He was taken to the land of the Greeks, where he was raised with great care, and he matured quickly. Counts and dukes at the emperor's court had to wait upon him as did other young nobles. He became a handsome hero, and they all became his vassals. When young Theodoric came of age to bear weapons, the emperor entrusted his banner to him, and he brought many lands under his control, which then paid taxes to the emperor. All those under him were in awe of him. He became such a favorite of the emperor that he made him one of his counselors.

Now let us go back to where we left off with Aetius. While he was serving as judge, he made some mocking remarks about the queen, and for that she hated him. To counteract the humiliation she felt, she sent messengers to Aetius saying she could not regain peace of mind until he would agree to come to the ladies' chambers at the palace, to pluck wool among the other women there. If he refused, she would remain resentful.

"It appears that the queen will never be happy again," said Aetius in answer to the message. "I do not intend to pluck wool. Talk like this has made many orphans. You can tell her I am offended. Her tongue is just too long. I will pluck her some wool to spin into yarn, all right. Yes, I will carry out her request—which she will never get over—and maintain her honor. Go and tell that to Emperor Zeno."

Aetius hesitated no longer but hurried off to Styria, which was under the control of a brave and high-spirited prince named Odoakar, and he could well afford to recruit an army. "You are very cramped where you are," Aetius told him. "You rule over nothing but mountains and narrow passes through them, but will you ride with me? Win some broad terrain for yourself! I will make Rome subject to you, and then, by rights, you should wear the crown. The Romans will receive you well, and I dare predict boldly that you will hold the Empire ever afterwards with great honors. We don't need to worry about what old Zeno does."

Odoakar was very pleased to hear this, and he quickly sent out a call to arms. In a short time he had assembled five thousand knights. He rode to the fortified city of Pavia, where the Lombards offered him their fealty, then escorted him to Rome, where they put the crown on his head. They hailed him as their lord, saying that they were quite willing to bring shame upon Zeno in Greece.

When the emperor heard it told that the Romans had raised a king, his heart was greatly troubled, and he uttered these sad words: "Owî! I wish the Romans had killed me before this! Am I really to lose my honor this way now? I would prefer death any day. The Romans are an unfaithful people."

Heroic Theodoric consoled him well, saying, "Sire, you will gain greater respect if you will cease this dreary talk. So long as I am alive, I will fight to uphold your honor. Grant the disputed lands to me as a fief so that I have the right to rule by your grace. I will tell you truly: if I may have some help from you, it would be easy for me to bring Merano into willing obedience to you; my kinsmen are there in Lombardy. I will punish Odoakar's army with swords to the point that he will know that he would be better off at home. Aetius will have to pluck wool after all, or I will make a public display of him with weaver's tools. What made him ride in the wrong direction like a fool?"

Emperor Zeno rejoiced to hear this, and he granted the lands as fiefs to Theodoric, who sent for volunteers from people to people. Russians, Pomeranians, Petsenaere, Valwens, Wends, Slavs, Greeks, and Africans came willingly from everywhere to serve Theodoric the hero. They assembled such a large and powerful army that we may truly say that a bird flying above it in the air could not fly to where there were no soldiers below him before he became tired and fell to the ground.

We hear the books tell us that, with the exception of Julius Caesar, no one ever amassed so many loyal followers. When the Romans heard the news they assembled their forces, too—two hundred thousand men. Aetius took the Roman banner, and shouted at his men that they had the strength and the will to prevail.

Early one morning, near the fortified city of Ravenna, the armies met. Theodoric himself carried his banner and shouted, "Hail, you bold warriors! Today you shall win fame and honor. If you defend the emperor's honor with success, you will be given red gold—the emperor is devoted to you and will keep his word—fine silks and satins, beautifully embroidered coats, and good fiefs aplenty. Yes, you will have subdued their arrogance and will live in honor forever. Charge against them where you see their flag, and I have a feeling that the outcome will show that Aetius overreached himself when he first established himself in Rome. He will have cause to regret his mocking words." Theodoric spurred his horse forward and charged into Aetius. For his part, Aetius resembled a hero of old. They thrust their spears at each other until the shafts shattered. Theodoric drew his sword and cut off Aetius' head; his body went limp. "Never again will you insult the ladies," shouted Theodoric, "nor will you ever help your lord, Odoakar, to attain any honors."

This battle of the nations raged all over the fields. Squadron charged against squadron. The Romans held their ground, acquitting themselves well with their sharp swords while their brave warriors made the most out of their bows of horn and steel. The Roman rage swept over the Wendish men. So many were slain then that the Book has no number for the incredible hordes who all fell dead. How few of them survived! Odoakar's forces fled into the fortress at Ravenna, but Theodoric, the worthy hero, besieged the castle there. High spirits drove him on, and he destroyed all the buildings in Ravenna. The defenders would not surrender Odoakar, but Theodoric scorned their resistance. Every day he ordered attacks on the castle. His men filled in the moat, and the defenders could no longer resist. Thietmar's son won such a victory that it was the subject of talk as long as he lived.

Odoakar saw that nothing was of any help. He stepped up where the moat had been and shouted that Theodoric should be told he was not noble but the son of a concubine. If he were willing to fight with him, he was willing to risk his life in an ordeal by combat before so many good knights.

"Well, now," said the hero Theodoric, "I am really not a woman," and he strode forward like a lion.

His grim determination did not depart from him and he swung his sword with both hands. That was enough to show Odoakar once and for all that he had overreached himself. It was a hard way to lose all royal honors; he never had another chance to make the mistake of seeking them again.

Theodoric and his men rode with streaming banners into the land of the Romans. That warrior had eliminated the lord, Odoakar, as he had promised to do. No one else made the same mistake. All the lords became his vassals, and all the Roman territories served him in awe.

Chapter Thirty-six

In those days lived Boethius, Seneca [Symmachus is meant] and a holy pope called Saint John [I]. They sent a message to Emperor Zeno saying that it was unworthy of him to entrust the Roman Empire to a man of no birth, but the messengers were stopped and seized on their way. They had to reveal the secret of the pope and the other noblemen who had been taking part with him in the conspiracy.

Theodoric, the evil monster, ordered that the noblemen be seized. He ordered the pope led away from Saint Peter's throne and had him sent with a group of priests and laymen to Pavia. He had them all cast into a dungeon—no one was allowed to help them—until they all confessed to taking part in the conspiracy or would die of starvation.

The Christians complained about losing their dear master. God took vengeance for this great injury the Christians suffered and condemned Theodoric before him. Many people saw devils taking him and flying with him over Mount Aetna nearby, [where they dropped him into the volcano.] Saint John, that holy man, commanded them to do that, and he will burn there until the Last Day, and no one can help him

If there is anyone who insists that Theodoric ever saw Attila, let him have the Book brought out. It was forty-three years after King Attila was buried at Buda that Theodoric was born. He was raised in Greece, when he first buckled on his sword he was sent to Rome, and he was buried in Mount Aetna. And so you can see that lie put to rest!

Zeno held the Empire jointly with Theodoric for thirty-six years and five months. They buried that lord in Constantinople.

Constantine VI

Although our author calls the next emperor "Constantius," it is clear that he has in mind Constantine VI, nominal ruler of the Eastern Empire (780–97), whose mother, Irene, did most of the decision-making for him. The name "Herena" is probably a fusion of Irene and Helena, Constantine the Great's mother. Hoping to rule in his own right, Constantine VI had his mother arrested, but he later relented and released her. Irene then organized a plot in which Constantine was blinded and she resumed control. The sordid story of Irene's rule furnished justification for Pope Leo III to transfer imperial rulership from the Byzantine Empire to Charlemagne, although, of course, the Byzantines did not cede any powers. After Charlemagne's imperial coronation in 800 there were once again, for the first time since 476, two emperors, one Eastern, the other Western.

Our author is not content with discrediting the Greeks as rulers. His agenda includes justifying the transfer of imperial rulership from both Greeks and Romans to Germans. Consequently, while the main characters are recognizable as historically real ones in his story, the issue of faithlessness and the eye-gouging incident are used to discredit Romans; the Greeks in his story are discredited only by being abused and humiliated.

 he Book tells us that Constantius, born a Greek, ruled the Empire. They had chosen him to be judge. Herena [Irene] was his mother's name. She was quite a good woman among the descendants of Constantine the Great; there could not have have been a better one.

One night, lying in her bed the lady had a frightening dream. In it she was on a ship crossing the sea, when the ship went out of control and sank to the bottom. She barely escaped and, back on land, a bear dragged her into the woods. The dream greatly troubled the queen.

Day and night, the lady urged her son that he should visit [the graves of] the blessed apostles [Peter and Paul in Rome]. He really did not want to go, but finally he gave in to her pleading and diligently prepared for an expedition to the Roman lands. His mother came along with him. She was well prepared, as was her custom, and took along considerable treasure. The lady did this with the thought that rich gifts would placate the Romans and that old memories of misdeeds could be erased with gold.

The Romans did everything they could to give their guests a fine welcome, showing particular honor to Herena, the emperor's mother. Then the fabled king called for silks and other fine cloths to be brought out, also fine bowls and high-footed goblets with golden well-engraved cups. He gave these to his [Roman] vassals, who all affirmed that they had never seen such fabulous gifts and that they would never fail to support him in all his undertakings.

His mother, Herena, gave them very special gifts: bracelets and rings of red gold and the broadest of silk cloths as long as anything was left in the chamber. As long as the gift-giving went on, the princes liked Constantius and Herena better and better, but when the chamber was empty the Romans reverted to their old ways and began complaining about the grave injustices committed by the guests' forefathers long before, saying that it would be just for them to pay with their lives because of them.

The devil then made it come to pass that a prince was killed who was a member of the Senate. His friends took up the cry that Emperor Constantius should surrender the perpetrator to them; otherwise, they could not put this deed behind them. That made the emperor angry, and he proclaimed his ban over them, ordering that two of them be beheaded. The friends of these men stormed the palace where his mother was with him. No one could prevent this: the Romans seized the two of them by the hair and dragged them to an open field in front of the castle. There they severely assuaged their rage. They gouged out their victims' eyes and cut off their noses, bringing them to the utmost shame amid their loud screams.

From that time on the Roman Empire has been separated from that of the Greeks, so that they never again would lay claim to the imperial right to be judge or to any imperial honors.

XXXVIII

Charles I, "the Great"

Charles (Karl) the Great, king of the Franks (768-814) and emperor (800-814), figures very prominently in both French and German medieval history and legends. Familiar to the English-speaking world by his French name, Charlemagne, the French count him among their kings although without a number. His grandson, Charles the Bald, is the official French King Charles I. The German-speaking world calls him Karl I. He is the founder of the Carolingian Empire, which gave the Germanic Franks their claim to have succeeded the Romans and Byzantine Greeks as heirs to the Roman Empire.

True to form, the *Book of Emperors* treats Charlemagne as the leader whose prowess renewed the Roman Empire after the Greeks had failed to run it honorably. In the minds of most medieval Germans who thought about it, the coronation of Charlemagne as Roman emperor meant a transfer of imperial authority to German rulers. The *Book of Emperors* author correctly states that Charlemagne's coronation took place on Christmas Day, 800, after Charlemagne had invaded Italy to right the wrongs done to Pope Leo III. Making the two men into biological brothers is a new touch of our author—adopted in several subsequent works[1]—probably to make the two leaders' cooperation seem more natural or simply to make a better story. The historical Leo III (Pope 795-816) was probably born in Rome. Many earlier accounts, including

---

1. It is included in one of the stories in *Der Stricker*, an anonymous thirteenth-century collection of parables in verse form. Schröder, p. 380. Almost the whole *Book of Emperors'* Charlemagne chapter was included in *Deutsche Sagen - Gesammelt durch die Brüder Grimm* (Munich and Leipzig: Georg Müller, no date); first edition with introduction, 1816, Vol. II, pp. 107-115.

some from Charlemagne's own time, recorded that Leo had been blinded. Einhard and some others added that his tongue had been cut out—by supporters of a rival claimant to the papacy.[2]

Foremost on our author's mind is driving home the point of the re-fusion of church and state in the Christian Empire begun by Constantine I. Having Charlemagne rescue and restore the pope to his office, with his prayers restoring the pope's sight, has its symmetry in the pope's making Charlemagne into the new Roman emperor. As is true of other exemplary rulers in the *Book of Emperors*, the Imperial Law guides him as he promotes peace and justice throughout his realm. His responsibility is all the heavier, since the Greeks had allowed much of the Imperial Law to be forgotten during their poor stewardship of the Empire. An angel dictates the missing parts, however, and Charles establishes a law code complete down to details of sumptuary laws concerning peasants' clothing and details of permissible and non-permissible weapons for their position of subordination, as established by church-state cooperation. While Charlemagne had many legends to his name by the twelfth century, most of them centered on his battles or other adventures. The historical Charlemagne was, in fact, an effective lawgiver, and our book reintroduces a focus on him as a reformer of laws, which other sources would then pass on. Charlemagne's expedition in 778 against Muslims in Spain lived on in many medieval legends, including the *Song of Roland*. Various Amazon legends had entered medieval historiography since the eighth century. They are contained in the works of Fredegar and Paulus Diaconus, among others. The *Book of Emperors*, however, is the earliest surviving source to work the story of an army of maidens into the account of Charlemagne in Spain. This version was subsequently

---

2.   These include Einhard, *Vita Karoli* from 830 (Darmstadt: Wissenschaftliche Buchgesellschaft, 1955), *Quellen zur karolingischen Reichsgeschichte*, Vol. I, p. 198, and Angilbert (disputed author), *Karolus Magnus et Leo Papa* or *Carmen de Karolo Magno*, dated as early as 801 or 802 (Hannover: Hahn, 1892), *Monumenta Germaniae Historica Scriptores*. Vol. II, pp. 393-403.

passed on in several German sagas, and appeared as late as 1589 in the Saxon *Chronicle* of Panonius.

Many medieval Charlemagne legends dwell on a substantial sin he committed, usually a matter of sexual excess or deviance—in some sagas including sorcery-induced necrophilia.[3] Our author notes that Charlemagne had a sin—he was human and consequently not perfect—but his emphasis is entirely on the great man's repentance and forgiveness.

All in all, our author does not follow any surviving previous account closely. In his conclusion of this chapter, he alludes to the fact that Charlemagne has "many songs" written about him already as a reason for not going on with this hero. He has obviously felt free to incorporate what he wanted from them as well as from learned sources. It appears that he may have also been drawing on collections of miracles associated with Charlemagne that were later presented as evidence of enough saintly powers to deserve canonization.[4]

Т he Empire remained without a head. They set the crown on Saint Peter's Altar. The nobles of Rome all met together and swore before the people that never again would they choose a king—nor a judge nor anyone to rule them—from the kin of the preceding house, for they had proven unable to maintain relations of faith and honor with them. They

---

3.   Grimm, *Deutsche Sagen*, op. cit., Vol. II, pp. 104-6.

4.   While Charlemagne was not canonized until 1165 and some of the material justifying his sainthood was written at the direction of Emperor Frederick Barbarossa not long before that date, some of the sources drawn upon went back at least to the 1140s. They stress Charles's "wonders" and were quite possibly accessible to our author, but at least one of them, a letter by Archbishop Tulpin of Reims, "Epistola de meritis et miraculis Karoli magni," was requested by a leading cleric of Aachen, in order to clarify the miraculous "individual events of the Spanish expedition which are already known in a general way." In other words, stories of Charlemagne-related miracles were in general circulation at the time the *Book of Emperors* was written. Irmgard Möller, "Die deutsche Geschichte in der Kaiserchronik;" dissertation, University of Munich, 1957; pp, 31-4.

wanted to have kings from other lands. The Greek line would have to yield its place to them.

According to the custom still kept in those days, royal youths from all the dominions were brought up with great care at the Roman Court. By the time they reached the age when the Romans gave them the sword of knighthood, how loyal they would be to the Romans! These would then send the young knights back to their homelands, and in this way all the dominions continued to serve Rome in awe.

And so it happened that Pippin, a mighty king of Karlingen,[5] had two fine sons. One of them, whose name was Leo, was raised in Rome and came to hold Saint Peter's throne. Charles, the other son, however, remained at home.

One night when Charles fell asleep, a voice called out to him three times: "Arise, beloved Charles, and hasten to Rome! Your brother Leo needs you!" And quickly Charles made ready, revealing nothing of his intentions to anyone until he asked leave of the king to go. He said that he wanted to see the pope and also desired greatly to pray in Rome, the capital city.

When the young prince asked for leave, his father granted it to him gladly and bestowed gifts upon his son most generously in a manner worthy of a mighty king.

Charles really undertook his journey more because of the divine apostles than for his brother.[6] Both early and late in the day his thoughts, which he revealed to no one, were filled with love of God. Quite often he would

---

5. Karlingen or Kerlingen is the name given by the author and some other medieval German writers to the Frankish domain of Charlemagne and his family. He first introduces it as a locale of Diocletian's persecution of Christians. It is probably either a vernacular garble of *carolingorum*, which appeared in contemporary Latin texts in the phrase *regnum carolingorum* (Carolingian Empire), or a derivation by analogy on the assumption that the great Karl's name was given to his whole family domain in the same way the name of his grandson, Lothar or Lothaire, was applied to Lothringen (Lorraine). From subsequent references to Ripuaria as identical with Karlingen, it is clear that the author has Karlingen mentally located in the Lower Rhine Valley.

6. This is, for the opportunity of praying at the graves of both Saint Peter and Saint Paul.

stand alone and turn his whole mind toward God. His eyes wet, he would pray to God that the devil might never lead him astray. How well God was later to watch over him!

When Charles arrived in Rome, he was given a good reception by old and young, as God saw fit to grant him. Pope Leo sang a mass in honor of the Holy Ghost and to strengthen the prince's spirit. There he received God's body. All who were there praised God, saying that Charles by right should be ruler and judge, and that he was worthy and greatly to their liking.

Charles did not listen to what was being said. He had made his journey for the sake of prayer, and he let no commotion distract him. He entered the church barefoot and, imploring God's mercy, he prayed for the sake of his soul. But his steadfast devotion secured him worldly honor as well as what he prayed for.

Thus he spent four weeks so wrapped in prayer and meditation that no one could approach him to speak, until his brother, Pope Leo, and all the people with him fell at his feet. Then Charles pointed out to God in heaven that if he were to prove unworthy he should never have made this journey. Then he received the royal emblems, and they set a magnificent crown on his head. All those there in Rome rejoiced that day, and all said, "Amen."

Then the king sat in judgment, and the pope made complaint before him that church properties and the collection of tithes, entrusted to him by his predecessors for his use in the saving of souls, were being granted away from his jurisdiction, and that his benefices had been taken from him. His complaint angered a number of nobles.

Then Charles spoke these true ruler's words: "Never, I feel sure, has it ever happened in this world that someone made a gift to honor God in order that another might take it. That would indeed be a clear instance of robbery. No layman ever has the right to dare take any part of what is given to churches. Whoever would take anything away from gifts bestowed on God's houses, through which God's work is fulfilled, would be despised of God and could not remain a good Christian. We must postpone acting on this complaint for the present, for I cannot judge it well now, but if I do live long enough to be able to do so justly, then let Saint Peter call me to account that I will gladly judge it for you." Then those nobles departed, full of resentment. Charles did not desire them to remain there any longer either. He returned to Ripuaria. The Romans realized very well that he was their rightful judge. But stupid men among them ridiculed the others for ever having proclaimed him ruler; in fact, there were many who soon regretted having done so. In Saint Peter's Cathedral they caught the pope and punched his eyes out of their sockets—they had no real idea why they were seeking revenge on him—and sent him thus as a blind man to the king in Ripuaria.

There was nothing else for the pope to do but set out on the journey in his hapless condition. He rode on a donkey and took with him two of his chaplains, desiring no other escort but these two subordinates, who showed him his way and protected him on the donkey. And so the noble pope made his way to Ripuaria, where he would no longer be able to hide the shame that had befallen him. Along the way, he often lacked the barest necessities.

The pope arrived in Ingelheim with his two chaplains and rode into the king's courtyard. Even by this time no one else knew what had happened to him. As he sat motionless upon the donkey, he bade one of his chaplains to go secretly to the king saying, "Hold back with your words and make no harsh reproaches, but tell the mighty king only that a poor pilgrim would like to speak with him."

Leaving Pope Leo, the priest wept so violently that blood ran down over his beard. When the king saw him coming, he said to one of his men: "Something bad has happened to this pilgrim, and we shall do justice in his cause if we can. He is desperately in need of help. I imagine someone has robbed him."

The priest knelt down and with great difficulty spoke these words: "Hail to you, mighty king! Please, speak now with one of your chaplains alone, who wants to reveal distress to you; he has suffered grave misfortune." The king hesitated no longer but strode quickly across the courtyard following the priest. After telling his men to stand at a distance from him, he said, "Good pilgrim, if you wish to stay here with me, I will gladly take you in. Tell me if something is troubling you that I can remedy. Why don't you dismount?"

Then the noble pope wanted to draw closer to the king. His head hung at a strange angle and his eyes stared askew. "That God should have granted me your presence!" he began. "My tongue seeks words for this meeting. It has not been long since I sang a mass for you at Rome, when I could still see well." As he spoke these words the noble king recognized him and was so shocked that he could neither hear nor see. He did not know himself what was happening to him. His body went limp and he could not speak. His breath left him, and two of his men sprang to their lord's side to steady him and keep him from falling to the ground.

When the emperor had recovered, the pope made complaint before him, saying, "I have come here that you may show me mercy. It was because of you that I lost my eyes. Blinding me was done as an insult to you. Brother, you must pull yourself together. Weep no more! Let us praise Our Lord for all his mercies." Then the greatest wailing that you have ever heard tell of arose. No one could keep himself from weeping.

The emperor himself lifted him down and carried him across the courtyard into his private chamber. There they sat down together, and Charles told his men to go outside. "Brother," he said, "how did this happen to you? I want to hear your plaint, and then I will turn my forces of justice toward righting the wrong."

Pope Leo answered the king thus: "Brother, very soon after you left Rome the Romans betrayed their loyalty to me in a conspiracy. They caught me in the cathedral and committed a frightful crime upon me. Vengeance I seek only in heaven. Brother, we must bear this patiently. You must never injure any of them because of this crime."

To this the noble king replied, "It would be doing God a dishonor to spare those murderers. Hai! How sorely that would injure Christendom. I am called 'Judge' and 'Ruler.' And this means that I have the duty of judging over the peoples: Nations, be as God commands you! I must defend Christianity with the sword. You will have them sorely regret their crime against you. I will exact full vengeance for your eyes, or I will renounce my sword."

Then, dispatching his messengers to King Pippin he instructed that his great need be presented to him and that the nobles of Karlingen be told that—if they wanted to do God a loving service—they should come to him quickly. And there were none alive in Karlingen but that they proclaimed all of one voice: "Woe to the fatal hour and the instant that Rome was ever raised!" Their wailing and lamenting grew great indeed.

The messengers galloped ceaselessly from land to land and from lord to vassal, and all men were willing to come to the cause of Charles. Farmers and merchants, too—no one could hold them back. They left all their belongings and set out to join Charles. The mourning and grief over the news traveled through Christendom from people to people and the streams of warriors converged like clouds over Mount Jove.[7] Hai, how that army marched over the mountains and through the valleys of Trent! The Book does not even have any number for the army. This was the greatest military expedition that ever descended on Rome.

When the army had advanced to within sight of the Aventine Hill in Rome, the worthy king asked three days and nights for himself. This annoyed the nobles who went to the king and said that it was ill becoming to his office to pause there, now that they had come so close that they could see the city which had aggrieved them.

The king answered, "First we must fervently pray to God, for we must gain his leave for our undertaking: then we can fight with ease. Besides, I need one man on whom I can count when I need help most, who is a credit to the crown. May God be merciful and send him to me!"

Early one morning a voice from God spoke to him: "God in heaven commands you, king, to bide here no longer. Ride on to Rome. Judgment has been decreed before God, and just vengeance must be exacted from them."

At this the king's banner was made ready, and Charles let word pass through his whole army that when the knights were prepared for battle they should keep their eyes upon the banner and ride in close formation. Hearts swelling with high spirits, the soldiers swarmed over the mountain. Then Gerold [Duke of Swabia] rode toward him. When the king

---

7.   Probably the Great Saint Bernard Pass; Mount Jove may derive from the memory of a temple to Jupiter or Jove on the plain at the top of the pass.

looked at him, he spoke these words in lordly fashion: "I have been waiting for you a long time, dearest of all my men!" Raising the visor of his helmet, he kissed him affectionately. All the other knights wondered who this lone warrior might be, of whom the king thought so highly as to honor him with such a greeting. It was brave [Duke] Gerold, who led all of the Swabians.

Three mighty legions, magnificent to behold as fitted the service of the Empire, soon began to converge. They were under Gerold's command and distinguished themselves in such noble fashion that King Charles bestowed on heroic Gerold the perpetual right of the Swabians to fight in the front of ranks whenever the Empire needed help. Gerold, that worthy hero, earned this for them.

Owî! What an army this was that besieged Rome and the Lateran for seven days and seven nights, so menacingly that no one would fight against it! On the eighth day—I am telling you this as the truth—the Romans ordered the city gates opened and offered to let the king enter with this condition: that any man who could prove his innocence—that he had not committed the crime himself, nor furthered it, nor advised it—would remain in the king's favor, while the king would deal with the guilty ones after deciding a just sentence. The nobles unanimously agreed to accept the terms.

As the emperor was sitting in judgment and the document naming the guilty men was read, those accused all fervently denied their guilt when they were called forward. The king ordered them to submit to trial by combat for their unwillingness to confess. But then the Romans objected that this was not according to their law, and that no emperor ever forced such treatment on them before; instead, that they should prove their innocence by swearing with their two fingers.[8]

Then King Charles said, "I doubt that any crime so great was ever committed before. Don't be so overhasty. I feel certain that my brother saw the guilty ones himself." Still, when plenty of the accused offered their oaths

---

8.   A reflection of the Roman medieval conviction that even within the same empire different people are rightfully judged only according to their own law codes.

in the cathedral, the king said, "I will not deprive you of recourse to your own law any longer; however, I know of a youth here named Pancras.[9] If you are willing to swear an oath at his grave, and if he tolerates it, then I will be quite willing to believe you."

Icy fear seized the Romans at the mention of this test. As they came to the place dedicated to Saint Pancras and were supposed to hold up their fingers and keep asserting their innocence under oath, one man was overcome, and panic gripped all the rest. They retreated in fear and fled back over the bridge; a great many of them returned to Saint Peter's Cathedral.

Charles hesitated no longer but rode after them angrily. For three days he and his men struck them down and for three days they carried them out. Then they washed down the paving stones. The pope had been led inside the Cathedral by force. Charles fell before Saint Peter's resting place and made a fervent plea to Christ, saying, "Lord God in heaven, how could I be any good to you as king when you let such shame befall me? Sinner that I may be, I do make every attempt to judge people in a manner worthy of you. The Romans swore allegiance to a pope and you did grant him a portion of your power that he might loosen the people from their sins and bind them. What more can I do? I recall to you your sublime martyrdom and your divine resurrection, that you may give the evil people of Rome something by which to recognize your hidden power. Then they will know for certain that you are a true God. Grant me this, Holy Christ!"

Charles, the noble king, fell to the ground a second time and said, "Hail noble Saint Peter! You are really a divine stalwart of God, a watchman of Christendom. Think now, my lord, what I am going through! You are a summoner of the Kingdom of Heaven. Just look at your Pope! I left him sound of body in your care. Blinded was how I found him, and if you do not heal the blind man today I shall destroy your cathedral and shall ruin the buildings and grounds donated to you, and then I shall leave him for you, blind as he is, and go back to Ripuaria."

---

9.   Pancras was only fourteen, according to tradition, when he was martyred. His story is given, lines 6458-6485, in the reign of Diocletian.

Quickly the noble Pope Leo made himself ready and said his confession. As he spoke the last word, he saw a heavenly light with both of his eyes. Great are the hidden powers of God.

The pope turned around again and spoke to the multitude. "My dearest children gathered from afar, be glad of heart, for the Kingdom of God is drawing near to you. God has heard you and because of your holy prayer has turned his face toward you. Here, at this very place, you have been witnesses so that you may well confirm in public that a great miracle has happened. God has revealed His hidden power before you. I can see with both eyes better than I ever saw in this world." When he finished speaking, the king fell to the ground with arms outstretched in the form of a cross, and all the people did the same. *Omnis clerus* [all the clergy] sang "*Te deum laudamus*" [We praise you, God].

The pope consecrated him as emperor and granted absolution to all his comrades in arms. Owî! What joy there was in Rome then! The whole people rejoiced and sang "*Gloria in excelsis deo.*"

Then Charles laid down the Imperial Law, as an angel recited it, true words of God, to him. Quite often the heavenly messenger would help him with this in private. And so the mighty emperor left us many good laws, which God caused to be spoken before Charles, whose humility pleased him, while he ruled the Empire with great honor. All the lords who ruled the lands swore to him that they would defend the Imperial Law as they would their lives, and not even for the sake of wife or child would they shield injustice. From this day forward, every loyal subject has retrained himself in the knowledge that if he were convicted of sinful or shameful crimes he would forfeit his rights and be excluded from all honors ever afterward.

The very first laws the emperor established dealt with what seemed to him the most exalted matters, those concerning bishops and priests, for the Imperial Law of Constantine had been sorely neglected. At the same time, he established laws governing tithes and gifts of property to the Church and thus assured protection of the *sacrificia* [gifts made to the Church]. Then he issued decrees concerning the peasants' clothes and the pope confirmed these.

Now I shall tell you about what the peasant is to wear according to Imperial Law. His clothes may be black or gray, and he is allowed no others. To wear gores at the sides is compatible with his station in life. He is to have shoes of cow leather and that is all, also seven yards of towcloth for his shirts and breeches. If he wears gores in front or behind, then he has lost the rights of men of his station. He is to spend six days at the plow and doing plenty of other work. On Sunday he is to go to church, carrying his animal goad openly in his hand. If a sword is found on a peasant, he is to be led bound to the churchyard fence, where he is to be tied and his skin and hair flayed. If he is threatened by enemies, however, let him defend himself with a pitchfork. This law King Charles established for the peasants.

Charles, the son of Pippin and Bertha of blessed memory, gained great renown for himself as the first from the German lands to be made emperor at Rome. The Romans recognized him fully, and Charles's honors continued to increase from that day when he won victory with his sword and forced the Romans into obedience to God. He deprived the devil of many a soul.

When Charles had finished codifying his Imperial Law at Rome, including all the regulations governing property owned and fiefs and those governing vassals and their lords, he headed toward Apulia. A noble named Adelhart lived there, who was an enemy of God. Because he was a threat to the Empire, the noble was beheaded and his followers were taken captive, after which the emperor withdrew.[10]

There is a city in the same land called Susa, whose ruler was named Desiderius. He had prepared all his subjects to offer armed opposition to the emperor. But the emperor's forces so subdued him that he was com-

---

10. The historical Adelhard or Adelhart was a cousin of Charlemagne and loyal to him. The author is probably thinking of Adelgis, son of Desiderius, the last Lombard king, whose story follows immediately. Charlemagne had married Desiderata, daughter of Desiderius, whom the author calls "Ava." Desiderius attacked territory belonging to the pope, who asked aid of the Franks. Charlemagne defeated Desiderius and took him to what is now France as a prisoner. Susa is now in the Italian province of Turin, close to the French border, held in Charlemagne's day by the Lombards along with most of Italy north of Rome.

pelled to seek terms, offering his daughter to gain the emperor's favor. That lady's name was Ava. Charles took her and led her back to the Rhine. All his men cheered at the outcome of the expedition.

While the Westphalians submitted their country to Charles, the Frisians resisted fiercely, but their arrogance was soon laid low. The Saxons did not want to receive him. There were princes among them who fell back into the old custom of their nation and fought against the emperor. Charles was deprived of victory, but Wittekind [the Saxon duke] did not long profit by this, for Gerold, a worthy lord, cleverly devised a way to kill him afterwards.

The Saxons offered fierce resistance; they hoped never to become subject to the king. The emperor sent for his men, the princes of the Empire, and they came to join him most willingly, many a bold and daring vassal. The Saxons were defeated, with Gerold fighting in the front ranks, after which the princes of Saxony lost all their power.

Charles founded the Diocese of Bremen, and from there Saint Willehad had converted the Danes with his sweet teachings. After departing, the noble emperor turned toward Spain, where he made the people obedient to God. Then he went to Navarre, where the people wanted to offer resistance to him. I am telling you the facts. They fought for two whole days; then the emperor won victory on the battlefield, while the people of Navarre suffered grievous injuries.

Then Emperor Charles besieged a walled city called Arles, which actually took him more than seven years. The inhabitants had considered him unworthy of his office. An underground spring also served to carry wine in to them, so that they were plentifully supplied. At last Charles succeeded in cutting off their source with great cunning. When the inhabitants could not hold the city any longer they threw open the gates and fought in front of them, offering no terms at all. So many were slain on both sides that there is no man who can tell another how many—of either the Christians or the heathens—lay there dead after the battle. No one was able to distinguish among the dead until the emperor overcame the problem with God's help. He found the Christians lying separately in well adorned coffins. This story always meets with great interest when told.

Charles, God's servant, having won the people for Our Lord, departed for a walled city called Gerundo, which he besieged until the inhabitants were forced by hunger to surrender, and all who lived there were baptized.

The emperor and his men turned toward Galatia,[11] where the king of the heathens inflicted great losses upon them. The Christian soldiers were all slain, and Charles barely escaped from the battle. Today the stone is still wet on which Charles sat afterwards, weeping passionately as he lamented his sin, saying, "Hail to you, God sublime! Grant me mercy for my poor soul. Take me out of this world, so that my people will no longer be punished because of me. I can never be consoled again."

Then an angel comforted him, saying, "Charles, beloved of God, your joy will come to you quickly. Bid your messengers make haste to summon virgin women—leave the married ones at home—for God will reveal his power through them. If you will fear and love God, the maidens will win your honor back again for you."

The messengers made haste, and thoroughly searched throughout all the dominions. They gathered together the maidens and brought them together *ad portam Cesaris* where the emperor was waiting for them. And many a young maiden came to join this host: fifty-three thousand—I am telling you this as a fact—and sixty-six more. The emperor praised the Lord.

When all the maidens arrived in a valley since named for Charles, they readied themselves for battle in formations just like men. There the emperor took pleasure in the sight of many noble virgins.

Each heathen sentry was struck by wonder as to who this people could be, for it seemed very strange to all of them. They hurried back and said to their king, "Sire, even though we have slain the old ones, we can tell you with certainty that the young ones have now followed them here. I imagine they want to satisfy their thirst for vengeance. They are big around the chest. Sire, it will not come to any good end if you fight with them. They are fine knights indeed: their hair is long and their gait is very graceful.

---

11. Probably Galicia in northwestern Spain.

This is a terrifying people, and our warfare cannot cope with them. There is no force that could be grouped together on this earth that could ever resist them. Their whole bearing is most terrifying."

At the advice of his experienced councilors, their king turned over hostages to the emperor. The king then had himself and all his people baptized—how well all of them believed in God! He came to love Christianity. Thus God made Charles victorious without the thrust of a spear or the blow of a sword, and the maidens well realized that God in heaven was with them.

Charles and his heroines returned to their own homes back in their Empire. On the way the worthy maidens came to a green meadow. Tired from the expedition, these heroines stuck their spearshafts into the ground, after praising God for the goodness which He had shown them. They stayed there overnight, and a great wonder occurred. Their spearshafts had turned green and had sent forth leaves and blossoms. This is the reason that the place is called the *Sceftwalt* [Woods of the Spearshafts], which can be seen to this day.

Charles, the rich and powerful, built a beautiful city and strong church in praise of Holy Christ, to honor St. Mary and all the maidens of God, and for the solace of Christendom. Since it was because of chastity and spiritual purity that the maids achieved their victory, the church is called "*domini sanctitas*" [the Lord's purity].[12]

Charles had committed one sin, and he said that he did not intend to tell any man on this earth about it but would rather die in it. The burden seemed great and long to him, however, and finally when he heard it said that Saint Aegidius, who was a contemporary of his, was a holy man, fear compelled him to make his confession to him. When the emperor had told him everything else that he had done, he said "Aegidius, good man, I have committed one other sin, which has been concealed for a long time, and my heart is caught about with anxieties, but I cannot reveal it to you. Please advise me what to do."

---

12. The Emperor's Chapel, main and oldest part of the Aachen Cathedral, also called "Saint Mary's."

Saint Aegidius was greatly troubled and put off the answer until the next morning; however, he encouraged him well to hope in God. Then that pious messenger of God told the emperor to stay there, and the two dear comrades spent the night there, although neither of them was able to sleep.

And so, early the next morning, the emperor asked this true minister of God if he would grant him absolution with the holy rites, for he could not stay there any longer. The good Aegidius asked God with heart and mind to reveal to him the power of this mystery—that God will certainly show mercy to whoever shall trust in him. As he finished saying the mass and spoke the benediction, he saw a document written without human hand. It had been sent down here from heaven. He showed it to the king and said, "No one does such evil in the world but that, if he shows obedience to God, the kingdom of heaven is open to him."

When the emperor read the letter, he found this written: "You have God's favor. Whenever a man inwardly repents of his transgression, trusting in God all the while, from him God demands nothing else for it." This was mediated by Saint Aegidius, the holy lord.

If we were to tell of all the wonders connected with Charles we would have to have many hours—there is not time enough now, and Charles also has other songs. Charles was a true warrior of God, who compelled the heathens to Christianity. Charles was brave, Charles was handsome, Charles was merciful, Charles was blessed by fortune, Charles was humble, Charles was constant, and his goodness lasted him his whole life through. Charles earned great praise, Charles was to be feared, and, in the Roman domains, Charles was exalted with good reason above all other kings of the world, for he had the most virtues of all. The Book tells us with certainty that he held the Empire for forty-six years and nine months. This ruler was buried in Aachen.

XXXIX

Louis I, "the Pious"

Louis I (r. 813–840), sole surviving son of Charlemagne, was called "the Pious" because of his theological interests, liberality to the church and moral strictness, banishing even his sisters for sexual misconduct. Twice he sent his second wife, Judith, to a convent for infidelity. In 813, at his father's bidding, he crowned himself joint emperor, and, when Charlemagne died the following year, he became sole emperor. He was faced with sedition by his sons and presided over an Empire rocked by other revolts as well.

Our author appears to know very little about Louis except for his reputation for piety. This leads him to extrapolate on what the results of pious kingship must have been.

When that fabled emperor passed on, he left a good heir whose name was Louis. When it was time for him to assume the duties of manhood the princes acclaimed him to be their lord and ruler and to be the judge over Christians, saying that he was wise enough for this.

When Louis held the Empire, he had the princes told that they should have the young lords taught Imperial Law the way the Romans once taught it. His good vassals all confirmed how willing they were to do this, and the fabled king sent word to all the princes that he wanted to hold his first council at Mainz.

The high nobility from far and wide then gathered there, adding a large number to the council, but two brothers arrogantly asserted that they never wanted to see the king nor confirm him as ruler or as judge.

The book tells us as a fact that one brother was named Germar, the other Godwin. Many of the princes supported them in deserting the king and attacking the Empire.

Then King Louis thought over the fact that in his father's time no one did violence to anyone else, and his mood changed to an angry one. Because of the severe crisis he declared them to be outlaws. It was not long after that when they were caught in Oppenheim. A council was announced once again in the city of Mainz. The king judged according to Imperial Law, and those nobles were condemned. With the concurrence of the lords spiritual and temporal, he sentenced them to be beheaded, which cast proper fear into the hearts of the other princes.

The king judged the Empire, advised by wise counsel. He decreed a Peace of God: he punished robbery with the hangman's noose, murder with the wheel. Hai! What a peace that was! Yes, the robber went to the gallows, the thief paid with his eyes, the breaker of the peace with a hand, and the arsonist with his neck.

Peace grew in the Empire, as the king judged as powerfully as his father before him. The farms remained intact, unrobbed and unburned so that the son found his inheritance just pleasing to behold as when it had been his father's. He took care of his vassals very well, and they served in the king's forces well. He wielded his sword in a way that gained him honor. In a battle with other peoples, he would spare the life of a conquered leader. When one of his vassals died in battle or survived, his fief became his son's without his paying anything in gold or gems or other treasure.

Under King Louis no one could doubt that if anyone committed a crime he would pay for it on the spot, all as justice required, which served as a strong deterrent. There was fidelity and honor between vassals and lords. Pleasure and good manners abounded. No one belittled what he had inherited but manfully took up enlarging what his father had left him.

In King Louis's time—the Book makes this clear beyond a doubt—vassals were true and faithful to their lords. They oversaw their parts of the Empire well and always spoke the truth. What they were told to do— Owî!—how soon they let that come true! That fabled king mastered everything together. Liars could never press their way into his court and kneel before his nobles at trials or other open sessions to advance their evil conspiracies. Upright men gave advice, which evil men were unable to do; only a man who was distinguished for telling the truth would be allowed to speak, a mature man known for his virtues or who had displayed noble conduct in his youth. Older men were expected to display honor and virtue; young men to maintain good behavior. Thus the two ages of man made themselves welcome and praiseworthy at Louis's court.

In King Louis's time Christendom rejoiced far and wide; indeed the ruler busied himself looking for what deeds of honor he might perform in a manner that would be worthy service to God. He ordered children of the noblest families to be taught the sublime and rich Imperial Law, so that they would be able to give wise counsel. Mindful of his own noble birth, he declined to take fees or gifts from poor people. He judged the people well as the Imperial Law directed. He would give good advice himself to a rich man whom need was oppressing. He would order the wisest of his men to come to his chamber, where base-born men had to stand and wait at the door—those were men he did not recognize.

Louis judged the Empire with great wisdom. He was compassionate in dealing with evil, he was constant in his treatment of good people, and God's service was dear to him. He was beloved of all his people. For the sake of God, he loved the poor. In court proceedings he would accept neither silver nor gold. It is a fact that he held the Empire for thirty-seven years and twelve days more. That lord departed from us resting in his great goodness.

XL

Lothair I

Lothair I (r. 840–855) was the eldest son of Louis I, "the Pious," who made him joint emperor with himself in 817. Lothair, however, spent most of the 830s in conflict with his father over who ruled what. When Louis I died in 840, Lothair claimed the whole empire for himself, which was disputed by his younger half-brother, Charles the Bald, and his younger brother, Louis the German. In

843, the quarrel among the brothers was settled with the Treaty of Verdun, which divided the Empire into three portions. Charles received the western part, which developed into the Kingdom of France. Louis received the eastern part, which, very roughly, became Germany. Lothair received the title of sole emperor and the "Middle Kingdom," reaching from the Netherlands through Alsace-Lorraine into Italy. "Lorraine" is in fact the French and English adaptation of the Germanic "Lotharingen (Lothair's land)."

Lothair continued to be involved in alternating conflicts and periods of cooperation with his brothers. Eventually he turned Italy over to his son, Louis II. When he sensed that he had a fatal illness, he entered a monastery, where six days later he died. While he did some fighting in Bavaria, as presented below, there is no record of any Herman or Otto in roles of opposition to him.

When Louis departed from this world he left a worthy son named Lothair. The princes would not stop demanding that they continue to maintain their honor through choosing him for their ruler. Lothair was a worthy hero and soon he convoked a council at Regensburg.

There was one Duke Otto among the Bavarians who chose not to attend the council, saying that he had authority over his lands—or else what was his sword good for? That duke took up arms and assembled a great army. The Bavarians all confirmed that they would never leave him and that those who should desert would find that they never again could gain land on Bavarian soil, neither fiefs nor land of their own.

King Lothair and his men were well aware that things were taking place against him in the empire. Now hear a strange story: When he entered the land of the Bavarians, the duke readied his flag and entrusted it to Margrave Herman to carry. Many of the men dear to the king were slain, and the king was forced to depart without a victory.

The king ordered messengers to ride from the Rhine to the Rhone, and so messenger was flying after messenger. Burgundians and Swabians rose in revolt, but the wisest of the duke's counselors told him he could not hold out against the Empire. He would have to evacuate the land. The invaders began ravaging the land with fire. The king commanded greater forces as he rode into the city of Regensburg, where he revealed his might. The Bavarians sustained great damage from Lothair's men as they destroyed towers and other fortifications. Margrave Herman ordered the castle moat-ditch filled in; following judgment by all the Bavarians, he was slain. King Lothair left that place, and, taking a large part of his army with him, occupied Agest, where the duke was seeking refuge. The duke escaped, but his men were captured and killed.

The duke vacated the Empire. Lothair and his men turned toward the Rhine. The king took control over the Bavarians' land, and the Bavarians served him for more than five years. Duke Otto was unable to negotiate anything for himself; no men of authority could be guarantors for him, and so he began to waste away from sickness and died among the Greeks.

King Lothair had four noble sons: One, named Louis, possessed the Empire after him. The second, named Lothair, was a bold and energetic hero. The third was named Charles, and it would be tedious to recount how often they fought among themselves. The fourth was named Pippin. Lothair [I] had the Empire for exactly seventeen years; then he abdicated to enter a monastery, turning over body and soul to God.

XLI

Louis II

Louis II (r. 850 – 875) was the eldest son of Lothair I. In 850, he was crowned joint emperor with his father by Pope Leo IV, and, upon Lothair's death in 855, he became sole emperor. Later, Louis's power in Italy was sufficient to require Pope Adrian II to accept "tutelage" from him in secular affairs. Conflicts over divisions in the Empire continued. What was new in Louis's reign was a successful campaign by the emperor in 866 against invading "Saracens"

(Muslims), although he could not follow up his land victory with a naval one simply because the Empire did not have much of a fleet. Three years later in cooperation with the Byzantine emperor Basil I, he took Bari, the Muslim stronghold in southeastern Italy. Afterwards, when he was reorganizing his troops in Italy for a further campaign, he was treacherously taken prisoner by Adelchis, Prince of Benevento. He was released, and in Rome Pope Adrian II crowned him emperor a second time.

Massmann (see Introduction) assumed that this Ludwig or Louis is Louis the German; however, the fact that our author brings Pope Adrian into the story (even though in a different role from his historical one) and clearly gives this Louis the position of sole emperor would tend to support the idea that this second Louis is indeed the eldest son of Emperor Lothair I.

Louis then held the Empire, but great strife broke out between Charles and Pippin, and they enlisted friends and relations against each other—Owî! How many men soon lay dead! Huge numbers—lords and vassals alike—were slain in these conflicts, to which no one was able to bring peace or any separation of the combatants. With one voice the nobles addressed the king, saying that it was not fitting that he permit such widespread raiding and burning within the Empire.

The great suffering and need led him to convoke a council at Worms, but when he opened the proceedings there—the Book confirms this—such signs came from heaven that all his men deserted him. A lightning bolt struck Worms and set it ablaze. I am telling you truly: the people there saw huge flashes of lightning and heard louder thunder than ever. The king was so terrified that he was forced to flee from there; the others left, too, with no love for the king.

Right then other feuds and conflicts broke out, and King Louis was blamed for the hunger and loss of crops that accompanied them. It was said that it was his fault—that it came because of his misdeeds. Bishops and dukes summoned the king to Rome, and the exalted ruler made that journey.

The lords lodged a complaint with Pope Adrian against King Louis, saying that it was his fault that the Empire was torn apart and destruction wrought upon Christendom. He never wanted to hold court, and they could not put up with this state of affairs any longer.

Pope Adrian settled the conflict by directing Louis to judge again according to the Imperial Law of Charles [the Great], which was being neglected, and that expenses for restoring lords' estates, leaseholds and outlying rented lands back to the same way they were in that Charles's time should be paid for from the royal treasury.

That settled matters peacefully among the nobles, and great honor abounded all around as they departed. The pope consecrated the emperor. No argument was to be made against the need for Charles and Pippin to lay down arms. The king sent one of them to his old relatives of the house from which the whole family descended, the other to the land of the Burgundians, who—this is a known fact—killed him.

Louis judged the Empire in a way that was pleasing to the princes. The Book tells us that he ruled for thirty-six years and three months. The princes greatly lamented his passing.

XLII

Charles III, "the Fat"

Charles the Fat (Roman emperor 881–887) is numbered "the Third" in deference to Charles the Bald, skipped over by our author, who had received as king the western part of the three-way division of the Empire and later served as Emperor Charles II from 875 to his death in 877. Charles III was constantly at war in Italy, attempting in vain to pacify it. He brought disgrace upon himself by coming with a large army to defend Paris against the Normans, but eventually buying them off with the payment of a large sum as tribute and giving them permission to invade and plunder Burgundy with no interference from the Empire. This was enough to make the German princes convoke an assembly in 887 to demand that he abdicate, which he did. He died the following year.

The story that Charles's wife, variously recorded as Richardis or Richildis, was accused of adultery but proved her innocence through an ordeal by fire became a widespread legend in the German-speaking territories. The version that follows found its way over the centuries from the *Book of Emperors* into Grimm's *German Sagas*. Other versions have Richardis proving her innocence by walking barefoot over a bed of coals.

W hen Louis departed from this world, he left behind three sons—the fabled Charles [III, "the Fat"], brave Louis, and a third who was called Carloman. They all became praiseworthy and noble in their deeds.

Charles held the Empire, and the Book tells us that he took a wife whose soul, we should know by the trust we have in God, is with those of the just. She was free of any evil.

The lady was attractive and honorable, and she adorned herself with many virtues, but there were jealous people at the court, who, when they observed the queen's virtues, developed resentment toward her. They said that she had illicit relations with a man. They attacked her with lies, but afterwards they all suffered from what they did.

One morning quite early, the king was on his way to matins when he was followed by a senior servant named Siegerat, whose advising remarks were malicious. "Sire," he began. "What my queen has been doing is unworthy of the honors due you, but I dare say nothing further."

The king looked at him, and his words were sad. "Keep on talking— may God keep you in his care! You should reveal the truth to me. If you have observed anything that goes against the honor of the Empire, keep it secret no longer."

"Sire," answered the old man. "I am unable to regain peace of mind because of what I have seen. My queen loves another man. Sire, if I am found to be lying, have me hanged from a tree."

The king hurried back again to his chamber and lay down on the bed. His lady spoke to him. "Milord, I am unaccustomed to this. Why have you come back here so quickly? Until now you always were at prayers until daylight."

He hit her a rough blow with his fist and spoke thus: "O woe that I ever saw you! If I should be losing my honor because of you, it will cost you your life."

The lady began sobbing uncontrollably, and she said, "Milord, hold back words like these! Maintain your honor! I am sorely afraid that lies have been told about me. If this is happening because of guilt on my part, then let me lose my life. I really would like to know the source of this slander."

The rich and powerful Charles began to be persuaded by these words and suppressed his anger. Then, after a little while, he said, "If it is as I have heard, you have acted unlawfully in yielding to the temptation of illicit love. How can you be any good to the Empire as its queen?"

"Milord," she answered. "If I am guilty of what you say, then by rights I should lose my life. But I wish to prove my innocence by an ordeal. With God's help I shall prevail in it. I trust in God all the more when I recall how Susanna survived in the face of evil liars. God will think of me, too, poor sinner that I may be."

The lady lost no time in sending for four bishops, who heard her confession and stayed with her afterwards. She prayed and she fasted. She had her sins cancelled out; she kept falling on her knees in prayer, and she assigned herself to Our Lord's power.

When the day of her ordeal came, bishops and dukes all came together with a great crowd of other people. The queen prepared herself for her great trial, while by then the bishops and the dukes would have preferred to avoid it. "My Lord himself," said the noble queen, "would not want me to wear the crown any longer, if charges that are being made about me as guilty of that sin [of adultery] were true." The princes all sighed and groaned at hearing this.

Then the queen stepped forward with raised eyes and many a good blessing. She slipped on a tunic especially prepared for the purpose [in being coated with wax]. There was singing and reading aloud. Everyone there wished that God would show her his grace.

They ignited the tunic in front and back, right and left, even at her hands and feet, and within a short period of time the tunic completely burned off her and melted wax ran down onto the floor stones. The lady was completely innocent, and everyone there said, "*Deo gracias*! [Thanks be to God!]"

Then the bishops excused themselves, and the king ordered the liars seized. They were all hanged from a gallows. Joyfully the queen departed. She abdicated her imperial position and served God eagerly ever afterwards as a nun. Charles did not rule after that either. He had ruled for a year and a half.

XLIII

Arnulf

Arnulf (Roman emperor 895–899) was the illegitimate son of Carloman, king of Bavaria and Italy, who saw to it that Arnulf became margrave of Carynthia in southeastern Austria. In 882, Arnulf did homage to Charles the Fat as Roman emperor and led numerous expeditions against Slavs and Normans. In 887, sharing the disgust at the incompetence and cowardice of Charles the Fat, he took a leading role in the assembly that achieved his abdication. The following year, Arnulf was chosen King of the Germans.

Pope Formosus asked him to come to Italy and free him from the domination of Guido III, duke of Spoleto, who had had himself crowned emperor. Arnulf invaded Italy in 894, although so many of his men deserted that he was unsuccessful in helping Formosus. The pope was then forced to consecrate Lambert, Duke Guido's son, as emperor. Guido died the following year, however, and

Arnulf led another invasion of Italy. Formosus consecrated him as Roman emperor, and Arnulf spent his few remaining years attempting to expand his authority in Italy. During the course of one campaign he was stricken by paralysis and returned home to Bavaria, where he died in 899. He was buried in Regensburg.

At the time there was a widely praised prince named Arnulf, son of Carloman. The other princes were devoted to him and most willing to serve him. They agreed that they could make no better choice.

In his very first year, so the Book tells us truly, there was a bishop of Würzburg named Arn who was frequently at the king's court. Knowing well the evil among the Saxons, Arnulf sent this bishop to their land. He spoke God's true Word to them, which did not suit the people there. As he was speaking the concluding blessing at a service, he was slain over the altar. Hai! What a costly vengeance the king exacted for that crime!

The king subdued the Normans and did the same with the people of Italy. As a result, their country has been eager to serve the Roman Empire ever since.

In King Arnulf's time, hunger spread far and wide. The earth was so barren that people were sorely tempted to eat each other. The Hungarians invaded the land until the king dealt them a resounding defeat with God's help. So many Huns were slain that they had to depart from there in shame.

The king went from there to Rome, where Pope Formosus consecrated him with the imperial crown. The Romans agreed that since he forced the Huns to flight he would make a good judge for them. The Romans were very mindful of his great victory.

The emperor returned to Germany, where he found very bad tidings circulating. There was a bishop in Regensburg by the name of Emmeram, who, after overcoming great difficulties, was winning the people over to God. The duke of the Bavarians was then one Diete, who had a beautiful daughter. She was accused of scandalous behavior.

Without guilt and without recourse to law, Emmeram was murdered by Lambert, the duke [of Spoleto]'s son. He was to suffer great injury as the result of this crime. Emperor Arnulf destroyed him with everything that belonged to him. His relatives are scattered far and wide.

When Emperor Arnulf learned what a true stalwart of God the good Saint Emmeran was, he loved him more and more. He built him the best cathedral that he could in the city of Regensburg and willed money from his own inheritance to it. The Book tells us truly that he had the Empire for twelve years and five months; they buried that ruler in Regensburg.

XLIV

Louis III, "the Child"

Arnulf's son, Louis (Roman emperor 900–911), was given the imperial title at age seven, soon after his father's death. As long as he was still quite young, Bishop Hatto of Mainz oversaw the administration of the empire. The *Book of Emperors* is accurate enough in portraying Louis's reign as marked by Hungarian invasions and internal German conflicts, although individual names and events are sometimes arbitrarily handled. For instance, the historical Count Adalbert of Babensberg[1] becomes "Bishop Albrecht." Historically, Adalbert had killed Louis's brother, Conrad, and was captured by trickery planned by Bishop Hatto, brought before King Louis for judgment, and beheaded.

Our author continues to identify the Hungarians with the Huns, using the two names interchangeably, as if to associate the reputation of the Huns for savage conduct with that of the Hungarians of his own day. The etymology he uses for Frankfurt as "Ford of the Franks" has held up over the centuries, although today that city's inhabitants derive the name from an encampment there by

---

1.   Modern Bamberg.

Charlemagne, greatest king of the Franks, rather than Louis the Child. With the death of Louis the Child, the rule of members of Charlemagne's family as emperors came to an end in Germany.

W hen Emperor Arnulf departed this life, he left a son named Louis. It was not yet the right time for him to hold the Empire after his father; however, he did so in spite of being still a young child.

The Hungarians heard it told that Emperor Arnulf was dead, and they scorned the young ruler, raising great havoc in the Empire. They invaded Bavaria, plundering and burning as they went. They destroyed churches and carried the people off with them, but soon young King Louis was coming to be able to save his people.

The Hungarians wanted to cross a river called the Engesin. The young king fought them with his troops, and God's power helped him prevail over the Huns—eight thousand of them were slain.

A prince named Conrad—that is what is written here—was a brother of King Louis, with whom he engaged in conflict that grew to warfare within Bavaria. [In spite of this, when] Conrad lay slain, King Louis avenged his death.

A bishop named Albrecht suffered grave injustice in the eyes of God. Following a false accusation he was seized and brought before King Louis, and he was sentenced and beheaded. He lay dead with no guilt on his part.

In the fourth year of Louis's reign, the Hungarians truly gained revenge. The Bavarians fought them at a river called the Inn. The Bavarians survived with very little that was good for anything.

Those most evil Hungarians, together with Saxons and Thuringians, ravished the countryside with their swords, sparing neither women nor children. They rode into Frankish territory, plundering and burning as they went. The Eastern Franks attacked them in front and at their rear, as did the Ripuarian Franks. The Book tells us beyond any doubt that one Sunday the forces reached each other at Frankfurt. The Franks avenged their women and children with sword and spear—that is how the city got its name.[2] Many a fine hero lay fallen there; so many Christians fell in battle they could not be counted. Duke Burchart was slain along with his men who lay there beside him. The Christians struggled until nightfall, but the Huns maintained control of the area, using ferocious measures.

Louis ruled the Empire, the Book tells us for a fact, exactly twelve years. Then he fell out of a tower. Everything that happens is still God's will.

XLV

Conrad I

Conrad I (r. as German king 911–918) never was crowned emperor, but functioned as one nonetheless. Election as German king had the effect of making the recipient of that title into heir apparent for Roman emperor. Several German kings were never consecrated by the pope as emperors, but functioned as de facto emperors in the absence of consecrated ones.

Bishop Hatto orchestrated the election of Conrad, son of Count Conrad of Lahngau, soon after the death of Louis the Child. The younger Conrad had a reputation for fairness in peace and skill in war. He dealt successfully with the Magyars and the Normans but did not succeed in curbing the power of the stronger duchies, particularly Saxony, relative to the Empire. When he felt death approaching he asked that, in the interest of the people, German kingship be passed on to his arch-rival, Henry of Saxony.

Much of what follows, including the unexplained execution of dukes Erchenger and Perhtolt, is taken from the *Würzburg Chronicle*.

---

2.   Frankfurt is *Furt* (Ford) of the Franks.

hen King Louis died without an heir, bishops and dukes came to Mainz, where a great council was held. They all came to the same conclusion in choosing one Conrad. His father was also named Conrad, according to what is written here. He had been killed by Albrecht, who held Babensberg as his own. From this the hatred first arose that brought on the end for all time of the friendship between Conrad's house and his.

Conrad judged the Empire energetically enough. Once again the Hungarians rose in arms and invaded Bavaria. Whatever they found there became their plunder and booty. Everything was lost to them. Also the earth bore neither grapes nor grain, nor any other kind of crops, afflicting the Christians with more than enough sorrows.

King Conrad lost no time in assembling his forces in accordance with the advice of the dukes of Bavaria and Swabia. Because of their great suffering they prayed to God in heaven that he would give prosperity and victory to the king. They strongly resisted the Hungarian invasion.

The Book confirms beyond any doubt that the king and his followers prayed to their Creator, pointing out that he himself was their peace. Our Lord heard their prayers. At the Inn River, they set up an ambush, calling upon God's name as they located there.

The Huns were moved by their overconfidence—that is always the way of the unblessed—and in their arrogance could remember only their old honors. They charged at the king with their banner held high. Wisely, the king held back his troops hidden for the ambush until the forces were about to join in combat. Conrad's troops came at the Huns from behind and in front, until the Huns again were persuaded that it was time to flee. The Bavarians took vengeance for their slain wives and children, as the Huns were becoming exhausted. How many of those who knew no peace fell in battle no one can tell you. They all struck blows day and night until the conflict shifted to the Litach[1]. The Huns had never experienced such a stinging defeat before.

The wild Hungarians complained about their humiliation to the younger troops among them, saying that it would be better to ride into cer-

---

1.   The Litach River is also called the Leitha.

tain death than have to bear the disgrace of defeat. Unrealistic resolve inspired them for the moment. Before attacking again they took an oath that, whatever it might take to succeed in the battle, any man who rode away from danger—unless he was forced to do so by severe wounds—would have a stone tied around his neck and be drowned in the river, or he would be burned alive.

And, yes, the Hungarians gave evidence of living up to their oath. They wrought destruction as far as the west side of the Rhine. They destroyed a fortified city called Basel and went on to wreak destruction in Alsace, as they harried the people with their swords. No one was able to resist them, and they set fires all around, leaving the land completely laid low. Then they rode back to the Burgundians. Some Swabians and Bavarians agreed to serve them in return for land, violating their pledge under the Law of the Empire that no one should support an enemy in war.

Illness began to weaken King Conrad, and the princes were saying truly that he could not be of much service to the Empire. His vassals were also saying that they did not want to serve him any longer as their judge and lord.

A council was convoked at Würzburg, but it was postponed after Bishop Gebhart raised the objection that it was unfitting for the Empire to remove from office any Roman judge who had not been guilty of any misconduct—further that he should be asked to appear and testify himself at another council. The princes agreed to another council, this time in Aachen.

Both Duke Erchenger and his brother, Berthold, were beheaded.

Before the time set for the council at Aachen had arrived, King Conrad died, after holding the Empire for seven years.

XLVI

Henry I

Henry I (r. as German king 919–936) was duke of the Saxons, who had frequently opposed German kings and emperors since Charlemagne's day. Henry himself had been an adversary of Conrad I, who surprised the other princes by asking that Henry be his successor because of his talents and the possibility of uniting Saxon interests with those of other Germans. His interest in falconry led to his being called Henry the Fowler. Contrary to our author's account below of a consecration in Rome, Henry desired to stay free of unwelcome influence by the church and declined to have himself consecrated by the pope, remaining content with the title of German king and not Roman emperor.

Henry was careful to undertake military campaigns only when he had a good idea how they would end. He bribed the Hungarians with tribute into a ten-year truce from 923 to 933. When it expired he defeated them in two major battles. He also won victories against Danes and Slavs, leaving the empire considerably stronger than it had been under Conrad.

The princes lost no time in assembling for a council. With one voice they praised Henry, saying that this lord was true and reliable, descended as he was from such a trustworthy house. They comforted themselves with these thoughts, but they barely won him over. In fact, they had to exert pressure on him to induce him to take over the Empire. Hai! How long he was opposed to accepting their offer!

The Huns found out that a new king had been raised. They agreed they would give him a fine reception by riding through Bavaria, Swabia, Alsace, and Lorraine, setting them all ablaze. Duke Burchart fought against the Hungarians on Frankish soil, where the duke was killed and his men fled. The Huns ravished and burned the land, putting the Christians to shame.

Christendom could no longer bear doubts about the outcome of this conflict, and all Christians called upon God. His messenger appeared as Archbishop Heriger, who dispelled Christendom's fears. King Henry was fighting the Normans, and, using great force, he compelled them to accept baptism. It seemed to Christendom that this was taking a long time.

King Henry was made aware that the Hungarians were riding over his lands, their armies bringing destruction to his border territories. Day and night he hastened to make preparations for an expedition—Hai! How little he rested! Princes arrived who raised the complaint that churches were being burned down from land to land! The bishop proclaimed a summons to arms, and there was no man good for anything who could ignore that. While the princes sat deciding what to do, the Hungarians invaded the land of the Sorbs, where the king and his army were camped.

Very early one morning the princes were eager to take action, and the king gave orders to charge the Hungarians in their defensive positions. The Hungarians lost all their confidence and might. They were unable to raise a hand, and the Christians began killing them. That was a sure sign that it was Our Lord who was making them almost unable to move. Neither shields nor spears, hauberks nor helmets could do them any good. They lay about benumbed, and very few of them escaped. The Christians sang praises to God.

All the princes joined in telling King Henry that he should journey to Rome to the [graves of] the two holy apostles [Peter and Paul]. Following the advice of the princes, he did so, and the pope consecrated him as emperor, to give relief to widows and orphans and to protect Christendom. The ferocious Bohemians did not want to cease their attacks and committed serious crimes against the king, to which he put an end with God's help. He rode into the land of Bohemia—they could not resist him there—and he ordered the heads struck off many of the Bohemian princes, so that the rest of them were fearful of him forever more. Indeed, Henry judged his people severely but wisely. He held the Empire—the book tells us as a fact—for exactly seventeen years and one month. The princes sorely lamented his passing.

XLVII

Otto I, "the Great"

Henry I's son Otto succeeded in putting together the strongest European empire since that of Charlemagne. Often the German Empire of the Middle Ages is dated from his accession as emperor in 962. Born in 912, Otto was elected German king in 936 and made a serious attempt to keep the duchies under his control. Saxony, Lorraine, and Franconia at first resisted Otto's authority but later submitted to him, while Swabia and Bavaria were joined to Otto's house through marriage. Otto reduced the tribes between the Elbe and the Oder to tributary status, and, in 950, he personally led an expedition to Bohemia, which ended with the Bohemians losing their independence.

Once again, the Hungarians attacked German territories, and soon they threatened Augsburg. The victory of Otto's troops over them at the Battle of the Lechfeld (August 10, 955) was the greatest German or imperial victory over the Magyars in the nearly continual wars their invasions set off.

Otto's religious policy aimed at having church officials serve state interests as well as clerical ones. In Italy, Otto's control was challenged by Berengar, margrave of Ivrea, who had himself made king of Italy. In 960, Pope John XII complained of being hard-pressed by Berengar and asked Otto to come to Rome, which—after pacifying parts of northern Italy on the way—he did and was crowned Roman emperor, with Pope John taking an oath of loyalty to him. Men loyal to Otto subsequently intercepted letters from John XII that attempted to incite foreign powers to oppose the emperor. Otto returned to Rome, deposed John, and put in his own appointee as Leo VIII, after he had compelled the Romans to agree not to name any popes without imperial consent.

The Romans revolted against imperial authority when Otto returned to Germany, but Otto marched on Rome again and this time gave his soldiers permission to sack the city. He was resolved to move against Greeks and Muslims in southern Italy, but decided on diplomacy instead, sending Bishop Luitprand of Cremona to arrange a marriage between his son, the future Otto II, and a Byzantine princess. Those negotiations foundered largely because Byzantine Emperor Nicephorus II refused to recognize Otto's imperial title and treated Liutprand with abject contempt. The succeeding Byzantine emperor was conciliatory, however, and agreed to a marriage between a princess and the younger Otto, after which relations between the Greeks of southern Italy and the Empire improved.

The story of blinding captives, leaving one of them one-eyed to lead the rest home, was probably inspired by the actual atrocity of Byzantine Emperor Basil II, "Basil the Bulgar Killer," in 1014. After a long war culminating in a decisive victory, Basil ordered fifteen thousand Bulgar soldiers blinded, leaving one eye to one man in a hundred to lead the troops back to their own emperor, who fainted at the sight and died two days later. Although the cities of northern Italy revolted on several occasions to assert their independence from the Holy Roman Empire, there is no record of Otto's doing anything like this in Milan or elsewhere.

When Emperor Henry departed this life, he left a son whose name was Otto.

The princes would not depart for home until they were assured that they could have young Otto as their judge. They praised the son all the more highly since his father had been so able.

Otto convoked a council at Aachen. Pious messengers from Rome came to it, bringing an urgent complaint to him from the Pope: men of Milan were seizing Christians and forcing them to commit pagan acts; their army was ravaging the land in defiance of him. The pope asked him to force them to cease all this, since by rights he was the Roman ruler and judge.

The fabled King Otto lost no time in making preparations for an expedition against Milan, and the princes pledged to go with it to besiege Milan. The Milanese held that siege in the utmost contempt. Hai! How well they defended themselves with spears and with swords. The city-dwellers bore the brunt of injury from the attack, but many of the king's heroes were also lying there wounded or dead. Injury and misery abounded there.

The king thought that it would be too much of a disgrace for him to leave without assuaging his anger, and he ordered a tower constructed higher than the city walls. That helped bring about the defeat of the city-dwellers, who were also so hard pressed by hunger and soldiers coming at them from all directions that they were forced to negotiate, in hopes of winning back the king's favor. I tell you that there is no doubt but what the king and his men rode into the city in a formation. The inhabitants had to put up with much robbery and plunder, as the king deprived them of all their honors.

And, yes, the king's wise counselors advised him to take hostages from the city. He soon ordered twelve to be taken who seemed to him to be noble enough to prove his point. He ordered them bound with ropes and led out of the city into an open field, where he gave vent to his anger. Eleven had their eyes gouged out, and the twelfth was left with one eye to guide the others on the road back home. This gave the burgesses reason to worry.

The fabled King Otto issued laws regulating coinage and taxes so that these would better serve the interest of the Empire. There was no one among the Lombards but those who said, "The king, who liberated us from the Milanese, came into our land to bring us comfort and prosperity."

The Hungarians found out that the king was in Lombardy and rose again against the Empire, robbing, burning, and rendering the land desolate. Their ferocious behavior knew no limit: They destroyed churches, raped women, and tortured children with fire and sword.

Our Lord himself commanded that King Otto save the people from their oppression. He hurried back through the mountains and designated Augsburg as the assembly point. Very soon the Christians had twenty-six thousand volunteers against the heathen hordes of one hundred and twenty-eight thousand. That holy lord, Saint Udalrich, pleaded every hour the whole time with God for a good outcome, until God revealed to that holy bishop that the raging heathens stood condemned before him.

Very early one morning the bishop sang a mass, and the king took up his own flag. He charged the heathens with daring beyond measure, for God himself was with him. The king displayed his brave determination until, out of that massive horde of heathens, only seven were left.

Christendom then rejoiced, comforted in its suffering and well relieved of its oppression. The empire enjoyed peace with the Hungarian people ever afterwards. The king was unwilling to fail to honor God for the great love he had shown him. He proclaimed the honor and fame of God far and wide and founded the archdiocese of Magdeburg, the city in which he was buried afterwards. He held the Empire, it is a fact, for thirty-eight years and twelve days. The princes greatly lamented his passing.

XLVIII

Otto II

Otto II (r. as German king 961–983 and Roman emperor 967–983), son of Otto the Great, married Theophano, daughter of Byzantine Emperor Romanus II. He led a campaign against the Bohemians that had to be abandoned because fighting had broken out in Bavaria. Eventually he made a successful second expedition to Bohemia, which resulted in Polish King Boleslaus II's promise of allegiance to him.

His marriage to Princess Theophano did not mean good relations with the Greeks of southern Italy. Otto marched on Italy. In Rome he restored Pope Benedict XII, who had been deposed. Then, in an attempt to counter Islamic inroads in Italy, he continued south to Apulia. At first his efforts were successful, but then an alliance developed among Arabs, south-Italian Greeks, and the Byzantine Empire in reaction to Otto's taking of Apulia. Although the medieval and modern boundaries are not the same, Apulia (modern Puglia) is very roughly the heel of the Italian "boot;" Calabria is the "toe."

W hen King Otto departed this life, he left a worthy son also named Otto, who then held the Empire. There was a prince named Regenwart in a land called Calabria who let his men rob and burn at will. The Greeks had no intention of putting up with this and did not rest until they had chased him to Apulia. He had to experience being badly shamed in his own country.

Regenwart sent out letters and in one of them he asked King Otto if he would help him regain his honor. If he would, then he would become the king's vassal and serve him evermore. He would surrender his lands to the king. How helpful and fitting that would be for the Roman Empire!

At the advice of his princes, King Otto assembled his forces. The Romans assured him how willing they were to serve. Quickly and energetically they arranged for ships to be constructed and well outfitted. The pope, however, voiced his opposition, telling the king it would be against his will if they sent an expedition to Apulia.

Some of the Romans advised the Greeks that they should reconsider what they were doing and fight against the king; he would be forced to withdraw if they did. [The Greeks agreed, and] to assure the good will of those Romans the Greeks also gave them silver and gold. Those Romans insisted that they admired the Greeks and would not help the king anymore to regain his honor.

When the king and his men arrived in Calabria, the Greek forces challenged them on the sea. Those who were with the king, having falsely pledged to serve him, fled before the conflict began without even being threatened. The king himself was hard pressed, and many of his men soon lay dead. Still the young warriors committed to him fought fiercely. We know the truth about this from the books. More than thirty thousand Greeks were slain, so that the Greeks paid dearly for that victory.

The king and his men forced the galleys' oars hard through the water; it was time to get away. They hurried and rowed—how little they spared themselves! It was really a miracle that any German survived this.

When they arrived back on land and the pope discovered what had happened, he complained to the Senate that the king had been betrayed—the oaths of loyalty had been badly kept. Young people joined older ones in demanding that those who had sold out the king should be killed, as the law required.

There were twenty of them who had sold out the king, although they strongly denied it until they were killed. They fought ordeals of combat, which ended badly for them. Fourteen were rich and prominent nobles, the rest commoners; they were all beheaded.

Not long after the king fled from the Greeks, he fell ill. For a fact, he held the Empire exactly nine years. He was buried in Rome. Many Germans were slain [in the conflict at the end of his reign].

XLIX

Otto III

Otto III (r. as German king 983–1002 and Roman emperor 996–1002) was the son of Otto II and the Byzantine Princess Theophano. He was elected German king at age three. Having accompanied his troops in expeditions against the Wends and the Bohemians in his early teens, he undertook an expedition to Italy in the course of which he appointed a cousin to the vacant papacy as Gregory V, who crowned him Roman emperor at age fifteen (not twelve).

Otto took his Roman connection quite seriously. He built a palace on the Aventine and ornamented it with art works resembling those of ancient Greeks and Romans. He also revived some ancient-Roman titles for himself. The Romans were on the whole less than enthusiastic about him and eventually besieged him in his palace. After a temporary truce, Otto escaped and rallied some troops, but he died in the course of a military campaign against the Romans.

When King Otto departed this life, he left a son, the third Otto, who was not yet of age, since he was twelve years old. The princes assembled at Mainz for a council, where bishops and dukes agreed that since his father was so true and trustworthy, they would choose the son even though he was still a child. This led to a great conflict breaking out in the Empire.

On the Rhine there were two rich and powerful counts, one a mighty prince named Theodoric, the other one named William. They did not want to pledge themselves as vassals and were scornful of the boy as a ruler. They raised a fierce revolt, saying that no child ever won control of the Empire in the manner of an apprentice and that, if the election had really been free, a king would have been chosen who could run the Empire on the basis of his own knowledge and experience. It was asking too much to expect someone still in childhood to know what to do or to be relied upon.

Young Otto would have preferred to overcome their opposition with conciliation. He offered them fiefs and treasure, but that did not help anything. At Würzburg there was a bishop named Hugo, who was often at the king's court, and the honor of the Empire was very dear to him. Since the rebel dukes destroyed so much with their fires, hunger spread throughout the land. What the rebel dukes did caused people to suffer greatly, and it was the cause of many deaths. Bishop Hugo had mercy on the suffering people. Very often he would ride out secretly, searching quietly for those rebel dukes until he caught them at Kassel and led them back to the king's court.

Everyone, poor and rich, praised the bishop the same way for what he had done.

After the lords temporal and spiritual had given their verdict, Theodoric and William were executed in Worms. Now let us hear what the books tell us: great unrest was then stirred up by the Wends. Fear of God made nothing sacred to them. In Prague—to this day the books contain documents proving this—there was a bishop named Albrecht. The Wends committed a great crime against him according to the laws of God while he was lying in his bed. It was the worst of crimes for King Otto—they martyred him to death. In the choir of martyrs he occupies a place in the Kingdom of Heaven.

God then avenged his stalwart. King Otto led an expedition into Wendish territory and laid waste the land with fire and sword. It is a fact that he held the Empire for exactly eighteen years and four months. Then he [died and] was buried at Aachen.

L

Henry II, "Saint Henry"

Otto III died childless, and upon his death Frankish and Bavarian princes elected Henry II as German king (r. 1002–1024; r. as Roman emperor 1014–1024). He bought the allegiance of the Saxons and Thuringians, and soon Lorrainian and Swabian princes did homage to him.

Boleslaus I, "the Great," king of Poland, invaded and occupied Bohemia and held Meissen in Saxony with the connivance of some discontented German nobles, including Bruno, bishop of Augsburg and brother of King Henry. Henry began to mobilize against Boleslaus but, instead of moving against him, led an expedition into Italy to put down a revolt by Arduin, margrave of Ivrea, who was claiming to be king of Italy. Arduin submitted to Henry's forces without much of a fight. Henry then drove the Poles from Bohemia, and Boleslav in 1005 asked for peace. Peace was finally concluded between Henry and Boleslav in 1013. In the same year Henry went to Rome, where Pope Benedict VIII, whom Henry had supported against a rival claimant to the papacy, crowned him Roman emperor in 1014.

In 1020, Pope Benedict visited Henry in Babenberg and asked Henry for assistance against rebellious Greeks in southern Italy.

Henry agreed to help and led another expedition to Italy, where with some Norman aid he defeated the Greeks, but had to take his troops back to Germany to escape the pestilence that broke out in southeastern Italy.

Henry was a strong patron of the church and supporter of church reform. He founded the see of Babenberg after providing for building a great cathedral there. Although not until the mid-thirteenth century, the bishops of Babenberg functioned as princes of the Empire. Henry backed Pope Benedict in his efforts to prohibit clerical marriage and the sale of spiritual offices, although he did appoint bishops on his own. In 1146, Pope Eugene III canonized him.

Without delay the princes praised one Henry, saying that he was faithful and reliable enough to fittingly head the Empire. He was duke of the Bavarians and renowned throughout for his compassion, his goodness and his great humility.

The princes refused to go home until they had succeeded in making him their ruler. At Regensburg a council was held, to which many bishops, dukes and counts came. Hai! How willingly they supported him! They conducted him to the throne at Aachen. Wherever the king went, when a poor man would reach out his hand, the king would slip off his shirt and give it to him. He reconciled the princes and resolved hostilities, giving the nobles fiefs and land of their own. What he bestowed on the poor he could never replace. Love for God grew within him. He was a true vassal of God, which won him abundant grace afterwards.

If we are correct in our understanding of this, he forced the Bohemians and the Poles to accept Christianity after a great struggle, along with all those who spoke Wendish. Then he turned his forces on the Hungarians. They were forced to flee before him and were not allowed to come to any terms with him until they had themselves baptized and believed in the one true God.

Since King Henry had victories over the foreign nations he went to Regensburg. The Bavarians were much in need of peace, which Henry established for them fairly and firmly. He was ever mindful of the best way he might serve God while on earth and in a way that would provide those who came after him with a good model when he was no longer there.

That ruler thought often and long about how he could do something good and useful so that afterwards people would remember that it was his work. Finally he decided to undertake a magnificent work in founding a diocese at Babenberg in the name of the Father, the Son, and the Holy Ghost. He served God early and late. He donated broad acres of land with many outlying fields to churches, providing them also with rich furnishings. As a result Babenberg has become a much-admired bishopric as well befits the Empire.

After that the king hastened to set out for Rome. In a beautiful ceremony Pope Benedict [VIII] consecrated him emperor. Afterwards the emperor invited the pope to his own home in Babenberg so that he could see his work there with his own eyes. Bishop Henry [of Regensburg] opposed all of this, saying that it was contrary to custom that this bishopric be taken away from him and that separating Babenberg from his jurisdiction amounted to a robbery. With the princes promising to help, they advised the king—Pope Benedict helped also—and they settled the dispute this way: the emperor should give the Franconian duchy to the bishop of Regensburg. Whoever holds power has jurisdiction in two ways—he is both bishop and duke. This agreement may still be seen today as it was written out.

When the dispute was settled, the pope consecrated a cathedral in the city of Babenberg to honor good Saint Stephen. All the nobles rejoiced, but there came an earthquake, and they began to fear for their safety. The stone building wobbled and the people who delayed getting out lay there as if dead, having no idea what they had done. The princes thought for the most part that it was the Final Day of Judgment.

The emperor remained as the head of the Empire—the Book tells us truly—for twenty-three years and two months. Angels conducted his soul away.

He was buried in Saint Peter's Cathedral, and we can tell you truly that at his grave the blind become seeing, he helps sinners expunge their sins, and the crooked in body and those who are lame are healed. Saint Henry, save us in body and soul!

LI

Conrad II

A descendant of Otto I, Conrad II (r. 1027–1039) founded the Salian or Franconian dynasty. He solidified imperial power in Germany and northern Italy, although frequent revolts by the German nobility hindered him.

King Stephen I ruled Hungary as a contemporary of Conrad I. According to most accounts he wanted peaceful relations with the German Empire, but Conrad attempted to invade Hungary, where his forces were defeated by those of Stephen. The Liutzen were a loose federation of Slavic tribes frequently at war with the Empire.

The princes of the Empire mourned Henry with great devotion. They met in council and elected one Conrad. Then many great conflicts broke out—lord against lord and land against land with plundering and burning. There was a bishop of Augsburg named Bruno, who was in a feud with Welf. As a result of the violence they stirred up, the land lay in ruins. Widows and orphans came close to starving to death, but then God had mercy on the people. One of those lords was sitting at the table—the book gives us proof of that—when suddenly his eyesight left him. The feud ended with him never being able to see anything again. How well God avenged his own!

King Stephen of Hungary had badly injured the Empire, which made the princes very angry. They reported this to King Conrad, who ordered an expedition to march to Hungary. All through Austria, Bavaria, and Swabia, the princes were eager to join the march. Hai! How willingly they served him!

King Stephen ordered his Hungarian warriors forward, and he spoke to them. "Now listen, old and young. I have heard it told, and it is true, that my forefathers ravaged the land on the other side of the Rhine. Should we be so cowardly now that our enemies think they want to invade us? And are we unable to defend ourselves against them? Whoever helps me preserve my honor today I will be glad to reward forever. Wherever God sends him, he goes with my love."

King Conrad withdrew with one of his men from his assembled forces and walked to a cliff from which he could see the Hungarians riding towards them. At that point, the Hungarians numbered one hundred and eight thousand men.

The king hurried back from his lookout place to his troops, and the princes rushed to meet him. "At dawn, yesterday," he began, "I dreamed that King Stephen intended to sail against me in a huge ship, but when he wanted to speak to me his ship sank to the bottom. Then a black dog came and swallowed up his men, but I don't know what all that means."

All the princes spoke up. "We will interpret that dream for you. The Hungarians will see a miserable end today. They are all condemned to death unless they are able to run away from us. Their land shall burn, and no building in it shall be left standing. The dream shall come true today as it spells their doom."

The armies streamed together with many a warrior from each Empire. They did not fight equally well, however. The Bavarians succeeded with their spear thrusts in breaking through the enemy ranks. King Stephen barely escaped with very few of his men. He recovered at Rammerswert[1]— but what misery reigned among the Huns! The cries of the poor wounded and dying began to soften King Conrad's heart, and he ordered the great slaughter to cease and no more booty to be taken from those wretched dogs. Then he turned and headed back to the Souwe.

Now the books tell us that while the king was on his expedition, the ferocious heathens were doing him great harm at home. Our Lord let it come to pass that the heathens took by stealth a castle called Wirbina. They hanged all the Christians they found there from a gallows, keeping the

---

1.   A fortified outpost on or in the Danube.

worthiest among them to take back home with them as hostages. Then they set fire to the castle. King Conrad exacted vengeance for this. Our Lord gave him the power to do so. He rode to the Liutzen, where he wrought great destruction on those heathens. Most of them were killed. He released the Christians captured by the heathens and took them back with him. The remaining heathens agreed to pay a tax to the king as long as he lived. The war the heathens waged was over.

King Stephen sent some of his men to King Conrad, asking for peace, which King Conrad granted, and the peace treaty was sealed with oaths. Conrad had the Empire exactly fifteen years. He is buried at Speyer.

LII

Henry III, "the Black," also "the Good"

Henry III (r. as German king 1028–1056 and as Roman emperor 1046–1056) was the only son of Conrad II. As German king, he took part in a successful expedition to Burgundy. Not long before he died, Conrad gave his son the additional title of King of Burgundy. He married Princess Kunigunde, daughter of Canute, king of both Denmark and England. Kunigunde died in 1038, and Henry married Agnes of Poitou, daughter of Duke William V of Guienne. As the mother of young Henry IV, Agnes was later to play an advisory role in imperial affairs.

Henry's military talents were substantial, and he succeeded in bringing both Bohemia and Hungary under German control. He promoted the building of several cathedrals and generally was generous towards the church; however, he saw nothing wrong with intervening in church affairs as secular ruler, setting an example for Henry IV that would lead to massive church-state conflict. In 1046, he marched into Italy to settle a conflict between two claimants to the papacy at the Council of Sutri, where both contestants were deposed, and Henry named Suidger, Bishop of Babenberg, as Clement II, who crowned Henry Roman emperor. When Clement died at the end of 1047, Henry named Damasus II, who lived only a few months as pope, after which Henry appointed Leo IX. Henry's deposition of two claimants to the papacy and his appointment of three popes in two years had considerable influence on the creation of the College of Cardinals, which aimed at making the church, not the German emperor, responsible for selecting new pontiffs.

When he departed this life, King Conrad left a son, good Henry. The princes soon decided to take that lord to be their judge. To their great misfortune, the evil Bohemians, with the help of the Hungarians, rose in opposition to the king.

King Stephen [of Hungary] was buried at Weissenburg and Peter held his Empire after him. That angered the princes there, who would not rest until they had driven Peter into exile. With the help of the Bohemians, they then put another man in his place, called Otto the Cross-Eyed. This turned out badly for all of them.

Peter fled to Margrave Adalbert of Austria, but the Hungarians came after him with their army. They came through the borderlands and killed his people. Peter and Adalbert were unable to defend themselves, and so they fled to Henry the Good, who received them graciously, as was befitting for such a lord. He helped them regain their honor.

The king complained to the princes of the Empire and all spoke with one voice. First of all, they would see to it that the Bohemians were punished, and afterwards, they would deal with the Hungarians. And, yes, they advised the king to have the people in the countryside root up the forest there. This was done very quickly. All those who were with the lord landgraves hewed a wide stretch through the woods, making it unsafe for the Bohemians to stay in their country. The king's forces invaded and burned Wiscerat and Prague. They also beheaded the *supp ne*.[1] The duke [Otto the Cross-Eyed] just barely got away. Later, in Regensburg, he was to gain the king's good graces for a while through distributing great treasure among the princes.

Every day, Peter would complain to King Henry about his enormous suffering. The king held a council in Vienna, where those loyal to him swore to support him on an expedition, and they rode off to Hungary. The king led many a fine hero and first besieged Pressburg. Events unfolded rapidly. The city-dwellers were taken prisoner. Otto escaped in time; taking wife and child he ran off to the Russians, but the rest of his house were all killed.

Peter sat again on his throne. King Henry never forgot the services that Adalbert had rendered him. He took Leopold, who was Adalbert's son, and placed all his borderlands under his royal protection until Leopold was grown and the king would give him his sword and entrust him with his fiefs. How could he have treated him any better? The lordly princes all praised his goodness, saying that he had the true royal spirit in him.

Meanwhile it came to pass that the Romans raised three different men to the papal throne, setting off a conflict that was more than Christendom could bear. The people complained to the king about this terrible problem. In Babenberg there was a bishop named Suidger, a well-educated master who was frequently at the king's court. He advised King Henry to proceed peacefully by convoking a synod in Rome, where he could render proper judgment according to synodal custom. All the nobles followed this advice.

The king took the bishop and others who were close to him and rode to Rome. Some people raised objections, but what the king did pleased others. Queen Agnes went along, too.

The king presided at the court in Rome, where three hundred and forty-six bishops had gathered. After much discussion of God's teachings a common judgment was reached. The three popes were dismissed, and Suidger, who was bishop of Babenberg, became pope [as Leo IX]. That

---

1.   Slavic chiefs

ended the strife, and the pope consecrated Henry as emperor. The empress also received his blessing and everyone joined in praising Our Lord.

Meanwhile it happened that while the emperor was in Rome, grave misfortune overtook the king of Hungary. He was seized from his throne and his eyes were gouged out. Throughout the land, Hungarians were unwilling to let anyone who had come there from Germany live any longer.

There was nothing else for the emperor to do but command a military expedition. He divided Hungarian territory into two parts, and one he gave to the man with sight, the other to the blind man. Still they burned each other's lands and buildings. The Bavarian Duke Conrad helped to keep the conflict going, and was later exiled from the Roman Empire. Later he died in Hungary in great shame.

There was a bishop of Regensburg named Gebhart, whose story is still told. From the prompting of the devil it happened that he was seized by his personal servants and thrown into a dungeon. The emperor himself had to help relieve him from that wicked treatment. The princes all complained about what he had suffered, particularly since he was the emperor's uncle. He regained his bishop's throne in Regensburg.

The Liutzen rose again and killed many Christians, drowning some of them and setting the lands of others ablaze. The emperor was overtaken by illness and announced that any person to whom he might have done any wrong should bring it to his attention. How quickly he sent for them! He ordered restitution and gifts beyond those first ordered to be given, and he transformed his earthly life into one with God. He had the Empire exactly seventeen years and eight days. Our Lord has his soul.

LIII

Henry IV

Henry IV (r. 1056–1106) is one of the better-remembered German emperors, in considerable part because he personified secular claims against the reform attempts of Gregory VII, particularly in the dispute over whether kings or emperors could appoint bishops in the "Investiture Controversy."

The historical Henry IV became German king at the age of six; his mother, Agnes, served as his regent until 1062, when Archbishop Anno of Cologne—the subject of the *Annolied*—kidnapped him and made himself regent. The powerful Archbishop Adalbert of Hamburg and Bremen, who also oversaw Scandinavian church affairs for the papacy, at first supported Anno, but then competed with him. Anno's value system was rather ascetic, Adalbert's more worldly, and contemporary clerics saw Adalbert's victory over Anno as Henry's main advisor—when the later began ruling in his own right in 1065—as the cause of Henry's turn toward ways of the flesh.

Henry IV attempted to do what he could to consolidate his power, which necessarily brought him into conflict with the feudal lords of his realm, who were naturally distrustful of imperial power, which could only lessen their own. In his conflicts with them and with the papacy, much of his support came from bishops he and his father had appointed—and who consequently opposed any exclusive investiture right by the papacy. Support also came from townspeople, who—as often elsewhere in Europe—preferred kings who might give them local charters of liberties, to the feudal nobility who were more grudging with regard for townspeople's modest freedoms.

Henry's conflict with Gregory VII led him to persuade many of the German bishops to renounce their obedience to the pope in

1076. A month later, Gregory excommunicated Henry. When Henry's secular vassals sided with the pope, he felt forced to submit to Gregory at Canossa. His German princes nonetheless elected Rudolf of Swabia as counter-king. Henry defeated him in 1080 and declared Gregory deposed, after which he appointed the counter-pope Clement III. It took him three years of military efforts to gain entrance to Rome, but in 1084, he did so, and Clement crowned him emperor. In later years Henry had to fight his older son, Conrad, who had been crowned as joint king in 1087, and then his younger son, the future Emperor Henry V, who had been crowned in 1098 as joint king. In 1105, young Henry defeated his father and forced him to promise to abdicate, but Henry IV escaped, rallied his followers, and was attempting to reassert his authority when he died of natural causes the following year.

For our author, Henry's reign should be remembered not so much for the interminable power struggles it featured as for the opening of the Crusades. His account of Godfrey of Boullion, who led the First Crusade and became the first ruler of the Latin Kingdom of Jerusalem, is typical of contemporary accounts, which had the streets of Jerusalem flowing with blood. He was probably relying on oral accounts he had heard as a younger man. Godfrey's virtues as a ruler in single-mindedly serving the triumph of the Cross contrast with Henry's vices in one of the author's many "mirrors of princes."

The author draws on the *Würzburg Chronicle* for his introductory words about the Saxons fighting the Liutzen, that confederation of pagan Slavs to the northeast of Saxony resolutely hostile to church and Empire, and Ekkehard of Aura's *World Chronicle*. He may have used a Guelph history that told how one Marquess Ida of Austria went on a pilgrimage to the Holy Land, where she was taken prisoner and eventually became the mother of Zangi ("Sangwin" or Imad-al-Din, 1084–1146). Our author calls Henry IV's mother "Agnes" correctly, but gives her the title "Duchess of Bavaria" as a matter of pure fiction. Then, by calling Zangi's supposed mother both "Agnes" and "Duchess of Bavaria," the author appears to conflate her with Henry IV's mother, Agnes (but of Poitou, not Bavaria, as our author has it). In the unfinished final chapter of the *Book of Emperors*—this time more or less as in real history—Zangi slaughters crusaders and clerics in Edessa; it is the first Crusader kingdom to be re-conquered by Muslims, setting off the Second Crusade.

The princes consulted together with each other and agreed on a Henry who was the son of the previous one. They were influenced by the fine record of the father's deeds to give the same office to the son.

His mother was Duchess of Bavaria. While the Saxons were unable to refuse obedience to the young king, they later caused him no end of trouble. At the king's bidding the Saxons raised an expedition against the Liutzen. They liberated Christians the Liutizi had captured and deprived the Liutzen of all their means for waging war, after which they had to pay regular tribute to the king.

When King Henry grew a little older, he sadly neglected his duties and let himself become reckless. He ignored the princes and treated the nobility with contempt, allowing himself to become a stranger to learning and committing offenses against chastity. He would ride through the countryside with a great courtly display, which ended in treating noble ladies shamefully, sometimes allowing men to strip them.[1] He constantly gave himself over to excess and often sat at the gaming table when he was supposed to be governing the Empire, all of which aroused anger in the princes.

The lords began to plot against him, often laying ambushes in hopes of killing him. Henry had a chaplain who was archbishop of Bremen, and the princes blamed him most severely, saying that Henry's bad conduct was his fault and that the Empire could not tolerate his role in it.

Off in Merseburg a council was called, at which the archbishop asserted his position successfully, but then a terrible feud broke out when the

---

1. The manuscripts all have "*die sine liez er rouben*" ("he would let his men rob them") here, but Massmann argues convincingly for "*rouben*" used in parallel sources for both "*spoliare*" and "*denudare*," the latter of which makes the best sense here. Op. cit., Vol. III, p.1100

Saxons deserted the king and conspired with all their kinsmen to attack the Empire. Their armies thoroughly ravaged and burned Thuringia.

There were princes at that time, particularly in Bavaria, Swabia, and the Rhine Valley, who bitterly resented how the Saxons had gone through the Empire with such destruction, burning their lands. They called a great meeting and set after them with an army. The Saxons at first defended themselves well, but then nothing was heard but cries of anguish, as a lake of blood floated onto the Unstrut River, turning the whole river into one of blood. The king was victorious, and the Saxons were killed except for a small number who escaped in the battle. He subdued all Saxony, whose people had turned over hostages to him.

There was a duchess of Bavaria whom Our Lord inspired to take vassals closest to her and journey to the Holy Sepulchre, which she desired to do. They set sail from the port city of Bari [in Apulia], but when they came to the port of their destination the heathens found out who they were, and the lady was captured with her ladies-in-waiting and vassals. Duchess Agnes was detained at a city called Rages,[2] where she took a heathen husband to whom she later bore a son named Zangi; however, for now, we will interrupt that story and take it up at the proper point, presenting then what happened in some detail.

The time soon came when Duke Godfrey set out for the Holy Sepulchre [on the First Crusade], leaving behind all his worldly possessions in honor of the true God, and great was the number of lords who set out with him. They journeyed through Hungary, then through Bulgaria and through desolate Romania. The heathen forces fled from him to the city of Antioch, which the duke then besieged. Inside, the heathen chieftain named Milian was unable to continue defending the city to save himself. Heathen forces were coming to his aid, but they delayed so long that Godfrey took the fortifications by storm, captured Milian, and put all his men to death together.

When the heathens found out that the Christians had won the fortress, five of their kings rode against them with all their forces. It would take too

---

2. "Rages" cannot be identified with certainty. It could conceivably be "Ramusi" an old name for Dubrovnik, which might have fit in for the author as a place where crusaders landed on the other side of the Adriatic on their way to the Holy Land, even though it was not in Muslim hands in the late-eleventh century.

long to tell you how vast the forces were with which they put their own siege in place. Their monstrous numbers were so great—this is what we have all heard, now—that no one could see the end of them. They put the Christians under great stress from hunger with their siege. Things were so bad that a donkey's head—however hard it may be for you to believe this—was sold for three bizendinge, [Byzantine gold coins]. Hunger pressed them so hard that the Christians dragged off those heathens they had killed and ate their stinking bodies. That is how they kept themselves alive.

Still, God deigned to save his own, and no armies would help the heathens indefinitely. Very early one morning the duke put on his armor, even as the Christians were dying of starvation. Many had slipped into a faint and never gotten up again. Then, however, he who redeemed us from hell came to the aid of the Christians and gave them joy, for they found the Holy Lance. The knights in that far-off land raised high their hands and, hungry as they were, they plunged into battle. Within a short, time they had killed more than fifty thousand heathens. Our Lord himself was helping them, giving them such power that a Christian man could have easily killed a thousand heathens if they had not all been running away from him. The Christians sang praises to God, and—I will tell you a really interesting thing—the price of cleaned wheat fell to a penny a bushel. That was the way God redeemed his warriors with his divine power.

After Our Lord had requited them for their suffering and they had undisputed control of Antioch, they pressed on further. Duke Godfrey besieged Jerusalem, where the heathens inside the city were aroused to such a savage fury that they soon threw open the city gates and fought the Christians in front of the walls. The Christians forced them back inside and took over that fortified city. Wicger and Frederick displayed their prowess particularly well; all the heathens who came within their reach had to pay with their lives.

Some of them tried to save their lives by fleeing up to the towers, hurling down rocks and shooting arrows, but to no avail, for nothing could keep the fire from sweeping over them. Both women and children were killed. That was a time when God was helping his own.

The king of Babylonia gathered great forces together, for he wanted to free that fortified city from the Christians. Duke Godfrey heard about this and gathered his Christian warriors together, intending to postpone battle with them no longer. He said, "Our Lord has the good and certain trait that he never lets his own down—those who call upon him in their need. We shall share the way with him, and the doomed heathens will never escape us."

The heathens were encamped by a river called Salkatha in such force as no one can properly describe to you. The Christians were unable to find water, and imploringly they complained about this to God. Their people were dripping with sweat and overheated by the sun, all suffering miserably. Then a great miracle happened: such clouds of cool vapors passed over them that they languished no longer and drank the heavenly dew. Who should ever fail to trust God?

When the heathens heard that the Christians were beginning to draw near, they left in flight, but a hundred thousand of them soon lay dead not from the sword blows or spears but from thirst. Some of them had sought shade beneath the thorn bushes, but some [who escaped later] drowned as their ships sank in the sea. The Christians who arrived first on the scene found that the heathens had left such fine booty for them to seize as words cannot accurately describe. The Christians went on to invade the lands of Babylonia up to the very gates of the capital itself. The heathens outside were trampled to death or struck down in such numbers that it is quite possible to assure you that this heathen land was stinking with carrion. There was great joy among the Christians as they set out on the return journey to the Holy City.

We are not able to tell you every single miracle that God worked for the sake of his children. The fear of God was spread throughout that whole region; since God had rendered his own victorious, the forces of heathendom were left in despair and did not try anything after that. And so the Word of God was spread.

The Christians demanded a king. They held church services, worshipping God diligently with matins and masses and with almsgiving and prayer. From city to city and from province to province the Christians secured the whole kingdom with their swords, and the heathens had to yield before hem. Duke Godfrey achieved all this. Where can you find, before or since, any man of like capability who deserved all worldly honors as much as he? His soul has gone to grace, and, just as I am telling you now, his bones are resting there by the Holy Sepulchre while his soul is holy and purified.

Now let us resume the story of Emperor Henry. At the instigation of the princes he led an expedition to Apulia, where he remained many days. He followed his custom there of riding out alone to hunt deer, but early one morning he fell into the hands of his enemies. He was held there, beset with worries, until the fourth morning afterwards. The princes all began to mourn for him, for they thought they had lost him.

The news reached Germany that the emperor had been lost. The princes gathered at Bonn, where they unanimously elected young Henry [V], entrusting the Empire to him so that he might sit in judgment now that his father had been lost.

A short time after that the old king was found again. He rode into the city of Rome, where he was consecrated as emperor. Then he returned to Germany, but when he reached the mountains he heard correctly that there was a plot afoot to kill him. He was resourceful enough, however, to escape with a few of his men.

At Regensburg, the main city, a council of angry nobles met, which threatened the peace. The old king had arrived there [by then], leading great forces. The Saxons, Bohemians, and others who generally supported him joined in giving him aid, while the Bavarians, Swabians, and all those who had pledged their support to his son at Bonn continued to aid him instead.

A river called the Regen runs by the place where they met each other, leading very large forces. Bavarians and Swabians were giving really extensive support to young Henry. The Bohemians barely escaped with their lives, and Hartwig was killed. Unable to withstand his enemies, the old king had to yield. He governed the Empire, the book tells us with certainty, for forty-eight years before he was repudiated in the forty-ninth. He died in Speyer, where his remains are buried.

LIV

Henry V

With Henry IV opposed by much of the German nobility but generally supported by bishops whom he had appointed, his rebellious son, Henry V, found many allies among the German nobles and opponents among the bishops. At a council held in Worms, the conflict came to an end when Henry V agreed not to appoint bishops as such to their church or "spiritual" offices, as long as church officials did not object to the German ruler giving them their "regalian rights" (secular jurisdiction over their dioceses) as fiefs from him.

The bishops then sent messages from land to land. They hated what they were faced with and did not want to submit to the young king ever. In fact, the papal ban flew over everywhere in Christendom. At the same time the secular princes were grieved by the thought of deserting young Henry, the man they had already praised and agreed to have as their ruler and judge.

The Empire began to divide along the lines of priests and laymen. The laymen were eager to support young Henry. A council was convoked in Regensburg. Dukes and counts with many a proven hero attended, but no bishops came. Count Sigihart was slain in the city. The princes generally advised the king that he should ride to Rome and have his crown confirmed.

An archbishop named Albrecht helped the king in everything, even if it was crooked or evil. The pope and the lords spiritual began to criticize him for this. The archbishop set off a serious conflict [in Rome]. He advised the king—an evil deed held against him—to station men in the cathedral, capture the pope and take him away with them as their prisoner.

[They did this, but] then the Romans wanted to free their overlord. They were quick to arm themselves with white hauberks and rush across the Tiber River. In the conflict there were more then seven thousand confirmed casualties among them, wounded or dead. They led the pope away from there with them. The king himself wanted only to get away from there, but the Romans would not let him. The city gates were narrow so the Romans knocked down some walls. The Germans did not want to be caught by the mob, and they cleared a broad path in front of them so that they could ride through, just as they wanted to do. Only their heroes' strength enabled them to do this.

The king and his men then rode through the countryside, robbing and burning and seizing castles. He caught the men he was looking for and punished them most severely. Even the pope suffered grave indignities from him. Wise counselors advised him that the dispute could be settled with the king giving up all the bishoprics. [He did this and] the pope invited him back into the city of Rome, where the Romans gave him and all those traveling with him a grand reception. The pope removed his ban of excommunication and consecrated him as the new emperor; he then rejoiced and departed.

Decrees flew about the countryside, as the king ordered punishments for robbing and burning. The ruler of Mainz received bitter criticism. He was accused of setting off such unrest in the Empire as to do permanent damage to Christendom.

The princes who had opposed the emperor now had to yield to him and sought his grace. Good and just men among them blamed Bishop Albrecht as responsible. The lords spiritual were very sorry that the son had ever risen against his father. It is known that he had the Empire for exactly seventeen years and six months more. At Speyer they buried their lord.

Lothair II

Lothair II (r. as German king 1125–1137 and as emperor 1133–1137) along with his father had supported Henry V against Henry IV. Henry V made him duke of Saxony. Although they had some quarrels, Lothair was in good standing with Henry when the latter died, and he was elected the next German king. In the struggle between the houses of Welf and Hohenstaufen, which would later become the Guelph-Ghibelline conflict, Lothair sided with the Welf faction, which enjoyed the support of the papal party most of the time in the twelfth century.

Not long after becoming king, Lothair attempted to get Frederick of Hohenstaufen to return to him some lands that Henry V had bequeathed to him. Frederick refused, and conflict broke out between them. Lothair's forces did well against those of Frederick, but, in 1127, the German princes elected Frederick's brother, Conrad of Hohenstaufen, counter-king of Germany. More conflict followed, but, by 1131, Lothair had overcome most of the Hohenstaufen resistance to his rule.

That same year, two claimants to the papacy, Innocent II and Anaclete II, asked for Lothair's support, but Innocent visited Lothair at Liége and won him over to his side. In 1133, Lothair arrived in Rome, where Innocent crowned him emperor and bestowed large papal fiefs in Tuscany on him. Lothair returned to Germany and had considerable success in overcoming Hohenstaufen opposition. After defeating them, he allowed Frederick and Conrad to keep their estates. For several years Lothair presided over a relatively peaceful and secure Empire, although at the end of his reign the desire of some Lombard cities for more independence and a dispute with Roger II of Sicily over Apulia led him to invade Italy. At first he was successful, but a breach with Innocent over Lothair's control of Apulia and mutiny among his German troops led him to begin returning to Germany. He died in a Tirolean village on the way back.

The princes agreed to a council away at the throne of Aachen. The secular princes met there along with many bishops. They drew upon the wisdom of all of them as they discussed where in the Empire they might find any prince who would be a worthy head of the Empire. They had heard frequent and favorable mention of good Lothair, a Saxon duke, and they showed him the greatest honor in extending him their offer to become their ruler.

It took the messengers considerable effort, searching early and late, before they found him in Brunswick. As soon as he understood the message he sent out some of his own men, telling them to go and get advice about how he might avoid accepting the title—that he did not think himself capable of any more great undertakings. The lords all spoke against his doubts. In fact, the lords all told him he should appreciate the faith of the nobles in choosing him as their judge and ruler. In a discussion with him they convinced him to change his mind and ride with them to Mainz. Two brothers, one named Conrad, the other Frederick, did not like this turn of events at all. Arrogantly they allowed themselves to swear that he would never ever be their king or lord.

There was a second source of trouble. The Duke of Bohemia drove out Otto of Moravia, a brave and spirited prince, and he fled to the king, which the Saxons took much amiss, saying that Otto's expulsion was against the interests of the Empire and reflected badly on all of them. The princes came to the conclusion that the king should ride to Bohemia. At that time passage through the Bohemian woods was blocked with trees cut down and forming barriers everywhere so that no knight could ride through without losing his life [to defenders] very soon.

Otto was a resourceful man. He took one thousand mounted knights with him, who then dismounted and went on foot, letting their horses go. They thought to slip through that way, but there was so much snow and neither roads nor paths, which brought those heroes into grave straits, particularly since they were very tired from carrying their own weapons. The Bohemians became aware of them and lost no time in exacting vengeance from them. Most of the Saxons were killed, and Otto himself never came out of those woods.

One morning just at daybreak, Duke Ulrich stopped the king and his men as they rode. The princes began to raise fervent objections, pointing out that bishops and counts were among those stopped, and they advised Count Ulrich that he should make way for the king—saying that he was the lord of the Empire. Duke Ulrich took that advice and gained the king's favor. Afterwards he became his privy counselor, the imperial adviser. At Nuremberg he sat beside the king as he was holding court.

Those two dukes, Conrad and Frederick, did not let up from their efforts to find what they could do more and more damaging to the king. They called upon friends and relations who gave them considerable help. The princes were slow in coming to the king's aid. Those dukes and their men with banners held high laid waste large parts of the Empire. The king and, yes, the blessed queen also, often implored Our Lord for aid. Through long hours they prayed to God that for his mother's sake he would let the outcome be decided according to whose souls were right and true and also according to what would bring honor to the Empire.

Some princes within the Empire met and decided to elect Duke Conrad [as counter-king]. They rushed into doing this too recklessly, letting it be known throughout the whole Empire that they wanted to have Conrad as their king and lord. At Neuenburg they set off a conflict by acclaiming him as king. To the lords spiritual this seemed an evil thing to do.

The conflict went on until, making use of bans of excommunication, the bishops rallied to the side of King Lothair. The dukes then gave way, and Conrad fled to Milan, where he was pursued by Lothair's forces. Conrad made his way to Lombardy. Frederick of Falkenstein was his one true ally.

It was not long after that before King Lothair besieged that fortified city called Speyer, since it was serving as the rallying point for the outlaws. Conrad was sure they could survive the siege, but nothing was of any help to him. King Lothair did not raise the siege until they turned over the fortress to him. All the inhabitants swore allegiance to the Empire. Day by day, God multiplied all King Lothair's worldly honors.

Meanwhile a conflict broke out in Rome, where the Romans fanned hatred against one another in raising two claimants to the papal throne. King Lothair rode there with his army, and with the common advice of the princes they rejected the one called Pierleoni [Anaclete II] and confirmed Innocent [II]. No one can succeed in doing anything against God. The pope consecrated Lothair as emperor. It was decided then to take an imperial expedition to Apulia; that is what the princes wanted to do. There they found a prince named Ruocher [Roger], whom King Lothair expelled to Sicily. Conrad the Swabian carried the king's banner, and all those who had earlier been opposed to him now served him loyally. He succeeded in taking over a tower in Bari after many setbacks. God the Good was helping him take it.

There was a duke in Bavaria who was the subject of much praise, and he was such a noble prince that all his men served him very willingly. He was an in-law of the emperor and one of the worthiest lords temporal who lived at that time. Owî! What a great array of virtues he had! He conquered the border territories of a land called Tuscany; indeed he contributed mightily to the Empire so that the emperor quite willingly bestowed fiefs on him and lands of his own. The might of that rich and powerful duke was evident then in Apulia, where he carried out his will.

The Book tells us now with certainty that the duke took his heroes to a castle on St. Benedict's mountain, called Monte Cassino. When they arrived at the mountain they turned themselves into pilgrims. The men from the Abens [a tributary of the Danube near Regensburg] region in particular served brilliantly. They wore coats of steel armor, but over them they put on linen cloaks with hoods, and they carried their swords next to their bodies, sword–handles in their armpits. They went barefoot and performed good works, often falling to their knees in prayer. Stealthily they climbed the mountain; they captured their enemies and punished them without letting up. Then they turned the fortress over to the Empire.

Chapter Fifty-five

The duke and his men departed rejoicing. Benevento was the name of a city that he won with his warshield. He moved on from there—I am telling you this truly—to Monte Gargano, where his heroes acquitted themselves well. They charged in a stormy attack on Troy [in southern Italy], pressing their way into the city in high spirits. The mighty emperor thanked them for that.

At the walls of the fortified city of Bari the emperor ordered a wall-scaling tower device built. It was big and strong, and it is called an "Ebenhöhe [even with the heights];" it was solidly made and impressive to look at. In addition, he ordered digging under their walls. As fire broke out below, the heathens were unable to maintain themselves in the fortress. Those who were defending it paid dearly for their resistance—the emperor ordered them hanged.

With the approval of all the princes the emperor installed a duke there, good Reinulf, but the emperor was still not ready to return home. He rode to Otranto and hurled his lance into the sea. Emperor Lothair served as judge—the Book tells us truly—exactly twelve years, twelve weeks and twelve days. Let him who hears this song say a pater noster for the love of God Almighty and Emperor Lothair's soul. When he ruled the Empire, the earth bore plenty of fruit. He loved all divine teaching and retained all worldly honor. He feared Our Lord as did the blessed queen. They clothed the poor and took care of others in need. They overcame heathendom, and what they gained for the Empire honored God. God's grace upon the souls of both of them!

Conrad III

Conrad III (r. as German counter-king 1127–1135 and as German king 1137–1152) was the first German ruler of the Hohenstaufen dynasty. He had been elected by many of the German princes as king in opposition to Lothair II in 1127. He and his brother Frederick fought Lothair off and on, but, in 1135, he submitted to Lothair, who pardoned him and allowed him to take back his lost estates.

When Lothair died two years later, most of the German princes again elected Conrad king, this time not in opposition to any other claimant. The major holdouts were Bavarian and Saxon dukes from the Welf dynasty, who refused his allegiance. One of them, Henry the Proud, was made an outlaw through Conrad's imperial ban. He died in 1139, but Henry's brother, Welf, continued the family struggle. Conrad prevailed over Welf in the siege of Weinsburg, as our author indicates, although he does not record the episode that became probably the most famous emperor-legend associated with Conrad. According to that story, Conrad promised the women of Weinsburg that they could leave without interference, taking with them only what they could carry on their backs. Welf's wife, the duchess, left carrying him on her shoulders, and the other women of Weinsburg followed, each carrying a husband or other close male relative on her back. A nephew of Conrad protested that no one had intended this outcome, at which Conrad shouted loud and clear, "A word—an emperor!"

Conrad was never actually consecrated emperor by a pope. In spite of repeated invitations from Romans he always found himself too busy to go to Rome for the ceremony, but like Henry I and a fair number of other German kings, he functioned *de facto* as one.

Conflict continued intermittently in Bavaria and Saxony until in 1146 Bernard of Clairvaux succeeded in persuading many European nobles to answer his call to what became the Second Crusade, instead of fighting among themselves. Both Conrad and King Louis VII of France heeded the call and set out in 1147. This is the point where the *Book of Emperors* breaks off. The army was decimated by defeats and disease, and Conrad returned to Constantinople and then Italy. The French king turned against Conrad and allied himself with Roger of Sicily and Welf of Bavaria, his old adversary.

The princes met and agreed on a Conrad, who earlier had been against the Empire. Bishop Henry of Regensburg from the noble house of Diessen advised them to make this choice as did the Bohemian spokesman. That was done against the wishes of Duke Henry of Bavaria and his brother, Welf. They obtained considerable help from exploiting old resentments from when they were held in great honor in Emperor Lothair's time. The princes sought ways to entrap him.

It was the advice of the princes that King Conrad give Duke Henry a court reception that was less than gracious. He had him come to Regensburg, where Henry entrusted the spear and also the crown to him for the sake of the Empire's honor. He never saw him again.

The king ordered that he surrender the land of Bavaria to him. Leopold was already holding that land and took it much amiss since he was lord of that land and held it as part of his inheritance.

Duke Henry rode to Swabia, where Conrad's men treated him very badly. The duke was driven out and made his way to Saxony. That lord then departed this world—may God in heaven grant mercy to his soul!

Welf then rose in rebellion against the Empire. Duke Leopold besieged Vallei, and Welf fought against him there. Leopold was defeated in the conflict because so many of his men were killed and he barely escaped himself; however, Leopold was a determined hero and lost no time in rising in revolt once again, this time sustaining severe injuries. He was unable to retain support. How quickly all those who had pledged allegiance to him completely deserted him! Again he had to flee and was unable to obtain any honor for himself.

It soon came to pass that the king became angry with the noble prince Welf. Neither friends nor relations wanted to help him. They were slow to respond because Welf was opposing the Empire. King Conrad besieged Weinsberg. Welf re-gathered his heroes, planning to raise the siege of that fortified city. In his conflict with the king, Welf had greater forces, but that did not help him, and the Empire prevailed over him. Welf barely escaped. His men were captured and taken away from him. The siege was withdrawn from Weinsberg, but Welf had had enough of fighting.

Meanwhile, Our Lord allowed it to come to pass that the heathen named Zangi stealthily led forces to Edessa, when it was looked after by the Christians. On Christmas Day it happened just as I will tell you: the bishop [Archbishop Hugo] there was singing the first mass of the day when sounds of a great scuffle were heard at the doors. The heathens pushed their way through. The Christians suffered casualties. The heathens killed the bishop, whose head fell from his body. Once again the reigning God was martyred, as the martyrdom of Christians was great—blood was flowing all the way to the tower, and very few men or women survived, although we cannot tell you exactly how many Christians were slain. The devil was later to regret the whole scheme, since he got nothing out of it. Our Lord gathered all the souls unto himself.

Pope Eugene decided on this course of action: he ordered that this crime be reported to King Conrad and King Louis [VII of France]. Very soon, Abbot Bernard [of Clairvaux] presented the expedition [Second Crusade] in a way that made the princes eager to join it. He came before King Conrad and admonished him of his duty firmly but kindly, saying that Our Lord himself had chosen him. The king hesitated no longer. . . .

Bibliography

Frequent Abbreviations:

MGH – Monumenta Germaniae Historica
WBG – Wissenschaftliche Buchgesellschaft

1. Editions of the Book of Emperors and excerpts
(whole text and excerpts given in order of publication)

Docen, Bernhard Josef. "Abschnitt einer Kaiser-Chronik in deutschen Versen aus dem XII Jahrhundert," *Arentins Beyträge zur Geschichte und Literatur*, Vol. IX (1807), pp. 1063-1076. Charlemagne story.

Massmann, Hans Ferdinand, ed. *Der keiser und der kunige buoch oder die sogenannte Kaiserchronik*, ed. Hans Ferdinand Massmann. Quedlinburg and Leipzig: Gottfried Basse, 1848-1854. Three volumes: synoptic text in first two; very extensive (1192 pages) commentary in third.

Diemer, Josef. *Die Kaiserchronik nach der ältesten Handschrift des Stifles Vorau.* Wien: W. Braumüller, 1849.

Maier, Oberappelationsgerichts-Sekretär Joseph Maria. *Der Kaiser und der Könige Buch oder die sogenannte Kaiserchronik in freier Prosa-Bearbeitung.* Munich: L. Unflad, 1878. A very free reworking of the text into modern German with many unidentified, sometimes drastic, changes, additions and subtractions.

Schröder, Edward, ed. *Die Kaiserchronik eines Regensburger Geistlichen,* in MGH: *Deutsche Chroniken.* Vol. I. Hannover, 1892; repr. Darmstadt: WBG, 1964 and 1969. The standard version of the MHG text with manuscript variations.

Bulst, Walter, ed. *Die Kaiserchronik,* No. 18 of the series, *Deutsche Volkheit,* Jena: Eugen Diederichs, 1926. Modern German version of lines 14307-17181, the chapters on Charlemagne through Lothair of Supplinburg.

Die Kaiserchronik: Ausgewählte Erzählungen, I: Faustinianus. Heidelberg: Carl Winter, 1946.

Die Kaiserchronik: Ausgewählte Erzählungen, II: Crescentia. Heidelberg: Carl Winter, 1946.

Fank, Pius, ed. *Die Vorauer Handschrift,* Vol. I, *Die Kaiserchronik*; facsimile reproduction of the original from 1185-1190. Graz: Akademische Druck- and Verlagsanstalt, 1953.

Schultz, James A., transl. and ed. excerpt of 420 lines from *"Die Kaiserchronik,"* verses 247-667, in *Sovereignty and Salvation in the Vernacular,* 1050-1150 Published for the Consortium for the Teaching of Middle Ages in the series: *Medieval German Texts in Bilingual Editions* by Medieval Publications, Western Michigan University, Kalamazoo, Michigan, 2000.

2. Other Primary Sources

Alighieri, Dante. *Monarchia,* ed. Prue Shaw. Cambridge University Press, 1995.

Anonymous. *Das Annolied,* ed. M. Roediger, in MGH: *Deutsche Chroniken.* Hannover: Hahn, 1892, Vol. I; included with Schröder's edition of the *Book of Emperors* (see above), but not included with later reprints of it.

Augustinus Aurelius, *De civitate dei libri xxii,* ed. Emanuel Hoffmann. Vienna: F. Tempsky, 1900.

Frutolfi et Ekkehardi. *Chronica, necnon Anonymi Chronica Imperatorum,* ed. and transl. (bilingual ed.) Franz-Josef Schmale and Irene Schmale-Ott. Darmstadt: WBG, 1972.

Marsilius of Padua. *Defensor Pacis—Der Verteidiger des Friedens,* ed. and transl. (bilingual ed.) Horst Kusch. Berlin: Rütten & Loening, 1958.

Orosius, Paulus, *Historiarum adversum paganos libri vii,* ed. Karl Zangemeister. Vienna: C. Gerold, 1882.

Otto, Bishop of Freising. *Chronica sive Historia de duabus civitatibus,* ed. Walter Lammers. Darmstadt: WBG, 1961.

Completed by Rahewin. *Gesta Friderici imperatoris.* MGH, ed. G. Waitt. Hanover and Leipzig: Hahn, 1912; repr. 1978.

Thegan, *Vita Hludowici.* In series: *Quellen zur karolingischen Reichsgeschichte,* ed. Reinhold Rau. Darmstadt, WBG, 1968. Vol. I, pp. 215-52

3. Secondary Sources

Angenendt, Arnold. *Geschichte der Religiosität im Mittlealter.* Darmstadt: WBG, 1997

Becher, Matthias. *Merovinger und Karolinger.* Darmstadt: WBG, 2000

Bauer, Georg Karl. *"Kaiserchronik* und *Rolandslied," Zeitschrift für deutsche Philologie,* Vol. LVI (1931), pp.114

Bosl, Karl. *"Kaiserchronik* und *Rolandslied," Frühformen der Gesellschaft im mittelalterlichen Europa.* Munich/Vienna: Oldenbourg, 1964.

Die Sozialstruktur der mittelalterlichen Residenzund Fernhandelsstadt Regensburg; die Entwicklung ihres Bürgertums vom 9.-14. Jahrhundert. Bayrische Akademie der Wissenschaften, Phil.-Histor. Klasse, neue Folge, Heft 63. Munich: Beck, 1966.

Brincken, Anna-Dorothee von den. *Studien zur lateinischen Weltchronistik bis in das Zeitalters Ottos von Freising.* Düsseldorf: Michael Triltsch Verlag, 1957.

Crossley, R. G. *Die Kaiserchronik: ein literarhistorisches Problem der altdeutschen Literatur.* Dissertation: Freiburg, 1937. Munich: R. Oldenbourg, 1939.

Debo, Felix. *ber die Einheit der Kaiserchronik: eine kritische Vorstudie.* Dissertation: University of Graz. Graz: Leuschner & Lubensky, 1877.

Dunphy, transl. and ed., R. Graeme, History as Literature: German World Chronicles of the thirteenth Century in Verse. Excerpts from Rudolf von Ems, Weltchronik. Anon., The Christherre-Chronik; Jans Enikel, Weltchronik: Published for the Consortium for the Teaching of Middle Ages in the series: *Medieval German Texts in Bilingual Editions* by Medieval Publications, Western Michigan University, Kalamazoo, Michigan, 2003.

Eilers, Helge. *Untersuchungen zum frühmitteldeutschen Sprachstil am Beispiel der Kaiserchronik.* Göppingen Arbeiten zur Germanistik, no. 76. Göppingen: Kümmerle, 1972.

Erb, Ewald. *Geschichte der deutschen Literatur van den Anfängen bis1160.* Berlin: Volk und Wissen Volkseigener Verlag, 1965. Vol. II.

Fank. Pius. *Die Vorauer Handschrift: Ihre Entstehung und ihr Schreiber.* Graz: Akademische Druck- und Verlagsanstalt, 1967.

Folz, Robert. *Le souvenir et la légende de Charlemagne dans l'empire germanique médiéval.* Paris: Publications de l'Université, VII, 1950.

Fueter, Eduard. *Geschichte der neueren Historiographie.* Munich: Oldenbourg, 1936.

Christian Gellinek. *Die deutsche Kaiserchronik: Erzähltechnik und Kritik.* Frankfurt: Athenum Verlag, 1971.

"The *German Emperors' Chronicle*: an Epic Fiction?" *Colloquia Germania Internationale,* Heft 3 (1971), pp. 230-236.

Goez. Elke, *Papsttum und Kaisertum im Mittelalter.* Darmstadt: WBG, 2009.

Helff, Marta Maria. *Studien zur Kaiserchronik.* Leipzig and Berlin: B. G. Teubner, 1924.

Kienast, Dietmar. *Rmische Kaisertabelle: Grundzüge zu einer rmischen Kaiserchronologie.* Darmstadt: WBG, 1990; 1996.

Körntgen, Ludger. *Ottonen und Salier.* Darmstadt: WBG, 2002; 3rd ed. 2010.

Möller, Irmgard. *Die deutsche Geschichte in der Kaiserchronik.* Dissertation: University of Munich, 1958; typescript.

Mohr, Wolfgang. "Lucretia in der Kaiserchronik," *Deutsche Vierteljahrsschrift für Literaturwissenschaft und Geistesgeschichte,* Vol. XXVI (1952), pp. 433-446.

Müller, Stephan. *Vom Annolied zur Kaiserchronik: Zu Text- und Forschungsgeschichte einer verlorenen deutschen Reimchronik.* Heidelberg: Universittsverlag C. Winter, 1999.

Müller-Mertens, Eckhard. *Regnum Teutonicum: Aufkommen und Verbreitung der deutschen Reichs- und Königsauffassung im frühen Mittelalter.* Berlin: Akademie-Verlag, 1970.

Myers, Henry A. "The Concept of Kingship in the *Book of Emperors (Kaiserchronik).* *Traditio,* Vol. XXVII (1971), pp. 205-230.

Medieval Kingship: The Origins and Development of Western Monarchy in All Stages from the Fall of Rome to the Fifteenth Century; in cooperation with Herwig Wolfram. Chicago: Nelson-Hall, 1982.

"The Origin of Popular History in Twelfth-Century Germany," *Journal of Popular Culture,* Vol. X 1977), pp. 840-847.

Nellmann, Eberhard. *Die Reichsidee in deutschen Dichtungen der Salier- und frühen Stauferzeit: Annolied - Kaiserchronik - Rolandslied - Eraclius.* Philologische Studien und Quellen, Heft 16. Berlin: Erich Schmidt, 1963.

Ohly, Ernst Friedrich. *Sage und Legende in der Kaiserchronik.* Münster 1940; repr. Darmstadt: WBG, 1968.

O'Walshe, M. C., *Medieval German Literature.* Cambridge, Massachusetts: Harvard University Press, 1962.

Polheim, Karl Konrad. "Die Struktur der Vorauer Handschrift," an introduction to the second volume of the facsimile printing of the twenty-three MHG works in that manuscript. Graz: Akademische Druck- und Verlagsanstalt, 1958.

Robinson, I.S. *Henry IV of Germany, 1056-1106.* Cambridge University Press, 1999.

Rogge, Jörg. *Die deutschen Könige im Mittelalter.* Darmstadt: WBG, 2006; with updated bibliography, 2011.

Scherer, Wilhelm. "*Rolandslied, Kaiserchronik, Rother,*" *Zeitschrift für das Altertum und deutsche Literatur,* Vol. XVIII (1875), pp. 298-306.

Schmale-Ott, Irene. "Ekkehard von Aura," in *Die deutsche Literatur des Mittelalters: Verfasserlexikon,* ed. Karl Langosch. Berlin: De Gruyter, 1955, Vol. 5, cols. 185-191.

"Die Recension C der *Weltchronik* Ekkehards," *Deutsches Archiv für Erforschung des Mittelalters,* Vol. XII (1956), pp. 363-387.

"Untersuchungen zu Ekkehard von Aura und zur Kaiserchronik," *Zeitschrift für bayrische Landesgeschichte,* Vol. XXXIV (1971), pp. 363-387.

Schnell, Rudier, and Skoukje Vedder. "'Kunic' und 'Keiser'" in Schnell, ed., *Die Reichsidee in der deutschen Dichtung des Mittelalters.* Darmstadt: WBG, 1983, pp. 428-429

Singer, Samuel. *Wolframs Willehalm.* Bern: A. Francke, 1918.

Stackmann, Karl. "Dietrich von Bern in der *Kaiserchronik;* Struktur als Anweisung zur Deutung." In: *Idee - Gestalt - Geschichte; Festschrift Klaus van See.* Studies in European Cultural Tradition. Odense: G. W. Weber, 1988, pp. 137-142.

"Erzählstrategie und Sinnvermittlung in der deutscben *Kaiserchronik*. In: *Erscheinungsformen kultureller Prozesse*. Jahrbuch 1988 des Sonderforschungsbereichs, "bergange und Spannungsfelder zwischen Mündlichkeit und Schriftlichkeit." Tbingen; Wolfgang Raible, 1990, pp. 63-82.

Stengel, Edmund. E. "Die Entstehung del *Kaiserchronik* und der Aufgang der stauferschen Zeit." *Deutsches Archiv fr Erfassung des Mittelalters*, Vol. XIV (1958), pp. 395417.

"Nochmals die Datierung der *Kaiserchronik*." *Deutsches Archiv für Erfassung des Mittelalters*, Vol. XVI (1960), pp. 226-228.

Teske, Hans. "Die andere Seite: Der Reichsgedanke des Mittelalters in welfischer Dichtung." *Deutsches Volkstum*, 1935, pp. 813-817.

Todd, Malcolm, *The Early Germans*. London: Blackwell Publishers, 1992.

Tulasiewicz, W. F., *Index Verborum zur deutschen Kaiserchronik*. Berlin: Akademie-Verlag, 1972.

Urbanek, Ferdinand. "Zur Datierung del *Kaiserchronik*," *Euphorion*, Vol. LIII (1959), pp. 113-152.

"Herrscherzahl und Regierungszeiten in der *Kaiserchronik*," *Euphorion*, Vol. LXVI (1972), pp. 219-237.

Vogt, Friedrich. "Zur *Kaiserchronik*," *Zeitschrift für deutsche Philologie*, Vol. XXVII (1895), pp. 145-148.

Voswinckel, Hiltrud, "Repräsentation in der *Kaiserchronik*." Dissertation: University of Tbingen, 1955; typescript.

Weleda, Jutta. "*Die Kaiserchronik:* Untersuchung am Lautstand. Alphabetisches Reimwrterbuch." Dissertation: University of Vienna, 1974; Dissertationen der Universitt Wien, #106.

Welzhofer, Heinrich. *Untersuchungen ber die deutsche Kaiserchronik des zwöften Jahrhunderts*. Munich: Ackermann, 1874.

Wentzlaff-Eggebert, Friedrich-Wilhelm. *Kreuzzugsdichtung des Mittelalters: Studien zu ihrer geschichtlichen und dichterischen Wirklichkeit*. Berlin: Walter de Gruyter, 1960.

Wesle, Carl. "*Kaiserchronik* und *Rolandslied*," *Beiträge zur Geschichte der deutschen Sprache und Literatur*, Vol. XLVIII (1924), pp. 223-258.

Wolfram, Herwig. "Constantin als Vorbild für den Herrscher des hochmittelalterlichen Reiches," *Mitteilungen des Instituts fur sterreichische Geschichtsforschung*, Vol. LXVIII (1960), pp. 226-243.

Review of Nellmann, *Die Reichsidee . . .* (above), *Mitteilungunen des Instituts für Österreichische Geschichtsforschung*, Vol. LXXII (1964), pp. 226-243.

Zink, Georges. "*Rolandslied* et *Kaiserchronik*," *Études Germaniques*, Vol. XIX (1964), pp. 1-8.

Index

A

Accommodus, Lucius, Rom. emp., story of, 197-200

Achilleus, story of, 201

Adrian II, Pope, 338-340

Aegidius, Saint, Charles I's (Charlemagne's) confessor, 332-33

Agnes of Poitou, (fictitious) title of Duchess of Bavaria, 370-71; mother and regent for Henry IV, 364, 368; second wife of Emperor Henry III, 364

Alsatian Chronicle, 47

Alaric, king of the Visigoths, fictional treatment of, 198; story of, 198-200

Alighieri, Dante, and church and empire, 16-22

Ambrose, Saint, and church and empire, 294

Angels: "good," 3; in Charles I's (Charlemagne's) story, 310, 328, 331; in Constantine's story, 213, 217, 224, 225, 227, 228, 231, 232, 238, 239, 247, 251; in Decius' story, 180; in Domitian's story, 165; in Faustinian's story, 104-6, 110, 112,122, 127, 139; in Heraclius' story, 264, 266; in Julian's story, 258, 259; in Trajan's story, 174-5; medieval role of, 13, 29

Anno, Bishop of Cologne, 2, 72, 368

Annolied, 2, 72, 368

Aquila, and Niceta, 96, 105, 106, 117, 125

Arab, "Philip the," 176-7; 209

Arians, and the Trinity, 208-210, 300

Arius, and the Trinity, 295, 301-2

Arnulf, Rom. emp., story of, 343-5

Attila, and accuracy, 12, 315

Augustine of Hippo, Saint: and world historiography, 3-7; and Orosius, 3; and Otto of Freising, 3; as source, 90; eschatological concerns of, 7-9; and heavenly city and earthly city, 3; otherworldly focus of, 7; and Roman Empire, 6

Augustus Caesar, first Roman emperor, 80: and *Annolied*, 72, and *Book of Emperors*, 16; and Christmas story, 80; and Alighieri, Dante, 16; and Early Roman Empire and Christianity, 80; and Orosius, 3, 80

Author, *Book of Emperors*, 1-2, 30-2: Age 33; anonymous cleric (or monk) of Regensburg, 1, 10, 32, 54; Bavaria, 1; death of, 32, 34; educated, 52; fear of disease 33; patriotism of, 32; Second Crusade 33, *see also* Conrad, Priest

B

Bamberg Chronicle, The, 63

Barnabas, Saint, 102-4

Basil, Saint, 254, 260, 261

Basil I, Byz. emp., 339

Basil II, Byz. emp., "Basil the Bulgar-Killer," 353

Bavaria, and *Book of Emperors'* author, 1

"Bells that warned of revolt," 51, 67, 70

Benedict VIII, Pope, 360-361

Benedict XII, Pope, 355

Bernard, Abbot of Clairvaux, and *Book of Emperors'* last words, 33-5;. and Second Crusade, 383-4

Boleslav II, King of Poland, 359

Book of the Kings Under the Old Covenant, 46

Book of Emperors, authorship of, 1-2, 30-2: and abrupt end, 32; accepted theory of, 31; and Conrad, Priest, 31; and continuators, 44; and Debo, Felix, 32; and *Die Kaiserchronik eines Regensburger Geistlichen*, 31; and last words, 33; and *Monumenta Germaniae Historica*, 31; and *Song of Roland*, 31; and Regensburg, anonymous cleric (or monk) of, 1, 2, 32; and Scherer, Wilhelm, 31; and Schroeder, Edward, 31, 34; and Second Crusade, 35; and death, 32, 34

Book of Emperors, and Christianity: 2-4, 6, 28-9, 93: and Arius, 300-14; and Charles I, 324-5, 332, 333; and Constantine I, 209-10, 214-19, 241; and Constantine Chlorus, 20-6; and Diocletian and Maximus, 184-5; and Domitian, 164-5; and Henry II, Saint, 360; and pagan religion, 67; and peace, 80, 82; and Roman Empire, 82; and Saint Peter, 104-33; and Sixtus, 178; and Sylvester, 250; and Theodosius, 296, 300-14; medieval, 26

Book of Emperors, and kingship (or rulership), 13, 19-21: and Arnulf, 21; and attributes, 20, 156; and Charles I, 332-3; and Conrad, I, 21, 347; and Conrad II, 21; and Constantine I, 210; Constantine VI, 316; and Christian, 210; and Domitian, 21, 164; and embodiments of virtues, 13, 16-18; and Henry I, 21; and Henry II, Saint, 361; and Henry IV, 21; and Julius Caesar, 73, 76-77; and Justinian, 20-1, 53, 290; and Louis the Child, 21; and Louis I, the Pious, 334; and Müller-Mertens, Eckhard, 62; and Narcissus, 267; and Nero, 20; and Nerva, 167; and Otto II, 21; and Philip the Arab, 13; and pagan rulers, 210; and royal functions, 21; and Tarquin, 140; and Theodosius I, 21; and Titus, 21; and Trajan, 20, 171; and Vespasian, 21, 156; models and prototypes of, 19-20, 61-3; uniting the people, 21

Book of Emperors, last words of, 33, 384: abrupt end, 32; style, 33

Book of Emperors, patronage of, 35: and *History of Two Cities*, 38; and Otto V, Count Palatine, 36-7

Book of Emperors, source material, 38-47, 140, 205, 254-5: Augustine of Hippo, Saint, 90; and Bernard, Abbot of Clairvaux, 33-5; and Charlemagne (or Charles I), 40; and Cassiodorus, 4, 290; Christianity, 26; current events, 33-5; and Eusebius, 22, 47, 71; and Ekkehard of Aura, 369; and Frutolf, 22; and Hagen, F. H. von der, 49; and Hoffmann von Fallersleben, Heinrich, 49; and Josephus, 38; and Kuno, Bishop of Regensburg, 35; and Lachmann, Karl, 49; legend, Amazon, 319-20; and Massmann, Hans Ferdinand, 38; observation, 33, 35; and Ohly, Ernst Friedrich, 39; Orosius, 22, 39; *Recognitions of Saint Clement*, 93; and Repgow, Eike von 43;

sermons, 13 n. 13, 51, 67; and *Sage und Legende in der Kaiserchronik*, 39; saints, lives of, 38; songs, 320; *Song of Roland*, 42; and Suetonius, 39, 71; *Würzburg Chronicle*, 369

Book of Emperors, and influence of, 41-50: and continuator, 44; and Alighieri, Dante, 16, 16-22; and Conrad the Priest, 42; historically minded poets, 42; intellectual history, ix, 14-15, 41, 60-1; and Hoffmann von Fallersleben, Heinrich, 49; and Massmann, Ferdinand, 49; and Veldeke, Heinrich von, 42; copied in verse form, 43; German south, 44; legendary nature of narrative, 48; source for law and theology, 45; prose rewrite, 46; scholarly patriots; 49

Book of Emperors, stylistic considerations of, 52: and accuracy, 10-13, 22-3, 52; 140, 60, 151; action and imagery, 54; and audience, 11, 12, 13-14, 34, 45, 50, 52, 60; biographies of great men, 53; and evangelism, 53; and fiction, ix, 12-13, 15, 24, 47, 140, 198, 205, 309, 370; and "gleeman" elements, 54; instruct and entertain, 55; and minnesingers, 54; and techniques of, 11-14, 16, 20, 40; use of etymology, 53; use of Latin phrases, 57; vocabulary, 10; *see also* popular history

Book of Emperors, title, 59-63: and author, 60; vs. *Chronicle of Emperors*, 59; *Cronica* as sourcebook, 60-1; chronology, 60; definition of chronicle, 59; general usage, 62; medieval and present-day standards, 62; mirror-for-princes genre, 60

Book of Emperors, translation: emperor and king distinctions, 57; parataxis, 55; names, familiar and foreign, 58; subjectivity, 56; Vorau Manuscript, 45, 56; translation difficulties, 18

Book of Emperors, and treatment of history: Christianization of pagan Roman emperors, 17; "Donation of Constantine," 21-4; concept of empire, 1, 10; ideals of empire, 14, 15; ideology, 15-6, 17, 60; Imperial law, 15, 15-9, 23-5; law enforcement, 24-26

C

Caius (or Gaius) Caligula, Rom. emp., 90-2

Caius Mucius, adaptation of, 151

Cardinals, College of, 365-6

Cardinals and patriarchs, 214, 220

Charlemagne (*see also*, Charles I, "the Great") 7, 11, 318-20; and *Book of Emperors* dialogue, 43; and *Book of Emperors* patron, 36; and Pope Leo 24, 316; crowning of, 15, 23; Ford of the Franks, 345; sources for, 40; talks to God and Saint Peter, 28

Charles I, the Great, story of, 318-33

Charles, "the Bald," King of France, Brother of Lothair I, 336; grandson of Charlemagne, 318; historical Charles II, 340

Charles III, "the Fat," Rom. emp.," son of Louis, 340; story of, 340-343

Christ, *see also* Jesus; and Charles I, 327, 332; and Constantine, 209-216, 219; divine nature of, 295; as redeemer, 104, 107, 117, 119, 178, 221-6; and miracles, 247; prayers to, 118, 219, 327; and Theodosius, 296, 302, 303

Church, and empire (or state), 4, 6, 7, 10, 14, 15, 16, 17, 21-2, 294, 319; Ambrose, Saint, 294; Miracles and wonders, 26: and Barnabas, Saint, 102-4; and Simon the Magician, 28, 105-12, 134-5; and Sylvester, Pope, 245-6

Claudius, Rom. emp., 134-5

Clemency, Christian, 26; and law enforcement, 23, 26

Imperial Law, 17; and Otho, 150; and Trajan, 172; and Vespasian, 156; and Vitellius, 151; author's source of Lateran Palace name, 53;

Nerva, Rom. emp., story of, 167-70

New Testament, 27, 28, 239

Niceta, and Aquila, 96, 105, 106, 117, 125

O

Odnatus, legend, 151-55

Odoakar, and Zeno, 309, 312-4

Ohly, Ernst Friedrich, 40, 49, 58

Old Testament, 3, 27, 28, 46, 239

Orosius, Paulus, and Achilleus, 201; and Augustus Caesar, 80; and Donation of Constantine, 22; and Julius Caesar, 71; and source material, 39; and Trajan, 171; and world historiography, 3-7

Otho, Rom. emp., and name forms, 58; and Vitellius, 151; in story of Galba and Piso, 149; story of, 150

Otto I , the Great, HR emp., 151, 352-5; 362

Otto II, HR emp., 355-7

Otto III, HR emp., 357-9

Otto, Bishop of Bamberg, 63

Otto, Duke of Bavaria, 337-9

Otto, Margrave of Moravia, 378

Otto the Cross-eyed, King of Hungary, 365-6

Otto V, Count Palatine, and *Book of Emperors*, 36-8

Otto VI, Wittelsbach dynasty, 38

Ovid, and Tarquin, 140-1

P

Pancratius, Saint, 183

Paul, Saint, and Constantine I, 211-12; and divine contract, 28; and Eusebius, 298; and Peter, Saint, 28, 211-12; defies Julian, 258-59; executed, 136-8; grave of, 317, 351;

Peter, Saint, and Charles I, 320-4, 327; and Claudius, 135; and Constantine I, 211-15, 249; and contest of wonders, 105-33; and Decius, 178; and divine contract, 28; and Henry I, 351; and Henry II, 362; and Henry III, 365-6; and Narcissus, 267, 282; and Nero, 136-9; and Paul, Saint, 28, 211-12; and Simon the Magician, 28, 105-33, 134-5, 137-8; and Sylvester, 252-3; and Trajan, 174; and Zeno, 315, 317;

Philip the Arab, Rom. emp., 176-177

Pippin, King of the Franks, 15, and Charles I (Charlemagne), 321, 324, 329

Pippin, son of HR emp. Lothair I, 338

Piso, R emp., 149

Plato, 120, 122

Pontius Pilate, 94

Prayer, and Christian contract, 26, 28; and Charlemagne, Saint, 29; and Pope Leo and Trajan, 29-30;

Promise, Christian, 26-8; and divine intervention, 26; and eternal salvation, 26; and prayer, 27, 28; and saints, 28; and Testament, Old, 28; and Testament, New, 28; reminding God of, 28

R

Rachel, mother of Simon the Magician, 105-6; disposition of soul of, 111-2;

Regensburg, and Arnulf, 344, 345; councils at, 337, 360, 374-5; Lothair besieges, 338; and news of Second Crusade, 34-5; and story of Henry II, 361; and Henry III, 366-7

Roger II, king of Sicily, and Conrad III, 383; and Lothair II, 377–81, 390; in story of Lothair II, 392

Robinson, I. S., and this title, 63

Romans, abolish kingship in Rome,

Ulrich or Sobeslaw, Duke of Bohemia, 379
Urbanek, Ferdinand, 36, 37; *see also* patronage

V

Vercingetorix or Signator, 58, in story of Julius Caesar, 76
Vernacular, 1, 36, 39, 43, 47, 45, 50, 51, 54, 60
Veronica, 82, legend of, 84
Vespasian, Rom. emp., as general of Tiberius, 83, 86, 88; as rival of Vitellius, 150, 155; healed, 82; wins "Jewish War," 21; story of, 156-160
Vitellius, Rom. emp., story of, 151-5; 156
Vitus, Saint, 182, 183
Vogelweide, Walther von der, 54; *see also* vernacular
Volusianus, searches for Jesus, 84
Vorau Manuscript, earliest surviving *Book of Emperors*, x, 41; and *Gesta Friderici*, 45; production of, 42; precedence of, xii, 56; as source material for history, law and theology, 45

W

Wace, Master, canon of Bayeux, 2

Weinsberg, Battle of, 384
Welf (Guelph) II, Swabian-Bavarian count, 363
Welf III, Duke of Bavaria, son of HR emp. Henry III, 383-4
Weltchronik, incorporates *Book of Emperors* episodes, 43-4
Book of Emperors, as source material for, Conrad's *Song of Roland*, 31; continuators, 44-5; Enenkel's *Weltchronik*, 43-4; for Ottokar's *Weltchronik*, 45; Eschenbach's *Parzival*, 42-3
Wesle, Carl, and Conrad's *Song of Roland*, 31
Welzhofer, Heinrich, and *Book of Emperors* authorship, 31; search for earlier chronicle, 61
Wittelsbach, dynasty, *Book of Emperors* patron, 36-8
Worms, city, council at, 339, 375
Würzburg, city, council at, 349
Würzburg Chronicle, as source material, 347, 36

Z

Zacheus, 97, 113
Zambri, and Sylvester, 243-48
Zeno, Rom. emp., story of, 308-15
Zenophilus, 221, 227

About the Author

Henry A. Myers is Professor Emeritus of History at James Madison University. Dr. Myers earned the B.A. from Swarthmore College, the M.A. from Boston University, and the Ph.D. from Brandeis University. He also studied at the Free University of Berlin and the Institut for Österreiche Geschichtsforschung. Dr. Myers taught at JMU for 42 years in global and intellectual history. His published books include *Medieval Kingship* (Nelson-Hall, 1982), *Postwar Trade in Divided Germany* co-authored with Karel Holbik (Johns Hopkins, 1964), and *West German Foreign Aid, 1956-1966: Its Economic and Political Aspects* co-authored with Karel Holbik (Boston University, 1969). He also co-edited several editions of *The Global Experience*, a two-volume reader in World history, and authored numerous scholarly articles. In addition to scholarly pursuits, Dr. Myers was a competitive equestrian athlete for many years. He and his wife are proud parents and grandparents, who reside in Churchville, Virginia.